THE MESSAGE:
THE OLD TESTAMENT
BOOKS OF MOSES

ᗧᗤ

*The Message is a contemporary rendering
of the Bible from the original languages,
crafted to present its tone, rhythm, events,
and ideas in everyday language.*

ᗧᗤ

The MESSAGE

The New Testament with Psalms and Proverbs

The Old Testament Wisdom Books
Job, Psalms, Proverbs, Ecclesiastes, Song of Songs

The Old Testament Prophets
Isaiah, Jeremiah, Lamentations, Ezekiel, Daniel, Hosea, Joel, Amos, Obadiah, Jonah, Micah, Nahum, Habakkuk, Zephaniah, Haggai, Zechariah, Malachi

The Old Testament Books of Moses
Genesis, Exodus, Leviticus, Numbers, Deuteronomy

The Old Testament History Books Available June 2002
Joshua, Judges, Ruth, 1 Samuel, 2 Samuel, 1 Kings, 2 Kings, 1 Chronicles, 2 Chronicles, Ezra, Nehemiah, Esther

The Message Bible Available July 2002
Old and New Testaments combined into one volume

For a free Message/NavPress catalog or to inquire about large quantity purchases for your business, ministry, church, or organization, please call 1-800-366-7788; send an e-mail to themessage@navpress.com; or write to The Message, P.O. Box 35001, Colorado Springs, CO 80935.
www.messagebible.com

THE BOOKS OF MOSES: INTRODUCTION

An enormous authority and dignity have, through the centuries, developed around the first five books of the Bible, commonly known as The Books of Moses. Over the course of many centuries, they account for a truly astonishing amount of reading and writing, study and prayer, teaching and preaching.

God is the primary concern of these books. That accounts for the authority and the dignity. But it is not only God; we get included. That accounts for the widespread and intense human interest. We want to know what's going on. We want to know how we fit into things. We don't want to miss out.

The Books of Moses are made up mostly of stories and signposts. The stories show us God working with and speaking to men and women in a rich variety of circumstances. God is presented to us not in ideas and arguments but in events and actions that involve each of us personally. The signposts provide immediate and practical directions to guide us into behavior that is appropriate to our humanity and honoring to God.

The simplicity of the storytelling and signposting in these books makes what is written here as accessible to children as to adults. But the simplicity (as in so many simple things) is also profound, inviting us into a lifetime of growing participation in God's saving ways with us.

An image of human growth suggests a reason for the powerful pull of these stories and signposts on so many millions of men, women, and children to live as *God's* people. The sketch shows the five books as five stages of growth in which God creates first a cosmos and then a people for his glory.

Genesis is Conception. After establishing the basic elements by which God will do his work of creation and salvation and judgment in the midst of human sin and rebellion (chapters 1-11), God conceives a People to whom he will reveal himself as a God of salvation and through them, over time, to everyone on earth. God begins small, with one man: Abraham. The embryonic People of God grow in the womb. Gradually details and then more details become evident as the embryo takes shape: Sarah, Isaac, Rebekah, Jacob and Esau, Rachel, Joseph and his brothers. The pregnancy develops. Life is obviously developing in that womb but there is also much that is not clear and visible. The background history is vague, the surrounding nations and customs veiled in a kind of mist. But the presence of life, God-conceived life, is kicking and robust.

Exodus is Birth and Infancy. The gestation of the People of God lasts a long time, but finally the birth pangs start. Egyptian slavery gives the first intimations of the contractions to come. When Moses arrives on the scene to preside over the birth itself, ten fierce plagues on Egypt accompany the contractions that bring the travail to completion: at the Red Sea the waters break, the People of God tumble out of the womb onto dry ground, and their life as a free People of God begins. Moses leads them crawling and toddling to Sinai. They are fed. God reveals himself to them at the mountain. They begin to get a sense of their Parent. They learn the language of freedom and salvation—a word here, a word there, the Ten Words (commandments) as a beginning, their basic vocabulary. The signposts begin to go up: do this; don't do that. But the largest part of their infant life is God, the living God. As they explore the deep and wide world of God, worship becomes their dominant and most important activity. An enormous amount of attention is given to training them in worship, building the structures for worship, mastering the procedures. They are learning how to give their full attention in obedience and adoration to God.

Leviticus is Schooling. As infancy develops into childhood, formal schooling takes place. There's a lot to know; they need some structure and arrangement to keep things straight: reading, writing, arithmetic. But for the People of God the basic curriculum has to do with God and their relationship with God. Leviticus is the *McGuffey's Reader* of the People of God. It is an almost totally audio-visual book, giving a picture and ritual in the sacrifices and feasts for the pivotal ways in which God's people keep alert and observant to the ways their relationship with God goes awry (sin) and the ways they are restored to forgiveness and innocence (salvation). Everyday life consists of endless and concrete detail, much of it having to do with our behavior before God and with one another, and so, of course, Leviticus necessarily consists also of endless detail.

Numbers is Adolescence. The years of adolescence are critical to understanding who we are. We are advanced enough physically to be able, for the most part, to take care of ourselves. We are developed enough mentally, with some obvious limitations, to think for ourselves. We discover that we are not simply extensions of our parents; and we are not just mirror images of our culture. But who are we? Especially, who are we as a People of God? The People of God in Numbers are new at these emerging independent operations of behaving and thinking and so inevitably make a lot of mistakes. Rebellion is one of the more conspicuous mistakes. They test out their unique identity by rejecting the continuities with parents and culture. It's the easiest and cheapest way to "be myself" as we like to say. But it turns out that there isn't much to the "self" that is thus asserted. Maturity requires the integration, not the amputation, of what we have received through our

The MESSAGE

THE OLD TESTAMENT
BOOKS OF MOSES

EUGENE H. PETERSON

NAVPRESS

Bringing Truth to Life
P.O. Box 35001, Colorado Springs, Colorado 80935

The Old Testament Books of Moses Exegetical Consultants:

Dr. Robert L Hubbard Jr.
Chairman
North Park Theological Seminary

Dr. Richard E. Averbeck
Trinity Evangelical Divinity School

Dr. Peter Enns
Westminster Theological Seminary

Dr. Duane A. Garrett
Gordon-Conwell Theological Seminary

Dr. Prescott H. Williams Jr.
Austin Presbyterian Theological Seminary

Library of Congress Catalog Card Number: 2001042578
ISBN 1-57683-196-5

Bible, O.T. Pentateuch. English. Peterson. 2001.
    The message : the Old Testament books of Moses / Eugene H. Peterson.
       p. cm.
    ISBN 1-57683-196-5
     I. Title: Old Testament books of Moses. II. Peterson, Eugene H., 1932- III. Title.

BS1223 2001
222'.105209—dc21

                                         2001042578

Published in association with the literary agency of Alive Communications, Inc., 7680 Goddard St., Suite 200, Colorado Springs, CO 80920.

Printed in the United States of America

1 2 3 4 5 6 7 8 9 10 11 12 13 14 15 16 17 / 10 09 08 07 06 05 04 03 02 01

CONTENTS

conception and birth, our infancy and schooling. The People of God have an extraordinarily long adolescence in the wilderness—nearly forty years of it.

Deuteronomy is Adulthood. The mature life is a complex operation. Growing up is a long process. And growing up in God takes the longest time. During their forty years spent in the wilderness, the People of God developed from that full-term embryo brought to birth on the far shore of the Red Sea, are carried and led, nourished and protected under Moses to the place of God's Revelation at Sinai, taught and trained, disciplined and blessed. Now they are ready to live as free and obedient men and women in the new land, the Promised Land. They are ready for adulthood, ready to be as grown up inwardly as they are outwardly. They are ready to live as a free people, formed by God, as a holy people, transformed by God. They still have a long way to go (as do we all), but all the conditions for maturity are there. The book of Deuteronomy gathers up that entire process of becoming a People of God and turns it into a sermon and a song and a blessing. The strongest and key word in Deuteronomy is *love*. Love is the most characteristic and comprehensive act of the human being. We are most ourselves when we love; we are most the People of God when we love. But love is not an abstract word defined out of a dictionary. In order to love maturely we have to live and absorb and enter into this world of salvation and freedom, find ourselves in the stories, become familiar with and follow the signposts, learn the life of worship, and realize our unique identity as the People of God who love.

☞

The Books of Moses are foundational to the sixty-one books that follow in our Bibles. A foundation, though, is not a complete building but the anticipation of one. An elaborate moral infrastructure is provided here for what is yet to come. Each book that follows, in one way or another, picks up and develops some aspect of the messianic salvation involved in becoming the People of God, but it is always on this foundation. This foundation of stories and signposts has proved over and over to be solid and enduring.

☞

A note on translating the name of God. In the original Hebrew text of the Old Testament, the generic name for divinity used by both Israel and its neighbors is translated God (or god). But the unique and distinctively personal name for God that was revealed to Moses at the burning bush (Exodus 3:13-14) I have translated as GOD. The Jewish community early on substituted "LORD" for the unique name out of reverence (our lips are not worthy to speak The Name) and caution (lest we inadvertently blaspheme by saying God's name "in vain"). Most Christian translators continue that practice.

GENESIS

First, God. God is the subject of life. God is foundational for living. If we don't have a sense of the primacy of God, we will never get it right, get life right, get *our* lives right. Not God at the margins; not God as an option; not God on the weekends. God at center and circumference; God first and last; God, God, God.

Genesis gets us off on the right foot. Genesis pulls us into a sense of reality that is God-shaped and God-filled. It gives us a vocabulary for speaking accurately and comprehensively about our lives, where we come from and where we are going, what we think and what we do, the people we live with and how to get along with them, the troubles we find ourselves in and the blessings that keep arriving.

Genesis uses words to make a foundation that is solid and true. Everything we think and do and feel is material in a building operation in which we are engaged all our life long. There is immense significance in everything that we do. Our speech and our actions and our prayers are all, every detail of them, involved in this vast building operation comprehensively known as the Kingdom of God. But we don't build the foundation. The foundation is given. The foundation is firmly in place.

Jesus concluded his most famous teaching by telling us that there are two ways to go about our lives, we can build on sand or we can build on rock. No matter how wonderfully we build, if we build on sand it will all fall to pieces like a house of cards. We build on what is already there, on the rock. Genesis is a verbal witness to that rock: God's creative acts, God's intervening and gracious judgments, God's call to a life of faith, God's making covenant with us.

But Genesis presents none of this to us as an abstract, bloodless "truth" or "principle." We are given a succession of stories with named people, people who loved and quarreled, believed and doubted, had children and married, experienced sin and grace. If we pay attention, we find that we ourselves are living variations on these very stories: Adam and Eve, Cain and Abel, Noah and his sons, Abraham and Sarah, Isaac and Rebekah, Jacob and Rachel, Joseph and his brothers. The stories show clearly that we are never outsiders or spectators to anything in "heaven and earth." God doesn't work impersonally from space; he works with us where we are, as he finds us. No matter what we do, whether good or bad, we continue to be part of everything that God is doing. Nobody can drop out—there's no place to drop out to. So we may as well get started and take our place in the story—at the beginning.

GENESIS

HEAVEN AND EARTH

1 First this: God created the Heavens and Earth—all you see, all you don't see. Earth was a soup of nothingness, a bottomless emptiness, an inky blackness. God's Spirit brooded like a bird above the watery abyss.

God spoke: "Light!"
    And light appeared.
God saw that light was good
    and separated light from dark.
God named the light Day,
    he named the dark Night.
It was evening, it was morning—
Day One.

God spoke: "Sky! In the middle of the waters;
    separate water from water!"
God made sky.
He separated the water under sky
    from the water above sky.
And there it was:
    he named sky the Heavens;
It was evening, it was morning—
Day Two.

God spoke: "Separate!
    Water-beneath-Heaven, gather into one place;
Land, appear!"
    And there it was.
God named the land Earth.
    He named the pooled water Ocean.
God saw that it was good.

God spoke: "Earth, green up! Grow all varieties
    of seed-bearing plants,
Every sort of fruit-bearing tree."

And there it was.
Earth produced green seed-bearing plants,
    all varieties,
And fruit-bearing trees of all sorts.
    God saw that it was good.
It was evening, it was morning—
Day Three.

God spoke: "Lights! Come out!
    Shine in Heaven's sky!
Separate Day from Night.
    Mark seasons and days and years,
Lights in Heaven's sky to give light to Earth."
    And there it was.

God made two big lights, the larger
    to take charge of Day,
The smaller to be in charge of Night;
    and he made the stars.
God placed them in the heavenly sky
    to light up Earth
And oversee Day and Night,
    to separate light and dark.
God saw that it was good.
    It was evening, it was morning—
Day Four.

God spoke: "Swarm, Ocean, with fish and all sea life!
    Birds, fly through the sky over Earth!"
God created the huge whales,
    all the swarm of life in the waters,
And every kind and species of flying birds.
    God saw that it was good.
God blessed them: "Prosper! Reproduce! Fill Ocean!
    Birds, reproduce on Earth!"
It was evening, it was morning—
Day Five.

God spoke: "Earth, generate life! Every sort and kind:
        cattle and reptiles and wild animals—all kinds."

13

And there it was:
  wild animals of every kind,
Cattle of all kinds, every sort of reptile and bug.
  God saw that it was good.

God spoke: "Let us make human beings in our image, make them
  reflecting our nature
So they can be responsible for the fish in the sea,
  the birds in the air, the cattle,
And, yes, Earth itself,
  and every animal that moves on the face of Earth."
God created human beings;
  he created them godlike,
Reflecting God's nature.
  He created them male and female.
God blessed them:
  "Prosper! Reproduce! Fill Earth! Take charge!
Be responsible for fish in the sea and birds in the air,
  for every living thing that moves on the face of Earth."

Then God said, "I've given you
  every sort of seed-bearing plant on Earth
And every kind of fruit-bearing tree,
  given them to you for food.
To all animals and all birds,
  everything that moves and breathes,
I give whatever grows out of the ground for food."
  And there it was.

God looked over everything he had made;
  it was so good, so very good!
It was evening, it was morning—
Day Six.

2 Heaven and Earth were finished,
  down to the last detail.

By the seventh day
  God had finished his work.

On the seventh day
> he rested from all his work.
God blessed the seventh day.
> He made it a Holy Day
Because on that day he rested from his work,
> all the creating God had done.

This is the story of how it all started,
> of Heaven and Earth when they were created.

ADAM AND EVE

At the time GOD made Earth and Heaven, before any grasses or shrubs had sprouted from the ground—GOD hadn't yet sent rain on Earth, nor was there anyone around to work the ground (the whole Earth was watered by underground springs)—GOD formed Man out of dirt from the ground and blew into his nostrils the breath of life. The Man came alive—a living soul!

Then GOD planted a garden in Eden, in the east. He put the Man he had just made in it. GOD made all kinds of trees grow from the ground, trees beautiful to look at and good to eat. The Tree-of-Life was in the middle of the garden, also the Tree-of-Knowledge-of-Good-and-Evil.

A river flows out of Eden to water the garden and from there divides into four rivers. The first is named Pishon; it flows through Havilah where there is gold. The gold of this land is good. The land is also known for a sweet-scented resin and the onyx stone. The second river is named Gihon; it flows through the land of Cush. The third river is named Hiddekel and flows east of Assyria. The fourth river is the Euphrates.

GOD took the Man and set him down in the Garden of Eden to work the ground and keep it in order.

GOD commanded the Man, "You can eat from any tree in the garden, except from the Tree-of-Knowledge-of-Good-and-Evil. Don't eat from it. The moment you eat from that tree, you're dead."

GOD said, "It's not good for the Man to be alone; I'll make him a helper, a companion." So GOD formed from the dirt of the ground all the animals of the field and all the birds of the air. He brought them to the Man to see what he would name them. Whatever the Man called each living creature, that was its name. The Man named the cattle, named the birds of the air, named the wild animals; but he didn't find a suitable companion.

15

GOD put the Man into a deep sleep. As he slept he removed one of his ribs and replaced it with flesh. GOD then used the rib that he had taken from the Man to make Woman and presented her to the Man.

> The Man said,
> "Finally! Bone of my bone,
>   flesh of my flesh!
> Name her Woman
>   for she was made from Man."
>   Therefore a man leaves his father and mother and embraces his wife. They become one flesh.
>   The two of them, the Man and his Wife, were naked, but they felt no shame.

3 The serpent was clever, more clever than any wild animal GOD had made. He spoke to the Woman: "Do I understand that God told you not to eat from any tree in the garden?"

The Woman said to the serpent, "Not at all. We can eat from the trees in the garden. It's only about the tree in the middle of the garden that God said, 'Don't eat from it; don't even touch it or you'll die.'"

The serpent told the Woman, "You won't die. God knows that the moment you eat from that tree, you'll see what's really going on. You'll be just like God, knowing everything, ranging all the way from good to evil."

When the Woman saw that the tree looked like good eating and realized what she would get out of it—she'd know everything!—she took and ate the fruit and then gave some to her husband, and he ate.

Immediately the two of them did "see what's really going on"—saw themselves naked! They sewed fig leaves together as makeshift clothes for themselves.

When they heard the sound of GOD strolling in the garden in the evening breeze, the Man and his Wife hid in the trees of the garden, hid from GOD.

GOD called to the Man: "Where are you?"

He said, "I heard you in the garden and I was afraid because I was naked. And I hid."

GOD said, "Who told you you were naked? Did you eat from that tree I told you not to eat from?"

The Man said, "The Woman you gave me as a companion, she gave me fruit from the tree, and, yes, I ate it."

GOD said to the Woman, "What is this that you've done?"

"The serpent seduced me," she said, "and I ate."

GOD told the serpent:
"Because you've done this, you're cursed,
    cursed beyond all cattle and wild animals,
Cursed to slink on your belly
    and eat dirt all your life.
I'm declaring war between you and the Woman,
    between your offspring and hers.
He'll wound your head,
    you'll wound his heel."

He told the Woman:
"I'll multiply your pains in childbirth;
    you'll give birth to your babies in pain.
You'll want to please your husband,
    but he'll lord it over you."

He told the Man:
"Because you listened to your wife
    and ate from the tree
That I commanded you not to eat from,
    'Don't eat from this tree,'
The very ground is cursed because of you;
    getting food from the ground
Will be as painful as having babies is for your wife;
    you'll be working in pain all your life long.
The ground will sprout thorns and weeds,
    you'll get your food the hard way,
Planting and tilling and harvesting,
    sweating in the fields from dawn to dusk,
Until you return to that ground yourself, dead and buried;
    you started out as dirt, you'll end up dirt."

The Man, known as Adam, named his wife Eve because she was the mother of all the living.

GOD made leather clothing for Adam and his wife and dressed them.

17

GOD said, "The Man has become like one of us, capable of knowing everything, ranging from good to evil. What if he now should reach out and take fruit from the Tree-of-Life and eat, and live forever? Never—this cannot happen!"

So GOD expelled them from the Garden of Eden and sent them to work the ground, the same dirt out of which they'd been made. He threw them out of the garden and stationed angel-cherubim and a revolving sword of fire east of it, guarding the path to the Tree-of-Life.

4 Adam slept with Eve his wife. She conceived and had Cain. She said, "I've gotten a man, with GOD's help!"

Then she had another baby, Abel. Abel was a herdsman and Cain a farmer.

Time passed. Cain brought an offering to GOD from the produce of his farm. Abel also brought an offering, but from the firstborn animals of his herd, choice cuts of meat. GOD liked Abel and his offering, but Cain and his offering didn't get his approval. Cain lost his temper and went into a sulk.

GOD spoke to Cain: "Why this tantrum? Why the sulking? If you do well, won't you be accepted? And if you don't do well, sin is lying in wait for you, ready to pounce; it's out to get you, you've got to master it."

Cain had words with his brother. They were out in the field; Cain came at Abel his brother and killed him.

GOD said to Cain, "Where is Abel your brother?"

He said, "How should I know? Am I his babysitter?"

GOD said, "What have you done! The voice of your brother's blood is calling to me from the ground. From now on you'll get nothing but curses from this ground; you'll be driven from this ground that has opened its arms to receive the blood of your murdered brother. You'll farm this ground, but it will no longer give you its best. You'll be a homeless wanderer on Earth."

Cain said to GOD, "My punishment is too much. I can't take it! You've thrown me off the land and I can never again face you. I'm a homeless wanderer on Earth and whoever finds me will kill me."

GOD told him, "No. Anyone who kills Cain will pay for it seven times over." GOD put a mark on Cain to protect him so that no one who met him would kill him.

Cain left the presence of GOD and lived in No-Man's-Land, east of Eden.

Cain slept with his wife. She conceived and had Enoch. He then built a city and named it after his son, Enoch.

Enoch had Irad,
Irad had Mehujael,
Mehujael had Methushael,
Methushael had Lamech.

Lamech married two wives, Adah and Zillah. Adah gave birth to Jabal, the ancestor of all who live in tents and herd cattle. His brother's name was Jubal, the ancestor of all who play the lyre and flute. Zillah gave birth to Tubal-Cain, who worked at the forge making bronze and iron tools. Tubal-Cain's sister was Naamah.

Lamech said to his wives,
Adah and Zillah, listen to me;
    you wives of Lamech, hear me out:
I killed a man for wounding me,
    a young man who attacked me.
If Cain is avenged seven times,
    for Lamech it's seventy-seven!

Adam slept with his wife again. She had a son whom she named Seth. She said, "God has given me another child in place of Abel whom Cain killed." And then Seth had a son whom he named Enosh.

That's when men and women began praying and worshiping in the name of GOD.

THE FAMILY TREE OF THE HUMAN RACE

5 This is the family tree of the human race: When God created the human race, he made it godlike, with a nature akin to God. He created both male and female and blessed them, the whole human race.

When Adam was 130 years old, he had a son who was just like him, his very spirit and image, and named him Seth. After the birth of Seth, Adam lived another 800 years, having more sons and daughters. Adam lived a total of 930 years. And he died.

When Seth was 105 years old, he had Enosh. After Seth had Enosh, he lived another 807 years, having more sons and daughters. Seth lived a total of 912 years. And he died.

When Enosh was ninety years old, he had Kenan. After he had

Kenan, he lived another 815 years, having more sons and daughters. Enosh lived a total of 905 years. And he died.

When Kenan was seventy years old, he had Mahalalel. After he had Mahalalel, he lived another 840 years, having more sons and daughters. Kenan lived a total of 910 years. And he died.

When Mahalalel was sixty-five years old, he had Jared. After he had Jared, he lived another 830 years, having more sons and daughters. Mahalalel lived a total of 895 years. And he died.

When Jared was 162 years old, he had Enoch. After he had Enoch, he lived another 800 years, having more sons and daughters. Jared lived a total of 962 years. And he died.

When Enoch was sixty-five years old, he had Methuselah. Enoch walked steadily with God. After he had Methuselah, he lived another 300 years, having more sons and daughters. Enoch lived a total of 365 years.

Enoch walked steadily with God. And then one day he was simply gone: God took him.

When Methuselah was 187 years old, he had Lamech. After he had Lamech, he lived another 782 years. Methuselah lived a total of 969 years. And he died.

When Lamech was 182 years old, he had a son. He named him Noah, saying, "This one will give us a break from the hard work of farming the ground that GOD cursed." After Lamech had Noah, he lived another 595 years, having more sons and daughters. Lamech lived a total of 777 years. And he died.

When Noah was 500 years old, he had Shem, Ham, and Japheth.

GIANTS IN THE LAND

6When the human race began to increase, with more and more daughters being born, the sons of God noticed that the daughters of men were beautiful. They looked them over and picked out wives for themselves.

Then GOD said, "I'm not going to breathe life into men and women endlessly. Eventually they're going to die; from now on they can expect a life span of 120 years."

This was back in the days (and also later) when there were giants in the land. The giants came from the union of the sons of God and the daughters of men. These were the mighty men of ancient lore, the famous ones.

Noah and His Sons

God saw that human evil was out of control. People thought evil, imagined evil—evil, evil, evil from morning to night. God was sorry that he had made the human race in the first place; it broke his heart. God said, "I'll get rid of my ruined creation, make a clean sweep: people, animals, snakes and bugs, birds—the works. I'm sorry I made them."

But Noah was different. God liked what he saw in Noah.

This is the story of Noah: Noah was a good man, a man of integrity in his community. Noah walked with God. Noah had three sons: Shem, Ham, and Japheth.

As far as God was concerned, the Earth had become a sewer; there was violence everywhere. God took one look and saw how bad it was, everyone corrupt and corrupting—life itself corrupt to the core.

God said to Noah, "It's all over. It's the end of the human race. The violence is everywhere; I'm making a clean sweep.

"Build yourself a ship from teakwood. Make rooms in it. Coat it with pitch inside and out. Make it 450 feet long, seventy-five feet wide, and forty-five feet high. Build a roof for it and put in a window eighteen inches from the top; put in a door on the side of the ship; and make three decks, lower, middle, and upper.

"I'm going to bring a flood on the Earth that will destroy everything alive under Heaven. Total destruction.

"But I'm going to establish a covenant with you: You'll board the ship, and your sons, your wife and your sons' wives will come on board with you. You are also to take two of each living creature, a male and a female, on board the ship, to preserve their lives with you: two of every species of bird, mammal, and reptile—two of everything so as to preserve their lives along with yours. Also get all the food you'll need and store it up for you and them."

Noah did everything God commanded him to do.

7 Next God said to Noah, "Now board the ship, you and all your family—out of everyone in this generation, you're the righteous one.

"Take on board with you seven pairs of every clean animal, a male and a female; one pair of every unclean animal, a male and a female; and seven pairs of every kind of bird, a male and a female, to insure their survival on Earth. In just seven days I will dump rain on Earth for forty days and forty nights. I'll make a clean sweep of everything that I've made."

Noah did everything GOD commanded him.

Noah was 600 years old when the floodwaters covered the Earth. Noah and his wife and sons and their wives boarded the ship to escape the flood. Clean and unclean animals, birds, and all the crawling creatures came in pairs to Noah and to the ship, male and female, just as God had commanded Noah. In seven days the floodwaters came.

It was the six-hundredth year of Noah's life, in the second month, on the seventeenth day of the month that it happened: all the underground springs erupted and all the windows of Heaven were thrown open. Rain poured for forty days and forty nights.

That's the day Noah and his sons Shem, Ham, and Japheth, accompanied by his wife and his sons' wives, boarded the ship. And with them every kind of wild and domestic animal, right down to all the kinds of creatures that crawl and all kinds of birds and anything that flies. They came to Noah and to the ship in pairs—everything and anything that had the breath of life in it, male and female of every creature came just as God had commanded Noah. Then GOD shut the door behind him.

The flood continued forty days and the waters rose and lifted the ship high over the Earth. The waters kept rising, the flood deepened on the Earth, the ship floated on the surface. The flood got worse until all the highest mountains were covered—the high water mark reached twenty feet above the crest of the mountains. Everything died. Anything that moved—dead. Birds, farm animals, wild animals, the entire teeming exuberance of life—dead. And all people—dead. Every living, breathing creature that lived on dry land died; he wiped out the whole works—people and animals, crawling creatures and flying birds, every last one of them, gone. Only Noah and his company on the ship lived.

The floodwaters took over for 150 days.

8 Then God turned his attention to Noah and all the wild animals and farm animals with him on the ship. God caused the wind to blow and the floodwaters began to go down. The underground springs were shut off, the windows of Heaven closed and the rain quit. Inch by inch the water lowered. After 150 days the worst was over.

On the seventeenth day of the seventh month, the ship landed on the Ararat mountain range. The water kept going down until the tenth month. On the first day of the tenth month the tops of the mountains came into view. After forty days Noah opened the window that he had built into the ship.

He sent out a raven; it flew back and forth waiting for the flood-waters to dry up. Then he sent a dove to check on the flood conditions, but it couldn't even find a place to perch—water still covered the Earth. Noah reached out and caught it, brought it back into the ship.

He waited seven more days and sent out the dove again. It came back in the evening with a freshly picked olive leaf in its beak. Noah knew that the flood was about finished.

He waited another seven days and sent the dove out a third time. This time it didn't come back.

In the six-hundred-first year of Noah's life, on the first day of the first month, the flood had dried up. Noah opened the hatch of the ship and saw dry ground. By the twenty-seventh day of the second month, the Earth was completely dry.

God spoke to Noah: "Leave the ship, you and your wife and your sons and your sons' wives. And take all the animals with you, the whole menagerie of birds and mammals and crawling creatures, all that brimming prodigality of life, so they can reproduce and flourish on the Earth."

Noah disembarked with his sons and wife and his sons' wives. Then all the animals, crawling creatures, birds—every creature on the face of the Earth—left the ship family by family.

Noah built an altar to GOD. He selected clean animals and birds from every species and offered them as burnt-offerings on the altar. GOD smelled the sweet fragrance and thought to himself, "I'll never again curse the ground because of people. I know they have this bent toward evil from an early age, but I'll never again kill off everything living as I've just done.

> For as long as Earth lasts,
>> planting and harvest, cold and heat,
> Summer and winter, day and night
>> will never stop."

9 God blessed Noah and his sons: He said, "Prosper! Reproduce! Fill the Earth! Every living creature—birds, animals, fish—will fall under your spell and be afraid of you. You're responsible for them. All living creatures are yours for food; just as I gave you the plants, now I give you everything else. Except for meat with its lifeblood still in it—don't eat that.

"But your own lifeblood I will avenge; I will avenge it against both animals and other humans.

Whoever sheds human blood,
>by humans let his blood be shed,
Because God made humans in his image
>reflecting God's very nature.
You're here to bear fruit, reproduce,
>lavish life on the Earth, live bountifully!"

Then God spoke to Noah and his sons: "I'm setting up my covenant with you including your children who will come after you, along with everything alive around you—birds, farm animals, wild animals—that came out of the ship with you. I'm setting up my covenant with you that never again will everything living be destroyed by floodwaters; no, never again will a flood destroy the Earth."

God continued, "This is the sign of the covenant I am making between me and you and everything living around you and everyone living after you. I'm putting my rainbow in the clouds, a sign of the covenant between me and the Earth. From now on, when I form a cloud over the Earth and the rainbow appears in the cloud, I'll remember my covenant between me and you and everything living, that never again will floodwaters destroy all life. When the rainbow appears in the cloud, I'll see it and remember the eternal covenant between God and everything living, every last living creature on Earth."

And God said, "This is the sign of the covenant that I've set up between me and everything living on the Earth."

The sons of Noah who came out of the ship were Shem, Ham, and Japheth. Ham was the father of Canaan. These are the three sons of Noah; from these three the whole Earth was populated.

Noah, a farmer, was the first to plant a vineyard. He drank from its wine, got drunk and passed out, naked in his tent. Ham, the father of Canaan, saw that his father was naked and told his two brothers who were outside the tent. Shem and Japheth took a cloak, held it between them from their shoulders, walked backwards and covered their father's nakedness, keeping their faces turned away so they did not see their father's exposed body.

When Noah woke up with his hangover, he learned what his youngest son had done. He said,

> Cursed be Canaan! A slave of slaves,
>   a slave to his brothers!
> Blessed be GOD, the God of Shem,
>   but Canaan shall be his slave.
> God prosper Japheth,
>   living spaciously in the tents of Shem.
> But Canaan shall be his slave.

Noah lived another 350 years following the flood. He lived a total of 950 years. And he died.

THE FAMILY TREE OF NOAH'S SONS

10 This is the family tree of the sons of Noah: Shem, Ham, and Japheth. After the flood, they themselves had sons.

The sons of Japheth: Gomer, Magog, Madai, Javan, Tubal, Meshech, Tiras.

The sons of Gomer: Ashkenaz, Riphath, Togarmah.

The sons of Javan: Elishah, Tarshish, Kittim, Rodanim. The seafaring peoples developed from these, each in its own place by family, each with its own language.

The sons of Ham: Cush, Egypt, Put, Canaan.

The sons of Cush: Seba, Havilah, Sabtah, Raamah, Sabteca.

The sons of Raamah: Sheba, Dedan.

Cush also had Nimrod. He was the first great warrior on Earth. He was a great hunter before GOD. There was a saying, "Like Nimrod, a great hunter before GOD." His kingdom got its start with Babel; then Erech, Akkad, and Calneh in the country of Shinar. From there he went up to Asshur and built Nineveh, Rehoboth Ir, Calah, and Resen between Nineveh and the great city Calah.

Egypt was ancestor to the Ludim, the Anamim, the Lehabim, the Naphtuhim, the Pathrusim, the Casluhim (the origin of the Philistines), and the Kaphtorim.

Canaan had Sidon his firstborn, Heth, the Jebusites, the Amorites, the Girgashites, the Hivites, the Arkites, the Sinites, the Arvadites, the Zemarites, and the Hamathites. Later the Canaanites spread out, going from Sidon toward Gerar, as far south as Gaza, and then east all the way over to Sodom, Gomorrah, Admah, Zeboiim, and on to Lasha.

These are the descendants of Ham by family, language, country, and nation.

Shem, the older brother of Japheth, also had sons. Shem was ancestor to all the children of Eber.

The sons of Shem: Elam, Asshur, Arphaxad, Lud, and Aram.

The sons of Aram: Uz, Hul, Gether, Meshech.

Arphaxad had Shelah and Shelah had Eber. Eber had two sons, Peleg (so named because in his days the human race divided) and Joktan.

Joktan had Almodad, Sheleph, Hazarmaveth, Jerah, Hadoram, Uzal, Diklah, Obal, Abimael, Sheba, Ophir, Havilah, and Jobab—all sons of Joktan. Their land goes from Mesha toward Sephar as far as the mountain ranges in the east.

These are the descendants of Shem by family, language, country, and nation.

This is the family tree of the sons of Noah as they developed into nations. From them nations developed all across the Earth after the flood.

"GOD TURNED THEIR LANGUAGE INTO 'BABBLE'"

11 At one time, the whole Earth spoke the same language. It so happened that as they moved out of the east, they came upon a plain in the land of Shinar and settled down.

They said to one another, "Come, let's make bricks and fire them well." They used brick for stone and tar for mortar.

Then they said, "Come, let's build ourselves a city and a tower that reaches Heaven. Let's make ourselves famous so we won't be scattered here and there across the Earth."

GOD came down to look over the city and the tower those people had built.

GOD took one look and said, "One people, one language; why, this is only a first step. No telling what they'll come up with next—they'll stop at nothing! Come, we'll go down and garble their speech so they won't understand each other." Then GOD scattered them from there all over the world. And they had to quit building the city. That's how it came to be called Babel, because there GOD turned their language into "babble." From there GOD scattered them all over the world.

✝

This is the story of Shem. When Shem was 100 years old, he had Arphaxad. It was two years after the flood. After he had Arphaxad, he lived 600 more years and had other sons and daughters.

When Arphaxad was thirty-five years old, he had Shelah. After Arphaxad had Shelah, he lived 403 more years and had other sons and daughters.

When Shelah was thirty years old, he had Eber. After Shelah had Eber, he lived 403 more years and had other sons and daughters.

When Eber was thirty-four years old, he had Peleg. After Eber had Peleg, he lived 403 more years and had other sons and daughters.

When Peleg was thirty years old, he had Reu. After he had Reu, he lived 209 more years and had other sons and daughters.

When Reu was thirty-two years old, he had Serug. After Reu had Serug, he lived 207 more years and had other sons and daughters.

When Serug was thirty years old, he had Nahor. After Serug had Nahor, he lived 200 more years and had other sons and daughters.

When Nahor was twenty-nine years old, he had Terah. After Nahor had Terah, he lived 119 more years and had other sons and daughters.

When Terah was seventy years old, he had Abram, Nahor, and Haran.

THE FAMILY TREE OF TERAH

This is the story of Terah. Terah had Abram, Nahor, and Haran.

Haran had Lot. Haran died before his father, Terah, in the country of his family, Ur of the Chaldees.

Abram and Nahor each got married. Abram's wife was Sarai; Nahor's wife was Milcah, the daughter of his uncle Haran. Haran had two daughters, Milcah and Iscah.

Sarai was barren; she had no children.

Terah took his son Abram, his grandson Lot (Haran's son), and Sarai his daughter-in-law (his son Abram's wife) and set out with them from Ur of the Chaldees for the land of Canaan. But when they got as far as Haran, they settled down there.

Terah lived 205 years. He died in Haran.

ABRAM AND SARAH

12 GOD told Abram: "Leave your country, your family, and your father's home for a land that I will show you.

I'll make you a great nation
    and bless you.
I'll make you famous;
    you'll be a blessing.
I'll bless those who bless you;
    those who curse you I'll curse.
All the families of the Earth
    will be blessed through you."

So Abram left just as GOD said, and Lot left with him. Abram was seventy-five years old when he left Haran. Abram took his wife Sarai and his nephew Lot with him, along with all the possessions and people they had gotten in Haran, and set out for the land of Canaan and arrived safe and sound.

Abram passed through the country as far as Shechem and the Oak of Moreh. At that time the Canaanites occupied the land.

GOD appeared to Abram and said, "I will give this land to your children." Abram built an altar at the place GOD had appeared to him.

He moved on from there to the hill country east of Bethel and pitched his tent between Bethel to the west and Ai to the east. He built an altar there and prayed to GOD.

Abram kept moving, steadily making his way south, to the Negev.

Then a famine came to the land. Abram went down to Egypt to live; it was a hard famine. As he drew near to Egypt, he said to his wife, Sarai, "Look. We both know that you're a beautiful woman. When the Egyptians see you they're going to say, 'Aha! That's his wife!' and kill me. But they'll let you live. Do me a favor: tell them you're my sister. Because of you, they'll welcome me and let me live."

When Abram arrived in Egypt, the Egyptians took one look and saw that his wife was stunningly beautiful. Pharaoh's princes raved over her to Pharaoh. She was taken to live with Pharaoh.

Because of her, Abram got along very well: he accumulated sheep and cattle, male and female donkeys, men and women servants, and camels. But GOD hit Pharaoh hard because of Abram's wife Sarai; everybody in the palace got seriously sick.

Pharaoh called for Abram, "What's this that you've done to me? Why didn't you tell me that she's your wife? Why did you say, 'She's my sister' so that I'd take her as my wife? Here's your wife back—take her and get out!"

Pharaoh ordered his men to get Abram out of the country. They sent him and his wife and everything he owned on their way.

13 So Abram left Egypt and went back to the Negev, he and his wife and everything he owned, and Lot still with him. By now Abram was very rich, loaded with cattle and silver and gold.

He moved on from the Negev, camping along the way, to Bethel, the place he had first set up his tent between Bethel and Ai and built his first altar. Abram prayed there to GOD.

Lot, who was traveling with Abram, was also rich in sheep and cattle and tents. But the land couldn't support both of them; they had too many possessions. They couldn't both live there—quarrels broke out between Abram's shepherds and Lot's shepherds. The Canaanites and Perizzites were also living on the land at the time.

Abram said to Lot, "Let's not have fighting between us, between your shepherds and my shepherds. After all, we're family. Look around. Isn't there plenty of land out there? Let's separate. If you go left, I'll go right; if you go right, I'll go left."

Lot looked. He saw the whole plain of the Jordan spread out, well watered (this was before GOD destroyed Sodom and Gomorrah), like GOD's garden, like Egypt, and stretching all the way to Zoar. Lot took the whole plain of the Jordan. Lot set out to the east.

That's how they came to part company, uncle and nephew. Abram settled in Canaan; Lot settled in the cities of the plain and pitched his tent near Sodom.

The people of Sodom were evil—flagrant sinners against GOD.

After Lot separated from him, GOD said to Abram, "Open your eyes, look around. Look north, south, east, and west. Everything you see, the whole land spread out before you, I will give to you and your children forever. I'll make your descendants like dust—counting your descendants will be as impossible as counting the dust of the Earth. So—on your feet, get moving! Walk through the country, its length and breadth; I'm giving it all to you."

Abram moved his tent. He went and settled by the Oaks of Mamre in Hebron. There he built an altar to GOD.

✝

14 Then this: Amraphel king of Shinar, Arioch king of Ellasar, Kedorlaomer king of Elam, and Tidal king of Goiim went off to war to fight Bera king of Sodom, Birsha king of Gomorrah, Shinab king of Admah, Shemeber king of Zeboiim, and the king of Bela, that is, Zoar.

This second group of kings, the attacked, came together at the Valley of Siddim, that is, the Salt Sea. They had been under the thumb of Kedorlaomer for twelve years. In the thirteenth year, they revolted.

In the fourteenth year, Kedorlaomer and the kings allied with him set out and defeated the Rephaim in Ashteroth Karnaim, the Zuzim in Ham, the Emim in Shaveh Kiriathaim, and the Horites in their hill country of Seir as far as El Paran on the far edge of the desert. On their way back they stopped at En Mishpat, that is, Kadesh, and conquered the whole region of the Amalekites as well as that of the Amorites who lived in Hazazon Tamar.

That's when the king of Sodom marched out with the king of Gomorrah, the king of Admah, the king of Zeboiim, and the king of Bela, that is, Zoar. They drew up in battle formation against their enemies in the Valley of Siddim—against Kedorlaomer king of Elam, Tidal king of Goiim, Amraphel king of Shinar, and Arioch king of Ellasar, four kings against five.

The Valley of Siddim was full of tar pits. When the kings of Sodom and Gomorrah fled, they fell into the tar pits, but the rest escaped into the mountains. The four kings captured all the possessions of Sodom and Gomorrah, all their food and equipment, and went on their way. They captured Lot, Abram's nephew who was living in Sodom at the time, taking everything he owned with them.

A fugitive came and reported to Abram the Hebrew. Abram was living at the Oaks of Mamre the Amorite, brother of Eshcol and Aner. They were allies of Abram. When Abram heard that his nephew had been taken prisoner, he lined up his servants, all of them born in his household—there were 318 of them—and chased after the captors all the way to Dan. Abram and his men split into small groups and attacked by night. They chased them as far as Hobah, just north of Damascus. They recovered all the plunder along with nephew Lot and his possessions, including the women and the people.

After Abram returned from defeating Kedorlaomer and his allied kings, the king of Sodom came out to greet him in the Valley of Shaveh, the King's Valley. Melchizedek, king of Salem, brought out bread and wine—he was priest of The High God—and blessed him:

Blessed be Abram by The High God,
Creator of Heaven and Earth.

And blessed be The High God,
　　who handed your enemies over to you.

Abram gave him a tenth of all the recovered plunder.

The king of Sodom said to Abram, "Give me back the people but keep all the plunder for yourself."

But Abram told the king of Sodom, "I swear to GOD, The High God, Creator of Heaven and Earth, this solemn oath, that I'll take nothing from you, not so much as a thread or a shoestring. I'm not going to have you go around saying, 'I made Abram rich.' Nothing for me other than what the young men ate and the share of the men who went with me, Aner, Eshcol, and Mamre; they're to get their share of the plunder."

✝

15 After all these things, this word of GOD came to Abram in a vision: "Don't be afraid, Abram. I'm your shield. Your reward will be grand!"

Abram said, "GOD, Master, what use are your gifts as long as I'm childless and Eliezer of Damascus is going to inherit everything?" Abram continued, "See, you've given me no children, and now a mere house servant is going to get it all."

Then GOD's Message came: "Don't worry, he won't be your heir; a son from your body will be your heir."

Then he took him outside and said, "Look at the sky. Count the stars. Can you do it? Count your descendants! You're going to have a big family, Abram!"

And he believed! Believed GOD! God declared him "Set-Right-with-God."

GOD continued, "I'm the same GOD who brought you from Ur of the Chaldees and gave you this land to own."

Abram said, "Master GOD, how am I to know this, that it will all be mine?"

GOD said, "Bring me a heifer, a goat, and a ram, each three years old, and a dove and a young pigeon."

He brought all these animals to him, split them down the middle and laid the halves opposite each other. But he didn't split the birds. Vultures swooped down on the carcasses, but Abram scared them off.

As the sun went down a deep sleep overcame Abram and then a sense of dread, dark and heavy.

GOD said to Abram, "Know this: your descendants will live as outsiders in a land not theirs; they'll be enslaved and beaten down for 400 years. Then I'll punish their slave masters; your offspring will march out of there loaded with plunder. But not you; you'll have a long and full life and die a good and peaceful death. Not until the fourth generation will your descendants return here; sin is still a thriving business among the Amorites."

When the sun was down and it was dark, a smoking firepot and a flaming torch moved between the split carcasses. That's when GOD made a covenant with Abram: "I'm giving this land to your children, from the Nile River in Egypt to the River Euphrates in Assyria—the country of the Kenites, Kenizzites, Kadmonites, Hittites, Perizzites, Rephaim, Amorites, Canaanites, Girgashites, and Jebusites."

✢

16 Sarai, Abram's wife, hadn't yet produced a child. She had an Egyptian maid named Hagar. Sarai said to Abram, "GOD has not seen fit to let me have a child. Sleep with my maid. Maybe I can get a family from her." Abram agreed to do what Sarai said.

So Sarai, Abram's wife, took her Egyptian maid Hagar and gave her to her husband Abram as a wife. Abram had been living ten years in Canaan when this took place. He slept with Hagar and she got pregnant. When she learned she was pregnant, she looked down on her mistress.

Sarai told Abram, "It's all your fault that I'm suffering this abuse. I put my maid in bed with you and the minute she knows she's pregnant, she treats me like I'm nothing. May GOD decide which of us is right."

"You decide," said Abram. "Your maid is your business."

Sarai was abusive to Hagar and she ran away.

An angel of GOD found her beside a spring in the desert; it was the spring on the road to Shur. He said, "Hagar, maid of Sarai, what are you doing here?"

She said, "I'm running away from Sarai my mistress."

The angel of GOD said, "Go back to your mistress. Put up with her abuse." He continued, "I'm going to give you a big family, children past counting.

From this pregnancy, you'll get a son: Name him Ishmael;
    for GOD heard you, GOD answered you.

He'll be a bucking bronco of a man,
  a real fighter, fighting and being fought,
Always stirring up trouble,
  always at odds with his family."

She answered God by name, praying to the God who spoke to her, "You're the God who sees me!"

"Yes! He saw me; and then I saw him!"

That's how that desert spring got named "God-Alive-Sees-Me Spring." That spring is still there, between Kadesh and Bered.

Hagar gave Abram a son. Abram named him Ishmael. Abram was eighty-six years old when Hagar gave him his son, Ishmael.

✛

17 When Abram was ninety-nine years old, God showed up and said to him, "I am The Strong God, live entirely before me, live to the hilt! I'll make a covenant between us and I'll give you a huge family."

Overwhelmed, Abram fell flat on his face.

Then God said to him, "This is my covenant with you: You'll be the father of many nations. Your name will no longer be Abram, but Abraham, meaning that 'I'm making you the father of many nations.' I'll make you a father of fathers—I'll make nations from you, kings will issue from you. I'm establishing my covenant between me and you, a covenant that includes your descendants, a covenant that goes on and on and on, a covenant that commits me to be your God and the God of your descendants. And I'm giving you and your descendants this land where you're now just camping, this whole country of Canaan, to own forever. And I'll be their God."

God continued to Abraham, "And you: You will honor my covenant, you and your descendants, generation after generation. This is the covenant that you are to honor, the covenant that pulls in all your descendants: Circumcise every male. Circumcise by cutting off the foreskin of the penis; it will be the sign of the covenant between us. Every male baby will be circumcised when he is eight days old, generation after generation—this includes house-born slaves and slaves bought from outsiders who are not blood kin. Make sure you circumcise both your own children and anyone brought in from the outside. That way my covenant will be cut into your body, a permanent mark of my permanent covenant. An uncircumcised male, one who has not had the foreskin of his penis cut off, will be cut off from his people—he has broken my covenant."

God continued speaking to Abraham, "And Sarai your wife: Don't call her Sarai any longer; call her Sarah. I'll bless her—yes! I'll give you a son by her! Oh, how I'll bless her! Nations will come from her; kings of nations will come from her."

Abraham fell flat on his face. And then he laughed, thinking, "Can a hundred-year-old man father a son? And can Sarah, at ninety years, have a baby?"

Recovering, Abraham said to God, "Oh, keep Ishmael alive and well before you!"

But God said, "That's not what I mean. Your wife, Sarah, will have a baby, a son. Name him Isaac (Laughter). I'll establish my covenant with him and his descendants, a covenant that lasts forever.

"And Ishmael? Yes, I heard your prayer for him. I'll also bless him; I'll make sure he has plenty of children—a huge family. He'll father twelve princes; I'll make him a great nation. But I'll establish my covenant with Isaac whom Sarah will give you about this time next year."

God finished speaking with Abraham and left.

Then Abraham took his son Ishmael and all his servants, whether houseborn or purchased—every male in his household—and circumcised them, cutting off their foreskins that very day, just as God had told him.

Abraham was ninety-nine years old when he was circumcised. His son Ishmael was thirteen years old when he was circumcised. Abraham and Ishmael were circumcised the same day together with all the servants of his household, those born there and those purchased from outsiders—all were circumcised with him.

✢

18 GOD appeared to Abraham at the Oaks of Mamre while he was sitting at the entrance of his tent. It was the hottest part of the day. He looked up and saw three men standing. He ran from his tent to greet them and bowed before them.

He said, "Master, if it please you, stop for a while with your servant. I'll get some water so you can wash your feet. Rest under this tree. I'll get some food to refresh you on your way, since your travels have brought you across my path."

They said, "Certainly. Go ahead."

Abraham hurried into the tent to Sarah. He said, "Hurry. Get three cups of our best flour; knead it and make bread."

Then Abraham ran to the cattle pen and picked out a nice plump calf and gave it to the servant who lost no time getting it ready. Then he got curds and milk, brought them with the calf that had been roasted, set the meal before the men, and stood there under the tree while they ate.

The men said to him, "Where is Sarah your wife?"

He said, "In the tent."

One of them said, "I'm coming back about this time next year. When I arrive, your wife Sarah will have a son." Sarah was listening at the tent opening, just behind the man.

Abraham and Sarah were old by this time, very old. Sarah was far past the age for having babies. Sarah laughed within herself, "An old woman like me? Get pregnant? With this old man of a husband?"

GOD said to Abraham, "Why did Sarah laugh saying, 'Me? Have a baby? An old woman like me?' Is anything too hard for GOD? I'll be back about this time next year and Sarah will have a baby."

Sarah lied. She said, "I didn't laugh," because she was afraid.

But he said, "Yes you did; you laughed."

✛

When the men got up to leave, they set off for Sodom. Abraham walked with them to say goodbye.

Then GOD said, "Shall I keep back from Abraham what I'm about to do? Abraham is going to become a large and strong nation; all the nations of the world are going to find themselves blessed through him. Yes, I've settled on him as the one to train his children and future family to observe GOD's way of life, live kindly and generously and fairly, so that GOD can complete in Abraham what he promised him."

GOD continued, "The cries of the victims in Sodom and Gomorrah are deafening; the sin of those cities is immense. I'm going down to see for myself, see if what they're doing is as bad as it sounds. Then I'll know."

The men set out for Sodom, but Abraham stood in GOD's path, blocking his way.

Abraham confronted him, "Are you serious? Are you planning on getting rid of the good people right along with the bad? What if there are fifty decent people left in the city; will you lump the good with the bad and get rid of the lot? Wouldn't you spare the city for the sake of those fifty innocents? I can't believe you'd do that, kill off the good and the bad alike as if there were no difference between them. Doesn't the Judge of all the Earth judge with justice?"

GOD said, "If I find fifty decent people in the city of Sodom, I'll spare the place just for them."

Abraham came back, "Do I, a mere mortal made from a handful of dirt, dare open my mouth again to my Master? What if the fifty fall short by five—would you destroy the city because of those missing five?"

He said, "I won't destroy it if there are forty-five."

Abraham spoke up again, "What if you only find forty?"

"Neither will I destroy it if for forty."

He said, "Master, don't be irritated with me, but what if only thirty are found?"

"No, I won't do it if I find thirty."

He pushed on, "I know I'm trying your patience, Master, but how about for twenty?"

"I won't destroy it for twenty."

He wouldn't quit, "Don't get angry, Master—this is the last time. What if you only come up with ten?"

"For the sake of only ten, I won't destroy the city."

When GOD finished talking with Abraham, he left. And Abraham went home.

19 The two angels arrived at Sodom in the evening. Lot was sitting at the city gate. He saw them and got up to welcome them, bowing before them and said, "Please, my friends, come to my house and stay the night. Wash up. You can rise early and be on your way refreshed."

They said, "No, we'll sleep in the street."

But he insisted, wouldn't take no for an answer; and they relented and went home with him. Lot fixed a hot meal for them and they ate.

Before they went to bed men from all over the city of Sodom, young and old, descended on the house from all sides and boxed them in. They yelled to Lot, "Where are the men who are staying with you for the night? Bring them out so we can have our sport with them!"

Lot went out, barring the door behind him, and said, "Brothers, please, don't be vile! Look, I have two daughters, virgins; let me bring them out; you can take your pleasure with them, but don't touch these men—they're my guests."

They said, "Get lost! You drop in from nowhere and now you're going to tell us how to run our lives. We'll treat you worse than them!" And they charged past Lot to break down the door.

But the two men reached out and pulled Lot inside the house, locking the door. Then they struck blind the men who were trying to break down the door, both leaders and followers, leaving them groping in the dark.

The two men said to Lot, "Do you have any other family here? Sons, daughters—anybody in the city? Get them out of here, and now! We're going to destroy this place. The outcries of victims here to GOD is deafening; we've been sent to blast this place into oblivion."

Lot went out and warned the fiancés of his daughters, "Evacuate this place; GOD is about to destroy this city!" But his daughters' would-be husbands treated it as a joke.

At break of day, the angels pushed Lot to get going, "Hurry. Get your wife and two daughters out of here before it's too late and you're caught in the punishment of the city."

Lot was dragging his feet. The men grabbed Lot's arm, and the arms of his wife and daughters—GOD was so merciful to them!—and dragged them to safety outside the city. When they had them outside, Lot was told, "Now run for your life! Don't look back! Don't stop anywhere on the plain—run for the hills or you'll be swept away."

But Lot protested, "No, masters, you can't mean it! I know that you've taken a liking to me and have done me an immense favor in saving my life, but I can't run for the mountains—who knows what terrible thing might happen to me in the mountains and leave me for dead. Look over there—that town is close enough to get to. It's a small town, hardly anything to it. Let me escape there and save my life—it's a mere wide place in the road."

He said to him, "All right. If you insist. I'll let you have your way. And I won't stamp out the town you've spotted. But hurry up. Run for it! I can't do anything until you get there." That's why the town was called Zoar, that is, Smalltown.

The sun was high in the sky when Lot arrived at Zoar.

Then GOD rained brimstone and fire down on Sodom and Gomorrah—a river of lava from GOD out of the sky!—and destroyed these cities and the entire plain and everyone who lived in the cities and everything that grew from the ground.

But Lot's wife looked back and turned into a pillar of salt.

Abraham got up early the next morning and went to the place he had so recently stood with GOD. He looked out over Sodom and Gomorrah, surveying the whole plain. All he could see was smoke belching from the Earth, like smoke from a furnace.

And that's the story: When God destroyed the Cities of the Plain, he was mindful of Abraham and first got Lot out of there before he blasted those cities off the face of the Earth.

Lot left Zoar and went into the mountains to live with his two daughters; he was afraid to stay in Zoar. He lived in a cave with his daughters.

One day the older daughter said to the younger, "Our father is getting old and there's not a man left in the country by whom we can get pregnant. Let's get our father drunk with wine and lie with him. We'll get children through our father—it's our only chance to keep our family alive."

They got their father drunk with wine that very night. The older daughter went and lay with him. He was oblivious, knowing nothing of what she did. The next morning the older said to the younger, "Last night I slept with my father. Tonight, it's your turn. We'll get him drunk again and then you sleep with him. We'll both get a child through our father and keep our family alive." So that night they got their father drunk again and the younger went in and slept with him. Again he was oblivious, knowing nothing of what she did.

Both daughters became pregnant by their father, Lot. The older daughter had a son and named him Moab, the ancestor of the present-day Moabites. The younger daughter had a son and named him Ben-Ammi, the ancestor of the present-day Ammonites.

✢

20 Abraham traveled from there south to the Negev and settled down between Kadesh and Shur. While he was camping in Gerar, Abraham said of his wife Sarah, "She's my sister."

So Abimelech, king of Gerar, sent for Sarah and took her. But God came to Abimelech in a dream that night and told him, "You're as good as dead—that woman you took, she's a married woman."

Now Abimelech had not yet slept with her, hadn't so much as

touched her. He said, "Master, would you kill an innocent man? Didn't he tell me, 'She's my sister'? And didn't she herself say, 'He's my brother'? I had no idea I was doing anything wrong when I did this."

God said to him in the dream, "Yes, I know your intentions were pure, that's why I kept you from sinning against me; I was the one who kept you from going to bed with her. So now give the man's wife back to him. He's a prophet and will pray for you—pray for your life. If you don't give her back, know that it's certain death both for you and everyone in your family."

Abimelech was up first thing in the morning. He called all his house servants together and told them the whole story. They were shocked. Then Abimelech called in Abraham and said, "What have you done to us? What have I ever done to you that you would bring on me and my kingdom this huge offense? What you've done to me ought never to have been done."

Abimelech went on to Abraham, "Whatever were you thinking of when you did this thing?"

Abraham said, "I just assumed that there was no fear of God in this place and that they'd kill me to get my wife. Besides, the truth is that she is my halfsister; she's my father's daughter but not my mother's. When God sent me out as a wanderer from my father's home, I told her, 'Do me a favor; wherever we go, tell people that I'm your brother.'"

Then Abimelech gave Sarah back to Abraham, and along with her sent sheep and cattle and servants, both male and female. He said, "My land is open to you; live wherever you wish."

And to Sarah he said, "I've given your brother a thousand pieces of silver—that clears you of even a shadow of suspicion before the eyes of the world. You're vindicated."

Then Abraham prayed to God and God healed Abimelech, his wife and his maidservants, and they started having babies again. For GOD had shut down every womb in Abimelech's household on account of Sarah, Abraham's wife.

✛

21 GOD visited Sarah exactly as he said he would; GOD did to Sarah what he promised: Sarah became pregnant and gave Abraham a son in his old age, and at the very time God had set. Abraham named him Isaac. When his son was eight days old, Abraham circumcised him just as God had commanded.

Abraham was a hundred years old when his son Isaac was born. Sarah said,

> God has blessed me with laughter
> and all who get the news will laugh with me!

She also said,

> Whoever would have suggested to Abraham
> that Sarah would one day nurse a baby!
> Yet here I am! I've given the old man a son!

The baby grew and was weaned. Abraham threw a big party on the day Isaac was weaned.

One day Sarah saw the son that Hagar the Egyptian had borne to Abraham, poking fun at her son Isaac. She told Abraham, "Get rid of this slave woman and her son. No child of this slave is going to share inheritance with my son Isaac!"

The matter gave great pain to Abraham—after all, Ishmael was his son. But God spoke to Abraham, "Don't feel badly about the boy and your maid. Do whatever Sarah tells you. Your descendants will come through Isaac. Regarding your maid's son, be assured that I'll also develop a great nation from him—he's your son too."

Abraham got up early the next morning, got some food together and a canteen of water for Hagar, put them on her back and sent her away with the child. She wandered off into the desert of Beersheba. When the water was gone, she left the child under a shrub and went off, fifty yards or so. She said, "I can't watch my son die." As she sat, she broke into sobs.

Meanwhile, God heard the boy crying. The angel of God called from Heaven to Hagar, "What's wrong Hagar? Don't be afraid. God has heard the boy and knows the fix he's in. Up now; go get the boy. Hold him tight. I'm going to make of him a great nation."

Just then God opened her eyes, she looked. She saw a well of water. She went to it and filled her canteen and gave the boy a long, cool drink.

God was on the boy's side as he grew up. He lived out in the desert and became a skilled archer. He lived in the Paran wilderness. And his mother got him a wife from Egypt.

At about that same time, Abimelech and the captain of his troops, Phicol, spoke to Abraham: "No matter what you do, God is on your side. So swear to me that you won't do anything underhanded to me or any of my family. For as long as you live here, swear that you'll treat me and my land as well as I've treated you."

Abraham said, "I swear it."

At the same time, Abraham confronted Abimelech over the matter of a well of water that Abimelech's servants had taken. Abimelech said, "I have no idea who did this; you never told me about it; this is the first I've heard of it."

So the two of them made a covenant. Abraham took sheep and cattle and gave them to Abimelech. Abraham set aside seven sheep from his flock.

Abimelech said, "What does this mean? These seven sheep you've set aside."

Abraham said, "It means that when you accept these seven sheep, you take it as proof that I dug this well, that it's my well."

That's how the place got named Beersheba (the Oath-Well), because the two of them swore a covenant oath there. After they had made the covenant at Beersheba, Abimelech and his commander, Phicol, left and went back to Philistine territory.

Abraham planted a tamarisk tree in Beersheba and worshiped GOD there, praying to the Eternal God. Abraham lived in Philistine country for a long time.

⊹

22 After all this, God tested Abraham. God said, "Abraham!" "Yes?" answered Abraham. "I'm listening."

He said, "Take your dear son Isaac whom you love and go to the land of Moriah. Sacrifice him there as a burnt offering on one of the mountains that I'll point out to you."

Abraham got up early in the morning and saddled his donkey. He took two of his young servants and his son Isaac. He had split wood for the burnt offering. He set out for the place God had directed him. On the third day he looked up and saw the place in the distance. Abraham told his two young servants, "Stay here with the donkey. The boy and I are going over there to worship; then we'll come back to you."

Abraham took the wood for the burnt offering and gave it to Isaac his son to carry. He carried the flint and the knife. The two of them went off together.

Isaac said to Abraham his father, "Father?"

"Yes, my son."

"We have flint and wood, but where's the sheep for the burnt offering?"

Abraham said, "Son, God will see to it that there's a sheep for the burnt offering." And they kept on walking together.

They arrived at the place to which God had directed him. Abraham built an altar. He laid out the wood. Then he tied up Isaac and laid him on the wood. Abraham reached out and took the knife to kill his son.

Just then an angel of GOD called to him out of Heaven, "Abraham! Abraham!"

"Yes, I'm listening."

"Don't lay a hand on that boy! Don't touch him! Now I know how fearlessly you fear God; you didn't hesitate to place your son, your dear son, on the altar for me."

Abraham looked up. He saw a ram caught by its horns in the thicket. Abraham took the ram and sacrificed it as a burnt offering instead of his son.

Abraham named that place, GOD-Yireh (GOD-Sees-to-It). That's where we get the saying, "On the mountain of GOD, he sees to it."

The angel of GOD spoke from Heaven a second time to Abraham: "I swear—GOD's sure word!—because you have gone through with this, and have not refused to give me your son, your dear, dear son, I'll bless you—oh, how I'll bless you! And I'll make sure that your children flourish—like stars in the sky! like sand on the beaches! And your descendants will defeat their enemies. All nations on Earth will find themselves blessed through your descendants because you obeyed me."

Then Abraham went back to his young servants. They got things together and returned to Beersheba. Abraham settled down in Beersheba.

✛

After all this, Abraham got the news: "Your brother Nahor is a father! Milcah has given him children: Uz, his firstborn, his brother Buz, Kemuel (he was the father of Aram), Kesed, Hazo, Pildash, Jidlaph, and Bethuel." (Bethuel was the father of Rebekah.) Milcah gave these eight sons to Nahor, Abraham's brother.

His concubine, Reumah, gave him four more children: Tebah, Gaham, Tahash, and Maacah.

✛

23 Sarah lived 127 years. Sarah died in Kiriath Arba, present-day Hebron, in the land of Canaan. Abraham mourned for Sarah and wept.

Then Abraham got up from mourning his dead wife and spoke to the Hittites: "I know I'm only an outsider here among you, but sell me a burial plot so that I can bury my dead decently."

The Hittites responded, "Why, you're no mere outsider here with us, you're a prince of God! Bury your dead wife in the best of our burial sites. None of us will refuse you a place for burial."

Then Abraham got up, bowed respectfully to the people of the land, the Hittites, and said, "If you're serious about helping me give my wife a proper burial, intercede for me with Ephron son of Zohar. Ask him to sell me the cave of Machpelah that he owns, the one at the end of his land. Ask him to sell it to me at its full price for a burial plot, with you as witnesses."

Ephron was part of the local Hittite community. Then Ephron the Hittite spoke up, answering Abraham with all the Hittites who were part of the town council listening: "Oh no, my master! I couldn't do that. The field is yours—a gift. I'll give it and the cave to you. With my people as witnesses, I give it to you. Bury your deceased wife."

Abraham bowed respectfully before the assembled council and answered Ephron: "Please allow me—I want to pay the price of the land; take my money so that I can go ahead and bury my wife."

Then Ephron answered Abraham, "If you insist, master. What's four hundred silver shekels between us? Now go ahead and bury your wife."

Abraham accepted Ephron's offer and paid out the sum that Ephron had named before the town council of Hittites—four hundred silver shekels at the current exchange rate.

That's how Ephron's field next to Mamre—the field, its cave and all the trees within its borders—became Abraham's property. The town council of Hittites witnessed the transaction. Abraham then proceeded to bury his wife Sarah in the cave in the field of Machpelah that is next to Mamre, present-day Hebron, in the land of Canaan. The field and its cave went from the Hittites into Abraham's possession as a burial plot.

Isaac and Rebekah

24 Abraham was now an old man. God had blessed Abraham in every way.

Abraham spoke to the senior servant in his household, the one in charge of everything he had, "Put your hand under my thigh and swear by God—God of Heaven, God of Earth—that you will not get a wife for my son from among the young women of the Canaanites here, but will go to the land of my birth and get a wife for my son Isaac."

The servant answered, "But what if the woman refuses to leave home and come with me? Do I then take your son back to your home country?"

Abraham said, "Oh no. Never. By no means are you to take my son back there. God, the God of Heaven, took me from the home of my father and from the country of my birth and spoke to me in solemn promise, 'I'm giving *this* land to your descendants.' This God will send his angel ahead of you to get a wife for my son. And if the woman won't come, you are free from this oath you've sworn to me. But under no circumstances are you to take my son back there."

So the servant put his hand under the thigh of his master Abraham and gave his solemn oath.

The servant took ten of his master's camels and, loaded with gifts from his master, traveled to Aram Naharaim and the city of Nahor. Outside the city, he made the camels kneel at a well. It was evening, the time when the women came to draw water. He prayed, "O God, God of my master Abraham, make things go smoothly this day; treat my master Abraham well! As I stand here by the spring while the young women of the town come out to get water, let the girl to whom I say, 'Lower your jug and give me a drink,' and who answers, 'Drink, and let me also water your camels'—let her be the woman you have picked out for your servant Isaac. Then I'll know that you're working graciously behind the scenes for my master."

It so happened that the words were barely out of his mouth when Rebekah, the daughter of Bethuel whose mother was Milcah the wife of Nahor, Abraham's brother, came out with a water jug on her shoulder. The girl was stunningly beautiful, a pure virgin. She went down to the spring, filled her jug and came back up. The servant ran to meet her and said, "Please, can I have a sip of water from your jug?"

She said, "Certainly, drink!" And she held the jug so that he could drink. When he had satisfied his thirst she said, "I'll get water for your camels, too, until they've drunk their fill." She promptly emptied her jug into the trough and ran back to the well to fill it, and she kept at it until she had watered all the camels.

The man watched, silent. Was this GOD's answer? Had GOD made his trip a success or not?

When the camels had finished drinking, the man brought out gifts, a gold nose ring weighing a little over a quarter of an ounce and two arm bracelets weighing about four ounces, and gave them to her. He asked her, "Tell me about your family? Whose daughter are you? Is there room in your father's house for us to stay the night?"

She said, "I'm the daughter of Bethuel the son of Milcah and Nahor. And there's plenty of room in our house for you to stay—and lots of straw and feed besides."

At this the man bowed in worship before GOD and prayed, "Blessed be GOD, God of my master Abraham: How generous and true you've been to my master; you've held nothing back. You led me right to the door of my master's brother!"

And the girl was off and running, telling everyone in her mother's house what had happened.

Rebekah had a brother named Laban. Laban ran outside to the man at the spring. He had seen the nose ring and the bracelets on his sister and had heard her say, "The man said this and this and this to me." So he went to the man and there he was, still standing with his camels at the spring. Laban welcomed him: "Come on in, blessed of GOD! Why are you standing out here? I've got the house ready for you; and there's also a place for your camels."

So the man went into the house. The camels were unloaded and given straw and feed. Water was brought to bathe the feet of the man and the men with him. Then Laban brought out food. But the man said, "I won't eat until I tell my story."

Laban said, "Go ahead; tell us."

The servant said, "I'm the servant of Abraham. GOD has blessed my master—he's a great man; GOD has given him sheep and cattle, silver and gold, servants and maidservants, camels and donkeys. And then to top it off, Sarah, my master's wife, gave him a son in her old age and he has passed everything on to his son. My master made me promise, 'Don't get a wife for my son from the daughters of the Canaanites in whose land I live. No, go to my father's home, back to my family, and get a wife for my son there.' I said to my master, 'But what if the woman won't come with me?' He said, 'GOD before whom I've walked faithfully will send his angel with you and he'll make things work out so that you'll bring back a wife for my son from my family, from the house of my father. Then you'll be free from the oath. If you go to my family and they won't give her to you, you will also be free from the oath.'

"Well, when I came this very day to the spring, I prayed, 'GOD, God of my master Abraham, make things turn out well in this task I've been given. I'm standing at this well. When a young woman comes here to draw water and I say to her, Please, give me a sip of water from your jug, and she says, Not only will I give you a drink, I'll also water your camels—let that woman be the wife GOD has picked out for my master's son.'

"I had barely finished offering this prayer, when Rebekah arrived, her jug on her shoulder. She went to the spring and drew water and I said, 'Please, can I have a drink?' She didn't hesitate. She held out her jug and said, 'Drink; and when you're finished I'll also water your camels.' I drank, and she watered the camels. I asked her, 'Whose daughter are you?' She said, 'The daughter of Bethuel whose parents were Nahor and Milcah.' I gave her a ring for her nose, bracelets for her arms, and bowed in worship to GOD. I praised GOD, the God of my master Abraham who had led me straight to the door of my master's family to get a wife for his son.

"Now, tell me what you are going to do. If you plan to respond with a generous *yes*, tell me. But if not, tell me plainly so I can figure out what to do next."

Laban and Bethuel answered, "This is totally from GOD. We have no say in the matter, either yes or no. Rebekah is yours: Take her and go; let her be the wife of your master's son, as GOD has made plain."

When Abraham's servant heard their decision, he bowed in worship before GOD. Then he brought out gifts of silver and gold and clothing and gave them to Rebekah. He also gave expensive gifts to her brother and mother. He and his men had supper and spent the night. But first thing in the morning they were up. He said, "Send me back to my master."

Her brother and mother said, "Let the girl stay a while, say another ten days, and then go."

He said, "Oh, don't make me wait! GOD has worked everything out so well—send me off to my master."

They said, "We'll call the girl; we'll ask her."

They called Rebekah and asked her, "Do you want to go with this man?"

She said, "I'm ready to go."

So they sent them off, their sister Rebekah with her nurse, and Abraham's servant with his men. And they blessed Rebekah saying,

> You're our sister—live bountifully!
> And your children, triumphantly!

Rebekah and her young maids mounted the camels and followed the man. The servant took Rebekah and set off for home.

Isaac was living in the Negev. He had just come back from a visit to Beer Lahai Roi. In the evening he went out into the field; while meditating he looked up and saw camels coming. When Rebekah looked up and saw Isaac, she got down from her camel and asked the servant, "Who is that man out in the field coming toward us?"

"That is my master."

She took her veil and covered herself.

After the servant told Isaac the whole story of the trip, Isaac took Rebekah into the tent of his mother Sarah. He married Rebekah and she became his wife and he loved her. So Isaac found comfort after his mother's death.

✠

25 Abraham married a second time; his new wife was named Keturah. She gave birth to Zimran, Jokshan, Medan, Midian, Ishbak, and Shuah.

Jokshan had Sheba and Dedan.

Dedan's descendants were the Asshurim, the Letushim, and the Leummim.

Midian had Ephah, Epher, Hanoch, Abida, and Eldaah—all from the line of Keturah.

But Abraham gave everything he possessed to Isaac. While he was still living, he gave gifts to the sons he had by his concubines, but then sent them away to the country of the east, putting a good distance between them and his son Isaac.

Abraham lived 175 years. Then he took his final breath. He died happy at a ripe old age, full of years, and was buried with his family. His sons Isaac and Ishmael buried him in the cave of Machpelah in the field of Ephron son of Zohar the Hittite, next to Mamre. It was the field that Abraham had bought from the Hittites. Abraham was buried next to his wife Sarah. After Abraham's death, God blessed his son Isaac. Isaac lived at Beer Lahai Roi.

THE FAMILY TREE OF ISHMAEL

This is the family tree of Ishmael son of Abraham, the son that Hagar the Egyptian, Sarah's maid, bore to Abraham.

These are the names of Ishmael's sons in the order of their births: Nebaioth, Ishmael's first-born, Kedar, Adbeel, Mibsam, Mishma, Dumah, Massa, Hadad, Tema, Jetur, Naphish, and Kedemah—all the sons of Ishmael. Their settlements and encampments were named after them. Twelve princes with their twelve tribes.

Ishmael lived 137 years. When he breathed his last and died he was buried with his family. His children settled down all the way from Havilah near Egypt eastward to Shur in the direction of Assyria. The Ishmaelites didn't get along with any of their kin.

JACOB AND RACHEL

This is the family tree of Isaac son of Abraham: Abraham had Isaac. Isaac was forty years old when he married Rebekah daughter of Bethuel the Aramean of Paddan Aram. She was the sister of Laban the Aramean.

Isaac prayed hard to GOD for his wife because she was barren. GOD answered his prayer and Rebekah became pregnant. But the children tumbled and kicked inside her so much that she said, "If this is the way it's going to be, why go on living?" She went to GOD to find out what was going on. GOD told her,

> Two nations are in your womb,
>   two peoples butting heads while still in your body.
> One people will overpower the other,
>   and the older will serve the younger.

When her time to give birth came, sure enough, there were twins in her womb. The first came out reddish, as if snugly wrapped in a hairy blanket; they named him Esau (Hairy). His brother followed, his fist clutched tight to Esau's heel; they named him Jacob (Heel). Isaac was sixty years old when they were born.

The boys grew up. Esau became an expert hunter, an outdoorsman. Jacob was a quiet man preferring life indoors among the tents. Isaac loved Esau because he loved his game, but Rebekah loved Jacob.

One day Jacob was cooking a stew. Esau came in from the field, starved. Esau said to Jacob, "Give me some of that red stew — I'm starved!" That's how he came to be called Edom (Red).

Jacob said, "Make me a trade: my stew for your rights as the firstborn."

Esau said, "I'm starving! What good is a birthright if I'm dead?"

Jacob said, "First, swear to me." And he did it. On oath Esau traded away his rights as the firstborn. Jacob gave him bread and the stew of lentils. He ate and drank, got up and left. That's how Esau shrugged off his rights as the firstborn.

⊹

26 There was a famine in the land, as bad as the famine during the time of Abraham. And Isaac went down to Abimelech, king of the Philistines, in Gerar.

GOD appeared to him and said, "Don't go down to Egypt; stay where I tell you. Stay here in this land and I'll be with you and bless you. I'm giving you and your children all these lands, fulfilling the oath that I swore to your father Abraham. I'll make your descendants as many as the stars in the sky and give them all these lands. All the nations of the Earth will get a blessing for themselves through your descendants. And why? Because Abraham obeyed my summons and kept my charge — my commands, my guidelines, my teachings."

So Isaac stayed put in Gerar.

The men of the place questioned him about his wife. He said, "She's my sister." He was afraid to say "She's my wife." He was thinking, "These men might kill me to get Rebekah, she's so beautiful."

One day, after they had been there quite a long time, Abimelech, king of the Philistines, looked out his window and saw Isaac fondling his wife Rebekah. Abimelech sent for Isaac and said, "So, she's your wife. Why did you tell us 'She's my sister'?"

Isaac said, "Because I thought I might get killed by someone who wanted her."

Abimelech said, "But think of what you might have done to *us*!

Given a little more time, one of the men might have slept with your wife; you would have been responsible for bringing guilt down on us."

Then Abimelech gave orders to his people: "Anyone who so much as lays a hand on this man or his wife dies."

Isaac planted crops in that land and took in a huge harvest. GOD blessed him. The man got richer and richer by the day until he was very wealthy. He accumulated flocks and herds and many, many servants, so much so that the Philistines began to envy him. They got back at him by throwing dirt and debris into all the wells that his father's servants had dug back in the days of his father Abraham, clogging up all the wells.

Finally, Abimelech told Isaac: "Leave. You've become far too big for us."

So Isaac left. He camped in the valley of Gerar and settled down there. Isaac dug again the wells which were dug in the days of his father Abraham but had been clogged up by the Philistines after Abraham's death. And he renamed them, using the original names his father had given them.

One day, as Isaac's servants were digging in the valley, they came on a well of spring water. The shepherds of Gerar quarreled with Isaac's shepherds, claiming, "This water is ours." So Isaac named the well Esek (Quarrel) because they quarreled over it. They dug another well and there was a difference over that one also, so he named it Sitnah (Accusation). He went on from there and dug yet another well. But there was no fighting over this one so he named it Rehoboth (Wide-Open Spaces), saying, "Now GOD has given us plenty of space to spread out in the land." From there he went up to Beersheba. That very night GOD appeared to him and said,

> I am the God of Abraham your father;
>> don't fear a thing because I'm with you.
> I'll bless you and make your children flourish
>> because of Abraham my servant.

Isaac built an altar there and prayed, calling on GOD by name. He pitched his tent and his servants started digging another well.

Then Abimelech came to him from Gerar with Ahuzzath his advisor and Phicol the head of his troops. Isaac asked them, "Why did you come to me? You hate me; you threw me out of your country."

They said, "We've realized that GOD is on your side. We'd like to make a deal between us—a covenant that we maintain friendly relations. We haven't bothered you in the past; we treated you kindly and let you leave us in peace. So—GOD's blessing be with you!"

Isaac laid out a feast and they ate and drank together. Early in the morning they exchanged oaths. Then Isaac said good-bye and they parted as friends.

Later that same day, Isaac's servants came to him with news about the well they had been digging, "We've struck water!" Isaac named the well Sheba (Oath), and that's the name of the city, Beersheba (Oath-Well), to this day.

✠

When Esau was forty years old he married Judith, daughter of Beeri the Hittite, and Basemath, daughter of Elon the Hittite. They turned out to be thorns in the sides of Isaac and Rebekah.

✠

27 When Isaac had become an old man and was nearly blind, he called his eldest son, Esau, and said, "My son."

"Yes, Father?"

"I'm an old man," he said; "I might die any day now. Do me a favor: Get your quiver of arrows and your bow and go out in the country and hunt me some game. Then fix me a hearty meal, the kind that you know I like, and bring it to me to eat so that I can give you my personal blessing before I die."

Rebekah was eavesdropping as Isaac spoke to his son Esau. As soon as Esau had gone off to the country to hunt game for his father, Rebekah spoke to her son Jacob. "I just overheard your father talking with your brother, Esau. He said, 'Bring me some game and fix me a hearty meal so that I can eat and bless you with GOD's blessing before I die.'

"Now, my son, listen to me. Do what I tell you. Go to the flock and get me two young goats. Pick the best; I'll prepare them into a hearty meal, the kind that your father loves. Then you'll take it to your father, he'll eat and bless you before he dies."

"But Mother," Jacob said, "my brother Esau is a hairy man and I have smooth skin. What happens if my father touches me? He'll think I'm playing games with him. I'll bring down a curse on myself instead of a blessing."

"If it comes to that," said his mother, "I'll take the curse on myself. Now, just do what I say. Go and get the goats."

So he went and got them and brought them to his mother and she cooked a hearty meal, the kind his father loved so much.

Rebekah took the dress-up clothes of her older son Esau and put them on her younger son Jacob. She took the goatskins and covered his hands and the smooth nape of his neck . Then she placed the hearty meal she had fixed and fresh bread she'd baked into the hands of her son Jacob.

He went to his father and said, "My father!"

"Yes?" he said. "Which son are you?"

Jacob answered his father, "I'm your firstborn son Esau. I did what you told me. Come now; sit up and eat of my game so you can give me your personal blessing."

Isaac said, "So soon? How did you get it so quickly?"

"Because your GOD cleared the way for me."

Jacob said, "Come close, son; let me touch you—are you really my son Esau?"

So Jacob moved close to his father Isaac. Isaac felt him and said, "The voice is Jacob's voice but the hands are the hands of Esau." He didn't recognize him because his hands were hairy, like his brother Esau's.

But as he was about to bless him he pressed him, "You're sure? *You* are my son Esau?"

"Yes. I am."

Isaac said, "Bring the food so I can eat of my son's game and give you my personal blessing." Jacob brought it to him and he ate. He also brought him wine and he drank.

Then Isaac said, "Come close, son, and kiss me."

He came close and kissed him and Isaac smelled the smell of his clothes. Finally, he blessed him,

> Ahhh. The smell of my son
>> is like the smell of the open country
>> blessed by GOD.
> May God give you
>> of Heaven's dew
>> and Earth's bounty of grain and wine.
> May peoples serve you
>> and nations honor you.
> You will master your brothers,

and your mother's sons will honor you.
Those who curse you will be cursed,
    those who bless you will be blessed.

And then right after Isaac had blessed Jacob and Jacob had left, Esau showed up from the hunt. He also had prepared a hearty meal. He came to his father and said, "Let my father get up and eat of his son's game, that he may give me his personal blessing."

His father Isaac said, "And who are you?"

"I am your son, your firstborn, Esau."

Isaac started to tremble, shaking violently. He said, "Then who hunted game and brought it to me? I finished the meal just now, before you walked in. And I blessed him—he's blessed for good!"

Esau, hearing his father's words, sobbed violently and most bitterly, and cried to his father, "My father! Can't you also bless me?"

"Your brother," he said, "came here falsely and took your blessing."

Esau said, "Not for nothing was he named Jacob, the Heel. Twice now he's tricked me: first he took my birthright and now he's taken my blessing."

He begged, "Haven't you kept back any blessing for me?"

Isaac answered Esau, "I've made him your master, and all his brothers his servants, and lavished grain and wine on him. I've given it all away. What's left for you, my son?"

"But don't you have just one blessing for me, father? Oh, bless me my father! Bless me!" Esau sobbed inconsolably.

Isaac said to him,

You'll live far from Earth's bounty,
    remote from Heaven's dew.
You'll live by your sword, hand-to-mouth,
    and you'll serve your brother.
But when you can't take it any more
    you'll break loose and run free.

Esau seethed in anger against Jacob because of the blessing his father had given him; he brooded, "The time for mourning my father's death is close. And then I'll kill my brother Jacob."

When these words of her older son Esau were reported to Rebekah, she called her younger son Jacob and said, "Your brother Esau is plotting vengeance against you. He's going to kill you. Son, listen to me. Get out of here. Run for your life to Haran, to my brother Laban. Live with him for a while until your brother cools down, until his anger subsides and he forgets what you did to him. I'll then send for you and bring you back. Why should I lose both of you the same day?"

Rebekah spoke to Isaac, "I'm sick to death of these Hittite women. If Jacob also marries a native Hittite woman, why live?"

28 So Isaac called in Jacob and blessed him. Then he ordered him, "Don't take a Caananite wife. Leave at once. Go to Paddan Aram to the family of your mother's father, Bethuel. Get a wife for yourself from the daughters of your uncle Laban.

"And may The Strong God bless you and give you many, many children, a congregation of peoples; and pass on the blessing of Abraham to you and your descendants so that you will get this land in which you live, this land God gave Abraham."

So Isaac sent Jacob off. He went to Paddan Aram, to Laban son of Bethuel the Aramean, the brother of Rebekah who was the mother of Jacob and Esau.

Esau learned that Isaac had blessed Jacob and sent him to Paddan Aram to get a wife there, and while blessing him commanded, "Don't marry a Canaanite woman," and that Jacob had obeyed his parents and gone to Paddan Aram. When Esau realized how deeply his father Isaac disliked the Canaanite women, he went to Ishmael and married Mahalath the sister of Nebaioth and daughter of Ishmael, Abraham's son. This was in addition to the wives he already had.

✠

Jacob left Beersheba and went to Haran. He came to a certain place and camped for the night since the sun had set. He took one of the stones there, set it under his head and lay down to sleep. And he dreamed: A stairway was set on the ground and it reached all the way to the sky; angels of God were going up and going down on it.

Then GOD was right before him, saying, "I am GOD, the God of Abraham your father and the God of Isaac. I'm giving the ground on which you are sleeping to you and to your descendants. Your descendants will be as the dust of the Earth; they'll stretch from west to east and from north to south. All the families of the Earth will bless themselves in you and your descendants. Yes. I'll stay with you, I'll protect you wherever you go, and I'll bring you back to this very ground. I'll stick with you until I've done everything I promised you."

Jacob woke up from his sleep. He said, "GOD is in this place — truly. And I didn't even know it!" He was terrified. He whispered in awe, "Incredible. Wonderful. Holy. This is God's House. This is the Gate of Heaven."

Jacob was up first thing in the morning. He took the stone he had used for his pillow and stood it up as a memorial pillar and poured oil over it. He christened the place Bethel (God's House). The name of the town had been Luz until then.

Jacob vowed a vow: "If God stands by me and protects me on this journey on which I'm setting out, keeps me in food and clothing, and brings me back in one piece to my father's house, *this* GOD will be my God. This stone that I have set up as a memorial pillar will mark this as a place where God lives. And everything you give me, I'll return a tenth to you."

✛

29 Jacob set out again on his way to the people of the east. He noticed a well out in an open field with three flocks of sheep bedded down around it. This was the common well from which the flocks were watered. The stone over the mouth of the well was huge. When all the flocks were gathered, the shepherds would roll the stone from the well and water the sheep; then they would return the stone, covering the well.

Jacob said, "Hello friends. Where are you from?"

They said, "We're from Haran."

Jacob asked, "Do you know Laban son of Nahor?"

"We do."

"Are things well with him?" Jacob continued.

"Very well," they said. "And here is his daughter Rachel coming with the flock."

Jacob said, "There's a lot of daylight still left; it isn't time to round up the sheep yet, is it? So why not water the flocks and go back to grazing?"

"We can't," they said. "Not until all the shepherds get here. It takes all of us to roll the stone from the well. Not until then can we water the flocks."

While Jacob was in conversation with them, Rachel came up with her father's sheep. She was the shepherd. The moment Jacob spotted Rachel, daughter of Laban his mother's brother, saw her arriving with his uncle Laban's sheep, he went and single-handedly rolled the stone from the mouth of the well and watered the sheep of his uncle Laban. Then he kissed Rachel and broke into tears. He told Rachel that he was related to her father, that he was Rebekah's son. She ran and told her father. When Laban heard the news—Jacob, his sister's son!—he ran out to meet him, embraced and kissed him and brought him home. Jacob told Laban the story of everything that had happened.

Laban said, "You're family! My flesh and blood!"

When Jacob had been with him for a month, Laban said, "Just because you're my nephew, you shouldn't work for me for nothing. Tell me what you want to be paid. What's a fair wage?"

Now Laban had two daughters; Leah was the older and Rachel the younger. Leah had nice eyes, but Rachel was stunningly beautiful. And it was Rachel that Jacob loved.

So Jacob answered, "I will work for you seven years for your younger daughter Rachel."

"It is far better," said Laban, "that I give her to you than marry her to some outsider. Yes. Stay here with me."

So Jacob worked seven years for Rachel. But it only seemed like a few days, he loved her so much.

Then Jacob said to Laban, "Give me my wife; I've completed what we agreed I'd do. I'm ready to consummate my marriage." Laban invited everyone around and threw a big feast. At evening, though, he got his daughter Leah and brought her to the marriage bed, and Jacob slept with her. (Laban gave his maid Zilpah to his daughter Leah as her maid.)

Morning came: There was Leah in the marriage bed!

Jacob confronted Laban, "What have you done to me? Didn't I work all this time for the hand of Rachel? Why did you cheat me?"

"We don't do it that way in our country," said Laban. "We don't marry off the younger daughter before the older. Enjoy your week of honeymoon, and then we'll give you the other one also. But it will cost you another seven years of work."

Jacob agreed. When he'd completed the honeymoon week, Laban gave him his daughter Rachel to be his wife. (Laban gave his maid Bilhah to his daughter Rachel as her maid.) Jacob then slept with her. And he loved Rachel more than Leah. He worked for Laban another seven years.

When GOD realized that Leah was unloved, he opened her womb.

But Rachel was barren. Leah became pregnant and had a son. She named him Reuben (Look-It's-a-Boy!). "This is a sign," she said, "that GOD has seen my misery; and a sign that now my husband will love me."

She became pregnant again and had another son. "GOD heard," she said, "that I was unloved and so he gave me this son also." She named this one Simeon (GOD-Heard). She became pregnant yet again — another son. She said, "Now maybe my husband will connect with me — I've given him three sons!" That's why she named him Levi (Connect). She became pregnant a final time and had a fourth son. She said, "This time I'll praise GOD." So she named him Judah (Praise-GOD). Then she stopped having children.

⁘

30 When Rachel realized that she wasn't having any children for Jacob, she became jealous of her sister. She told Jacob, "Give me sons or I'll die!"

Jacob got angry with Rachel and said, "Am I God? Am I the one who refused you babies?"

Rachel said, "Here's my maid Bilhah. Sleep with her. Let her substitute for me so I can have a child through her and build a family." So she gave him her maid Bilhah for a wife and Jacob slept with her. Bilhah became pregnant and gave Jacob a son.

Rachel said, "God took my side and vindicated me. He listened to me and gave me a son." She named him Dan (Vindication). Rachel's maid Bilhah became pregnant again and gave Jacob a second son. Rachel said, "I've been in an all-out fight with my sister — and I've won." So she named him Naphtali (Fight).

When Leah saw that she wasn't having any more children, she gave her maid Zilpah to Jacob for a wife. Zilpah had a son for Jacob. Leah said, "How fortunate!" and she named him Gad (Lucky). When Leah's maid Zilpah had a second son for Jacob, Leah said, "A happy day! The women will congratulate me in my happiness." So she named him Asher (Happy).

One day during the wheat harvest Reuben found some mandrakes in the field and brought them home to his mother Leah. Rachel asked Leah, "Could I please have some of your son's mandrakes?"

Leah said, "Wasn't it enough that you got my husband away from me? And now you also want my son's mandrakes?"

Rachel said, "All right. I'll let him sleep with you tonight in exchange for your son's love-apples."

When Jacob came home that evening from the fields, Leah was there to meet him: "Sleep with me tonight; I've bartered my son's mandrakes for a night with you." So he slept with her that night. God listened to Leah; she became pregnant and gave Jacob a fifth son. She said, "God rewarded me for giving my maid to my husband." She named him Issachar (Bartered). Leah became pregnant yet again and gave Jacob a sixth son, saying, "God has given me a great gift. This time my husband will honor me with gifts—I've given him six sons!" She named him Zebulun (Honor). Last of all she had a daughter and named her Dinah.

And then God remembered Rachel. God listened to her and opened her womb. She became pregnant and had a son. She said, "God has taken away my humiliation." She named him Joseph (Add), praying, "May GOD add yet another son to me."

⊹

After Rachel had had Joseph, Jacob spoke to Laban, "Let me go back home. Give me my wives and children for whom I've served you. You know how hard I've worked for you."

Laban said, "If you please, I have learned through divine inquiry that GOD has blessed me because of you." He went on, "So name your wages. I'll pay you."

Jacob replied, "You know well what my work has meant to you and how your livestock has flourished under my care. The little you had when I arrived has increased greatly; everything I did resulted in blessings for you. Isn't it about time that I do something for my own family?"

"So, what should I pay you?"

Jacob said, "You don't have to pay me a thing. But how about this? I will go back to pasture and care for your flocks. Go through your entire flock today and take out every speckled or spotted sheep, every dark-colored lamb, every spotted or speckled goat. They will be my wages. That way you can check on my honesty when you assess my wages. If you find any goat that's not speckled or spotted or a sheep that's not black, you will know that I stole it."

"Fair enough," said Laban. "It's a deal."

But that very day Laban removed all the mottled and spotted billy-goats and all the speckled and spotted nanny-goats, every animal that had even a touch of white on it plus all the black sheep and placed them under the care of his sons. Then he put a three day journey between himself and Jacob. Meanwhile Jacob went on tending what was left of Laban's flock.

But Jacob got fresh branches from poplar, almond, and plane trees and peeled the bark, leaving white stripes on them. He stuck the peeled branches in front of the watering troughs where the flocks came to drink. When the flocks were in heat, they came to drink and mated in front of the streaked branches. Then they gave birth to young that were streaked or spotted or speckled. Jacob placed the ewes before the dark-colored animals of Laban. That way he got distinctive flocks for himself which he didn't mix with Laban's flocks. And when the sturdier animals were mating, Jacob placed branches at the troughs in view of the animals so that they mated in front of the branches. But he wouldn't set up the branches before the feebler animals. That way the feeble animals went to Laban and the sturdy ones to Jacob.

The man got richer and richer, acquiring huge flocks, lots and lots of servants, not to mention camels and donkeys.

31 Jacob learned that Laban's sons were talking behind his back: "Jacob has used our father's wealth to make himself rich at our father's expense." At the same time, Jacob noticed that Laban had changed toward him. He wasn't treating him the same.

That's when GOD said to Jacob, "Go back home where you were born. I'll go with you."

So Jacob sent word for Rachel and Leah to meet him out in the field where his flocks were. He said, "I notice that your father has changed toward me; he doesn't treat me the same as before. But the God of my father hasn't changed; he's still with me. You know how hard I've worked for your father. Still, your father has cheated me over and over, changing my wages time and again. But God never let him really hurt me. If he said, 'Your wages will consist of speckled animals' the whole flock would start having speckled lambs and kids. And if he said, 'From now on your wages will be streaked animals' the whole flock would have streaked ones. Over and over God used your father's livestock to reward me.

"Once, while the flocks were mating, I had a dream and saw the billy-goats, all of them streaked, speckled, and mottled, mounting their mates. In the dream an angel of God called out to me, 'Jacob!'

"I said, 'Yes?'

"He said, 'Watch closely. Notice that all the goats in the flock that are mating are streaked, speckled, and mottled. I know what Laban's been doing to you. I'm the God of Bethel where you consecrated a pillar and made a vow to me. Now be on your way, get out of this place, go home to your birthplace.'"

Rachel and Leah said, "Has he treated us any better? Aren't we treated worse than outsiders? All he wanted was the money he got from selling us, and he's spent all that. Any wealth that God has seen fit to return to us from our father is justly ours and our children's. Go ahead. Do what God told you."

Jacob did it. He put his children and his wives on camels and gathered all his livestock and everything he had gotten, everything acquired in Paddan Aram, to go back home to his father Isaac in the land of Canaan.

Laban was off shearing sheep. Rachel stole her father's household gods. And Jacob had concealed his plans so well that Laban the Aramean had no idea what was going on—he was totally in the dark. Jacob got away with everything he had and was soon across the Euphrates headed for the hill country of Gilead.

Three days later, Laban got the news: "Jacob's run off." Laban rounded up his relatives and chased after him. Seven days later they caught up with him in the hill country of Gilead. That night God came to Laban the Aramean in a dream and said, "Be careful what you do to Jacob, whether good or bad."

When Laban reached him, Jacob's tents were pitched in the Gilead mountains; Laban pitched his tents there too.

"What do you mean," said Laban, "by keeping me in the dark and sneaking off, hauling my daughters off like prisoners of war? Why did you run off like a thief in the night? Why didn't you tell me? Why, I would have sent you off with a great celebration—music, timbrels, flutes! But you wouldn't permit me so much as a kiss for my daughters and grandchildren. It was a stupid thing for you to do. If I had a mind to, I could destroy you right now, but the God of your father spoke to me last night, 'Be careful what you do to Jacob, whether good or bad.' I understand. You left because you were homesick. But why did you steal my household gods?"

Jacob answered Laban, "I was afraid. I thought you would take your daughters away from me by brute force. But as far as your gods are concerned, if you find that anybody here has them, that person dies. With all of us watching, look around. If you find anything here that belongs to you, take it." Jacob didn't know that Rachel had stolen the gods.

Laban went through Jacob's tent, Leah's tent, and the tents of the two maids but didn't find them. He went from Leah's tent to Rachel's. But Rachel had taken the household gods, put them inside a camel cushion, and was sitting on them. When Laban had gone through the tent, searching high and low without finding a thing, Rachel said to her father, "Don't think I'm being disrespectful, my master, that I can't stand before you, but I'm having my period." So even though he turned the place upside down in his search, he didn't find the household gods.

Now it was Jacob's turn to get angry. He lit into Laban: "So what's my crime, what wrong have I done you that you badger me like this? You've ransacked the place. Have you turned up a single thing that's yours? Let's see it — display the evidence. Our two families can be the jury and decide between us.

"In the twenty years I've worked for you, ewes and she-goats never miscarried. I never feasted on the rams from your flock. I never brought you a torn carcass killed by wild animals but that I paid for it out of my own pocket — actually, you made me pay whether it was my fault or not. I was out in all kinds of weather, from torrid heat to freezing cold, putting in many a sleepless night. For twenty years I've done this: I slaved away fourteen years for your two daughters and another six years for your flock and you changed my wages ten times. If the God of my father, the God of Abraham and the Fear of Isaac, had not stuck with me, you would have sent me off penniless. But God saw the fix I was in and how hard I had worked and last night rendered his verdict."

Laban defended himself: "The daughters are my daughters, the children are my children, the flock is my flock — everything you see is mine. But what can I do about my daughters or for the children they've had? So let's settle things between us, make a covenant — God will be the witness between us."

Jacob took a stone and set it upright as a pillar.

Jacob called his family around, "Get stones!" They gathered stones and heaped them up and then ate there beside the pile of stones. Laban named it in Aramaic, Yegar-sahadutha (Witness Monument); Jacob echoed the naming in Hebrew, Galeed (Witness Monument).

Laban said, "This monument of stones will be a witness, beginning now, between you and me." (That's why it is called Galeed — Witness Monument.) It is also called Mizpah (Watchtower) because Laban said, "GOD keep watch between you and me when we are out of each other's sight. If you mistreat my daughters or take other wives when there's no one around to see you, God will see you and stand witness between us."

Laban continued to Jacob, "This monument of stones and this stone pillar that I have set up is a witness, a witness that I won't cross this line to hurt you and you won't cross this line to hurt me. The God of Abraham and the God of Nahor (the God of their ancestor) will keep things straight between us."

Jacob promised, swearing by the Fear, the God of his father Isaac. Then Jacob offered a sacrifice on the mountain and worshiped, calling in all his family members to the meal. They ate and slept that night on the mountain.

32 Laban got up early the next morning, kissed his grandchildren and his daughters, blessed them, and then set off for home.

And Jacob went his way. Angels of God met him. When Jacob saw them he said, "Oh! God's Camp!" And he named the place Mahanaim (Campground).

Then Jacob sent messengers on ahead to his brother Esau in the land of Seir in Edom. He instructed them: "Tell my master Esau this, 'A message from your servant Jacob: I've been staying with Laban and couldn't get away until now. I've acquired cattle and donkeys and sheep; also men and women servants. I'm telling you all this, my master, hoping for your approval.'"

The messengers came back to Jacob and said, "We talked to your brother Esau and he's on his way to meet you. But he has four hundred men with him."

Jacob was scared. Very scared. Panicked, he divided his people, sheep, cattle, and camels into two camps. He thought, "If Esau comes on the first camp and attacks it, the other camp has a chance to get away."

And then Jacob prayed, "God of my father Abraham, God of my father Isaac, GOD who told me, 'Go back to your parents' homeland and I'll treat you well.' I don't deserve all the love and loyalty you've shown me. When I left here and crossed the Jordan I only had the clothes on my back, and now look at me—two camps! Save me, please, from the violence of my brother, my angry brother! I'm afraid he'll come and attack us all, me, the mothers and the children. You yourself said, 'I will treat you well; I'll make your descendants like the sands of the sea, far too many to count.'"

He slept the night there. Then he prepared a present for his brother Esau from his possessions: two hundred female goats, twenty male goats, two hundred ewes and twenty rams, thirty camels with their nursing young, forty cows and ten bulls, twenty female donkeys and ten male donkeys. He put a servant in charge of each herd and said, "Go ahead of me and keep a healthy space between each herd."

Then he instructed the first one out: "When my brother Esau comes close and asks, 'Who is your master? Where are you going? Who owns these?'—answer him like this, 'Your servant Jacob. They are a gift to my master Esau. He's on his way.'"

He gave the same instructions to the second servant and to the third—to each in turn as they set out with their herds: "Say 'Your servant Jacob is on his way behind us.'" He thought, "I will soften him up with the succession of gifts. Then when he sees me face-to-face, maybe he'll be glad to welcome me."

So his gifts went before him while he settled down for the night in the camp.

But during the night he got up and took his two wives, his two maidservants, and his eleven children and crossed the ford of the Jabbok. He got them safely across the brook along with all his possessions.

But Jacob stayed behind by himself, and a man wrestled with him until daybreak. When the man saw that he couldn't get the best of Jacob as they wrestled, he deliberately threw his hip out of joint.

The man said, "Let me go; it's daybreak."

Jacob said, "I'm not letting you go 'til you bless me."

The man said, "What's your name?"

He answered, "Jacob."

The man said, "But no longer. Your name is no longer Jacob. From now on it's Israel (God-Wrestler); you've wrestled with God and you've come through."

Jacob asked, "And what's your name?"

The man said, "Why do you want to know my name?" And then, right then and there, he blessed him.

Jacob named the place Peniel (God's Face) because, he said, "I saw God face-to-face and lived to tell the story!"

The sun came up as he left Peniel, limping because of his hip. (This is why Israelites to this day don't eat the hip muscle; because Jacob's hip was thrown out of joint.)

33 Jacob looked up and saw Esau coming with his four hundred men. He divided the children between Leah and Rachel and the two maidservants. He put the maidservants out in front, Leah and her children next, and Rachel and Joseph last. He led the way and, as he approached his brother, bowed seven times, honoring his brother. But Esau ran up and embraced him, held him tight and kissed him. And they both wept.

Then Esau looked around and saw the women and children: "And who are these with you?"

Jacob said, "The children that God saw fit to bless me with."

Then the maidservants came up with their children and bowed; then Leah and her children, also bowing; and finally, Joseph and Rachel came up and bowed to Esau.

Esau then asked, "And what was the meaning of all those herds that I met?"

"I was hoping that they would pave the way for my master to welcome me."

Esau said, "Oh, brother. I have plenty of everything—keep what is yours for yourself."

Jacob said, "Please. If you can find it in your heart to welcome me, accept these gifts. When I saw your face, it was as the face of God smiling on me. Accept the gifts I have brought for you. God has been good to me and I have more than enough." Jacob urged the gifts on him and Esau accepted.

Then Esau said, "Let's start out on our way; I'll take the lead."

But Jacob said, "My master can see that the children are frail. And the flocks and herds are nursing, making for slow going. If I push them too hard, even for a day, I'd lose them all. So, master, you go on ahead of your servant, while I take it easy at the pace of my flocks and children. I'll catch up with you in Seir."

Esau said, "Let me at least lend you some of my men."

"There's no need," said Jacob. "Your generous welcome is all I need or want."

So Esau set out that day and made his way back to Seir.

And Jacob left for Succoth. He built a shelter for himself and sheds for his livestock. That's how the place came to be called Succoth (Sheds).

And that's how it happened that Jacob arrived all in one piece in Shechem in the land of Canaan—all the way from Paddan Aram. He camped near the city. He bought the land where he pitched his tent from the sons of Hamor, the father of Shechem. He paid a hundred silver coins for it. Then he built an altar there and named it El-Elohe-Israel (Mighty Is the God of Israel).

✠

34 One day Dinah, the daughter Leah had given Jacob, went to visit some of the women in that country. Shechem, the son of Hamor the Hivite who was chieftain there, saw her and raped her. Then he felt a strong attraction to Dinah, Jacob's daughter, fell in love with her and wooed her. Shechem went to his father Hamor, "Get me this girl for my wife."

Jacob heard that Shechem had raped his daughter Dinah, but his sons were out in the fields with the livestock so he didn't say anything until they got home. Hamor, Shechem's father, went to Jacob to work out marriage arrangements. Meanwhile Jacob's sons on their way back from the fields heard what had happened. They were outraged, explosive with anger. Shechem's rape of Jacob's daughter was intolerable in Israel and not to be put up with.

Hamor spoke with Jacob and his sons, "My son Shechem is head over heels in love with your daughter—give her to him as his wife. Intermarry with us. Give your daughters to us and we'll give our daughters to you. Live together with us as one family. Settle down among us and make yourselves at home. Prosper among us."

Shechem then spoke for himself, addressing Dinah's father and brothers: "Please, say yes. I'll pay anything. Set the bridal price as high as you will—the sky's the limit! Only give me this girl for my wife."

Jacob's sons answered Shechem and his father with cunning. Their sister, after all, had been raped. They said, "This is impossible. We could never give our sister to a man who was uncircumcised. Why, we'd be disgraced. The only condition on which we can talk business is if all your men become circumcised like us. Then we will freely exchange daughters in marriage and make ourselves at home among you and become one big, happy family. But if this is not an acceptable condition, we will take our sister and leave."

That seemed fair enough to Hamor and his son Shechem.

The young man was so smitten with Jacob's daughter that he proceeded to do what had been asked. He was also the most admired son in his father's family.

So Hamor and his son Shechem went to the public square and spoke to the town council: "These men like us; they are our friends. Let them settle down here and make themselves at home; there's plenty of room in the country for them. And, just think, we can even exchange our daughters in marriage. But these men will only accept our invitation to live with us and become one big family on one condition, that all our males become circumcised just as they themselves are. This is a very good deal for us—these people are very wealthy with great herds of livestock and we're going to get our hands on it. So let's do what they ask and have them settle down with us."

Everyone who was anyone in the city agreed with Hamor and his son, Shechem; every male was circumcised.

Three days after the circumcision, while all the men were still very sore, two of Jacob's sons, Simeon and Levi, Dinah's brothers, each with his sword in hand, walked into the city as if they owned the place and murdered every man there. They also killed Hamor and his son Shechem, rescued Dinah from Shechem's house, and left. When the rest of Jacob's sons came on the scene of slaughter, they looted the entire city in retaliation for Dinah's rape. Flocks, herds, donkeys, belongings— everything, whether in the city or the fields—they took. And then they took all the wives and children captive and ransacked their homes for anything valuable.

Jacob said to Simeon and Levi, "You've made my name stink to high heaven among the people here, these Canaanites and Perizzites. If they decided to gang up on us and attack, as few as we are we wouldn't stand a chance; they'd wipe me and my people right off the map."

They said, "Nobody is going to treat our sister like a whore and get by with it."

✛

35 God spoke to Jacob: "Go back to Bethel. Stay there and build an altar to the God who revealed himself to you when you were running for your life from your brother Esau."

Jacob told his family and all those who lived with him, "Throw out all the alien gods which you have, take a good bath and put on clean clothes, we're going to Bethel. I'm going to build an altar there to the God who answered me when I was in trouble and has stuck with me everywhere I've gone since."

They turned over to Jacob all the alien gods they'd been holding on to, along with their lucky-charm earrings. Jacob buried them under the oak tree in Shechem. Then they set out. A paralyzing fear descended on all the surrounding villages so that they were unable to pursue the sons of Jacob.

Jacob and his company arrived at Luz, that is, Bethel, in the land of Canaan. He built an altar there and named it El-Bethel (God-of-Bethel) because that's where God revealed himself to him when he was running from his brother.

And that's when Rebekah's nurse, Deborah, died. She was buried just below Bethel under the oak tree. It was named Allon-Bacuth (Weeping-Oak).

God revealed himself once again to Jacob, after he had come back from Paddan Aram and blessed him: "Your name is Jacob (Heel); but that's your name no longer. From now on your name is Israel (God-Wrestler)."

God continued,

I am The Strong God.
　　Have children! Flourish!
A nation—a whole company of nations!—
　　will come from you.
Kings will come from your loins;
　　the land I gave Abraham and Isaac
I now give to you,
　　and pass it on to your descendants.

And then God was gone, ascended from the place where he had spoken with him.

Jacob set up a stone pillar on the spot where God had spoken with him. He poured a drink offering on it and anointed it with oil. Jacob dedicated the place where God had spoken with him, Bethel (God's-House).

✠

They left Bethel. They were still quite a ways from Ephrath when Rachel went into labor—hard, hard labor. When her labor pains were at their worst, the midwife said to her, "Don't be afraid—you have another boy."

With her last breath, for she was now dying, she named him Ben-oni (Son-of-My-Pain), but his father named him Ben-jamin (Son-of-Good-Fortune).

Rachel died and was buried on the road to Ephrath, that is, Bethlehem. Jacob set up a pillar to mark her grave. It is still there today, "Rachel's Grave Stone."

✝

Israel kept on his way and set up camp at Migdal Eder. While Israel was living in that region, Reuben went and slept with his father's concubine, Bilhah. And Israel heard of what he did.

✝

There were twelve sons of Jacob.
The sons by Leah:
    Reuben, Jacob's firstborn
    Simeon
    Levi
    Judah
    Issachar
    Zebulun.
The sons by Rachel:
    Joseph
    Benjamin.
The sons by Bilhah, Rachel's maid:
    Dan
    Naphtali.
The sons by Zilpah, Leah's maid:
    Gad
    Asher.
These were Jacob's sons, born to him in Paddan Aram.

✝

Finally, Jacob made it back home to his father Isaac at Mamre in Kiriath Arba, present-day Hebron, where Abraham and Isaac had lived. Isaac was now 180 years old. Isaac breathed his last and died—an old man full of years. He was buried with his family by his sons Esau and Jacob.

✝

36 This is the family tree of Esau, who is also called Edom. Esau married women of Canaan: Adah, daughter of Elon the Hittite; Oholibamah, daughter of Anah and the granddaughter of Zibeon the Hivite; and Basemath, daughter of Ishmael and sister of Nebaioth.
    Adah gave Esau Eliphaz;
    Basemath had Reuel;

Oholibamah had Jeush, Jalam, and Korah.

These are the sons of Esau who were born to him in the land of Canaan.

Esau gathered up his wives, sons and daughters, and everybody in his household, along with all his livestock—all the animals and possessions he had gotten in Canaan—and moved a considerable distance away from his brother Jacob. The brothers had too many possessions to live together in the same place; the land couldn't support their combined herds of livestock. So Esau ended up settling in the hill country of Seir (Esau and Edom are the same).

So this is the family tree of Esau, ancestor of the people of Edom, in the hill country of Seir. The names of Esau's sons:

Eliphaz, son of Esau's wife Adah;

Reuel, son of Esau's wife Basemath.

The sons of Eliphaz: Teman, Omar, Zepho, Gatam, and Kenaz. (Eliphaz also had a concubine Timna, who had Amalek.) These are the grandsons of Esau's wife Adah.

And these are the sons of Reuel: Nahath, Zerah, Shammah, and Mizzah—grandsons of Esau's wife Basemath.

These are the sons of Esau's wife Oholibamah, daughter of Anah the son of Zibeon. She gave Esau his sons Jeush, Jalam, and Korah.

These are the chieftains in Esau's family tree. From the sons of Eliphaz, Esau's firstborn, came the chieftains Teman, Omar, Zepho, Kenaz, Korah, Gatam, and Amalek—the chieftains of Eliphaz in the land of Edom; all of them sons of Adah.

From the sons of Esau's son Reuel, came the chieftains Nahath, Zerah, Shammah, and Mizzah. These are the chieftains of Reuel in the land of Edom; all these were sons of Esau's wife Basemath.

These are the sons of Esau's wife Oholibamah: the chieftains Jeush, Jalam, and Korah—chieftains born of Esau's wife Oholibamah, daughter of Anah.

These are the the the sons of Esau, that is, Edom, and these are their chieftains.

This is the family tree of Seir the Horite, who were native to that land: Lotan, Shobal, Zibeon, Anah, Dishon, Ezer, and Dishan. These are the chieftains of the Horites, the sons of Seir in the land of Edom.

The sons of Lotan were Hori and Homam; Lotan's sister was Timna.

The sons of Shobal were Alvan, Manahath, Ebal, Shepho, and Onam.

The sons of Zibeon were Aiah and Anah—this is the same Anah who found the hot springs in the wilderness while herding his father Zibeon's donkeys.

The children of Anah were Dishon and his daughter Oholibamah.

The sons of Dishon were Hemdan, Eshban, Ithran, and Keran.

The sons of Ezer: Bilhan, Zaavan, and Akan.

The sons of Dishan: Uz and Aran.

And these were the Horite chieftains: Lotan, Shobal, Zibeon, Anah, Dishon, Ezer, and Dishan—the Horite chieftains clan by clan in the land of Seir.

And these are the kings who ruled in Edom before there was a king in Israel: Bela son of Beor was the king of Edom; the name of his city was Dinhabah. When Bela died, Jobab son of Zerah from Bozrah became the next king. When Jobab died, he was followed by Hushan from the land of the Temanites. When Hushan died, he was followed by Hadad son of Bedad; he was the king who defeated the Midianites in Moab; the name of his city was Avith. When Hadad died, Samlah of Masrekah became the next king. When Samlah died, Shaul from Rehoboth-on-the-River became king. When Shaul died, he was followed by Baal-Hanan son of Acbor. When Baal-Hanan son of Acbor died, Hadad became king; the name of his city was Pau; his wife's name was Mehetabel daughter of Matred, daughter of Me-Zahab.

And these are the chieftains from the line of Esau, clan by clan, region by region: Timna, Alvah, Jetheth, Oholibamah, Elah, Pinon, Kenaz, Teman, Mibzar, Magdiel, and Iram—the chieftains of Edom as they occupied their various regions.

This accounts for the family tree of Esau, ancestor of all Edomites.

37 Meanwhile Jacob had settled down where his father had lived, the land of Canaan.

JOSEPH AND HIS BROTHERS

This is the story of Jacob. The story continues with Joseph, seventeen years old at the time, helping out his brothers in herding the flocks. These were his half brothers actually, the sons of his father's wives Bilhah and Zilpah. And Joseph brought his father bad reports on them.

Israel loved Joseph more than any of his other sons because he was the child of his old age. And he made him an elaborately embroidered coat. When his brothers realized that their father loved him more than them, they grew to hate him—they wouldn't even speak to him.

Joseph had a dream. When he told it to his brothers, they hated him even more. He said, "Listen to this dream I had. We were all out in the field gathering bundles of wheat. All of a sudden my bundle stood straight up and your bundles circled around it and bowed down to mine."

His brothers said, "So! You're going to rule us? You're going to boss us around?" And they hated him more than ever because of his dreams and the way he talked.

He had another dream and told this one also to his brothers: "I dreamed another dream—the sun and moon and eleven stars bowed down to me!"

When he told it to his father and brothers, his father reprimanded him: "What's with all this dreaming? Am I and your mother and your brothers all supposed to bow down to you?" Now his brothers were really jealous; but his father brooded over the whole business.

His brothers had gone off to Shechem where they were pasturing their father's flocks. Israel said to Joseph, "Your brothers are with flocks in Shechem. Come, I want to send you to them."

Joseph said, "I'm ready."

He said, "Go and see how your brothers and the flocks are doing and bring me back a report." He sent him off from the valley of Hebron to Shechem.

A man met him as he was wandering through the fields, and asked him, "What are you looking for?"

"I'm trying to find my brothers. Do you have any idea where they are grazing their flocks?"

The man said, "They've left here, but I overheard them say, 'Let's go to Dothan.'" So Joseph took off, tracked his brothers down, and found them in Dothan.

They spotted him off in the distance. By the time he got to them they had cooked up a plot to kill him. The brothers were saying, "Here comes that dreamer. Let's kill him and throw him into one of these old cisterns; we can say that a vicious animal ate him up. We'll see what his dreams amount to."

Reuben heard the brothers talking and intervened to save him, "We're not going to kill him. No murder. Go ahead and throw him in this cistern out here in the wild, but don't hurt him." Reuben planned to go back later and get him out and take him back to his father.

When Joseph reached his brothers, they ripped off the fancy coat he was wearing, grabbed him and threw him into a cistern. The cistern was dry; there wasn't any water in it.

Then they sat down to eat their supper. Looking up, they saw a caravan of Ishmaelites on their way from Gilead, their camels loaded with spices, ointments, and perfumes to sell in Egypt. Judah said, "Brothers, what are we going to get out of killing our brother and concealing the evidence? Let's sell him to the Ishmaelites, but let's not kill him—he is, after all, our brother, our own flesh and blood." His brothers agreed.

By that time the Midianite traders were passing by. His brothers pulled Joseph out of the cistern and sold him for twenty pieces of silver to the Ishmaelites who took Joseph with them down to Egypt.

Later Reuben came back and went to the cistern—no Joseph! He ripped his clothes in despair. Beside himself, he went to his brothers. "The boy's gone! What am I going to do!"

They took Joseph's coat, butchered a goat and dipped the coat in the blood. They took the fancy coat back to their father and said, "We found this. Look it over—do you think this is your son's coat?"

He recognized it at once. "My son's coat—a wild animal has eaten him. Joseph torn limb from limb!"

Jacob tore his clothes in grief, dressed in rough burlap, and mourned his son a long, long time. His sons and daughters tried to comfort him but he refused their comfort. "I'll go to the grave mourning my son." Oh, how his father wept for him.

In Egypt the Midianites sold Joseph to Potiphar, one of Pharaoh's officials, manager of his household affairs.

✛

38 About that time, Judah separated from his brothers and hooked up with a man in Adullam named Hirah. While there, Judah met the daughter of a Canaanite named Shua. He married her, they went to bed, she became pregnant and had a son named Er. She got pregnant again and had a son named Onan. She had still another son; she named this one Shelah. They were living at Kezib when she had him.

Judah got a wife for Er, his firstborn. Her name was Tamar. But Judah's firstborn, Er, grievously offended GOD and GOD took his life.

So Judah told Onan, "Go and sleep with your brother's widow; it's the duty of a brother-in-law to keep your brother's line alive." But Onan knew that the child wouldn't be his, so whenever he slept with his brother's widow he spilled his semen on the ground so he wouldn't produce a child for his brother. GOD was much offended by what he did and also took his life.

So Judah stepped in and told his daughter-in-law Tamar, "Live as a widow at home with your father until my son Shelah grows up." He was worried that Shelah would also end up dead, just like his brothers. So Tamar went to live with her father.

Time passed. Judah's wife, Shua's daughter, died. When the time of mourning was over, Judah with his friend Hirah of Adullam went to Timnah for the sheep shearing.

Tamar was told, "Your father-in-law has gone to Timnah to shear his sheep." She took off her widow's clothes, put on a veil to disguise herself and sat at the entrance to Enaim which is on the road to Timnah. She realized by now that even though Shelah was grown up, she wasn't going to be married to him.

Judah saw her and assumed she was a prostitute since she had veiled her face. He left the road and went over to her. He said, "Let me sleep with you." He had no idea that she was his daughter-in-law.

She said, "What will you pay me?"

"I'll send you," he said, "a kid goat from the flock."

She said, "Not unless you give me a pledge until you send it."

"So what would you want in the way of a pledge?"

She said, "Your personal seal-and-cord and the staff you carry."

He handed them over to her and slept with her. And she got pregnant.

She then left and went home. She removed her veil and put her widow's clothes back on.

Judah sent the kid goat by his friend from Adullam to recover the pledge from the woman. But he couldn't find her. He asked the men of that place, "Where's the prostitute that used to sit by the road here near Enaim?"

They said, "There's never been a prostitute here."

He went back to Judah and said, "I couldn't find her. The men there said there never has been a prostitute there."

Judah said, "Let her have it then. If we keep looking, everyone will be poking fun at us. I kept my part of the bargain—I sent the kid goat but you couldn't find her."

Three months or so later, Judah was told, "Your daughter-in-law has been playing the whore—and now she's a pregnant whore."

Judah yelled, "Get her out here. Burn her up!"

As they brought her out, she sent a message to her father-in-law, "I'm pregnant by the man who owns these things. Identify them, please. Who's the owner of the seal-and-cord and the staff?"

Judah saw they were his. He said, "She's in the right; I'm in the wrong—I wouldn't let her marry my son Shelah." He never slept with her again.

When her time came to give birth, it turned out that there were twins in her womb. As she was giving birth, one put his hand out; the midwife tied a red thread on his hand, saying, "This one came first." But then he pulled it back and his brother came out. She said, "Oh! A breakout!" So she named him Perez (Breakout). Then his brother came out with the red thread on his hand. They named him Zerah (Bright).

✠

39 After Joseph had been taken to Egypt by the Ishmaelites, Potiphar an Egyptian, one of Pharaoh's officials and the manager of his household, bought him from them.

As it turned out, GOD was with Joseph and things went very well with him. He ended up living in the home of his Egyptian master. His master recognized that GOD was with him, saw that GOD was working for good in everything he did. He became very fond of Joseph and made him his personal aide. He put him in charge of all his personal affairs, turning everything over to him. From that moment on, GOD blessed the home of the Egyptian—all because of Joseph. The blessing of GOD spread over everything he owned, at home and in the fields, and all Potiphar had to concern himself with was eating three meals a day.

Joseph was a strikingly handsome man. As time went on, his master's wife became infatuated with Joseph and one day said, "Sleep with me."

He wouldn't do it. He said to his master's wife, "Look, with me here, my master doesn't give a second thought to anything that goes on here—he's put me in charge of everything he owns. He treats me as an equal. The only thing he hasn't turned over to me is you. You're his wife, after all! How could I violate his trust and sin against God?"

She pestered him day after day after day, but he stood his ground. He refused to go to bed with her.

On one of these days he came to the house to do his work and none of the household servants happened to be there. She grabbed him by his cloak, saying, "Sleep with me!" He left his coat in her hand and ran out of the house. When she realized that he had left his coat in her hand and run outside, she called to her house servants: "Look—this Hebrew shows up and before you know it he's trying to seduce us. He tried to make love to me but I yelled as loud as I could. With all my yelling and screaming, he left his coat beside me here and ran outside."

She kept his coat right there until his master came home. She told him the same story. She said, "The Hebrew slave, the one you brought to us, came after me and tried to use me for his plaything. When I yelled and screamed, he left his coat with me and ran outside."

When his master heard his wife's story, telling him, "These are the things your slave did to me," he was furious. Joseph's master took him and threw him into the jail where the king's prisoners were locked up. But there in jail GOD was still with Joseph: He reached out in kindness to him; he put him on good terms with the head jailer. The head jailer put Joseph in charge of all the prisoners—he ended up managing the whole operation. The head jailer gave Joseph free rein, never even checked on him, because GOD was with him; whatever he did GOD made sure it worked out for the best.

⁘

40As time went on, it happened that the cupbearer and the baker of the king of Egypt crossed their master, the king of Egypt. Pharaoh was furious with his two officials, the head cupbearer and the head baker, and put them in custody under the captain of the guard; it was the same jail where Joseph was held. The captain of the guard assigned Joseph to see to their needs.

After they had been in custody for a while, the king's cupbearer and baker, while being held in the jail, both had a dream on the same night, each dream having its own meaning. When Joseph arrived in the morning, he noticed that they were feeling low. So he asked them, the two officials of Pharaoh who had been thrown into jail with him, "What's wrong? Why the long faces?"

They said, "We dreamed dreams and there's no one to interpret them."

Joseph said, "Don't interpretations come from God? Tell me the dreams."

First the head cupbearer told his dream to Joseph: "In my dream there was a vine in front of me with three branches on it: It budded, blossomed, and the clusters ripened into grapes. I was holding Pharaoh's cup; I took the grapes, squeezed them into Pharaoh's cup, and gave the cup to Pharaoh."

Joseph said, "Here's the meaning. The three branches are three days. Within three days, Pharaoh will get you out of here and put you back to your old work—you'll be giving Pharaoh his cup just as you used to do when you were his cupbearer. Only remember me when things are going well with you again—tell Pharaoh about me and get me out of this place. I was kidnapped from the land of the Hebrews. And since I've been here, I've done nothing to deserve being put in this hole."

When the head baker saw how well Joseph's interpretation turned out, he spoke up: "My dream went like this: I saw three wicker baskets on my head; the top basket had assorted pastries from the bakery and birds were picking at them from the basket on my head."

Joseph said, "This is the interpretation: The three baskets are three days; within three days Pharaoh will take off your head, impale you on a post and the birds will pick your bones clean."

And sure enough, on the third day it was Pharaoh's birthday and he threw a feast for all his servants. He set the head cupbearer and the head baker in places of honor in the presence of all the guests. Then he restored the head cupbearer to his cupbearing post; he handed Pharaoh his cup just as before. And then he impaled the head baker on a post, following Joseph's interpretations exactly.

But the head cupbearer never gave Joseph another thought; he forgot all about him.

41 Two years passed and Pharaoh had a dream: He was standing by the Nile River. Seven cows came up out of the Nile, all shimmering with health, and grazed on the marsh grass. Then seven other cows, all skin and bones, came up out of the river after them and stood by them on the bank of the Nile. The skinny cows ate the seven healthy cows. Then Pharaoh woke up.

He went back to sleep and dreamed a second time: Seven ears of grain, full-bodied and lush, grew out of a single stalk. Then seven more ears grew up, but these were thin and dried out by the east wind. The thin ears swallowed up the full, healthy ears. Then Pharaoh woke up—another dream.

When morning came, he was upset. He sent for all the magicians and sages of Egypt. Pharaoh told them his dreams, but they couldn't interpret them to him.

The head cupbearer then spoke up and said to Pharaoh, "I just now remembered something—I'm sorry, I should have told you this long ago. Once when Pharaoh got angry with his servants, he locked me and the head baker in the house of the captain of the guard. We both had dreams on the same night, each dream with its own meaning. It so happened that there was a young Hebrew slave there with us; he belonged to the captain of the guard. We told him our dreams and he interpreted them for us, each dream separately. Things turned out just as he interpreted. I was returned to my position and the head baker was impaled."

Pharaoh at once sent for Joseph. They brought him on the run from the jail cell. He cut his hair, put on clean clothes, and came to Pharaoh.

"I dreamed a dream," Pharaoh told Joseph. "Nobody can interpret it. But I've heard that just by hearing a dream you can interpret it."

Joseph answered, "Not I, but God. God will set Pharaoh's mind at ease."

Then Pharaoh said to Joseph, "In my dream I was standing on the bank of the Nile. Seven cows, shimmering with health, came up out of the river and grazed on the marsh grass. On their heels seven more cows, all skin and bones, came up. I've never seen uglier cows anywhere in Egypt. Then the seven skinny, ugly cows ate up the first seven healthy cows. But you couldn't tell by looking—after eating them up they were just as skinny and ugly as before. Then I woke up.

"In my second dream I saw seven ears of grain, full-bodied and lush, growing out of a single stalk, and right behind them, seven other ears, shriveled, thin, and dried out by the east wind. And the thin ears swallowed up the full ears. I've told all this to the magicians but they can't figure it out."

Joseph said to Pharaoh, "Pharaoh's two dreams both mean the same thing. God is telling Pharaoh what he is going to do. The seven healthy cows are seven years and the seven healthy ears of grain are seven years—they're the same dream. The seven sick and ugly cows that followed them up are seven years and the seven scrawny ears of grain dried out by the east wind are the same—seven years of famine.

"The meaning is what I said earlier: God is letting Pharaoh in on what he is going to do. Seven years of plenty are on their way throughout Egypt. But on their heels will come seven years of famine, leaving no trace of the Egyptian plenty. As the country is emptied by famine, there won't be even a scrap left of the previous plenty—the famine will be total. The fact that Pharaoh dreamed the same dream twice emphasizes God's determination to do this and do it soon.

"So: Pharaoh needs to look for a wise and experienced man and put him in charge of the country. Then Pharaoh needs to appoint managers throughout the country of Egypt to organize it during the years of plenty. Their job will be to collect all the food produced in the good years ahead and stockpile the grain under Pharaoh's authority, storing it in the towns for food. This grain will be held back to be used later during the seven years of famine that are coming on Egypt. This way the country won't be devastated by the famine."

This seemed like a good idea to Pharaoh and his officials.

Then Pharaoh said to his officials, "Isn't this the man we need? Are we going to find anyone else who has God's spirit in him like this?"

So Pharaoh said to Joseph, "You're the man for us. God has given you the inside story—no one is as qualified as you in experience and wisdom. From now on, you're in charge of my affairs; all my people will report to you. Only as king will I be over you."

So Pharaoh commissioned Joseph: "I'm putting you in charge of the entire country of Egypt." Then Pharaoh removed his signet ring from his finger and slipped it on Joseph's hand. He outfitted him in robes of the best linen and put a gold chain around his neck. He put the second-in-command chariot at his disposal, and as he rode people shouted "Bravo!"

Joseph was in charge of the entire country of Egypt.

Pharaoh told Joseph, "I am Pharaoh, but no one in Egypt will make a single move without your stamp of approval."

Then Pharaoh gave Joseph an Egyptian name, Zaphenath-Paneah (God Speaks and He Lives). He also gave him an Egyptian wife, Asenath, the daughter of Potiphera, the priest of On (Heliopolis).

And Joseph took up his duties over the land of Egypt.

Joseph was thirty years old when he went to work for Pharaoh the king of Egypt. As soon as Joseph left Pharaoh's presence, he began his work in Egypt.

✛

During the next seven years of plenty the land produced bumper crops. Joseph gathered up the food of the seven good years in Egypt and stored the food in cities. In each city he stockpiled surplus from the surrounding fields. Joseph collected so much grain—it was like the sand of the ocean!—that he finally quit keeping track.

Joseph had two sons born to him before the years of famine came. Asenath, daughter of Potiphera the priest of On, was their mother. Joseph named the firstborn Manasseh (Forget), saying, "God made me forget all my hardships and my parental home." He named his second son Ephraim (Double Prosperity), saying, "God has prospered me in the land of my sorrow."

Then Egypt's seven good years came to an end and the seven years of famine arrived, just as Joseph had said. All countries experienced famine; Egypt was the only country that had bread.

When the famine spread throughout Egypt, the people called out in distress to Pharaoh, calling for bread. He told the Egyptians, "Go to Joseph. Do what he tells you."

As the famine got worse all over the country, Joseph opened the storehouses and sold emergency supplies to the Egyptians. The famine was very bad. Soon the whole world was coming to buy supplies from Joseph. The famine was bad all over.

⊹

42 When Jacob learned that there was food in Egypt, he said to his sons, "Why do you sit around here and look at one another? I've heard that there is food in Egypt. Go down there and buy some so that we can survive and not starve to death."

Ten of Joseph's brothers went down to Egypt to get food. Jacob didn't send Joseph's brother Benjamin with them; he was afraid that something bad might happen to him. So Israel's sons joined everyone else that was going to Egypt to buy food, for Canaan, too, was hit hard by the famine.

Joseph was running the country; he was the one who gave out rations to all the people. When Joseph's brothers arrived, they treated him with honor, bowing to him. Joseph recognized them immediately, but treated them as strangers and spoke roughly to them.

He said, "Where do you come from?"

"From Canaan," they said. "We've come to buy food."

Joseph knew who they were, but they didn't know who he was.

Joseph, remembering the dreams he had dreamed of them, said, "You're spies. You've come to look for our weak spots."

"No, master," they said. "We've only come to buy food. We're all the sons of the same man; we're honest men; we'd never think of spying."

He said, "No. You're spies. You've come to look for our weak spots."

They said, "There were twelve of us brothers—sons of the same father in the country of Canaan. The youngest is with our father, and one is no more."

But Joseph said, "It's just as I said, you're spies. This is how I'll test you. As Pharaoh lives, you're not going to leave this place until your younger brother comes here. Send one of you to get your brother while the rest of you stay here in jail. We'll see if you're telling the truth or not. As Pharaoh lives, I say you're spies."

Then he threw them into jail for three days.

On the third day, Joseph spoke to them. "Do this and you'll live. I'm a God-fearing man. If you're as honest as you say you are, one of your brothers will stay here in jail while the rest of you take the food back to your hungry families. But you have to bring your youngest brother back to me, confirming the truth of your speech—and not one of you will die." They agreed.

Then they started talking among themselves. "Now we're paying for what we did to our brother—we saw how terrified he was when he was begging us for mercy. We wouldn't listen to him and now we're the ones in trouble."

Reuben broke in. "Didn't I tell you, 'Don't hurt the boy'? But no, you wouldn't listen. And now we're paying for his murder."

Joseph had been using an interpreter, so they didn't know that Joseph was understanding every word. Joseph turned away from them and cried. When he was able to speak again, he took Simeon and had him tied up, making a prisoner of him while they all watched.

Then Joseph ordered that their sacks be filled with grain, that their money be put back in each sack, and that they be given rations for the road. That was all done for them.

They loaded their food supplies on their donkeys and set off.

When they stopped for the night, one of them opened his sack to get food for his donkey; there at the mouth of his bag was his money. He called out to his brothers, "My money has been returned; it's right here in my bag!" They were puzzled—and frightened. "What's God doing to us?"

When they got back to their father Jacob, back in the land of Canaan, they told him everything that had happened, saying, "The man who runs the country spoke to us roughly and accused us of being spies. We told him, 'We are honest men and in no way spies. There were twelve of us brothers, sons of one father; one is gone and the youngest is with our father in Canaan.'

"But the master of the country said, 'Leave one of your brothers with me, take food for your starving families, and go. Bring your youngest brother back to me, proving that you're honest men and not spies. And then I'll give your brother back to you and you'll be free to come and go in this country.'"

As they were emptying their food sacks, each man came on his purse of money. On seeing their money, they and their father were upset.

Their father said to them, "You're taking everything I've got! Joseph's gone, Simeon's gone, and now you want to take Benjamin. If you have your way, I'll be left with nothing."

Reuben spoke up: "I'll put my two sons in your hands as hostages. If I don't bring Benjamin back, you can kill them. Trust me with Benjamin; I'll bring him back."

But Jacob refused. "My son will not go down with you. His brother is dead and he is all I have left. If something bad happens to him on the road, you'll put my gray, sorrowing head in the grave."

43 The famine got worse. When they had eaten all the food they had brought back from Egypt, their father said, "Go back and get some more food."

But Judah said, "The man warned us most emphatically, 'You won't so much as see my face if you don't have your brother with you.' If you're ready to release our brother to go with us, we'll go down and get you food. But if you're not ready, we aren't going. What would be the use? The man told us, 'You won't so much as see my face if you don't have your brother with you.'"

Israel said, "Why are you making my life so difficult! Why did you ever tell the man you had another brother?"

They said, "The man pressed us hard, asking pointed questions about our family: 'Is your father alive? Do you have another brother?' So we answered his questions. How did we know that he'd say, 'Bring your brother here'?"

Judah pushed his father Israel. "Let the boy go; I'll take charge of him. Let us go and be on our way—if we don't get going, we're all going to starve to death—we and you and our children too! I'll take full responsibility for his safety; it's my life on the line for his. If I don't bring him back safe and sound, I'm the guilty one; I'll take all the blame.

If we had gone ahead in the first place instead of procrastinating like this, we could have been there and back twice over."

Their father Israel gave in. "If it has to be, it has to be. But do this: stuff your packs with the finest products from the land you can find and take them to the man as gifts—some balm and honey, some spices and perfumes, some pistachios and almonds. And take plenty of money—pay back double what was returned to your sacks; that might have been a mistake. Take your brother and get going. Go back to the man. And may The Strong God give you grace in that man's eyes so that he'll send back your other brother along with Benjamin. For me, nothing's left; I've lost everything."

The men took the gifts, double the money, and Benjamin. They lost no time in getting to Egypt and meeting Joseph. When Joseph saw that they had Benjamin with them, he told his house steward, "Take these men into the house and make them at home. Butcher an animal and prepare a meal; these men are going to eat with me at noon."

The steward did what Joseph had said and took them inside. But they became anxious when they were brought into Joseph's home, thinking, "It's the money; he thinks we ran off with the money on our first trip down here. And now he's got us where he wants us—he's going to turn us into slaves and confiscate our donkeys."

So they went up to Joseph's house steward and talked to him in the doorway. They said, "Listen, master. We came down here one other time to buy food. On our way home, the first night out we opened our bags and found our money at the mouth of the bag—the exact amount we'd paid. We've brought it all back and have plenty more to buy more food with. We have no idea who put the money in our bags."

The steward said, "Everything's in order. Don't worry. Your God and the God of your father must have given you a bonus. I was paid in full." And with that, he presented Simeon to them.

He then took them inside Joseph's house and made them comfortable—gave them water to wash their feet and saw to the feeding of their donkeys. The brothers spread out their gifts as they waited for Joseph to show up at noon—they had been told that they were to have dinner with him.

When Joseph got home, they presented him with the gifts they had brought and bowed respectfully before him.

Joseph welcomed them and said, "And your old father whom you mentioned to me, how is he? Is he still alive?"

They said, "Yes—your servant our father is quite well, very much alive." And they again bowed respectfully before him.

Then Joseph picked out his brother Benjamin, his own mother's son. He asked, "And is this your youngest brother that you told me about?" Then he said, "God be gracious to you, my son."

Deeply moved on seeing his brother and about to burst into tears, Joseph hurried out into another room and had a good cry. Then he washed his face, got a grip on himself and said, "Let's eat."

Joseph was served at his private table, the brothers off by themselves and the Egyptians off by themselves (Egyptians won't eat at the same table with Hebrews; it's repulsive to them). The brothers were seated facing Joseph, arranged in order of their age, from the oldest to the youngest. They looked at one another wide-eyed, wondering what would happen next. When the brothers' plates were served from Joseph's table, Benjamin's plate came piled high, far more so than his brothers. And so the brothers feasted with Joseph, drinking freely.

44 Joseph ordered his house steward: "Fill the men's bags with food—all they can carry—and replace each one's money at the top of the bag. Then put my chalice, my silver chalice, in the top of the bag of the youngest, along with the money for his food." He did as Joseph ordered.

At break of day the men were sent off with their donkeys. They were barely out of the city when Joseph said to his house steward, "Run after them. When you catch up with them, say, 'Why did you pay me back evil for good? This is the chalice my master drinks from; he also uses it for divination. This is outrageous!'"

He caught up with them and repeated all this word for word.

They said, "What is my master talking about? We would never do anything like that! Why, the money we found in our bags earlier, we brought back all the way from Canaan—do you think we'd turn right around and steal it back from your master? If that chalice is found on any of us, he'll die; and the rest of us will be your master's slaves."

The steward said, "Very well then, but we won't go that far. Whoever is found with the chalice will be my slave; the rest of you can go free."

They outdid each other in putting their bags on the ground and opening them up for inspection. The steward searched their bags, going from oldest to youngest. The chalice showed up in Benjamin's bag.

They ripped their clothes in despair, loaded up their donkeys and went back to the city.

Joseph was still at home when Judah and his brothers got back. They threw themselves down on the ground in front of him.

Joseph accused them: "How can you have done this? You have to know that a man in my position would have discovered this."

Judah as spokesman for the brothers said, "What can we say, master? What is there to say? How can we prove our innocence? God is behind this, exposing how bad we are. We stand guilty before you and ready to be your slaves—we're all in this together, the rest of us as guilty as the one with the chalice."

"I'd never do that to you," said Joseph. "Only the one involved with the chalice will be my slave. The rest of you are free to go back to your father."

Judah came forward. He said, "Please, master; can I say just one thing to you? Don't get angry. Don't think I'm presumptuous—you're the same as Pharaoh as far as I'm concerned. You, master, asked us, 'Do you have a father and a brother?' And we answered honestly, 'We have a father who is old and a younger brother who was born to him in his old age. His brother is dead and he is the only son left from that mother. And his father loves him more than anything.'

"Then you told us, 'Bring him down here so I can see him.' We told you, master, that it was impossible: 'The boy can't leave his father; if he leaves, his father will die.'

"And then you said, 'If your youngest brother doesn't come with you, you won't be allowed to see me.'

"When we returned to our father, we told him everything you said to us. So when our father said, 'Go back and buy some more food,' we told him flatly, 'We can't. The only way we can go back is if our youngest brother is with us. We aren't allowed to even see the man if our youngest brother doesn't come with us.'

"Your servant, my father, told us, 'You know very well that my wife gave me two sons. One turned up missing. I concluded that he'd been ripped to pieces. I've never seen him since. If you now go and take this one and something bad happens to him, you'll put my old gray, grieving head in the grave for sure.'

"And now, can't you see that if I show up before your servant, my father without the boy, this son with whom his life is so bound up, the moment he realizes the boy is gone, he'll die on the spot. He'll die of

84

grief and we, your servants who are standing here before you, will have killed him. And that's not all. I got my father to release the boy to show him to you by promising, 'If I don't bring him back, I'll stand condemned before you, father, all my life.'

"So let me stay here as your slave, not this boy. Let the boy go back with his brothers. How can I go back to my father if the boy is not with me? Oh, don't make me go back and watch my father die in grief!"

45 Joseph couldn't hold himself in any longer, keeping up a front before all his attendants. He cried out, "Leave! Clear out—everyone leave!" So there was no one with Joseph when he identified himself to his brothers. But his sobbing was so violent that the Egyptians couldn't help but hear him. The news was soon reported to Pharaoh's palace.

Joseph spoke to his brothers: "I am Joseph. Is my father really still alive?" But his brothers couldn't say a word. They were speechless—they couldn't believe what they were hearing and seeing.

"Come closer to me," Joseph said to his brothers. They came closer. "I am Joseph your brother whom you sold into Egypt. But don't feel badly, don't blame yourselves for selling me. God was behind it. God sent me here ahead of you to save lives. There has been a famine in the land now for two years; the famine will continue for five more years—neither plowing nor harvesting. God sent me on ahead to pave the way and make sure there was a remnant in the land, to save your lives in an amazing act of deliverance. So you see, it wasn't you who sent me here but God. He set me in place as a father to Pharaoh, put me in charge of his personal affairs and made me ruler of all Egypt.

"Hurry back to my father. Tell him, 'Your son Joseph says: I'm master of all of Egypt. Come as fast as you can and join me here. I'll give you a place to live in Goshen where you'll be close to me—you, your children, your grandchildren, your flocks, your herds, and anything else you can think of. I'll take care of you there completely. There are still five more years of famine ahead; I'll make sure all your needs are taken care of, you and everyone connected with you—you won't want for a thing.'

"Look at me. You can see for yourselves, and my brother Benjamin can see for himself, that it's me, my own mouth, telling you all this. Tell my father all about the high position I hold in Egypt, tell him everything you've seen here, but don't take all day—hurry up and get my father down here."

Then Joseph threw himself on his brother Benjamin's neck and wept, and Benjamin wept on his neck. He then kissed all his brothers and wept over them. Only then were his brothers able to talk with him.

The story was reported in Pharaoh's palace: "Joseph's brothers have come." It was good news to Pharaoh and all who worked with him.

Pharaoh said to Joseph, "Tell your brothers, 'This is the plan: Load up your pack animals; go to Canaan, get your father and your families and bring them back here. I'll settle you on the best land in Egypt— you'll live off the fat of the land.'

"Also tell them this: 'Here's what I want you to do: Take wagons from Egypt to carry your little ones and your wives and load up your father and come back. Don't worry about having to leave things behind; the best in all of Egypt will be yours.'"

And they did just that, the sons of Israel. Joseph gave them the wagons that Pharaoh had promised and food for the trip. He outfitted all the brothers in brand-new clothes, but he gave Benjamin three hundred pieces of silver and several suits of clothes. He sent his father these gifts: ten donkeys loaded with Egypt's best products and another ten donkeys loaded with grain and bread, provisions for his father's journey back.

Then he sent his brothers off. As they left he told them, "Take it easy on the journey; try to get along with each other."

They left Egypt and went back to their father Jacob in Canaan. When they told him, "Joseph is still alive—and he's the ruler over the whole land of Egypt!" he went numb; he couldn't believe his ears. But the more they talked, telling him everything that Joseph had told them and when he saw the wagons that Joseph had sent to carry him back, the blood started to flow again—their father Jacob's spirit revived. Israel said, "I've heard enough—my son Joseph is still alive. I've got to go and see him before I die."

✛

46 So Israel set out on the journey with everything he owned. He arrived at Beersheba and worshiped, offering sacrifices to the God of his father Isaac.

God spoke to Israel in a vision that night: "Jacob! Jacob!"

"Yes?" he said. "I'm listening."

God said, "I am the God of your father. Don't be afraid of going down to Egypt. I'm going to make you a great nation there. I'll go with you down to Egypt; I'll also bring you back here. And when you die, Joseph will be with you; with his own hand he'll close your eyes."

Then Jacob left Beersheba. Israel's sons loaded their father and their little ones and their wives on the wagons Pharaoh had sent to carry him. They arrived in Egypt with the livestock and the wealth they had accumulated in Canaan. Jacob brought everyone in his family with him—sons and grandsons, daughters and granddaughters. Everyone.

These are the names of the Israelites, Jacob and his descendants, who went to Egypt:

Reuben, Jacob's firstborn.

Reuben's sons: Hanoch, Pallu, Hezron, and Carmi.

Simeon's sons: Jemuel, Jamin, Ohad, Jakin, Zohar, and Shaul the son of a Canaanite woman.

Levi's sons: Gershon, Kohath, and Merari.

Judah's sons: Er, Onan, Shelah, Perez, and Zerah (Er and Onan had already died in the land of Canaan). The sons of Perez were Hezron and Hamul.

Issachar's sons: Tola, Puah, Jashub, and Shimron.

Zebulun's sons: Sered, Elon, and Jahleel.

These are the sons that Leah bore to Jacob in Paddan Aram. There was also his daughter Dinah. Altogether, sons and daughters, they numbered thirty-three.

Gad's sons: Zephon, Haggi, Shuni, Ezbon, Eri, Arodi, and Areli.

Asher's sons: Imnah, Ishvah, Ishvi, and Beriah. Also their sister Serah, and Beriah's sons, Heber and Malkiel.

These are the children that Zilpah, the maid that Laban gave to his daughter Leah, bore to Jacob—sixteen of them.

The sons of Jacob's wife Rachel were Joseph and Benjamin. Joseph was the father of two sons, Manasseh and Ephraim, from his marriage to Asenath daughter of Potiphera, priest of On. They were born to him in Egypt. Benjamin's sons were Bela, Beker, Ashbel, Gera, Naaman, Ehi, Rosh, Muppim, Huppim, and Ard.

These are the children born to Jacob through Rachel—fourteen.

Dan's son: Hushim.

Naphtali's sons: Jahziel, Guni, Jezer, and Shillem.

These are the children born to Jacob through Bilhah, the maid Laban had given to his daughter Rachel—seven.

Summing up, all those who went down to Egypt with Jacob—his own children, not counting his sons' wives—numbered sixty-six. Counting in the two sons born to Joseph in Egypt, the members of Jacob's family who ended up in Egypt numbered seventy.

✛

Jacob sent Judah on ahead to get directions to Goshen from Joseph. When they got to Goshen, Joseph gave orders for his chariot and went to Goshen to meet his father Israel. The moment Joseph saw him, he threw himself on his neck and wept. He wept a long time.

Israel said to Joseph, "I'm ready to die. I've looked into your face—you are indeed alive."

Joseph then spoke to his brothers and his father's family. "I'll go and tell Pharaoh, 'My brothers and my father's family, all of whom lived in Canaan, have come to me. The men are shepherds; they've always made their living by raising livestock. And they've brought their flocks and herds with them, along with everything else they own.' When Pharaoh calls you in and asks what kind of work you do, tell him, 'Your servants have always kept livestock for as long as we can remember—we and our parents also.' That way he'll let you stay apart in the area of Goshen—for Egyptians look down on anyone who is a shepherd."

47 Joseph went to Pharaoh and told him, "My father and brothers with their flocks and herds and everything they own have come from Canaan. Right now they are in Goshen."

He had taken five of his brothers with him and introduced them to Pharaoh. Pharaoh asked them, "What kind of work do you do?"

"Your servants are shepherds, the same as our fathers were. We have come to this country to find a new place to live. There is no pasture for our flocks in Canaan. The famine has been very bad there. Please, would you let your servants settle in the region of Goshen?"

Pharaoh looked at Joseph. "So, your father and brothers have arrived—a reunion! Egypt welcomes them. Settle your father and brothers on the choicest land—yes, give them Goshen. And if you know any among them that are especially good at their work, put them in charge of my own livestock."

Next Joseph brought his father Jacob in and introduced him to Pharaoh. Jacob blessed Pharaoh. Pharaoh asked Jacob, "How old are you?"

Jacob answered Pharaoh, "The years of my sojourning are 130—a short and hard life and not nearly as long as my ancestors were given." Then Jacob blessed Pharaoh and left.

Joseph settled his father and brothers in Egypt, made them proud owners of choice land—it was the region of Rameses (that is, Goshen)—

just as Pharaoh had ordered. Joseph took good care of them—his father and brothers and all his father's family, right down to the smallest baby. He made sure they had plenty of everything.

✝

The time eventually came when there was no food anywhere. The famine was very bad. Egypt and Canaan alike were devastated by the famine. Joseph collected all the money that was to be found in Egypt and Canaan to pay for the distribution of food. He banked the money in Pharaoh's palace. When the money from Egypt and Canaan had run out, the Egyptians came to Joseph. "Food! Give us food! Are you going to watch us die right in front of you? The money is all gone."

Joseph said, "Bring your livestock. I'll trade you food for livestock since your money's run out." So they brought Joseph their livestock. He traded them food for their horses, sheep, cattle, and donkeys. He got them through that year in exchange for all their livestock.

When that year was over, the next year rolled around and they were back, saying, "Master, it's no secret to you that we're broke: our money's gone and we've traded you all our livestock. We've nothing left to barter with but our bodies and our farms. What use are our bodies and our land if we stand here and starve to death right in front of you? Trade us food for our bodies and our land. We'll be slaves to Pharaoh and give up our land—all we ask is seed for survival, just enough to live on and keep the farms alive."

So Joseph bought up all the farms in Egypt for Pharaoh. Every Egyptian sold his land—the famine was that bad. That's how Pharaoh ended up owning all the land and the people ended up slaves; Joseph reduced the people to slavery from one end of Egypt to the other.

Joseph made an exception for the priests. He didn't buy their land because they received a fixed salary from Pharaoh and were able to live off of that salary. So they didn't need to sell their land.

Joseph then announced to the people: "Here's how things stand: I've bought you and your land for Pharaoh. In exchange I'm giving you seed so you can plant the ground. When the crops are harvested, you must give a fifth to Pharaoh and keep four-fifths for yourselves, for seed for yourselves and your families—you're going to be able to feed your children!"

They said, "You've saved our lives! Master, we're grateful and glad to be slaves to Pharaoh."

Joseph decreed a land law in Egypt that is still in effect, *A Fifth Goes to Pharaoh.* Only the priests' lands were not owned by Pharaoh.

✛

And so Israel settled down in Egypt in the region of Goshen. They acquired property and flourished. They became a large company of people. Jacob lived in Egypt for seventeen years. In all, he lived 147 years.

When the time came for Israel to die, he called his son Joseph and said, "Do me this favor. Put your hand under my thigh, a sign that you're loyal and true to me to the end. Don't bury me in Egypt. When I lie down with my fathers, carry me out of Egypt and bury me alongside them."

"I will," he said. "I'll do what you've asked."

Israel said, "Promise me." Joseph promised.

Israel bowed his head in submission and gratitude from his bed.

48 Some time after this conversation, Joseph was told, "Your father is ill." He took his two sons, Manasseh and Ephraim, and went to Jacob. When Jacob was told, "Your son Joseph has come," he roused himself and sat up in bed.

Jacob said to Joseph, "The Strong God appeared to me at Luz in the land of Canaan and blessed me. He said, 'I'm going to make you prosperous and numerous, turn you into a congregation of tribes; and I'll turn this land over to your children coming after you as a permanent inheritance.' I'm adopting your two sons who were born to you here in Egypt before I joined you; they have equal status with Reuben and Simeon. But any children born after them are yours; they will come after their brothers in matters of inheritance. I want it this way because, as I was returning from Paddan, your mother Rachel, to my deep sorrow, died as we were on our way through Canaan when we were only a short distance from Ephrath, now called Bethlehem."

Just then Jacob noticed Joseph's sons and said, "Who are these?"

Joseph told his father, "They are my sons whom God gave to me in this place."

"Bring them to me," he said, "so I can bless them." Israel's eyesight was poor from old age; he was nearly blind. So Joseph brought them up close. Old Israel kissed and embraced them and then said to Joseph, "I never expected to see your face again, and now God has let me see your children as well!"

Joseph took them from Israel's knees and bowed respectfully, his face to the ground. Then Joseph took the two boys, Ephraim with his right hand setting him to Israel's left, and Manasseh with his left hand setting him to Israel's right, and stood them before him. But Israel crossed his arms and put his right hand on the head of Ephraim who was the younger and his left hand on the head of Manasseh, the first-born. Then he blessed them:

> The God before whom walked
>   my fathers Abraham and Isaac,
> The God who has been my shepherd
>   all my life-long to this very day,
> The Angel who delivered me from every evil,
>   Bless the boys.
> May my name be echoed in their lives,
>   and the names of Abraham and Isaac, my fathers,
> And may they grow
>   covering the Earth with their children.

When Joseph saw that his father had placed his right hand on Ephraim's head, he thought he had made a mistake, so he took hold of his father's hand to move it from Ephraim's head to Manasseh's, saying, "That's the wrong head, father; the other one is the firstborn; place your right hand on his head."

But his father wouldn't do it. He said, "I know, my son; but I know what I'm doing. He also will develop into a people, and he also will be great. But his younger brother will be even greater and his descendants will enrich nations." Then he blessed them both:

> Israel will use your names to give blessings:
>   May God make you like Ephraim and Manasseh.

In that he made it explicit: he put Ephraim ahead of Manasseh.

Israel then said to Joseph, "I'm about to die. God be with you and give you safe passage back to the land of your fathers. As for me, I'm presenting you, as the first among your brothers, the ridge of land I took from Amorites with my sword and bow."

✠

49 Jacob called his sons and said, "Gather around. I want to tell you what you can expect in the days to come."

Come together, listen sons of Jacob,
     listen to Israel your father.

Reuben, you're my firstborn,
     my strength, first proof of my manhood,
     at the top in honor and at the top in power,
But like a bucket of water spilled,
     you'll be at the top no more,
Because you climbed into your father's marriage bed,
     mounting that couch, and you defiled it.

Simeon and Levi are two of a kind,
     ready to fight at the drop of a hat.
I don't want anything to do with their vendettas,
     want no part in their bitter feuds;
They kill men in fits of temper,
     slash oxen on a whim.
A curse on their uncontrolled anger,
     on their indiscriminate wrath.
I'll throw them out with the trash;
     I'll shred and scatter them like confetti throughout Israel.

You, Judah, your brothers will praise you:
     Your fingers on your enemies' throat,
     while your brothers honor you.
You're a lion's cub, Judah,
     home fresh from the kill, my son.
Look at him, crouched like a lion, king of beasts;
     who dares mess with him?
The scepter shall not leave Judah;
     he'll keep a firm grip on the command staff
Until the ultimate ruler comes
     and the nations obey him.
He'll tie up his donkey to the grapevine,
     his purebred prize to a sturdy branch.
He will wash his shirt in wine

and his cloak in the blood of grapes,
His eyes will be darker than wine,
    his teeth whiter than milk.

Zebulun settles down on the seashore;
    he's a safe harbor for ships,
    right alongside Sidon.

Issachar is one tough donkey
    crouching between the corrals;
When he saw how good the place was,
    how pleasant the country,
He gave up his freedom
    and went to work as a slave.

Dan will handle matters of justice for his people;
    he will hold his own just fine among the tribes of Israel.
Dan is only a small snake in the grass,
    a lethal serpent in ambush by the road
When he strikes a horse in the heel,
    and brings its huge rider crashing down.

I wait in hope
    for your salvation, GOD.

Gad will be attacked by bandits,
    but he will trip them up.

Asher will become famous for rich foods,
    candies and sweets fit for kings.

Naphtali is a deer running free
    that gives birth to lovely fawns.

Joseph is a wild donkey,
    a wild donkey by a spring,
    spirited donkeys on a hill.
The archers with malice attacked,
    shooting their hate-tipped arrows;

But he held steady under fire,
    his bow firm, his arms limber,
With the backing of the Champion of Jacob,
    the Shepherd, the Rock of Israel.
The God of your father—may he help you!
    And may The Strong God—may he give you his blessings,
Blessings tumbling out of the skies,
    blessings bursting up from the Earth—
    blessings of breasts and womb.
May the blessings of your father
    exceed the blessings of the ancient mountains,
    surpass the delights of the eternal hills;
May they rest on the head of Joseph,
    on the brow of the one consecrated among his brothers.

Benjamin is a ravenous wolf;
    all morning he gorges on his kill,
    at evening divides up what's left over.

All these are the tribes of Israel, the twelve tribes. And this is what their father said to them as he blessed them, blessing each one with his own special farewell blessing.

☩

Then he instructed them: "I am about to be gathered to my people. Bury me with my fathers in the cave which is in the field of Ephron the Hittite, the cave in the field of Machpelah facing Mamre in the land of Canaan, the field Abraham bought from Ephron the Hittite for a burial plot. Abraham and his wife Sarah were buried there; Isaac and his wife Rebekah were buried there; I also buried Leah there. The field and the cave were bought from the Hittites."

Jacob finished instructing his sons, pulled his feet into bed, breathed his last, and was gathered to his people.

50 Joseph threw himself on his father, wept over him and kissed him.

☩

Joseph then instructed the physicians in his employ to embalm his father. The physicians embalmed Israel. The embalming took forty days, the period required for embalming. There was public mourning by the Egyptians for seventy days.

When the period of mourning was completed, Joseph petitioned Pharaoh's court: "If you have reason to think kindly of me, present Pharaoh with my request: My father made me swear, saying, 'I am ready to die. Bury me in the grave plot that I prepared for myself in the land of Canaan.' Please give me leave to go up and bury my father. Then I'll come back."

Pharaoh said, "Certainly. Go and bury your father as he made you promise under oath."

So Joseph left to bury his father. And all the high-ranking officials from Pharaoh's court went with him, all the dignitaries of Egypt, joining Joseph's family—his brothers and his father's family. Their children and flocks and herds were left in Goshen. Chariots and horsemen accompanied them. It was a huge funeral procession.

Arriving at the Atad Threshing Floor just across the Jordan River, they stopped for a period of mourning, letting their grief out in loud and lengthy lament. For seven days, Joseph engaged in these funeral rites for his father.

When the Canaanites who lived in that area saw the grief being poured out at the Atad Threshing Floor, they said, "Look how deeply the Egyptians are mourning." That is how the site at the Jordan got the name Abel Mizraim (Egyptian Lament).

Jacob's sons continued to carry out his instructions to the letter. They took him on into Canaan and buried him in the cave in the field of Machpelah facing Mamre, the field that Abraham had bought as a burial plot from Ephron the Hittite.

⊹

After burying his father, Joseph went back to Egypt. All his brothers who had come with him to bury his father returned with him. After the funeral, Joseph's brothers talked among themselves: "What if Joseph is carrying a grudge and decides to pay us back for all the wrong we did him?"

So they sent Joseph a message, "Before his death, your father gave this command: Tell Joseph, 'Forgive your brothers' sin—all that wrongdoing. They did treat you very badly.' Will you do it? Will you forgive the sins of the servants of your father's God?"

When Joseph received their message, he wept.

Then the brothers went in person to him, threw themselves on the ground before him and said, "We'll be your slaves."

Joseph replied, "Don't be afraid. Do I act for God? Don't you see, you planned evil against me but God used those same plans for my good, as you see all around you right now—life for many people. Easy now, you have nothing to fear; I'll take care of you and your children." He reassured them, speaking with them heart to heart.

Joseph continued to live in Egypt with his father's family. Joseph lived 110 years. He lived to see Ephraim's sons into the third generation. The sons of Makir, Manasseh's son, were also recognized as Joseph's.

At the end, Joseph said to his brothers, "I am ready to die. God will most certainly pay you a visit and take you out of this land and back to the land he so solemnly promised to Abraham, Isaac, and Jacob."

Then Joseph made the sons of Israel promise under oath, "When God makes his visitation, make sure you take my bones with you as you leave here."

Joseph died at the age of 110 years. They embalmed him and placed him in a coffin in Egypt.

EXODUS

The human race is in trouble. We've been in trouble for a long time. Enormous energies have been and continue to be expended by many, many men and women to get us out of the trouble we are in — to clean up the world's mess. The skill, the perseverance, the intelligence, the devotion of the people who put their shoulders to the wheel to pull us out of the muck — parents and teachers, healers and counselors, rulers and politicians, writers and pastors — are impressive.

At the center and core of this work is God. The most comprehensive term for what God is doing to get us out of the mess we are in is *salvation*. Salvation is God doing for us what we can't do for ourselves. Salvation is the biggest word in the vocabulary of the people of God. The Exodus is a powerful and dramatic and true story of God working salvation. The story has generated an extraordinary progeny through the centuries as it has reproduced itself in song and poem, drama and novel, politics and social justice, repentance and conversion, worship and holy living. It continues to capture the imagination of men and women, especially men and women in trouble.

It is significant that God does not present us with salvation in the form of an abstract truth, or a precise definition or a catchy slogan, but as *story*. Exodus draws us into a story with plot and characters, which is to say, with design and personal relationships. Story is an invitation to participate, first through our imagination and then, if we will, by faith — with our total lives in response to God. This Exodus story continues to be a major means that God uses to draw men and women in trouble out of the mess of history into the kingdom of salvation.

About half the book (chapters 1–19 and 32–34) is a gripping narrative of an obscure and severely brutalized people who are saved from slavery into a life of freedom. The other half (chapters 20–31 and 35–40) is a meticulous, some think tedious, basic instruction and training in living the saved, free life. The story of salvation is not complete without both halves.

EXODUS

1 These are the names of the Israelites who went to Egypt with Jacob, each bringing his family members:

Reuben, Simeon, Levi, and Judah,
Issachar, Zebulun, and Benjamin,
Dan and Naphtali, Gad and Asher.

Seventy persons in all generated by Jacob's seed. Joseph was already in Egypt.

Then Joseph died, and all his brothers—that whole generation. But the children of Israel kept on reproducing. They were very prolific—a population explosion in their own right—and the land was filled with them.

"A New King . . . Who Didn't Know Joseph"

A new king came to power in Egypt who didn't know Joseph. He spoke to his people in alarm, "There are way too many of these Israelites for us to handle. We've got to do something: Let's devise a plan to contain them, lest if there's a war they should join our enemies, or just walk off and leave us."

So they organized them into work-gangs and put them to hard labor under gang-foremen. They built the storage cities Pithom and Rameses for Pharaoh. But the harder the Egyptians worked them the more children the Israelites had—children everywhere! The Egyptians got so they couldn't stand the Israelites and treated them worse than ever, crushing them with slave labor. They made them miserable with hard labor—making bricks and mortar and back-breaking work in the fields. They piled on the work, crushing them under the cruel workload.

The king of Egypt had a talk with the two Hebrew midwives; one was named Shiphrah and the other Puah. He said, "When you deliver the Hebrew women, look at the sex of the baby. If it's a boy, kill him; if it's a girl, let her live."

But the midwives had far too much respect for God and didn't do what the king of Egypt ordered; they let the boy babies live. The king of Egypt called in the midwives. "Why didn't you obey my orders? You've let those babies live!"

The midwives answered Pharaoh, "The Hebrew women aren't like the Egyptian women; they're vigorous. Before the midwife can get there, they've already had the baby."

God was pleased with the midwives. The people continued to increase in number—a very strong people. And because the midwives honored God, God gave them families of their own.

So Pharaoh issued a general order to all his people: "Every boy that is born, drown him in the Nile. But let the girls live."

MOSES

2 A man from the family of Levi married a Levite woman. The woman became pregnant and had a son. She saw there was something special about him and hid him. She hid him for three months. When she couldn't hide him any longer she got a little basket-boat made of papyrus, waterproofed it with tar and pitch, and placed the child in it. Then she set it afloat in the reeds at the edge of the Nile.

The baby's older sister found herself a vantage point a little way off and watched to see what would happen to him. Pharaoh's daughter came down to the Nile to bathe; her maidens strolled on the bank. She saw the basket-boat floating in the reeds and sent her maid to get it. She opened it and saw the child—a baby crying! Her heart went out to him. She said, "This must be one of the Hebrew babies."

Then his sister was before her: "Do you want me to go and get a nursing mother from the Hebrews so she can nurse the baby for you?"

Pharaoh's daughter said, "Yes. Go." The girl went and called the child's mother.

Pharaoh's daughter told her, "Take this baby and nurse him for me. I'll pay you." The woman took the child and nursed him.

After the child was weaned, she presented him to Pharaoh's daughter who adopted him as her son. She named him Moses (Pulled-Out), saying, "I pulled him out of the water."

Time passed. Moses grew up. One day he went and saw his brothers, saw all that hard labor. Then he saw an Egyptian hit a Hebrew— one of his relatives! He looked this way and then that; when he realized there was no one in sight, he killed the Egyptian and buried him in the sand.

The next day he went out there again. Two Hebrew men were fighting. He spoke to the man who started it: "Why are you hitting your neighbor?"

The man shot back: "Who do you think you are, telling us what to do? Are you going to kill me the way you killed that Egyptian?"

Then Moses panicked: "Word's gotten out—people know about this."

✛

Pharaoh heard about it and tried to kill Moses, but Moses got away to the land of Midian. He sat down by a well.

The priest of Midian had seven daughters. They came and drew water, filling the troughs and watering their father's sheep. When some shepherds came and chased the girls off, Moses came to their rescue and helped them water their sheep.

When they got home to their father, Reuel, he said, "That didn't take long. Why are you back so soon?"

"An Egyptian," they said, "rescued us from a bunch of shepherds. Why, he even drew water for us and watered the sheep."

He said, "So where is he? Why did you leave him behind? Invite him so he can have something to eat with us."

Moses agreed to settle down there with the man, who then gave his daughter Zipporah (Bird) to him for his wife. She had a son, and Moses named him Gershom (Sojourner), saying, "I'm a sojourner in a foreign country."

✛

Many years later the king of Egypt died. The Israelites groaned under their slavery and cried out. Their cries for relief from their hard labor ascended to God:

God listened to their groanings.

God remembered his covenant with Abraham, with Isaac, and with Jacob.

God saw what was going on with Israel.

God understood.

✛

3 Moses was shepherding the flock of Jethro, his father-in-law, the priest of Midian. He led the flock to the west end of the wilderness and came to the mountain of God, Horeb. The angel of GOD appeared to him in flames of fire blazing out of the middle of a bush. He looked. The bush was blazing away but it didn't burn up.

Moses said, "What's going on here? I can't believe this! Amazing!

Why doesn't the bush burn up?"

GOD saw that he had stopped to look. God called to him from out of the bush, "Moses! Moses!"

He said, "Yes? I'm right here!"

God said, "Don't come any closer. Remove your sandals from your feet. You're standing on holy ground."

Then he said, "I am the God of your father: The God of Abraham, the God of Isaac, the God of Jacob."

Moses hid his face, afraid to look at God.

GOD said, "I've taken a good, long look at the affliction of my people in Egypt. I've heard their cries for deliverance from their slave masters; I know all about their pain. And now I have come down to help them, pry them loose from the grip of Egypt, get them out of that country and bring them to a good land with wide-open spaces, a land lush with milk and honey, the land of the Canaanite, the Hittite, the Amorite, the Perizzite, the Hivite, and the Jebusite.

"The Israelite cry for help has come to me, and I've seen for myself how cruelly they're being treated by the Egyptians. It's time for you to go back: I'm sending you to Pharaoh to bring my people, the People of Israel, out of Egypt."

Moses answered God, "But why me? What makes you think that I could ever go to Pharaoh and lead the children of Israel out of Egypt?"

"I'll be with you," God said. "And this will be the proof that I am the one who sent you: When you have brought my people out of Egypt, you will worship God right here at this very mountain."

Then Moses said to God, "Suppose I go to the People of Israel and I tell them, 'The God of your fathers sent me to you'; and they ask me, 'What is his name?' What do I tell them?"

God said to Moses, "I-AM-WHO-I-AM. Tell the People of Israel, 'I-AM sent me to you.'"

God continued with Moses: "This is what you're to say to the Israelites: 'GOD, the God of your fathers, the God of Abraham, the God of Isaac, and the God of Jacob sent me to you.' This has always been my name, and this is how I always will be known.

"Now be on your way. Gather the leaders of Israel. Tell them, 'GOD, the God of your fathers, the God of Abraham, Isaac, and Jacob, appeared to me, saying, "I've looked into what's being done to you in Egypt, and I've determined to get you out of the affliction of Egypt and take you to the land of the Canaanite, the Hittite, the Amorite, the Perizzite, the Hivite, and the Jebusite, a land brimming over with milk and honey.'"

"Believe me, they will listen to you. Then you and the leaders of Israel will go to the king of Egypt and say to him: 'GOD, the God of the Hebrews, has met with us. Let us take a three-day journey into the wilderness where we will worship GOD—*our* God.'

"I know that the king of Egypt won't let you go unless forced to, so I'll intervene and hit Egypt where it hurts—oh, my miracles will send them reeling!—after which they'll be glad to send you off. I'll see to it that this people get a hearty sendoff by the Egyptians—when you leave, you won't leave empty-handed! Each woman will ask her neighbor and any guests in her house for objects of silver and gold, for jewelry and extra clothes; you'll put them on your sons and daughters. Oh, you'll clean the Egyptians out!"

4 Moses objected, "They won't trust me. They won't listen to a word I say. They're going to say, 'GOD? Appear to him? Hardly!'"

So GOD said, "What's that in your hand?"

"A staff."

"Throw it on the ground." He threw it. It became a snake; Moses jumped back—fast!

GOD said to Moses, "Reach out and grab it by the tail." He reached out and grabbed it—and he was holding his staff again. "That's so they will trust that GOD appeared to you, the God of their fathers, the God of Abraham, the God of Isaac, and the God of Jacob."

GOD then said, "Put your hand inside your shirt." He slipped his hand under his shirt, then took it out. His hand had turned leprous, like snow.

He said, "Put your hand back under your shirt." He did it, then took it back out—as healthy as before.

"So if they don't trust you and aren't convinced by the first sign, the second sign should do it. But if it doesn't, if even after these two signs they don't trust you and listen to your message, take some water out of the Nile and pour it out on the dry land; the Nile water that you pour out will turn to blood when it hits the ground."

Moses raised another objection to GOD: "Master, please, I don't talk well. I've never been good with words, neither before nor after you spoke to me. I stutter and stammer."

GOD said, "And who do you think made the human mouth? And

who makes some mute, some deaf, some sighted, some blind? Isn't it I, GOD? So, get going. I'll be right there with you—with your mouth! I'll be right there to teach you what to say."

He said, "Oh, Master, please! Send somebody else!"

GOD got angry with Moses: "Don't you have a brother, Aaron the Levite? He's good with words, I know he is. He speaks very well. In fact, at this very moment he's on his way to meet you. When he sees you he's going to be glad. You'll speak to him and tell him what to say. I'll be right there with you as you speak and with him as he speaks, teaching you step by step. He will speak to the people for you. He'll act as your mouth, but you'll decide what comes out of it. Now take this staff in your hand; you'll use it to do the signs."

⊹

Moses went back to Jethro his father-in-law and said, "I need to return to my relatives who are in Egypt. I want to see if they're still alive."

Jethro said, "Go. And peace be with you."

GOD said to Moses in Midian: "Go. Return to Egypt. All the men who wanted to kill you are dead."

So Moses took his wife and sons and put them on a donkey for the return trip to Egypt. He had a firm grip on the staff of God.

GOD said to Moses, "When you get back to Egypt, be prepared: All the wonders that I will do through you, you'll do before Pharaoh. But I will make him stubborn so that he will refuse to let the people go. Then you are to tell Pharaoh, 'GOD's Message: Israel is my son, my first-born! I told you, "Free my son so that he can serve me." But you refused to free him. So now I'm going to kill *your* son, *your* firstborn.'"

⊹

On the journey back, as they camped for the night, GOD met Moses and would have killed him but Zipporah took a flint knife and cut off her son's foreskin, and touched Moses' member with it. She said, "Oh! You're a bridegroom of blood to me!" Then GOD let him go. She used the phrase "bridegroom of blood" because of the circumcision.

⊹

GOD spoke to Aaron, "Go and meet Moses in the wilderness." He went and met him at the mountain of God and kissed him. Moses told Aaron

103

the message that GOD had sent him to speak and the wonders he had commanded him to do.

So Moses and Aaron proceeded to round up all the leaders of Israel. Aaron told them everything that GOD had told Moses and demonstrated the wonders before the people. And the people trusted and listened believingly that GOD was concerned with what was going on with the Israelites and knew all about their affliction. They bowed low and they worshiped.

MOSES AND AARON AND PHARAOH

5 After that Moses and Aaron approached Pharaoh. They said, "GOD, the God of Israel, says, 'Free my people so that they can hold a festival for me in the wilderness.'"

Pharaoh said, "And who is GOD that I should listen to him and send Israel off? I know nothing of this so-called 'GOD' and I'm certainly not going to send Israel off."

They said, "The God of the Hebrews has met with us. Let us take a three-day journey into the wilderness so we can worship our GOD lest he strike us with either disease or death."

But the king of Egypt said, "Why on earth, Moses and Aaron, would you suggest the people be given a holiday? Back to work!" Pharaoh went on, "Look, I've got all these people bumming around, and now you want to reward them with time off?"

Pharaoh took immediate action. He sent down orders to the slave-drivers and their underlings: "Don't provide straw for the people for making bricks as you have been doing. Make them get their own straw. And make them produce the same number of bricks—no reduction in their daily quotas! They're getting lazy. They're going around saying, 'Give us time off so we can worship our God.' Crack down on them. That'll cure them of their whining, their god-fantasies."

The slave-drivers and their underlings went out to the people with their new instructions. "Pharaoh's orders: No more straw provided. Get your own straw wherever you can find it. And not one brick less in your daily work quota!" The people scattered all over Egypt scrabbling for straw.

The slave-drivers were merciless, saying, "Complete your daily quota of bricks—the same number as when you were given straw."

The Israelite foremen whom the slave-drivers had appointed were beaten and badgered. "Why didn't you finish your quota of bricks yesterday or the day before—and now again today!"

The Israelite foremen came to Pharaoh and cried out for relief: "Why are you treating your servants like this? Nobody gives us any straw and they tell us, 'Make bricks!' Look at us—we're being beaten. And it's not our fault."

But Pharaoh said, "Lazy! That's what you are! Lazy! That's why you whine, 'Let us go so we can worship GOD.' Well then, go—go back to work. Nobody's going to give you straw, and at the end of the day you better bring in your full quota of bricks."

The Israelite foremen saw that they were in a bad way, having to go back and tell their workers, "Not one brick short in your daily quota."

As they left Pharaoh, they found Moses and Aaron waiting to meet them. The foremen said to them, "May GOD see what you've done and judge you—you've made us stink before Pharaoh and his servants! You've put a weapon in his hand that's going to kill us!"

Moses went back to GOD and said, "My Master, why are you treating this people so badly? And why did you ever send me? From the moment I came to Pharaoh to speak in your name, things have only gotten worse for this people. And rescue? Does this look like rescue to you?"

6 GOD said to Moses, "Now you'll see what I'll do to Pharaoh: With a strong hand he'll send them out free; with a strong hand he'll drive them out of his land."

God continued speaking to Moses, reassuring him, "I am GOD. I appeared to Abraham, Isaac, and Jacob as The Strong God, but by my name GOD (I-Am-Present) I was not known to them. I also established my covenant with them to give them the land of Canaan, the country in which they lived as sojourners. But now I've heard the groanings of the Israelites whom the Egyptians continue to enslave and I've remembered my covenant. Therefore tell the Israelites:

"'I am GOD. I will bring you out from under the cruel hard labor of Egypt. I will rescue you from slavery. I will redeem you, intervening with great acts of judgment. I'll take you as my own people and I'll be God to you. You'll know that I am GOD, *your* God who brings you out from under the cruel hard labor of Egypt. I'll bring you into the land that I promised to give Abraham, Isaac, and Jacob and give it to you as your own country. *I AM GOD.*'"

But when Moses delivered this message to the Israelites, they didn't even hear him—they were that beaten down in spirit by the harsh slave conditions.

Then GOD said to Moses, "Go and speak to Pharaoh king of Egypt so that he will release the Israelites from his land."

Moses answered GOD, "Look—the Israelites won't even listen to me. How do you expect Pharaoh to? And besides, I stutter."

But GOD again laid out the facts to Moses and Aaron regarding the Israelites and Pharaoh king of Egypt, and he again commanded them to lead the Israelites out of the land of Egypt.

THE FAMILY TREE OF MOSES AND AARON

These are the heads of the tribes:

The sons of Reuben, Israel's firstborn: Hanoch, Pallu, Hezron, and Carmi—these are the families of Reuben.

The sons of Simeon: Jemuel, Jamin, Ohad, Jakin, Zohar, and Saul, the son of a Canaanite woman—these are the families of Simeon.

These are the names of the sons of Levi in the order of their birth: Gershon, Kohath, and Merari. Levi lived 137 years.

The sons of Gershon by family: Libni and Shimei.

The sons of Kohath: Amram, Izhar, Hebron, and Uzziel. Kohath lived to be 133.

The sons of Merari: Mahli and Mushi.

These are the sons of Levi in the order of their birth.

Amram married his aunt Jochebed and she had Aaron and Moses. Amram lived to be 137.

The sons of Izhar: Korah, Nepheg, and Zicri.

The sons of Uzziel: Mishael, Elzaphan, and Sithri.

Aaron married Elisheba, the daughter of Amminadab and sister of Nahshon, and she had Nadab and Abihu, Eleazar and Ithamar.

The sons of Korah: Assir, Elkanah, and Abiasaph. These are the families of the Korahites.

Aaron's son Eleazar married one of the daughters of Putiel and she had Phinehas.

These are the heads of the Levite families, family by family.

This is the Aaron and Moses whom GOD ordered: "Bring the Israelites out of the land of Egypt clan by clan." These are the men, Moses and Aaron, who told Pharaoh king of Egypt to release the Israelites from Egypt.

"I'll Make You As a God to Pharaoh"

And that's how things stood when GOD next spoke to Moses in Egypt.

God addressed Moses, saying, "I am GOD. Tell Pharaoh king of Egypt everything I say to you."

And Moses answered, "Look at me. I stutter. Why would Pharaoh listen to me?"

7 GOD told Moses, "Look at me. I'll make you as a god to Pharaoh and your brother Aaron will be your prophet. You are to speak everything I command you, and your brother Aaron will tell it to Pharaoh. Then he will release the Israelites from his land. At the same time I am going to put Pharaoh's back up and follow it up by filling Egypt with signs and wonders. Pharaoh is not going to listen to you, but I will have my way against Egypt and bring out my soldiers, my people the Israelites, from Egypt by mighty acts of judgment. The Egyptians will realize that I am GOD when I step in and take the Israelites out of their country."

Moses and Aaron did exactly what GOD commanded. Moses was eighty and Aaron eighty-three when they spoke to Pharaoh.

✝

Then GOD spoke to Moses and Aaron. He said, "When Pharaoh speaks to you and says, 'Prove yourselves. Perform a miracle,' then tell Aaron, 'Take your staff and throw it down in front of Pharaoh: It will turn into a snake.'"

Moses and Aaron went to Pharaoh and did what GOD commanded. Aaron threw his staff down in front of Pharaoh and his servants, and it turned into a snake.

Pharaoh called in his wise men and sorcerers. The magicians of Egypt did the same thing by their incantations: each man threw down his staff and they all turned into snakes. But then Aaron's staff swallowed their staffs.

Yet Pharaoh was as stubborn as ever — he wouldn't listen to them, just as GOD had said.

Strike One: Blood

GOD said to Moses: "Pharaoh is a stubborn man. He refuses to release the people. First thing in the morning, go and meet Pharaoh as he goes down to the river. At the shore of the Nile take the staff that turned into a snake and say to him, 'GOD, the God of the Hebrews, sent me to you with this message, "Release my people so that they can worship me in the wilderness." So far you haven't listened. This is how you'll know that I am GOD. I am going to take this staff that I'm holding and strike this Nile River water: The water will turn to blood; the fish in the Nile will die; the Nile will stink; and the Egyptians won't be able to drink the Nile water.'"

GOD said to Moses, "Tell Aaron, 'Take your staff and wave it over the waters of Egypt—over its rivers, its canals, its ponds, all its bodies of water—so that they turn to blood.' There'll be blood everywhere in Egypt—even in the pots and pans."

Moses and Aaron did exactly as GOD commanded them. Aaron raised his staff and hit the water in the Nile with Pharaoh and his servants watching. All the water in the Nile turned into blood. The fish in the Nile died; the Nile stank; and the Egyptians couldn't drink Nile water. The blood was everywhere in Egypt.

But the magicians of Egypt did the same thing with their incantations. Still Pharaoh remained stubborn. He wouldn't listen to them as GOD had said. He turned on his heel and went home, never giving it a second thought. But all the Egyptians had to dig inland from the river for water because they couldn't drink the Nile water.

STRIKE TWO: FROGS

8 Seven days went by after GOD had struck the Nile. GOD said to Moses, "Go to Pharaoh and tell him, 'GOD's Message: Release my people so they can worship me. If you refuse to release them, I'm warning you, I'll hit the whole country with frogs. The Nile will swarm with frogs—they'll come up into your houses, into your bedrooms and into your beds, into your servants' quarters, among the people, into your ovens and pots and pans. They'll be all over you, all over everyone—frogs everywhere, on and in everything!'"

GOD said to Moses, "Tell Aaron, 'Wave your staff over the rivers and canals and ponds. Bring up frogs on the land of Egypt.'"

Aaron stretched his staff over the waters of Egypt and a mob of frogs came up and covered the country.

But again the magicians did the same thing using their incantations—they also produced frogs in Egypt.

Pharaoh called in Moses and Aaron and said, "Pray to GOD to rid us of these frogs. I'll release the people so that they can make their sacrifices and worship GOD."

Moses said to Pharaoh, "Certainly. Set the time. When do you want the frogs out of here, away from your servants and people and out of your houses? You'll be rid of frogs except for those in the Nile."

"Make it tomorrow."

Moses said, "Tomorrow it is—so you'll realize that there is no God like our GOD. The frogs will be gone. You and your houses and your servants and your people, free of frogs. The only frogs left will be the ones in the Nile."

Moses and Aaron left Pharaoh, and Moses prayed to GOD about the frogs he had brought on Pharaoh. GOD responded to Moses' prayer: The frogs died off—houses, courtyards, fields, all free of frogs. They piled the frogs in heaps. The country reeked of dead frogs.

But when Pharaoh saw that he had some breathing room, he got stubborn again and wouldn't listen to Moses and Aaron. Just as GOD had said.

STRIKE THREE: GNATS

GOD said to Moses, "Tell Aaron, 'Take your staff and strike the dust. The dust will turn into gnats all over Egypt.'"

He did it. Aaron grabbed his staff and struck the dust of the Earth; it turned into gnats, gnats all over people and animals. All the dust of the Earth turned into gnats, gnats everywhere in Egypt.

The magicians tried to produce gnats with their incantations but this time they couldn't do it. There were gnats everywhere, all over people and animals.

The magicians said to Pharaoh, "This is God's doing." But Pharaoh was stubborn and wouldn't listen. Just as GOD had said.

STRIKE FOUR: FLIES

GOD said to Moses, "Get up early in the morning and confront Pharaoh as he goes down to the water. Tell him, 'GOD's Message: Release my people so they can worship me. If you don't release my people, I'll release swarms of flies on you, your servants, your people, and your homes. The houses of the Egyptians and even the ground under their feet will be thick with flies. But when it happens, I'll set Goshen where my people live aside as a sanctuary—no flies in Goshen. That will show you that I am GOD in this land. I'll make a sharp distinction between your people and mine. This sign will occur tomorrow.'"

And GOD did just that. Thick swarms of flies in Pharaoh's palace and the houses of his servants. All over Egypt, the country ruined by flies.

Pharaoh called in Moses and Aaron and said, "Go ahead. Sacrifice to your God—but do it here in this country."

Moses said, "That would not be wise. What we sacrifice to our GOD would give great offense to Egyptians. If we openly sacrifice what is so deeply offensive to Egyptians, they'll kill us. Let us go three days' journey into the wilderness and sacrifice to our GOD, just as he instructed us."

Pharaoh said, "All right. I'll release you to go and sacrifice to your GOD in the wilderness. Only don't go too far. Now pray for me."

Moses said, "As soon as I leave here, I will pray to GOD that tomorrow the flies will leave Pharaoh, his servants, and his people. But don't play games with us and change your mind about releasing us to sacrifice to GOD."

Moses left Pharaoh and prayed to GOD. GOD did what Moses asked. He got rid of the flies from Pharaoh and his servants and his people. There wasn't a fly left. But Pharaoh became stubborn once again and wouldn't release the people.

STRIKE FIVE: ANIMALS

9 GOD said to Moses, "Go to Pharaoh and tell him, 'GOD, the God of the Hebrews, says: Release my people so they can worship me. If you refuse to release them and continue to hold on to them, I'm giving you fair warning: GOD will come down hard on your livestock out in the fields—horses, donkeys, camels, cattle, sheep—striking them with a severe disease. GOD will draw a sharp line between the livestock of Israel and the livestock of Egypt. Not one animal that belongs to the Israelites will die.'"

Then GOD set the time: "Tomorrow GOD will do this thing."

And the next day GOD did it. All the livestock of Egypt died, but not one animal of the Israelites died. Pharaoh sent men to find out what had happened and there it was: none of the livestock of the Israelites had died—not one death. But Pharaoh stayed stubborn. He wouldn't release the people.

STRIKE SIX: BOILS

GOD said to Moses and Aaron, "Take fistfuls of soot from a furnace and have Moses throw it into the air right before Pharaoh's eyes; it will become a film of fine dust all over Egypt and cause sores, an eruption of boils on people and animals throughout Egypt." So they took soot from a furnace, stood in front of Pharaoh and threw it up into the air. It caused boils to erupt on people and animals. The magicians weren't able to compete with Moses this time because of the boils—they were covered with boils just like everyone else in Egypt.

GOD hardened Pharaoh in his stubbornness. He wouldn't listen, just as GOD had said to Moses.

STRIKE SEVEN: HAIL

GOD said to Moses, "Get up early in the morning and confront Pharaoh. Tell him, 'GOD, the God of the Hebrews, says: Release my people so they can worship me. This time I am going to strike you and your servants and your people with the full force of my power so you'll get it into your head that there's no one like me anywhere in all the Earth. You know that by now I could have struck you and your people with deadly disease and there would be nothing left of you, not a trace. But for one reason only I've kept you on your feet: To make you recognize my power so that my reputation spreads in all the Earth. You are still building yourself up at my people's expense. You are not letting them go. So here's what's going to happen: At this time tomorrow I'm sending a terrific hailstorm—there's never been a storm like this in Egypt from the day of its founding until now. So get your livestock under roof—everything exposed in the open fields, people and animals, will die when the hail comes down.'"

All of Pharaoh's servants who had respect for GOD's word got their workers and animals under cover as fast as they could, but those who didn't take GOD's word seriously left their workers and animals out in the field.

GOD said to Moses: "Stretch your hands to the skies. Signal the hail to fall all over Egypt on people and animals and crops exposed in the fields of Egypt."

Moses lifted his staff to the skies and GOD sent peals of thunder and hail shot through with lightning strikes. GOD rained hail down on the land of Egypt. The hail came, hail and lightning—a fierce hailstorm. There had been nothing like it in Egypt in its entire history. The hail hit hard all over Egypt. Everything exposed out in the fields, people and animals and crops, was smashed. Even the trees in the fields were shattered. Except for Goshen where the Israelites lived; there was no hail in Goshen.

Pharaoh summoned Moses and Aaron. He said, "I've sinned for sure this time—GOD is in the right and I and my people are in the wrong. Pray to GOD. We've had enough of GOD's thunder and hail. I'll let you go. The sooner you're out of here the better."

Moses said, "As soon as I'm out of the city, I'll stretch out my arms to GOD. The thunder will stop and the hail end so you'll know that the land is GOD's land. Still, I know that you and your servants have no respect for GOD."

(The flax and the barley were ruined, for they were just ripening, but the wheat and spelt weren't hurt—they ripen later.)

Moses left Pharaoh and the city and stretched out his arms to GOD. The thunder and hail stopped; the storm cleared.

But when Pharaoh saw that the rain and hail and thunder had stopped, he kept right on sinning, stubborn as ever, both he and his servants. Pharaoh's heart turned rock-hard. He refused to release the Israelites, as GOD had ordered through Moses.

STRIKE EIGHT: LOCUSTS

10 GOD said to Moses: "Go to Pharaoh. I've made him stubborn, him and his servants, so that I can force him to look at these signs and so you'll be able to tell your children and grandchildren how I toyed with the Egyptians, like a cat with a mouse; you'll tell them the stories of the signs that I brought down on them, so that you'll all know that I am GOD."

Moses and Aaron went to Pharaoh and said to him, "GOD, the God of the Hebrews, says, 'How long are you going to refuse to knuckle under? Release my people so that they can worship me. If you refuse to release my people, watch out; tomorrow I'm bringing locusts into your country. They'll cover every square inch of ground; no one will be able to see the ground. They'll devour everything left over from the hailstorm, even the saplings out in the fields—they'll clear-cut the trees. And they'll invade your houses, filling the houses of your servants, filling every house in Egypt. Nobody will have ever seen anything like this, from the time your ancestors first set foot on this soil until today.'"

Then he turned on his heel and left Pharaoh.

Pharaoh's servants said to him, "How long are you going to let this man harass us? Let these people go and worship their GOD. Can't you see that Egypt is on its last legs?"

So Moses and Aaron were brought back to Pharaoh. He said to them, "Go ahead then. Go worship your GOD. But just who exactly is going with you?"

Moses said, "We're taking young and old, sons and daughters, flocks and herds—this is our worship-celebration of GOD."

He said, "I'd sooner send you off with GOD's blessings than let you go with your children. Look, you're up to no good—it's written all over your faces. Nothing doing. Just the men are going—go ahead and worship GOD. That's what you want so badly." And they were thrown out of Pharaoh's presence.

GOD said to Moses: "Stretch your hand over Egypt and signal the locusts to cover the land of Egypt, devouring every blade of grass in the country, everything that the hail didn't get."

Moses stretched out his staff over the land of Egypt. GOD let loose an east wind. It blew that day and night. By morning the east wind had brought in the locusts.

The locusts covered the country of Egypt, settling over every square inch of Egypt; the place was thick with locusts. There never was an invasion of locusts like it in the past, and never will be again. The ground was completely covered, black with locusts. They ate everything, every blade of grass, every piece of fruit, anything that the hail didn't get. Nothing left but bare trees and bare fields—not a sign of green in the whole land of Egypt.

Pharaoh had Moses and Aaron back in no time. He said, "I've sinned against your GOD and against you. Overlook my sin one more time. Pray to your GOD to get me out of this—get death out of here!"

Moses left Pharaoh and prayed to GOD. GOD reversed the wind— a powerful west wind took the locusts and dumped them into the Red Sea. There wasn't a single locust left in the whole country of Egypt.

But GOD made Pharaoh stubborn as ever. He still didn't release the Israelites.

STRIKE NINE: DARKNESS

GOD said to Moses: "Stretch your hand to the skies. Let darkness descend on the land of Egypt—a darkness so dark you can touch it."

Moses stretched out his hand to the skies. Thick darkness descended on the land of Egypt for three days. Nobody could see anybody. For three days no one could so much as move. Except for the Israelites: they had light where they were living.

Pharaoh called in Moses: "Go and worship GOD. Leave your flocks and herds behind. But go ahead and take your children."

But Moses said, "You have to let us take our sacrificial animals and offerings with us so we can sacrifice them in worship to our GOD. Our livestock has to go with us with not a hoof left behind; they are part of the worship of our GOD. And we don't know just what will be needed until we get there."

But GOD kept Pharaoh stubborn as ever. He wouldn't agree to release them.

Pharaoh said to Moses: "Get out of my sight! And watch your step. I don't want to ever see you again. If I lay eyes on you again, you're dead."

Moses said, "Have it your way. You won't see my face again."

STRIKE TEN: DEATH

11 God said to Moses: "I'm going to hit Pharaoh and Egypt one final time, and then he'll let you go. When he releases you, that will be the end of Egypt for you; he won't be able to get rid of you fast enough.

"So here's what you do. Tell the people to ask, each man from his neighbor and each woman from her neighbor, for things made of silver and gold." GOD saw to it that the Egyptians liked the people. Also, Moses was greatly admired by the Egyptians, a respected public figure among both Pharaoh's servants and the people at large.

Then Moses confronted Pharaoh: "GOD's Message: 'At midnight I will go through Egypt and every firstborn child in Egypt will die, from the firstborn of Pharaoh, who sits on his throne, to the firstborn of the slave girl working at her hand mill. Also the firstborn of animals. Widespread wailing will erupt all over the country, lament such as has never been and never will be again. But against the Israelites—man, woman, or animal—there won't be so much as a dog's bark, so that you'll know that GOD makes a clear distinction between Egypt and Israel.'

"Then all these servants of yours will go to their knees, begging me to leave, 'Leave! You and all the people who follow you!' And I will most certainly leave."

Moses, seething with anger, left Pharaoh.

GOD said to Moses, "Pharaoh's not going to listen to a thing you say so that the signs of my presence and work are going to multiply in the land of Egypt."

Moses and Aaron had performed all these signs in Pharaoh's presence, but GOD turned Pharaoh more stubborn than ever—yet again he refused to release the Israelites from his land.

✛

12 GOD said to Moses and Aaron while still in Egypt, "This month is to be the first month of the year for you. Address the whole community of Israel; tell them that on the tenth of this month each man is to take a lamb for his family, one lamb to a house. If the family is too small for a lamb, then share it with a close neighbor, depending on the number of persons involved. Be mindful of how much each person will eat. Your lamb must be a healthy male, one year old; you can select it from either the sheep or the goats. Keep it penned until the fourteenth day of this month and then slaughter it—the entire community of Israel will do this—at dusk. Then take some of the blood and smear it on the two doorposts and the lintel of the houses in which you will eat it. You are to eat the meat, roasted in the fire, that night, along with bread, made without yeast, and bitter herbs. Don't eat any of it raw or boiled in water; make sure it's roasted—the whole animal, head, legs, and innards. Don't leave any of it until morning; if there are leftovers, burn them in the fire.

"And here is how you are to eat it: Be fully dressed with your sandals on and your stick in your hand. Eat in a hurry; it's the Passover to GOD.

"I will go through the land of Egypt on this night and strike down every firstborn in the land of Egypt, whether human or animal, and bring judgment on all the gods of Egypt. I am GOD. The blood will serve as a sign on the houses where you live. When I see the blood I will pass over you—no disaster will touch you when I strike the land of Egypt.

"This will be a memorial day for you; you will celebrate it as a festival to GOD down through the generations, a fixed festival celebration to be observed always. You will eat unraised bread (matzoth) for seven days: On the first day get rid of all yeast from your houses—anyone who eats anything with yeast from the first day to the seventh day will be cut off from Israel. The first and the seventh days are set aside as holy; do no work on those days. Only what you have to do for meals; each person can do that.

"Keep the Festival of Unraised Bread! This marks the exact day I brought you out in force from the land of Egypt. Honor the day down through your generations, a fixed festival to be observed always. In the first month, beginning on the fourteenth day at evening until the twenty-first day at evening, you are to eat unraised bread. For those seven days not a trace of yeast is to be found in your houses. Anyone, whether a visitor or a native of the land, who eats anything raised shall be cut off from the community of Israel. Don't eat anything raised. Only matzoth."

Moses assembled all the elders of Israel. He said, "Select a lamb for your families and slaughter the Passover lamb. Take a bunch of hyssop and dip it in the bowl of blood and smear it on the lintel and on the two doorposts. No one is to leave the house until morning. GOD will pass through to strike Egypt down. When he sees the blood on the lintel and the two door posts, GOD will pass over the doorway; he won't let the destroyer enter your house to strike you down with ruin.

"Keep this word. It's the law for you and your children, forever. When you enter the land which GOD will give you as he promised, keep doing this. And when your children say to you, 'Why are we doing this?' tell them: 'It's the Passover-sacrifice to GOD who passed over the homes of the Israelites in Egypt when he hit Egypt with death but rescued us.'"

The people bowed and worshiped.

The Israelites then went and did what GOD had commanded Moses and Aaron. They did it all.

✢

At midnight GOD struck every firstborn in the land of Egypt, from the firstborn of Pharaoh, who sits on his throne, right down to the firstborn of the prisoner locked up in jail. Also the firstborn of the animals.

Pharaoh got up that night, he and all his servants and everyone else in Egypt—what wild wailing and lament in Egypt! There wasn't a house in which someone wasn't dead.

Pharaoh called in Moses and Aaron that very night and said, "Get out of here and be done with you—you and your Israelites! Go worship GOD on your own terms. And yes, take your sheep and cattle as you've insisted, but go. And bless me."

The Egyptians couldn't wait to get rid of them; they pushed them to hurry up, saying, "We're all as good as dead."

The people grabbed their bread dough before it had risen, bundled their bread bowls in their cloaks and threw them over their shoulders. The Israelites had already done what Moses had told them; they had asked the Egyptians for silver and gold things and clothing. GOD saw to it that the Egyptians liked the people and so readily gave them what they asked for. Oh yes! They picked those Egyptians clean.

The Israelites moved on from Rameses to Succoth, about six hundred thousand on foot, besides their dependents. There was also a crowd of riffraff tagging along, not to mention the large flocks and herds of livestock. They baked unraised cakes with the bread dough they had brought out of Egypt; it hadn't raised—they'd been rushed out of Egypt and hadn't time to fix food for the journey.

THE PASSOVER

The Israelites had lived in Egypt 430 years. At the end of the 430 years, to the very day, GOD's entire army left Egypt. GOD kept watch all night, watching over the Israelites as he brought them out of Egypt. Because GOD kept watch, all Israel for all generations will honor GOD by keeping watch this night—a watchnight.

✠

GOD said to Moses and Aaron, "These are the rules for the Passover:
No foreigners are to eat it.
Any slave, if he's paid for and circumcised, can eat it.
No casual visitor or hired hand can eat it.
Eat it in one house—don't take the meat outside the house.
Don't break any of the bones.
The whole community of Israel is to be included in the meal.

"If an immigrant is staying with you and wants to keep the Passover to GOD, every male in his family must be circumcised, then he can participate in the Meal—he will then be treated as a native son. But no uncircumcised person can eat it.

"The same law applies both to the native and the immigrant who is staying with you."

All the Israelites did exactly as GOD commanded Moses and Aaron. That very day GOD brought the Israelites out of the land of Egypt, tribe by tribe.

✠

13 GOD spoke to Moses, saying, "Consecrate every firstborn to me— the first one to come from the womb among the Israelites,

whether person or animal, is mine."

Moses said to the people, "Always remember this day. This is the day when you came out of Egypt from a house of slavery. GOD brought you out of here with a powerful hand. Don't eat any raised bread.

"You are leaving in the spring month of Abib. When GOD brings you into the land of the Canaanite, the Hittite, the Amorite, the Hivite, and the Jebusite, which he promised to your fathers to give you, a land lavish with milk and honey, you are to observe this service during this month:

"You are to eat unraised bread for seven days; on the seventh day there is a festival celebration to GOD.

"Only unraised bread is to be eaten for seven days. There is not to be a trace of anything fermented—no yeast anywhere.

"Tell your child on that day: 'This is because of what GOD did for me when I came out of Egypt.'

"The day of observance will be like a sign on your hand, a memorial between your eyes, and the teaching of GOD in your mouth. It was with a powerful hand that GOD brought you out of Egypt. Follow these instructions at the set time, year after year after year.

"When GOD brings you into the land of the Canaanites, as he promised you and your fathers, and turns it over to you, you are to set aside the first birth out of every womb to GOD. Every first birth from your livestock belongs to GOD. You can redeem every first birth of a donkey if you want to by substituting a lamb; if you decide not to redeem it, you must break its neck.

"Redeem every firstborn child among your sons. When the time comes and your son asks you, 'What does this mean?' you tell him, 'GOD brought us out of Egypt, out of a house of slavery, with a powerful hand. When Pharaoh stubbornly refused to let us go, GOD killed every firstborn in Egypt, the firstborn of both humans and animals. That's why I make a sacrifice for every first male birth from the womb to GOD and redeem every firstborn son.' The observance functions like a sign on your hands or a symbol on the middle of your forehead: GOD brought us out of Egypt with a powerful hand."

It so happened that after Pharaoh released the people, God didn't lead them by the road through the land of the Philistines, which was the shortest route, for God thought, "If the people encounter war, they'll change their minds and go back to Egypt."

So God led the people on the wilderness road, looping around to the Red Sea. The Israelites left Egypt in military formation.

Moses took the bones of Joseph with him, for Joseph had made the Israelites solemnly swear to do it, saying, "God will surely hold you accountable, so make sure you bring my bones from here with you."

They moved on from Succoth and then camped at Etham at the edge of the wilderness. GOD went ahead of them in a Pillar of Cloud during the day to guide them on the way, and at night in a Pillar of Fire to give them light; thus they could travel both day and night. The Pillar of Cloud by day and the Pillar of Fire by night never left the people.

THE STORY AND SONG OF SALVATION

14 GOD spoke to Moses: "Tell the Israelites to turn around and make camp at Pi Hahiroth, between Migdol and the sea. Camp on the shore of the sea opposite Baal Zephon.

"Pharaoh will think, 'The Israelites are lost; they're confused. The wilderness has closed in on them.' Then I'll make Pharaoh's heart stubborn again and he'll chase after them. And I'll use Pharaoh and his army to put my Glory on display. Then the Egyptians will realize that I am GOD."

And that's what happened.

When the king of Egypt was told that the people were gone, he and his servants changed their minds. They said, "What have we done, letting Israel, our slave labor, go free?" So he had his chariots harnessed up and got his army together. He took six hundred of his best chariots, with the rest of the Egyptian chariots and their drivers coming along.

GOD made Pharaoh king of Egypt stubborn, determined to chase the Israelites as they walked out on him without even looking back. The Egyptians gave chase and caught up with them where they had made camp by the sea—all Pharaoh's horse-drawn chariots and their riders, all his foot soldiers there at Pi Hahiroth opposite Baal Zephon.

As Pharaoh approached, the Israelites looked up and saw them—Egyptians! Coming at them!

They were totally afraid. They cried out in terror to GOD. They told Moses, "Weren't the cemeteries large enough in Egypt so that you had to take us out here in the wilderness to die? What have you done to us, taking us out of Egypt? Back in Egypt didn't we tell you this would happen? Didn't we tell you, 'Leave us alone here in Egypt—we're better off as slaves in Egypt than as corpses in the wilderness.'"

Moses spoke to the people: "Don't be afraid. Stand firm and watch

GOD do his work of salvation for you today. Take a good look at the Egyptians today for you're never going to see them again.

> "GOD will fight the battle for you.
>   And you? You keep your mouths shut!"

✠

GOD said to Moses: "Why cry out to me? Speak to the Israelites. Order them to get moving. Hold your staff high and stretch your hand out over the sea: Split the sea! The Israelites will walk through the sea on dry ground.

"Meanwhile I'll make sure the Egyptians keep up their stubborn chase—I'll use Pharaoh and his entire army, his chariots and horsemen, to put my Glory on display so that the Egyptians will realize that I am GOD."

The angel of God that had been leading the camp of Israel now shifted and got behind them. And the Pillar of Cloud that had been in front also shifted to the rear. The Cloud was now between the camp of Egypt and the camp of Israel. The Cloud enshrouded one camp in darkness and flooded the other with light. The two camps didn't come near each other all night.

Then Moses stretched out his hand over the sea and GOD, with a terrific east wind all night long, made the sea go back. He made the sea dry ground. The seawaters split.

The Israelites walked through the sea on dry ground with the waters a wall to the right and to the left. The Egyptians came after them in full pursuit, every horse and chariot and driver of Pharaoh racing into the middle of the sea. It was now the morning watch. GOD looked down from the Pillar of Fire and Cloud on the Egyptian army and threw them into a panic. He clogged the wheels of their chariots; they were stuck in the mud.

The Egyptians said, "Run from Israel! GOD is fighting on their side and against Egypt!"

GOD said to Moses, "Stretch out your hand over the sea and the waters will come back over the Egyptians, over their chariots, over their horsemen."

Moses stretched his hand out over the sea: As the day broke and the Egyptians were running, the sea returned to its place as before. GOD dumped the Egyptians in the middle of the sea. The waters returned, drowning the chariots and riders of Pharaoh's army that had chased after Israel into the sea. Not one of them survived.

But the Israelites walked right through the middle of the sea on dry ground, the waters forming a wall to the right and to the left. GOD delivered Israel that day from the oppression of the Egyptians. And Israel looked at the Egyptian dead, washed up on the shore of the sea, and realized the tremendous power that GOD brought against the Egyptians. The people were in reverent awe before GOD and trusted in GOD and his servant Moses.

·✝·

15 Then Moses and the Israelites sang this song to GOD, giving voice together,

> I'm singing my heart out to GOD—what a victory!
>> He pitched horse and rider into the sea.
> GOD is my strength, GOD is my song,
>> and, yes! GOD is my salvation.
> *This* is the kind of God I have
>> and I'm telling the world!
> *This* is the God of my father—
>> I'm spreading the news far and wide!
> GOD is a fighter,
>> pure GOD, through and through.
> Pharaoh's chariots and army
>> he dumped in the sea,
> The elite of his officers
>> he drowned in the Red Sea.
> Wild ocean waters poured over them;
>> they sank like a rock in the deep blue sea.
> Your strong right hand, GOD, shimmers with power;
>> your strong right hand shatters the enemy.
> In your mighty majesty
>> you smash your upstart enemies,
> You let loose your hot anger
>> and burn them to a crisp.
> At a blast from your nostrils
>> the waters piled up;
> Tumbling streams dammed up,
>> wild oceans curdled into a swamp.

121

The enemy spoke,
    "I'll pursue, I'll hunt them down,
I'll divide up the plunder,
    I'll glut myself on them;
I'll pull out my sword,
    my fist will send them reeling."

You blew with all your might
    and the sea covered them.
They sank like a lead weight
    in the majestic waters.
Who compares with you
    among gods, O GOD?
Who compares with you in power,
    in holy majesty,
In awesome praises,
    wonder-working God?

You stretched out your right hand
    and the Earth swallowed them up.
But the people you redeemed,
    you led in merciful love;
You guided them under your protection
    to your holy pasture.

When people heard, they were scared;
    Philistines writhed and trembled;
Yes, even the head men in Edom were shaken,
    and the big bosses in Moab.
Everybody in Canaan
    panicked and fell faint.
Dread and terror
    sent them reeling.
Before your brandished right arm
    they were struck dumb like a stone,
Until your people crossed over and entered, O GOD,
    until the people you made crossed over and entered.
You brought them and planted them
    on the mountain of your heritage,

The place where you live,
      the place you made,
Your sanctuary, Master,
      that you established with your own hands.
Let GOD rule
      forever, for eternity!

Yes, Pharaoh's horses and chariots and riders went into the sea and GOD turned the waters back on them; but the Israelites walked on dry land right through the middle of the sea.

✠

Miriam the prophetess, Aaron's sister, took a tambourine, and all the women followed her with tambourines, dancing. Miriam led them in singing,

Sing to GOD—
      what a victory!
He pitched horse and rider
      into the sea!

TRAVELING THROUGH THE WILDERNESS

Moses led Israel from the Red Sea on to the Wilderness of Shur. They traveled for three days through the wilderness without finding any water. They got to Marah, but they couldn't drink the water at Marah; it was bitter. That's why they called the place Marah (Bitter). And the people complained to Moses, "So what are we supposed to drink?"

So Moses cried out in prayer to GOD. GOD pointed him to a stick of wood. Moses threw it into the water and the water turned sweet.

That's the place where GOD set up rules and procedures; that's where he started testing them.

GOD said, "If you listen, listen obediently to how GOD tells you to live in his presence, obeying his commandments and keeping all his laws, then I won't strike you with all the diseases that I inflicted on the Egyptians; I am GOD your healer."

They came to Elim where there were twelve springs of water and seventy palm trees. They set up camp there by the water.

16On the fifteenth day of the second month after they had left Egypt, the whole company of Israel moved on from Elim to the Wilderness of Sin which is between Elim and Sinai. The whole company of Israel complained against Moses and Aaron there in the wilderness. The Israelites said, "Why didn't GOD let us die in comfort in Egypt where we had lamb stew and all the bread we could eat? You've brought us out into this wilderness to starve us to death, the whole company of Israel!"

GOD said to Moses, "I'm going to rain bread down from the skies for you. The people will go out and gather each day's ration. I'm going to test them to see if they'll live according to my Teaching or not. On the sixth day, when they prepare what they have gathered, it will turn out to be twice as much as their daily ration."

Moses and Aaron told the People of Israel, "This evening you will know that it is GOD who brought you out of Egypt; and in the morning you will see the Glory of GOD. Yes, he's listened to your complaints against him. You haven't been complaining against us, you know, but against GOD."

Moses said, "Since it will be GOD who gives you meat for your meal in the evening and your fill of bread in the morning, it's GOD who will have listened to your complaints against him. Who are we in all this? You haven't been complaining to us—you've been complaining to GOD!"

Moses instructed Aaron: "Tell the whole company of Israel: 'Come near to GOD. He's heard your complaints.'"

When Aaron gave out the instructions to the whole company of Israel, they turned to face the wilderness. And there it was: the Glory of GOD visible in the Cloud.

GOD spoke to Moses, "I've listened to the complaints of the Israelites. Now tell them: 'At dusk you will eat meat and at dawn you'll eat your fill of bread; and you'll realize that I am GOD, *your* God.'"

That evening quail flew in and covered the camp and in the morning there was a layer of dew all over the camp. When the layer of dew had lifted, there on the wilderness ground was a fine flaky something, fine as frost on the ground. The Israelites took one look and said to one another, *man-hu* (What is it?). They had no idea what it was.

So Moses told them, "It's the bread GOD has given you to eat. And these are GOD's instructions: 'Gather enough for each person, about two quarts per person; gather enough for everyone in your tent.'"

The People of Israel went to work and started gathering, some more, some less, but when they measured out what they had gathered, those who gathered more had no extra and those who gathered less weren't short—each person had gathered as much as was needed.

Moses said to them, "Don't leave any of it until morning."

But they didn't listen to Moses. A few of the men kept back some of it until morning. It got wormy and smelled bad. And Moses lost his temper with them.

They gathered it every morning, each person according to need. Then the sun heated up and it melted. On the sixth day they gathered twice as much bread, about four quarts per person.

Then the leaders of the company came to Moses and reported.

Moses said, "This is what GOD was talking about: Tomorrow is a day of rest, a holy Sabbath to GOD. Whatever you plan to bake, bake today; and whatever you plan to boil, boil today. Then set aside the leftovers until morning." They set aside what was left until morning, as Moses had commanded. It didn't smell bad and there were no worms in it.

Moses said, "Now eat it; this is the day, a Sabbath for GOD. You won't find any of it on the ground today. Gather it every day for six days, but the seventh day is Sabbath; there won't be any of it on the ground."

On the seventh day, some of the people went out to gather anyway but they didn't find anything.

GOD said to Moses, "How long are you going to disobey my commands and not follow my instructions? Don't you see that GOD has given you the Sabbath? So on the sixth day he gives you bread for *two* days. So, each of you, stay home. Don't leave home on the seventh day."

So the people quit working on the seventh day.

The Israelites named it manna (What-is-it?). It looked like coriander seed, whitish. And it tasted like a cracker with honey.

Moses said, "This is GOD's command: 'Keep a two-quart jar of it, an omer, for future generations so they can see the bread that I fed you in the wilderness after I brought you out of Egypt.'"

Moses told Aaron, "Take a jar and fill it with two quarts of manna. Place it before GOD, keeping it safe for future generations."

Aaron did what GOD commanded Moses. He set it aside before The Testimony to preserve it.

The Israelites ate the manna for forty years until they arrived at the land where they would settle down. They ate manna until they reached the border into Canaan.

According to ancient measurements, an omer is one-tenth of an ephah.

✛

17 Directed by GOD, the whole company of Israel moved on by stages from the Wilderness of Sin. They set camp at Rephidim. And there wasn't a drop of water for the people to drink. The people took Moses to task: "Give us water to drink." But Moses said, "Why pester me? Why are you testing GOD?"

But the people were thirsty for water there. They complained to Moses, "Why did you take us from Egypt and drag us out here with our children and animals to die of thirst?"

Moses cried out in prayer to GOD, "What can I do with these people? Any minute now they'll kill me!"

GOD said to Moses, "Go on out ahead of the people, taking with you some of the elders of Israel. Take the staff you used to strike the Nile. And go. I'm going to be present before you there on the rock at Horeb. You are to strike the rock. Water will gush out of it and the people will drink."

Moses did what he said, with the elders of Israel right there watching. He named the place Massah (Testing-Place) and Meribah (Quarreling) because of the quarreling of the Israelites and because of their testing of GOD when they said, "Is GOD here with us, or not?"

✛

Amalek came and fought Israel at Rephidim. Moses ordered Joshua: "Select some men for us and go out and fight Amalek. Tomorrow I will take my stand on top of the hill holding God's staff."

Joshua did what Moses ordered in order to fight Amalek. And Moses, Aaron, and Hur went to the top of the hill. It turned out that whenever Moses raised his hands, Israel was winning, but whenever he lowered his hands, Amalek was winning. But Moses' hands got tired. So they got a stone and set it under him. He sat on it and Aaron and Hur held up his hands, one on each side. So his hands remained steady until the sun went down. Joshua defeated Amalek and its army in battle.

GOD said to Moses, "Write this up as a reminder to Joshua, to keep it before him, because I will most certainly wipe the very memory of Amalek off the face of the Earth."

Moses built an altar and named it "GOD My Banner." He said,

> Salute GOD's rule!
> GOD at war with Amalek
> Always and forever!

☩

18 Jethro, priest of Midian and father-in-law to Moses, heard the report of all that God had done for Moses and Israel his people, the news that GOD had delivered Israel from Egypt. Jethro, Moses' father-in-law, had taken in Zipporah, Moses' wife who had been sent back home, and her two sons. The name of the one was Gershom (Sojourner) for he had said, "I'm a sojourner in a foreign land"; the name of the other was Eliezer (God's-Help) because "The God of my father is my help and saved me from death by Pharaoh."

Jethro, Moses' father-in-law, brought Moses his sons and his wife there in the wilderness where he was camped at the mountain of God. He had sent a message ahead to Moses: "I, your father-in-law, am coming to you with your wife and two sons."

Moses went out to welcome his father-in-law. He bowed to him and kissed him. Each asked the other how things had been with him. Then they went into the tent. Moses told his father-in-law the story of all that GOD had done to Pharaoh and Egypt in helping Israel, all the trouble they had experienced on the journey, and how GOD had delivered them.

Jethro was delighted in all the good that GOD had done for Israel in delivering them from Egyptian oppression. Jethro said, "Blessed be GOD who has delivered you from the power of Egypt and Pharaoh, who has delivered his people from the oppression of Egypt. Now I know that GOD is greater than all gods because he's done this to all those who treated Israel arrogantly."

Jethro, Moses' father-in-law, brought a Whole-Burnt-Offering and sacrifices to God. And Aaron, along with all the elders of Israel, came and ate the meal with Moses' father-in-law in the presence of God.

The next day Moses took his place to judge the people. People were standing before him all day long, from morning to night. When Moses' father-in-law saw all that he was doing for the people, he said, "What's going on here? Why are you doing all this, and all by yourself, letting everybody line up before you from morning to night?"

Moses said to his father-in-law, "Because the people come to me with questions about God. When something comes up, they come to me. I judge between a man and his neighbor and teach them God's laws and instructions."

Moses' father-in-law said, "This is no way to go about it. You'll burn out, and the people right along with you. This is way too much for you—you can't do this alone. Now listen to me. Let me tell you how to do this so that God will be in this with you. Be there for the people before God, but let the matters of concern be presented to God. Your job is to teach them the rules and instructions, to show them how to live, what to do. And then you need to keep a sharp eye out for competent men—men who fear God, men of integrity, men who are incorruptible—and appoint them as leaders over groups organized by the thousand, by the hundred, by fifty, and by ten. They'll be responsible for the everyday work of judging among the people. They'll bring the hard cases to you, but in the routine cases they'll be the judges. They will share your load and that will make it easier for you. If you handle the work this way, you'll have the strength to carry out whatever God commands you, and the people in their settings will flourish also."

Moses listened to the counsel of his father-in-law and did everything he said. Moses picked competent men from all Israel and set them as leaders over the people who were organized by the thousand, by the hundred, by fifty, and by ten. They took over the everyday work of judging among the people. They brought the hard cases to Moses, but in the routine cases they were the judges. Then Moses said good-bye to his father-in-law who went home to his own country.

MOUNT SINAI

19 Three months after leaving Egypt the Israelites entered the Wilderness of Sinai. They followed the route from Rephidim, arrived at the Wilderness of Sinai, and set up camp. Israel camped there facing the mountain.

As Moses went up to meet God, GOD called down to him from the mountain: "Speak to the House of Jacob, tell the People of Israel: 'You have seen what I did to Egypt and how I carried you on eagles' wings and brought you to me. If you will listen obediently to what I say and keep my covenant, out of all peoples you'll be my special treasure. The whole Earth is mine to choose from, but you're special: a kingdom of priests, a holy nation.'

"This is what I want you tell the People of Israel."

Moses came back and called the elders of Israel together and set before them all these words which GOD had commanded him.

The people were unanimous in their response: "Everything GOD says, we will do." Moses took the people's answer back to GOD.

☩

GOD said to Moses, "Get ready. I'm about to come to you in a thick cloud so that the people can listen in and trust you completely when I speak with you." Again Moses reported the people's answer to GOD.

GOD said to Moses, "Go to the people. For the next two days get these people ready to meet the Holy GOD. Have them scrub their clothes so that on the third day they'll be fully prepared, because on the third day GOD will come down on Mount Sinai and make his presence known to all the people. Post boundaries for the people all around, telling them, 'Warning! Don't climb the mountain. Don't even touch its edge. Whoever touches the mountain dies—a certain death. And no one is to touch that person, he's to be stoned. That's right—stoned. Or shot with arrows, shot to death. Animal or man, whichever—put to death.'

"A long blast from the horn will signal that it's safe to climb the mountain."

Moses went down the mountain to the people and prepared them for the holy meeting. They gave their clothes a good scrubbing. Then he addressed the people: "Be ready in three days. Don't sleep with a woman."

On the third day at daybreak, there were loud claps of thunder, flashes of lightning, a thick cloud covering the mountain, and an ear-piercing trumpet blast. Everyone in the camp shuddered in fear.

Moses led the people out of the camp to meet God. They stood at attention at the base of the mountain.

Mount Sinai was all smoke because GOD had come down on it as fire. Smoke poured from it like smoke from a furnace. The whole mountain shuddered in huge spasms. The trumpet blasts grew louder and louder. Moses spoke and God answered in thunder. GOD descended to the peak of Mount Sinai. GOD called Moses up to the peak and Moses climbed up.

GOD said to Moses, "Go down. Warn the people not to break through the barricades to get a look at GOD lest many of them die. And the priests also, warn them to prepare themselves for the holy meeting, lest GOD break out against them."

Moses said to GOD, "But the people can't climb Mount Sinai. You've already warned us well telling us: 'Post boundaries around the mountain. Respect the holy mountain.'"

GOD told him, "Go down and then bring Aaron back up with you. But make sure that the priests and the people don't break through and come up to GOD, lest he break out against them."

So Moses went down to the people. He said to them:

20 GOD spoke all these words:

I am GOD, your God,
who brought you out of the land of Egypt,
out of a life of slavery.

No other gods, only me.

No carved gods of any size, shape, or form of anything whatever, whether of things that fly or walk or swim. Don't bow down to them and don't serve them because *I* am GOD, your God, and I'm a most jealous God, punishing the children for any sins their parents pass on to them to the third, and yes, even to the fourth generation of those who hate me. But I'm unswervingly loyal to the thousands who love me and keep my commandments.

No using the name of GOD, your God, in curses or silly banter; GOD won't put up with the irreverant use of his name.

Observe the Sabbath day, to keep it holy. Work six days and do everything you need to do. But the seventh day is a Sabbath to GOD, your God. Don't do any work—not you, nor your son, nor your daughter, nor your servant, nor your maid, nor your animals, not even the foreign guest visiting in your town. For in six days GOD made Heaven, Earth, and sea, and everything in them; he rested on the seventh day. Therefore GOD blessed the Sabbath day; he set it apart as a holy day.

Honor your father and mother so that you'll live a long time in the land that GOD, your God, is giving you.

No murder.

No adultery.

No stealing.

No lies about your neighbor.

No lusting after your neighbor's house—or wife or servant or maid or ox or donkey. Don't set your heart on anything that is your neighbor's.

⊹

All the people, experiencing the thunder and lightning, the trumpet blast and the smoking mountain, were afraid—they pulled back and stood at a distance. They said to Moses, "You speak to us and we'll listen, but don't have God speak to us or we'll die."

Moses spoke to the people: "Don't be afraid. God has come to test you and instill a deep and reverent awe within you so that you won't sin."

The people kept their distance while Moses approached the thick cloud where God was.

GOD said to Moses, "Give this Message to the People of Israel: 'You've experienced firsthand how I spoke with you from Heaven. Don't make gods of silver and gods of gold and then set them alongside me. Make me an earthen Altar. Sacrifice your Whole-Burnt-Offerings, your Peace-Offerings, your sheep, and your cattle on it. Every place where I cause my name to be honored in your worship, I'll be there myself and bless you. If you use stones to make my Altar, don't use dressed stones. If you use a chisel on the stones you'll profane the Altar. Don't use steps to climb to my Altar because that will expose your nakedness.'

⊹

21 "These are the laws that you are to place before them:

"When you buy a Hebrew slave, he will serve six years. The seventh year he goes free, for nothing. If he came in single he leaves single. If he came in married he leaves with his wife. If the master gives him a wife and she gave him sons and daughters, the wife and children stay with the master and he leaves by himself. But suppose the slave should say, 'I love my master and my wife and children—I don't want my freedom,' then his master is to bring him before God and to a door or doorpost and pierce his ear with an awl, a sign that he is a slave for life.

"When a man sells his daughter to be a handmaid, she doesn't go free after six years like the men. If she doesn't please her master, her family must buy her back; her master doesn't have the right to sell her to foreigners since he broke his word to her. If he turns her over to his son, he has to treat her like a daughter. If he marries another woman, she retains all her full rights to meals, clothing, and marital relations. If he won't do any of these three things for her, she goes free, for nothing.

"If someone hits another and death results, the penalty is death. But if there was no intent to kill—if it was an accident, an 'act of God'—I'll set aside a place to which the killer can flee for refuge. But if the murder was pre-meditated, cunningly plotted, then drag the killer away, even if it's from my Altar, to be put to death.

"If someone hits father or mother, the penalty is death.

"If someone kidnaps a person, the penalty is death, regardless of whether the person has been sold or is still held in possession.

"If someone curses father or mother, the penalty is death.

"If a quarrel breaks out and one hits the other with a rock or a fist and the injured one doesn't die but is confined to bed and then later gets better and can get about on a crutch, the one who hit him is in the clear, except to pay for the loss of time and make sure of complete recovery.

"If a slave owner hits a slave, male or female, with a stick and the slave dies on the spot, the slave must be avenged. But if the slave survives a day or two, he's not to be avenged—the slave is the owner's property.

"When there's a fight and in the fight a pregnant woman is hit so that she miscarries but is not otherwise hurt, the one responsible has to pay whatever the husband demands in compensation. But if there is further damage, then you must give life for life—eye for eye, tooth for tooth, hand for hand, foot for foot, burn for burn, wound for wound, bruise for bruise.

"If a slave owner hits the eye of a slave or handmaid and ruins it, the owner must let the slave go free because of the eye. If the owner knocks out the tooth of the male or female slave, the slave must be released and go free because of the tooth.

"If an ox gores a man or a woman to death, the ox must be stoned. The meat cannot be eaten but the owner of the ox is in the clear. But if the ox has a history of goring and the owner knew it and did nothing to guard against it, then if the ox kills a man or a woman, the ox is to be stoned and the owner given the death penalty. If a ransom is agreed upon instead of death, he must pay it in full as a redemption for his life. If a son or daughter is gored, the same judgment holds. If it is a slave or a handmaid the ox gores, thirty shekels of silver is to be paid to the owner and the ox stoned.

"If someone uncovers a cistern or digs a pit and leaves it open and an ox or donkey falls into it, the owner of the pit must pay whatever the animal is worth to its owner but can keep the dead animal.

"If someone's ox injures a neighbor's ox and the ox dies, they must sell the live ox and split the price; they must also split the dead animal. But if the ox had a history of goring and the owner knew it and did nothing to guard against it, the owner must pay an ox for an ox but can keep the dead animal.

22 "If someone steals an ox or a lamb and slaughters or sells it, the thief must pay five cattle in place of the ox and four sheep in place of the lamb. If the thief is caught while breaking in and is hit hard and dies, there is no bloodguilt. But if it happens after daybreak, there is bloodguilt.

"A thief must make full restitution for what is stolen. The thief who is unable to pay is to be sold for his thieving. If caught red-handed with the stolen goods, and the ox or donkey or lamb is still alive, the thief pays double.

"If someone grazes livestock in a field or vineyard but lets them loose so they graze in someone else's field, restitution must be made from the best of the owner's field or vineyard.

"If fire breaks out and spreads to the brush so that the sheaves of grain or the standing grain or even the whole field is burned up, whoever started the fire must pay for the damages.

"If someone gives a neighbor money or things for safekeeping and they are stolen from the neighbor's house, the thief, if caught, must pay back double. If the thief is not caught, the owner must be brought before God to determine whether the owner was the one who took the neighbor's goods.

"In all cases of stolen goods, whether oxen, donkeys, sheep, clothing, anything in fact missing of which someone says, 'That's mine,' both parties must come before the judges. The one the judges pronounce guilty must pay double to the other.

"If someone gives a donkey or ox or lamb or any kind of animal to another for safekeeping and it dies or is injured or lost and there is no witness, an oath before GOD must be made between them to decide whether one has laid hands on the property of the other. The owner must accept this and no damages are assessed. But if it turns out it was stolen, the owner must be compensated. If it has been torn by wild beasts, the torn animal must be brought in as evidence; no damages have to be paid.

"If someone borrows an animal from a neighbor and it gets injured or dies while the owner is not present, he must pay for it. But if the owner was with it, he doesn't have to pay. If the animal was hired, the payment covers the loss.

✠

"If a man seduces a virgin who is not engaged to be married and sleeps with her, he must pay the marriage price and marry her. If her father absolutely refuses to give her away, the man must still pay the marriage price for virgins.

"Don't let a sorceress live.

"Anyone who has sex with an animal gets the death penalty.

"Anyone who sacrifices to a god other than GOD alone must be put to death.

"Don't abuse or take advantage of strangers; you, remember, were once strangers in Egypt.

"Don't mistreat widows or orphans. If you do and they cry out to me, you can be sure I'll take them most seriously; I'll show my anger and come raging among you with the sword, and your wives will end up widows and your children orphans.

"If you lend money to my people, to any of the down-and-out among you, don't come down hard on them and gouge them with interest.

"If you take your neighbor's coat as security, give it back before nightfall; it may be your neighbor's only covering—what else does the person have to sleep in? And if I hear the neighbor crying out from the cold, I'll step in—I'm compassionate.

"Don't curse God; and don't damn your leaders.

"Don't be stingy as your wine vats fill up.

"Dedicate your firstborn sons to me. The same with your cattle and sheep—they are to stay for seven days with their mother, then give them to me.

"Be holy for my sake.

"Don't eat mutilated flesh you find in the fields; throw it to the dogs.

✠

23 "Don't pass on malicious gossip.
"Don't link up with a wicked person and give corrupt testimony. Don't go along with the crowd in doing evil and don't fudge

your testimony in a case just to please the crowd. And just because someone is poor, don't show favoritism in a dispute.

"If you find your enemy's ox or donkey loose, take it back to him. If you see the donkey of someone who hates you lying helpless under its load, don't walk off and leave it. Help it up.

"When there is a dispute concerning your poor, don't tamper with the justice due them.

"Stay clear of false accusations. Don't contribute to the death of innocent and good people. I don't let the wicked off the hook.

"Don't take bribes. Bribes blind perfectly good eyes and twist the speech of good people.

"Don't take advantage of a stranger. You know what it's like to be a stranger; you were strangers in Egypt.

"Sow your land for six years and gather in its crops, but in the seventh year leave it alone and give it a rest so that your poor may eat from it. What they leave, let the wildlife have. Do the same with your vineyards and olive groves.

"Work for six days and rest the seventh so your ox and donkey may rest and your servant and migrant workers may have time to get their needed rest.

"Listen carefully to everything I tell you. Don't pay attention to other gods—don't so much as mention their names.

✠

"Three times a year you are to hold a festival for me.

"Hold the spring Festival of Unraised Bread when you eat unraised bread for seven days at the time set for the month of Abib, as I commanded you. That was the month you came out of Egypt. No one should show up before me empty-handed.

"Hold the summer Festival of Harvest when you bring in the first-fuits of all your work in the fields.

"Hold the autumn Festival of Ingathering at the end of the season when you bring in the year's crops.

"Three times a year all your males are to appear before the Master, GOD.

"Don't offer the blood of a sacrifice to me with anything that has yeast in it.

"Don't leave the fat from my festival offering out overnight.

135

"Bring the choice first produce of the year to the house of your GOD.
"Don't boil a kid in its mother's milk.

✠

"Now get yourselves ready. I'm sending my Angel ahead of you to guard
you in your travels, to lead you to the place that I've prepared. Pay close
attention to him. Obey him. Don't go against him. He won't put up with
your rebellions because he's acting on my authority. But if you obey him
and do everything I tell you, I'll be an enemy to your enemies, I'll fight
those who fight you. When my Angel goes ahead of you and leads you
to the the land of the Amorites, the Hittites, the Perizzites, the
Canaanites, the Hivites, and the Jebusites, I'll clear the country of them.
So don't worship or serve their gods; don't do anything they do because
I'm going to wipe them right off the face of the Earth and smash their
sacred phallic pillars to bits.

"But you—you serve your GOD and he'll bless your food and your
water. I'll get rid of the sickness among you; there won't be any mis-
carriages nor barren women in your land. I'll make sure you live full
and complete lives.

"I'll send my Terror on ahead of you and throw those peoples you're
approaching into a panic. All you'll see of your enemies is the backs of
their necks.

"And I'll send Despair on ahead of you. It will push the Hivites,
the Canaanites, and the Hittites out of your way. I won't get rid of them
all at once lest the land grow up in weeds and the wild animals take
over. Little by little I'll get them out of there while you have a chance
to get your crops going and make the land your own. I will make your
borders stretch from the Red Sea to the Mediterranean Sea and from the
Wilderness to the Euphrates River. I'm turning everyone living in that
land over to you; go ahead and drive them out.

"Don't make any deals with them or their gods. They are not to
stay in the same country with you lest they get you to sin by worshiping their gods. Beware. That's a huge danger."

✠

24 He said to Moses, "Climb the mountain to GOD, you and
Aaron, Nadab, Abihu, and seventy of the elders of Israel. They
will worship from a distance; only Moses will approach GOD. The

rest are not to come close. And the people are not to climb the mountain at all."

So Moses went to the people and told them everything GOD had said—all the rules and regulations. They all answered in unison: "Everything GOD said, we'll do."

Then Moses wrote it all down, everything GOD had said. He got up early the next morning and built an Altar at the foot of the mountain using twelve pillar-stones for the twelve tribes of Israel. Then he directed young Israelite men to offer Whole-Burnt-Offerings and sacrifice Peace-Offerings of bulls. Moses took half the blood and put it in bowls; the other half he threw against the Altar.

Then he took the Book of the Covenant and read it as the people listened. They said, "Everything GOD said, we'll do. Yes, we'll obey."

Moses took the rest of the blood and threw it out over the people, saying, "This is the blood of the covenant which GOD has made with you out of all these words I have spoken."

✛

Then they climbed the mountain—Moses and Aaron, Nadab and Abihu, and seventy of the elders of Israel—and saw the God of Israel. He was standing on a pavement of something like sapphires—pure, clear sky-blue. He didn't hurt these pillar-leaders of the Israelites: They saw God; and they ate and drank.

GOD said to Moses, "Climb higher up the mountain and wait there for me; I'll give you tablets of stone, the teachings and commandments that I've written to instruct them." So Moses got up, accompanied by Joshua his aide. And Moses climbed up the mountain of God.

He told the elders of Israel, "Wait for us here until we return to you. You have Aaron and Hur with you; if there are any problems, go to them."

Then Moses climbed the mountain. The Cloud covered the mountain. The Glory of GOD settled over Mount Sinai. The Cloud covered it for six days. On the seventh day he called out of the Cloud to Moses. In the view of the Israelites below, the Glory of God looked like a raging fire at the top of the mountain.

Moses entered the middle of the Cloud and climbed the mountain. Moses was on the mountain forty days and forty nights.

INSTRUCTIONS ON THE MOUNTAIN: THE OFFERINGS

25 GOD spoke to Moses: "Tell the Israelites that they are to set aside offerings for me. Receive the offerings from everyone who is willing to give. These are the offerings I want you to receive from them: gold, silver, bronze; blue, purple, and scarlet material; fine linen; goats' hair; tanned rams' skins; dolphin skins; acacia wood; lamp oil; spices for anointing oils and for fragrant incense; onyx stones and other stones for setting in the Ephod and the Breastpiece. Let them construct a Sanctuary for me so that I can live among them. You are to construct it following the plans I've given you, the design for The Dwelling and the design for all its furnishings.

THE CHEST

"First let them make a Chest using acacia wood: make it three and three-quarters feet long and two and one-quarter feet wide and deep. Cover it with a veneer of pure gold inside and out and make a molding of gold all around it. Cast four gold rings and attach them to its four feet, two rings on one side and two rings on the other. Make poles from acacia wood and cover them with a veneer of gold and insert them into the rings on the sides of the Chest for carrying the Chest. The poles are to stay in the rings; they must not be removed.

"Place The Testimony that I give you in the Chest.

"Now make a lid of pure gold for the Chest, an Atonement-Cover, three and three-quarters feet long and two and one-quarter feet wide.

"Sculpt two winged angels out of hammered gold for either end of the Atonement-Cover, one angel at one end, one angel at the other. Make them of one piece with the Atonement-Cover. Make the angels with their wings spread, hovering over the Atonement-Cover, facing one another but looking down on it. Set the Atonement-Cover as a lid over the Chest and place in the Chest The Testimony that I will give you. I will meet you there at set times and speak with you from above the Atonement-Cover and from between the angel-figures that are on it, speaking the commands that I have for the Israelites.

THE TABLE

"Next make a Table from acacia wood. Make it three feet long, one and one-half feet wide and two and one-quarter feet high. Cover it with a veneer of pure gold. Make a molding all around it of gold. Make the border a handbreadth wide all around it and a rim of gold for the border.

Make four rings of gold and attach the rings to the four legs parallel to the table top. They will serve as holders for the poles used to carry the Table. Make the poles of acacia wood and cover them with a veneer of gold. They will be used to carry the Table.

"Make plates, bowls, jars, and jugs for pouring out offerings. Make them of pure gold.

"Always keep fresh Bread of the Presence on the Table before me.

THE LAMPSTAND

"Make a Lampstand of pure hammered gold. Make its stem and branches, cups, calyxes, and petals all of one piece. Give it six branches, three from one side and three from the other; put three cups shaped like almond blossoms, each with calyx and petals, on one branch, three on the next, and so on—the same for all six branches. On the main stem of the Lampstand, make four cups shaped like almonds, with calyx and petals, a calyx extending from under each pair of the six branches, the entire Lampstand fashioned from one piece of hammered pure gold.

"Make seven of these lamps for the Table. Arrange the lamps so they throw their light out in front. Make the candle snuffers and trays out of pure gold.

"Use a seventy-five-pound brick of pure gold to make the Lampstand and its accessories. Study the design you were given on the mountain and make everything accordingly.

THE DWELLING

26 "Make The Dwelling itself from ten panels of tapestry woven from fine twisted linen, blue and purple and scarlet material, with an angel-cherubim design. A skilled craftsman should do it. The panels of tapestry are each to be forty-six feet long and six feet wide. Join five of the panels together, and then the other five together. Make loops of blue along the edge of the outside panel of the first set and the same on the outside panel of the second set. Make fifty loops on each panel. Then make fifty gold clasps and join the tapestries together so that The Dwelling is one whole.

"Next make tapestries of goat hair for a tent that will cover The Dwelling. Make eleven panels of these tapestries. The length of each panel will be forty-five feet long and six feet wide. Join five of the panels together, and then the other six. Fold the sixth panel double at the front of the tent.

Now make fifty loops along the edge of the end panel and fifty loops along the edge of the joining panel. Make fifty clasps of bronze and connect the clasps with the loops, bringing the tent together.

"Hang half of the overlap of the tapestry panels over the rear of The Dwelling. The eighteen inches of overlap on either side will cover the sides of the tent. Finally, make a covering for the tapestries of tanned rams' skins died red and over that a covering of dolphin skins.

"Frame The Dwelling with planks of acacia wood, each section of frame fifteen feet long and two and one-quarter feet wide, with two pegs for securing them. Make all the frames identical: twenty frames for the south side with forty silver sockets to receive the two pegs from each of the twenty frames; the same construction on the north side of The Dwelling; for the rear of The Dwelling, which faces west, make six frames with two additional frames for the rear corners. Both of the two corner frames need to be double in thickness from top to bottom and fit into a single ring—eight frames altogether with sixteen sockets of silver, two under each frame.

"Now make crossbars of acacia wood, five for the frames on one side of The Dwelling, five for the other side, and five for the back side facing west. The center crossbar runs from end to end halfway up the frames. Cover the frames with a veneer of gold and make gold rings to hold the crossbars. And cover the crossbars with a veneer of gold. Then put The Dwelling together, following the design you were shown on the mountain.

"Make a curtain of blue, purple, and scarlet material and fine twisted linen. Have a design of angel-cherubim woven into it by a skilled craftsman. Fasten it with gold hooks to four posts of acacia wood covered with a veneer of gold, set on four silver bases. After hanging the curtain from the clasps, bring the Chest of The Testimony in behind the curtain. The curtain will separate the Holy Place from the Holy-of-Holies. Now place the Atonement-Cover lid on the Chest of The Testimony in the Holy-of-Holies. Place the Table and the Lampstand outside the curtain, the Lampstand on the south side of The Dwelling and the Table opposite it on the north side.

"Make a screen for the door of the tent. Weave it from blue, purple, and scarlet material and fine twisted linen. Frame the weaving with five poles of acacia wood covered with a veneer of gold and make gold hooks to hang the weaving. Cast five bronze bases for the poles.

The Altar

27 "Make an Altar of acacia wood. Make it seven and a half feet square and four and a half feet high. Make horns at each of the four corners. The horns are to be of one piece with the Altar and covered with a veneer of bronze. Make buckets for removing the ashes, along with shovels, basins, forks, and fire pans. Make all these utensils from bronze. Make a grate of bronze mesh and attach bronze rings at each of the four corners. Put the grate under the ledge of the Altar at the halfway point of the Altar. Make acacia wood poles for the Altar and cover them with a veneer of bronze. Insert the poles through the rings on the two sides of the Altar for carrying. Use boards to make the Altar, keeping the interior hollow.

The Courtyard

"Make a Courtyard for The Dwelling. The south side is to be 150 feet long. The hangings for the Courtyard are to be woven from fine twisted linen, with their twenty posts, twenty bronze bases, and fastening hooks and bands of silver. The north side is to be exactly the same.

"For the west end of the Courtyard you will need seventy-five feet of hangings with their ten posts and bases. Across the seventy-five feet at the front, or east end, you will need twenty-two and a half feet of hangings, with their three posts and bases on one side and the same for the other side. At the door of the Courtyard make a screen thirty feet long woven from blue, purple, and scarlet stuff, with fine twisted linen, embroidered by a craftsman, and hung on its four posts and bases. All the posts around the Courtyard are to be banded with silver, with hooks of silver and bases of bronze. The Courtyard is to be 150 feet long and seventy-five feet wide. The hangings of fine twisted linen set on their bronze bases are to be seven and a half feet high. All the tools used for setting up The Holy Dwelling, including all the pegs in it and the Courtyard, are to be made of bronze.

"Now, order the Israelites to bring you pure, clear olive oil for light so that the lamps can be kept burning. In the Tent of Meeting, the area outside the curtain that veils The Testimony, Aaron and his sons will keep this light burning from evening until morning before God. This is to be a permanent practice down through the generations for Israelites.

141

THE VESTMENTS

28 "Get your brother Aaron and his sons from among the Israelites to serve me as priests: Aaron and his sons Nadab, Abihu, Eleazar, Ithamar. Make sacred vestments for your brother Aaron to symbolize glory and beauty. Consult with the skilled craftsmen, those whom I have gifted in this work, and arrange for them to make Aaron's vestments, to set him apart as holy, to act as priest for me. These are the articles of clothing they are to make: Breastpiece, Ephod, robe, woven tunic, turban, sash. They are making holy vestments for your brother Aaron and his sons as they work as priests for me. They will need gold, blue, purple, and scarlet material and fine linen.

THE EPHOD

"Have the Ephod made from gold; blue, purple, and scarlet material; and fine twisted linen by a skilled craftsman. Give it two shoulder pieces at two of the corners so it can be fastened. The decorated band on it is to be just like it and of one piece with it: made of gold; blue, purple, and scarlet material; and of fine twisted linen. Next take two onyx stones and engrave the names of the sons of Israel on them in the order of their birth, six names on one stone and the remaining six on the other. Engrave the names of the sons of Israel on the two stones the way a jeweler engraves a seal. Then mount the stones in settings of filigreed gold. Fasten the two stones on the shoulder pieces of the Ephod—they are memorial stones for the Israelites. Aaron will wear these names on his shoulders as a memorial before GOD. Make the settings of gold filigree. Make two chains of pure gold and braid them like cords, then attach the corded chains to the settings.

THE BREASTPIECE

"Now make a Breastpiece of Judgment, using skilled craftsmen, the same as with the Ephod. Use gold; blue, purple, and scarlet material; and fine twisted linen. Make it nine inches square and folded double. Mount four rows of precious gemstones on it.

> First row: carnelian, topaz, emerald.
> Second row: ruby, sapphire, crystal.
> Third row: jacinth, agate, amethyst.
> Fourth row: beryl, onyx, jasper.

"Set them in gold filigree. The twelve stones correspond to the names of the Israelites, with twelve names engraved, one on each, as on a seal for the twelve tribes.

"Then make braided chains of pure gold for the Breastpiece, like cords. Make two rings of gold for the Breastpiece and fasten them to the two ends. Fasten the two golden cords to the rings at the ends of the Breastpiece. Then fasten the other ends of the two cords to the two settings of filigree, attaching them to the shoulder pieces of the Ephod in front. Then make two rings of gold and fasten them to the two ends of the Breastpiece on its inside edge facing the Ephod. Then make two more rings of gold and fasten them in the front of the Ephod to the lower part of the two shoulder pieces, near the seam above the decorated band. Fasten the Breastpiece in place by running a cord of blue through its rings to the rings of the Ephod so that it rests secure on the decorated band of the Ephod and won't come loose.

"Aaron will regularly carry the names of the sons of Israel on the Breastpiece of Judgment over his heart as he enters the Sanctuary into the presence of GOD for remembrance. Place the Urim and Thummim in the Breastpiece of Judgment. They will be over Aaron's heart when he enters the presence of GOD. In this way Aaron will regularly carry the Breastpiece of Judgment into the presence of GOD.

THE ROBE

"Make the robe for the Ephod entirely of blue, with an opening for the head at the center and a hem on the edge so that it won't tear. For the edge of the skirts make pomegranates of blue, purple, and scarlet material all around and alternate them with bells of gold — gold bell and pomegranate, gold bell and pomegranate — all around the hem of the robe. Aaron has to wear it when he does his priestly work. The bells will be heard when he enters the Holy Place and comes into the presence of GOD, and again when he comes out so that he won't die.

THE TURBAN, TUNIC, UNDERWEAR

"Make a plate of pure gold. Engrave on it as on a seal: 'Holy to GOD.' Tie it with a blue cord to the front of the turban. It is to rest there on Aaron's forehead. He'll take on any guilt involved in the sacred offerings that the Israelites consecrate, no matter what they bring. It will always be on Aaron's forehead so that the offerings will be acceptable before GOD.

"Weave the tunic of fine linen. Make the turban of fine linen. The sash will be the work of an embroiderer. Make tunics, sashes, and hats for Aaron's sons to express glory and beauty. Dress your brother Aaron and his sons in them. Anoint, ordain, and consecrate them to serve me as priests.

"Make linen underwear to cover their nakedness from waist to thigh. Aaron and his sons must wear it whenever they enter the Tent of Meeting or approach the Altar to minister in the Holy Place so that they won't incur guilt and die. This is a permanent rule for Aaron and all his priest-descendants.

CONSECRATION OF PRIESTS

29 "This is the ceremony for consecrating them as priests. Take a young bull and two rams, healthy and without defects. Using fine wheat flour but no yeast make bread and cakes mixed with oil and wafers spread with oil. Place them in a basket and carry them along with the bull and the two rams. Bring Aaron and his sons to the entrance of the Tent of Meeting and wash them with water.

"Then take the vestments and dress Aaron in the tunic, the robe of the Ephod, the Ephod, and the Breastpiece, belting the Ephod on him with the embroidered waistband. Set the turban on his head and place the sacred crown on the turban. Then take the anointing oil and pour it on his head, anointing him. Then bring his sons, put tunics on them and gird them with sashes, both Aaron and his sons, and set hats on them. Their priesthood is upheld by law and is permanent.

"This is how you will ordain Aaron and his sons: Bring the bull to the Tent of Meeting. Aaron and his sons will place their hands on the head of the bull. Then you will slaughter the bull in the presence of GOD at the entrance to the Tent of Meeting. Take some of the bull's blood and smear it on the horns of the Altar with your finger; pour the rest of the blood on the base of the Altar. Next take all the fat that covers the innards, fat from around the liver and the two kidneys, and burn it on the Altar. But the flesh of the bull, including its hide and dung, you will burn up outside the camp. It is an Absolution-Offering.

"Then take one of the rams. Have Aaron and his sons place their hands on the head of the ram. Slaughter the ram and take its blood and throw it against the Altar, all around. Cut the ram into pieces; wash its innards and legs, then gather the pieces and its head and burn the whole ram on the Altar. It is a Whole-Burnt-Offering to GOD, a pleasant fragrance, an offering by fire to GOD.

"Then take the second ram. Have Aaron and his sons place their hands on the ram's head. Slaughter the ram. Take some of its blood and rub it on Aaron's right earlobe and on the right earlobes of his sons, on the thumbs of their right hands and on the big toes of their right feet. Sprinkle the rest of the blood against all sides of the Altar. Then take some of the blood that is on the Altar, mix it with some of the anointing oil, and splash it on Aaron and his clothes and on his sons and their clothes so that Aaron and his clothes and his sons and his sons' clothes will be made holy.

"Take the fat from the ram, the fat tail, the fat that covers the innards, the long lobe of the liver, the two kidneys and the fat on them, and the right thigh: this is the ordination ram. Also take one loaf of bread, an oil cake, and a wafer from the breadbasket that is in the presence of GOD.

"Place all of these in the open hands of Aaron and his sons who will wave them before GOD, a Wave-Offering. Then take them from their hands and burn them on the Altar with the Whole-Burnt-Offering—a pleasing fragrance before GOD, a gift to GOD.

"Now take the breast from Aaron's ordination ram and wave it before GOD, a Wave-Offering. That will be your portion.

"Consecrate the Wave-Offering breast and the thigh that was held up. These are the parts of the ordination ram that are for Aaron and his sons. Aaron and his sons are always to get this offering from the Israelites; the Israelites are to make this offering regularly from their Peace-Offerings.

"Aaron's sacred garments are to be handed down to his descendants so they can be anointed and ordained in them. The son who succeeds him as priest is to wear them for seven days and enter the Tent of Meeting to minister in the Holy Place.

"Take the ordination ram and boil the meat in the Holy Place. At the entrance to the Tent of Meeting, Aaron and his sons will eat the boiled ram and the bread that is in the basket. Atoned by these offerings, ordained and consecrated by them, they are the only ones who are to eat them. No outsiders are to eat them; they're holy. Anything from the ordination ram or from the bread that is left over until morning you are to burn up. Don't eat it; it's holy.

"Do everything for the ordination of Aaron and his sons exactly as I've commanded you throughout the seven days. Offer a bull as an Absolution-Offering for atonement each day. Offer it on the Altar when you make atonement for it: Anoint and consecrate it. Make atonement for the Altar and consecrate it for seven days; the Altar will become soaked in holiness—anyone who so much as touches the Altar will become holy.

"This is what you are to offer on the Altar: two year-old lambs each and every day, one lamb in the morning and the second lamb at evening. With the sacrifice of the first lamb offer two quarts of fine flour with a quart of virgin olive oil, plus a quart of wine for a Drink-Offering. The sacrifice of the second lamb, the one at evening, is also to be accompanied by the same Grain-Offering and Drink-Offering of the morning sacrifice to give a pleasing fragrance, a gift to GOD.

"This is to be your regular, daily Whole-Burnt-Offering before GOD, generation after generation, sacrificed at the entrance of the Tent of Meeting. That's where I'll meet you; that's where I'll speak with you; that's where I'll meet the Israelites, at the place made holy by my Glory. I'll make the Tent of Meeting and the Altar holy. I'll make Aaron and his sons holy in order to serve me as priests. I'll move in and live with the Israelites. I'll be their God. They'll realize that I am their GOD who brought them out of the land of Egypt so that I could live with them. I am GOD, *your* God.

THE ALTAR OF INCENSE

30 "Make an Altar for burning incense. Construct it from acacia wood, one and one-half feet square and three feet high with its horns of one piece with it. Cover it with a veneer of pure gold, its top, sides, and horns, and make a gold molding around it with two rings of gold beneath the molding. Place the rings on the two opposing sides to serve as holders for poles by which it will be carried. Make the poles of acacia wood and cover them with a veneer of gold.

"Place the Altar in front of the curtain that hides the Chest of The Testimony, in front of the Atonement-Cover that is over The Testimony where I will meet you. Aaron will burn fragrant incense on it every morning when he polishes the lamps, and again in the evening as he prepares the lamps for lighting, so that there will always be incense burning before GOD, generation after generation. But don't burn on this Altar any unholy incense or Whole-Burnt-Offering or Grain-Offering. And don't pour out Drink-Offerings on it. Once a year Aaron is to purify the Altar horns. Using the blood of the Absolution-Offering of atonement, he is to make this atonement every year down through the generations. It is most holy to GOD."

THE ATONEMENT TAX

GOD spoke to Moses: "When you take a head count of the Israelites to keep track of them, all must pay an atonement-tax to GOD for their life at the time of being registered so that nothing bad will happen because of the registration. Everyone who gets counted is to give a half-shekel (using the standard Sanctuary shekel of a fifth of an ounce to the shekel)—a half-shekel offering to GOD. Everyone counted, age twenty and up, is to make the offering to GOD. The rich are not to pay more nor the poor less than the half-shekel offering to GOD, the atonement-tax for your lives. Take the atonement-tax money from the Israelites and put it to the maintenance of the Tent of Meeting. It will be a memorial fund for the Israelites in honor of GOD, making atonement for your lives."

THE WASHBASIN

GOD spoke to Moses: "Make a bronze Washbasin; make it with a bronze base. Place it between the Tent of Meeting and the Altar. Put water in it. Aaron and his sons will wash their hands and feet in it. When they enter the Tent of Meeting or approach the Altar to serve there or offer gift offerings to GOD, they are to wash so they will not die. They are to wash their hands and their feet so they will not die. This is the rule forever, for Aaron and his sons down through the generations."

HOLY ANOINTING OIL

GOD spoke to Moses: "Take the best spices: twelve and a half pounds of liquid myrrh; half that much, six and a quarter pounds, of fragrant cinnamon; six and a quarter pounds of fragrant cane; twelve and a half pounds of cassia—using the standard Sanctuary weight for all of them—and a gallon of olive oil. Make these into a holy anointing oil, a perfumer's skillful blend.

"Use it to anoint the Tent of Meeting, the Chest of The Testimony, the Table and all its utensils, the Lampstand and its utensils, the Altar of Incense, the Altar of Whole-Burnt-Offerings and all its utensils, and the Washbasin and its base. Consecrate them so they'll be soaked in holiness, so that anyone who so much as touches them will become holy.

"Then anoint Aaron and his sons. Consecrate them as priests to me. Tell the Israelites, 'This will be my holy anointing oil throughout your generations.' Don't pour it on ordinary men. Don't copy this mixture to use for yourselves. It's holy; keep it holy. Whoever mixes up anything like it, or puts it on an ordinary person, will be expelled."

HOLY INCENSE

GOD spoke to Moses: "Take fragrant spices—gum resin, onycha, gal-banum—and add pure frankincense. Mix the spices in equal proportions to make an aromatic incense, the art of a perfumer, salted and pure—holy. Now crush some of it into powder and place some of it before The Testimony in the Tent of Meeting where I will meet with you; it will be for you the holiest of holy places. When you make this incense, you are not to copy the mixture for your own use. It's holy to GOD; keep it that way. Whoever copies it for personal use will be excommunicated."

BEZALEL AND OHOLIAB

31 GOD spoke to Moses: "See what I've done; I've personally chosen Bezalel, son of Uri, son of Hur of the tribe of Judah. I've filled him with the Spirit of God, giving him skill and knowhow and expertise in every kind of craft to create designs and work in gold, silver, and bronze; to cut and set gemstones; to carve wood—he's an all-around craftsman.

"Not only that, but I've given him Oholiab, son of Ahisamach of the tribe of Dan, to work with him. And to all who have an aptitude for crafts I've given the skills to make all the things I've commanded you: the Tent of Meeting, the Chest of The Testimony and its Atonement-Cover, all the implements for the Tent, the Table and its implements, the pure Lampstand and all its implements, the Altar of Incense, the Altar of Whole-Burnt-Offering and all its implements, the Washbasin and its base, the official vestments, the holy vestments for Aaron the priest and his sons in their priestly duties, the anointing oil, and the aromatic incense for the Holy Place—they'll make everything just the way I've commanded you."

SABBATH

GOD spoke to Moses: "Tell the Israelites, 'Above all, keep my Sabbaths, the sign between me and you, generation after generation, to keep the knowledge alive that I am the GOD who makes you holy. Keep the Sabbath; it's holy to you. Whoever profanes it will most certainly be put to death. Whoever works on it will be excommunicated from the people. There are six days for work but the seventh day is Sabbath, pure rest, holy to GOD. Anyone who works on the Sabbath will most certainly be put to death. The Israelites will keep the Sabbath, observe Sabbath-keeping down through the generations, as a standing covenant. It's a fixed sign between me and the Israelites. Yes, because in six days GOD made the Heavens and the Earth and on the seventh day he stopped and took a long, deep breath.'"

When he finished speaking with him on Mount Sinai, he gave Moses two tablets of Testimony, slabs of stone, written with the finger of God.

"MAKE GODS FOR US"

32 When the people realized that Moses was taking forever in coming down off the mountain, they rallied around Aaron and said, "Do something. Make gods for us who will lead us. That Moses, the man who got us out of Egypt—who knows what's happened to him?"

So Aaron told them, "Take off the gold rings from the ears of your wives and sons and daughters and bring them to me." They all did it; they removed the gold rings from their ears and brought them to Aaron. He took the gold from their hands and cast it in the form of a calf, shaping it with an engraving tool.

The people responded with enthusiasm: "These are your gods, O Israel, who brought you up from Egypt!"

Aaron, taking in the situation, built an altar before the calf.

Aaron then announced, "Tomorrow is a feast day to GOD!"

Early the next morning, the people got up and offered Whole-Burnt-Offerings and brought Peace-Offerings. The people sat down to eat and drink and then began to party. It turned into a wild party!

GOD spoke to Moses, "Go! Get down there! Your people whom you brought up from the land of Egypt have fallen to pieces. In no time at all they've turned away from the way I commanded them: They made a molten calf and worshiped it. They've sacrificed to it and said, 'These are the gods, O Israel, that brought you up from the land of Egypt!'"

GOD said to Moses, "I look at this people—oh! what a stubborn, hard-headed people! Let me alone now, give my anger free reign to burst into flames and incinerate them. But I'll make a great nation out of you."

Moses tried to calm his GOD down. He said, "Why, GOD, would you lose your temper with your people? Why, you brought them out of Egypt in a tremendous demonstration of power and strength. Why let the Egyptians say, 'He had it in for them—he brought them out so he could kill them in the mountains, wipe them right off the face of the Earth.' Stop your anger. Think twice about bringing evil against your people! Think of Abraham, Isaac, and Israel, your servants to whom you gave your word, telling them 'I will give you many children, as many as the stars in the sky, and I'll give this land to your children as their land forever.'"

And GOD did think twice. He decided not to do the evil he had threatened against his people.

Moses turned around and came down from the mountain, carrying the two tablets of The Testimony. The tablets were written on both sides, front and back. God made the tablets and God wrote the tablets—engraved them.

When Joshua heard the sound of the people shouting noisily, he said to Moses, "That's the sound of war in the camp!"

But Moses said,

> Those aren't songs of victory,
> And those aren't songs of defeat,
> I hear songs of people throwing a party.

And that's what it was. When Moses came near to the camp and saw the calf and the people dancing, his anger flared. He threw down the tablets and smashed them to pieces at the foot of the mountain. He took the calf that they had made, melted it down with fire, pulverized it to powder, then scattered it on the water and made the Israelites drink it.

Moses said to Aaron, "What on Earth did these people ever do to you that you involved them in this huge sin?"

Aaron said, "Master, don't be angry. You know this people and how set on evil they are. They said to me, 'Make us gods who will lead us. This Moses, the man who brought us out of Egypt, we don't know what's happened to him.'

"So I said, 'Who has gold?' And they took off their jewelry and gave it to me. I threw it in the fire and out came this calf."

Moses saw that the people were simply running wild—Aaron had let them run wild, disgracing themselves before their enemies. He took up a position at the entrance to the camp and said, "Whoever is on GOD's side, join me!" All the Levites stepped up.

He then told them, "GOD's orders, the God of Israel: 'Strap on your swords and go to work. Crisscross the camp from one end to the other: Kill brother, friend, neighbor.'"

The Levites carried out Moses' orders. Three thousand of the people were killed that day.

Moses said, "You confirmed your ordination today—and at great cost, even killing your sons and brothers! And God has blessed you."

The next day Moses addressed the people: "You have sinned an enormous sin! But I am going to go up to GOD; maybe I'll be able to clear you of your sin."

Moses went back to GOD and said, "This is terrible. This people has sinned—it's an enormous sin! They made gods of gold for themselves. And now, if you will only forgive their sin. . . . But if not, erase me out of the book you've written."

GOD said to Moses, "I'll only erase from my book those who sin against me. For right now, you go and lead the people to where I told you. Look, my Angel is going ahead of you. On the day, though, when I settle accounts, their sins will certainly be part of the settlement."

GOD sent a plague on the people because of the calf they and Aaron had made.

✞

33 GOD said to Moses: "Now go. Get on your way from here, you and the people you brought up from the land of Egypt. Head for the land which I promised to Abraham, Isaac, and Jacob, saying 'I will give it to your descendants.' I will send an angel ahead of you and I'll drive out the Canaanites, Amorites, Hittites, Perizzites, Hivites, and Jebusites. It's a land flowing with milk and honey. But I won't be with you in person—you're such a stubborn, hard-headed people!—lest I destroy you on the journey."

When the people heard this harsh verdict, they were plunged into gloom and wore long faces. No one put on jewelry.

GOD said to Moses, "Tell the Israelites, 'You're one hard-headed people. I couldn't stand being with you for even a moment—I'd destroy you. So take off all your jewelry until I figure out what to do with you.'" So the Israelites stripped themselves of their jewelry from Mount Horeb on.

✞

Moses used to take the Tent and set it up outside the camp, some distance away. He called it the Tent of Meeting. Anyone who sought GOD

151

would go to the Tent of Meeting outside the camp. It went like this: When Moses would go to the Tent, all the people would stand at attention; each man would take his position at the entrance to his tent with his eyes on Moses until he entered the Tent; whenever Moses entered the Tent, the Pillar of Cloud descended to the entrance to the Tent and GOD spoke with Moses. All the people would see the Pillar of Cloud at the entrance to the Tent, stand at attention, and then bow down in worship, each man at the entrance to his tent.

And GOD spoke with Moses face-to-face, as neighbors speak to one another. When he would return to the camp, his attendant, the young man Joshua, stayed—he didn't leave the Tent.

✢

Moses said to GOD, "Look, you tell me, 'Lead this people,' but you don't let me know whom you're going to send with me. You tell me, 'I know you well and you are special to me.' If I am so special to you, let me in on your plans. That way, I will continue being special to you. Don't forget, this is *your* people, your responsibility."

GOD said, "My presence will go with you. I'll see the journey to the end."

Moses said, "If your presence doesn't take the lead here, call this trip off right now. How else will it be known that you're with me in this, with me and your people? Are you traveling with us or not? How else will we know that we're special, I and your people, among all other people on this planet Earth?"

GOD said to Moses: "All right. Just as you say; this also I will do, for I know you well and you are special to me. I know you by name."

Moses said, "Please. Let me see your Glory."

GOD said, "I will make my Goodness pass right in front of you; I'll call out the name, GOD, right before you. I'll treat well whomever I want to treat well and I'll be kind to whomever I want to be kind."

GOD continued, "But you may not see my face. No one can see me and live."

GOD said, "Look, here is a place right beside me. Put yourself on this rock. When my Glory passes by, I'll put you in the cleft of the rock and cover you with my hand until I've passed by. Then I'll take my hand away and you'll see my back. But you won't see my face."

✢

34 GOD spoke to Moses: "Cut out two tablets of stone just like the originals and engrave on them the words that were on the original tablets you smashed. Be ready in the morning to climb Mount Sinai and get set to meet me on top of the mountain. Not a soul is to go with you; the whole mountain must be clear of people, even animals—not even sheep or oxen can be grazing in front of the mountain."

So Moses cut two tablets of stone just like the originals. He got up early in the morning and climbed Mount Sinai as GOD had commanded him, carrying the two tablets of stone. GOD descended in the cloud and took up his position there beside him and called out the name, GOD. GOD passed in front of him and called out, "GOD, GOD, a God of mercy and grace, endlessly patient—so much love, so deeply true—loyal in love for a thousand generations, forgiving iniquity, rebellion, and sin. Still, he doesn't ignore sin. He holds sons and grandsons responsible for a father's sins to the third and even fourth generation."

At once, Moses fell to the ground and worshiped, saying, "Please, O Master, if you see anything good in me, please Master, travel with us, hard-headed as these people are. Forgive our iniquity and sin. Own us, possess us."

And GOD said, "As of right now, I'm making a covenant with you: In full sight of your people I will work wonders that have never been created in all the Earth, in any nation. Then all the people with whom you're living will see how tremendous GOD's work is, the work I'll do for you. Take careful note of all I command you today. I'm clearing your way by driving out Amorites, Canaanites, Hittites, Perizzites, Hivites, and Jebusites. Stay vigilant. Don't let down your guard lest you make covenant with the people who live in the land that you are entering and they trip you up.

"Tear down their altars, smash their phallic pillars, chop down their fertility poles. Don't worship any other god. GOD—his name is The-Jealous-One—is a jealous God. Be careful that you don't make a covenant with the people who live in the land and take up with their sex-and-religion life, join them in meals at their altars, marry your sons to their women, women who take up with any convenient god or goddess and will get your sons to do the same thing.

"Don't make molten gods for yourselves.

"Keep the Feast of Unraised Bread. Eat only unraised bread for seven days in the month of Abib—it was in the month of Abib that you came out of Egypt.

"Every firstborn from the womb is mine, all the males of your herds, your firstborn oxen and sheep.

"Redeem your firstborn donkey with a lamb. If you don't redeem it you must break its neck.

"Redeem each of your firstborn sons.

"No one is to show up in my presence empty-handed.

"Work six days and rest the seventh. Stop working even during plowing and harvesting.

"Keep the Feast of Weeks with the first cutting of the wheat harvest, and the Feast of Ingathering at the turn of the year.

"All your men are to appear before the Master, the GOD of Israel, three times a year. You won't have to worry about your land when you appear before your GOD three times each year, for I will drive out the nations before you and give you plenty of land. Nobody's going to be hanging around plotting ways to get it from you.

"Don't mix the blood of my sacrifices with anything fermented.

"Don't leave leftovers from the Passover Feast until morning.

"Bring the finest of the firstfruits of your produce to the house of your GOD.

"Don't boil a kid in its mother's milk."

GOD said to Moses: "Now write down these words, for by these words I've made a covenant with you and Israel."

Moses was there with GOD forty days and forty nights. He didn't eat any food; he didn't drink any water. And he wrote on the tablets the words of the covenant, the Ten Words.

When Moses came down from Mount Sinai carrying the two Tablets of The Testimony, he didn't know that the skin of his face glowed because he had been speaking with GOD. Aaron and all the Israelites saw Moses, saw his radiant face, and held back, afraid to get close to him.

Moses called out to them. Aaron and the leaders in the community came back and Moses talked with them. Later all the Israelites came up to him and he passed on the commands, everything that GOD had told him on Mount Sinai.

When Moses finished speaking with them, he put a veil over his face, but when he went into the presence of GOD to speak with him, he removed the veil until he came out. When he came out and told the Israelites what he had been commanded, they would see Moses' face, its skin glowing, and then he would again put the veil on his face until he went back in to speak with GOD.

BUILDING THE PLACE OF WORSHIP

35 Moses spoke to the entire congregation of Israel, saying, "These are the things that GOD has commanded you to do:

"Work six days, but the seventh day will be a holy rest day, GOD's holy rest day. Anyone who works on this day must be put to death. Don't light any fires in your homes on the Sabbath day."

THE OFFERINGS

Moses spoke to the entire congregation of Israel, saying, "This is what GOD has commanded:

"Gather from among you an offering for GOD. Receive on GOD's behalf what everyone is willing to give as an offering: gold, silver, bronze; blue, purple, and scarlet material; fine linen; goats' hair; tanned rams' skins; dolphin skins; acacia wood; lamp oil; spices for anointing oils and for fragrant incense; onyx stones and other stones for setting in the Ephod and the Breastpiece.

"Come—all of you who have skills—come and make everything that GOD has commanded: The Dwelling with its tent and cover, its hooks, frames, crossbars, posts, and bases; the Chest with its poles, the Atonement-Cover and veiling curtain; the Table with its poles and implements and the Bread of the Presence; the Lampstand for giving light with its furnishings and lamps and the oil for lighting; the Altar of Incense with its poles, the anointing oil, the fragrant incense; the screen for the door at the entrance to The Dwelling; the Altar of Whole-Burnt-Offering with its bronze grate and poles and all its implements; the Washbasin with its base; the tapestry hangings for the Courtyard with the posts and bases, the screen for the Courtyard gate; the pegs for The Dwelling, the pegs for the Courtyard with their cords; the official vestments for ministering in the Holy Place, the sacred vestments for Aaron the priest and for his sons serving as priests."

So everyone in the community of Israel left the presence of Moses. Then they came back, every one whose heart was roused, whose spirit was freely responsive, bringing offerings to GOD for building the Tent of Meeting, furnishing it for worship and making the holy vestments. They came, both men and women, all the willing spirits among them,

offering brooches, earrings, rings, necklaces—anything made of gold—
offering up their gold jewelry to GOD. And anyone who had blue, purple,
and scarlet fabrics; fine linen; goats' hair; tanned leather; and dolphin
skins brought them. Everyone who wanted to offer up silver or bronze
as a gift to GOD brought it. Everyone who had acacia wood that could be
used in the work, brought it. All the women skilled at weaving brought
their weavings of blue and purple and scarlet fabrics and their fine linens.
And all the women who were gifted in spinning, spun the goats' hair.

The leaders brought onyx and other precious stones for setting in
the Ephod and the Breastpiece. They also brought spices and olive oil
for lamp oil, anointing oil, and incense. Every man and woman in Israel
whose heart moved them freely to bring something for the work that
GOD through Moses had commanded them to make, brought it, a vol-
untary offering for GOD.

BEZALEL AND OHOLIAB

Moses told the Israelites, "See, GOD has selected Bezalel son of Uri, son
of Hur, of the tribe of Judah. He's filled him with the Spirit of God, with
skill, ability, and knowhow for making all sorts of things, to design and
work in gold, silver, and bronze; to carve stones and set them; to carve
wood, working in every kind of skilled craft. And he's also made him
a teacher, he and Oholiab son of Ahisamach, of the tribe of Dan. He's
gifted them with the knowhow needed for carving, designing, weaving,
and embroidering in blue, purple, and scarlet fabrics, and in fine linen.
They can make anything and design anything.

36 "Bezalel and Oholiab, along with everyone whom GOD has given
the skill and knowhow for making everything involved in the
worship of the Sanctuary as commanded by GOD, are to start to work."

Moses summoned Bezalel and Oholiab along with all whom GOD
had gifted with the ability to work skillfully with their hands. The men
were eager to get started and engage in the work. They took from Moses
all the offerings that the Israelites had brought for the work of constructing the Sanctuary. The people kept on bringing in their freewill
offerings, morning after morning.

All the artisans who were at work making everything involved in
constructing the Sanctuary came, one after another, to Moses, saying,
"The people are bringing more than enough for doing this work that
GOD has commanded us to do!"

So Moses sent out orders through the camp: "Men! Women! No more offerings for the building of the Sanctuary!"

The people were ordered to stop bringing offerings! There was plenty of material for all the work to be done. Enough and more than enough.

THE TAPESTRIES

Then all the skilled artisans on The Dwelling made ten tapestries of fine twisted linen and blue, purple, and scarlet fabric with an angel-cherubim design worked into the material. Each panel of tapestry was forty-six feet long and six feet wide. Five of the panels were joined together, and then the other five. Loops of blue were made along the edge of the outside panel of the first set, and the same on the outside panel of the second set. They made fifty loops on each panel, with the loops opposite each other. Then they made fifty gold clasps and joined the tapestries together so that The Dwelling was one whole.

Next they made tapestries of woven goat hair for a tent that will cover The Dwelling. They made eleven panels of these tapestries. The length of each panel was forty-five feet long and six feet wide. They joined five of the panels together, and then the other six, by making fifty loops along the edge of the end panel and fifty loops along the edge of the joining panel, then making fifty clasps of bronze, connecting the clasps to the loops, bringing the tent together. They finished it off by covering the tapestries with tanned rams' skins died red, and covered that with dolphin skins.

THE FRAMING

They framed The Dwelling with vertical planks of acacia wood, each section of frame fifteen feet long and two and a quarter feet wide, with two pegs for securing them. They made all the frames identical: twenty frames for the south side, with forty silver sockets to receive the two tenons from each of the twenty frames; they repeated that construction on the north side of The Dwelling. For the rear of The Dwelling facing west, they made six frames, with two additional frames for the rear corners. Both of the two corner frames were double in thickness from top to bottom and fit into a single ring—eight frames altogether with sixteen sockets of silver, two under each frame.

They made crossbars of acacia wood, five for the frames on one side of The Dwelling, five for the other side, and five for the back side facing west. The center crossbar ran from end to end halfway up the frames. They covered the frames with a veneer of gold, made gold rings to hold the crossbars, and covered the crossbars with a veneer of gold.

They made the curtain of blue, purple, and scarlet material and fine twisted linen. They wove a design of angel-cherubim into it. They made four posts of acacia wood, covered them with a veneer of gold, and cast four silver bases for them.

They made a screen for the door of the tent, woven from blue, purple, and scarlet material and fine twisted linen with embroidery. They framed the weaving with five poles of acacia wood covered with a veneer of gold, and made gold hooks to hang the weaving and five bronze bases for the poles.

THE CHEST

37 Bezalel made the Chest using acacia wood: He made it three and three-quarters feet long and two and a quarter feet wide and deep. He covered it inside and out with a veneer of pure gold and made a molding of gold all around it. He cast four gold rings and attached them to its four feet, two rings on one side and two rings on the other. He made poles from acacia wood, covered them with a veneer of gold, and inserted the poles for carrying the Chest into the rings on the sides.

Next he made a lid of pure gold for the Chest, an Atonement-Cover, three and three-quarters feet long and two and a quarter feet wide.

He sculpted two winged angel-cherubim out of hammered gold for the ends of the Atonement-Cover, one angel at one end, one angel at the other. He made them of one piece with the Atonement-Cover. The angels had outstretched wings and appeared to hover over the Atonement-Cover, facing one another but looking down on the Atonement-Cover.

THE TABLE

He made the Table from acacia wood. He made it three feet long, one and a half feet wide and two and a quarter feet high. He covered it with a veneer of pure gold and made a molding of gold all around it. He made a border a handbreadth wide all around it and a rim of gold for the border. He cast four rings of gold for it and attached the rings to the four legs parallel to the table top. They will serve as holders for the poles used to carry the Table. He made the poles of acacia wood and covered them with a veneer of gold. They will be used to carry the Table.

Out of pure gold he made the utensils for the Table: its plates, bowls, jars, and jugs used for pouring.

THE LAMPSTAND

He made a Lampstand of pure hammered gold, making its stem and branches, cups, calyxes, and petals all of one piece. It had six branches, three from one side and three from the other; three cups shaped like almond blossoms with calyxes and petals on one branch, three on the next, and so on—the same for all six branches. On the main stem of the Lampstand, there were four cups shaped like almonds, with calyxes and petals, a calyx extending from under each pair of the six branches. The entire Lampstand with its calyxes and stems was fashioned from one piece of hammered pure gold. He made seven of these lamps with their candle snuffers, all out of pure gold.

He used a seventy-five-pound brick of pure gold to make the Lampstand and its accessories.

THE ALTAR OF INCENSE

He made an Altar for burning incense from acacia wood. He made it a foot and a half square and three feet high, with its horns of one piece with it. He covered it with a veneer of pure gold, its top, sides, and horns, and made a gold molding around it with two rings of gold beneath the molding. He placed the rings on the two opposing sides to serve as holders for poles by which it will be carried. He made the poles of acacia wood and covered them with a veneer of gold.

He also prepared with the art of a perfumer the holy anointing oil and the pure aromatic incense.

THE ALTAR OF WHOLE-BURNT-OFFERING

38 He made the Altar of Whole-Burnt-Offering from acacia wood. He made it seven and a half feet square and four and a half feet high. He made horns at each of the four corners. The horns were made of one piece with the Altar and covered with a veneer of bronze. He made from bronze all the utensils for the Altar: the buckets for removing the ashes, shovels, basins, forks, and fire pans. He made a grate of bronze mesh under the ledge halfway up the Altar. He cast four rings at each of the four corners of the bronze grating to hold the poles. He made the poles of acacia wood and covered them with a veneer of bronze. He inserted the poles through the rings on the two sides of the Altar for carrying it. The Altar was made out of boards; it was hollow.

THE WASHBASIN

He made the Bronze Washbasin and its bronze stand from the mirrors of the women's work group who were assigned to serve at the entrance to the Tent of Meeting.

THE COURTYARD

And he made the Courtyard. On the south side the hangings for the Courtyard, woven from fine twisted linen, were 150 feet long, with their twenty posts and twenty bronze bases, and fastening hooks and bands of silver. The north side was exactly the same.

The west end of the Courtyard had seventy-five feet of hangings with ten posts and bases, and fastening hooks and bands of silver. Across the seventy-five feet at the front, or east end, were twenty-two and a half feet of hangings, with their three posts and bases on one side and the same for the other side. All the hangings around the Courtyard were of fine twisted linen. The bases for the posts were bronze and the fastening hooks and bands on the posts were of silver. The posts of the Courtyard were both capped and banded with silver. The screen at the door of the Courtyard was embroidered in blue, purple, and scarlet fabric with fine twisted linen. It was thirty feet long and seven and a half feet high, matching the hangings of the Courtyard. There were four posts with bases of bronze and fastening hooks of silver; they were capped and banded in silver. All the pegs for The Dwelling and the Courtyard were made of bronze.

✠

This is an inventory of The Dwelling that housed The Testimony drawn up by order of Moses for the work of the Levites under Ithamar, son of Aaron the priest. Bezalel, the son of Uri, son of Hur, of the tribe of Judah, made everything that GOD had commanded Moses. Working with Bezalel was Oholiab, the son of Ahisamach, of the tribe of Dan, an artisan, designer, and embroiderer in blue, purple, and scarlet fabrics and fine linen.

Gold. The total amount of gold used in construction of the Sanctuary, all of it contributed freely, weighed out at 1,900 pounds according to the Sanctuary standard.

Silver. The silver from those in the community who were registered in the census came to 6,437 pounds according to the Sanctuary
standard—that amounted to a *beka*, or half-shekel, for every registered
person aged twenty and over, a total of 603,550 men. They used the
three and three-quarters tons of silver to cast the bases for the Sanctuary
and for the hangings, one hundred bases at sixty-four pounds each.
They used the remaining forty-five pounds to make the connecting
hooks on the posts, and the caps and bands for the posts.

Bronze. The bronze that was brought in weighed 4,522 pounds. It
was used to make the door of the Tent of Meeting, the Bronze Altar
with its bronze grating, all the utensils of the Altar, the bases around
the Courtyard, the bases for the gate of the Courtyard, and all the pegs
for The Dwelling and the Courtyard.

39 Vestments. Using the blue, purple, and scarlet fabrics, they made the woven vestments for ministering in the Sanctuary. Also they made the sacred vestments for Aaron, as GOD had commanded Moses.

Ephod. They made the Ephod using gold and blue, purple, and
scarlet fabrics and finely twisted linen. They hammered out gold leaf
and sliced it into threads that were then worked into designs in the blue,
purple, and scarlet fabric and fine linen. They made shoulder pieces fastened at the two ends. The decorated band was made of the same material—gold, blue, purple, and scarlet material, and of fine twisted
linen—and of one piece with it, just as GOD had commanded Moses.

They mounted the onyx stones in a setting of filigreed gold and
engraved the names of the sons of Israel on them, then fastened them
on the shoulder pieces of the Ephod as memorial stones for the Israelites,
just as GOD had commanded Moses.

Breastpiece. They made a Breastpiece designed like the Ephod from
gold, blue, purple, and scarlet material and fine twisted linen. Doubled,
the Breastpiece was nine inches square. They mounted four rows of
precious gemstones on it.

First row: carnelian, topaz, emerald.

Second row: ruby, sapphire, crystal.

Third row: jacinth, agate, amethyst.

Fourth row: beryl, onyx, jasper.

The stones were mounted in a gold filigree. The twelve stones cor-
responded to the names of the sons of Israel, twelve names engraved
as on a seal, one for each of the twelve tribes.

They made braided chains of pure gold for the Breastpiece, like cords. They made two settings of gold filigree and two rings of gold, put the two rings at the two ends of the Breastpiece, and fastened the two ends of the cords to the two rings at the end of the Breastpiece. Then they fastened the cords to the settings of filigree, attaching them to the shoulder pieces of the Ephod in front. Then they made two rings of gold and fastened them to the two ends of the Breastpiece on its inside edge facing the Ephod. They made two more rings of gold and fastened them in the front of the Ephod to the lower part of the two shoulder pieces, near the seam above the decorated band of the Ephod. The Breastpiece was fastened by running a cord of blue through its rings to the rings of the Ephod so that it rested secure on the decorated band of the Ephod and wouldn't come loose, just as GOD had commanded Moses.

Robe. They made the robe for the Ephod entirely of blue. The opening of the robe at the center was like a collar, the edge hemmed so that it wouldn't tear. On the hem of the robe they made pomegranates of blue, purple, and scarlet material and fine twisted linen. They also made bells of pure gold and alternated the bells and pomegranates —a bell and a pomegranate, a bell and a pomegranate—all around the hem of the robe that was worn for ministering, just as GOD had commanded Moses.

They also made the tunics of fine linen, the work of a weaver, for Aaron and his sons, the turban of fine linen, the linen hats, the linen underwear made of fine twisted linen, and sashes of fine twisted linen, blue, purple, and scarlet material and embroidered, just as GOD had commanded Moses.

They made the plate, the sacred crown, of pure gold and engraved on it as on a seal: "Holy to GOD." They attached a blue cord to it and fastened it to the turban, just as GOD had commanded Moses.

That completed the work of The Dwelling, the Tent of Meeting. The People of Israel did what GOD had commanded Moses. They did it all.

They presented The Dwelling to Moses, the Tent and all its furnishings:

fastening hooks
frames
crossbars
posts
bases
tenting of tanned ram skins

tenting of dolphin skins
veil of the screen
Chest of The Testimony
    with its poles
    and Atonement-Cover
Table
    with its utensils
    and the Bread of the Presence
Lampstand of pure gold
    and its lamps all fitted out
    and all its utensils
    and the oil for the light
Gold Altar
anointing oil
fragrant incense
screen for the entrance to the Tent
Bronze Altar
    with its bronze grate
    its poles and all its utensils
Washbasin
    and its base
hangings for the Courtyard
    its posts and bases
screen for the gate of the Courtyard
    its cords and its pegs
utensils for ministry in The Dwelling, the Tent of Meeting
    woven vestments for ministering in the Sanctuary
sacred vestments for Aaron the priest,
    and his sons when serving as priests

The Israelites completed all the work, just as GOD had commanded. Moses saw that they had done all the work and done it exactly as GOD had commanded. Moses blessed them.

"MOSES FINISHED THE WORK"

40 GOD spoke to Moses: "On the first day of the first month, set up The Dwelling, the Tent of Meeting. Place the Chest of The Testimony in it and screen the Chest with the curtain.

"Bring in the Table and set it, arranging its Lampstand and lamps.

"Place the Gold Altar of Incense before the Chest of The Testimony and hang the curtain at the door of The Dwelling.

"Place the Altar of Whole-Burnt-Offering at the door of The Dwelling, the Tent of Meeting.

"Place the Washbasin between the Tent of Meeting and the Altar and fill it with water.

"Set up the Courtyard on all sides and hang the curtain at the entrance to the Courtyard.

"Then take the anointing oil and anoint The Dwelling and everything in it; consecrate it and all its furnishings so that it becomes holy. Anoint the Altar of Whole-Burnt-Offering and all its utensils, consecrating the Altar so that it is completely holy. Anoint the Washbasin and its base: consecrate it.

"Finally, bring Aaron and his sons to the entrance of the Tent of Meeting and wash them with water. Dress Aaron in the sacred vestments. Anoint him. Consecrate him to serve me as priest. Bring his sons and put tunics on them. Anoint them, just as you anointed their father, to serve me as priests. Their anointing will bring them into a perpetual priesthood, down through the generations."

Moses did everything God commanded. He did it all.

On the first day of the first month of the second year, The Dwelling was set up. Moses set it up: He laid its bases, erected the frames, placed the crossbars, set the posts, spread the tent over The Dwelling, and put the covering over the tent, just as God had commanded Moses.

He placed The Testimony in the Chest, inserted the poles for carrying the Chest, and placed the lid, the Atonement-Cover, on it. He brought the Chest into The Dwelling and set up the curtain, screening off the Chest of The Testimony, just as God had commanded Moses.

He placed the Table in the Tent of Meeting on the north side of The Dwelling, outside the curtain, and arranged the Bread there before God, just as God had commanded him.

He placed the Lampstand in the Tent of Meeting opposite the Table on the south side of The Dwelling and set up the lamps before God, just as God had commanded him.

Moses placed the Gold Altar in the Tent of Meeting in front of the curtain and burned fragrant incense on it, just as God had commanded him.

He placed the screen at the entrance to The Dwelling.

He set the Altar of Whole-Burnt-Offering at the door of The Dwelling, the Tent of Meeting, and offered up the Whole-Burnt-Offerings and the Grain-Offerings, just as GOD had commanded Moses.

He placed the Washbasin between the Tent of Meeting and the Altar, and filled it with water for washing. Moses and Aaron and his sons washed their hands and feet there. When they entered the Tent of Meeting and when they served at the Altar, they washed, just as GOD had commanded Moses.

Finally, he erected the Courtyard all around The Dwelling and the Altar, and put up the screen for the Courtyard entrance.

Moses finished the work.

The Cloud covered the Tent of Meeting, and the Glory of GOD filled The Dwelling. Moses couldn't enter the Tent of Meeting because the Cloud was upon it, and the Glory of GOD filled The Dwelling.

Whenever the Cloud lifted from The Dwelling, the People of Israel set out on their travels, but if the Cloud did not lift, they wouldn't set out until it did lift. The Cloud of GOD was over The Dwelling during the day and the fire was in it at night, visible to all the Israelites in all their travels.

LEVITICUS

O ne of the stubbornly enduring habits of the human race is to insist on domesticating God. We are determined to tame him. We figure out ways to harness God to our projects. We try to reduce God to a size that conveniently fits our plans and ambitions and tastes.

But our Scriptures are even more stubborn in telling us that we can't do it. God cannot be fit into our plans, we must fit into his. We can't use God—God is not a tool or appliance or credit card.

"Holy" is the word that sets God apart and above our attempts to enlist him in our wish-fulfillment fantasies or our utopian schemes for making our mark in the world. Holy means that God is alive on God's terms, alive in a way that exceeds our experience and imagination. Holy refers to life burning with an intense purity that transforms everything it touches into itself.

Because the core of all living is God, and God is a holy God, we require much teaching and long training for living in response to God as he is and not as we want him to be. The book of Leviticus is a narrative pause in the story of our ancestors as they are on their way, saved out of Egypt, to settle in the land of Canaan. It is a kind of extended time-out of instruction, a detailed and meticulous preparation for living "holy" in a culture that doesn't have the faintest idea what "holy" is. The moment these people enter Canaan they will be picking their way through a lethal mine field of gods and goddesses that are designed to appeal to our god-fantasies: "Give us what we want when we want it on our own terms." What these god-fantasies in fact do is cripple or kill us. Leviticus is a start at the "much teaching and long training" that continues to be adapted and reworked in every country and culture where God is forming a saved people to live as he created them to live—holy as God is holy.

The first thing that strikes us as we read Leviticus in this light is that this holy God is actually present with us and virtually every detail of our lives is affected by the presence of this holy God; nothing in us, our relation-ships, or environment is left out. The second thing is that God provides a way (the sacrifices and feasts and Sabbaths) to bring everything in and about us into his holy presence, transformed in the fiery blaze of the holy. It is an awesome thing to come into his presence and we, like ancient Israel, stand in his presence at every moment (Psalm 139). Our Lord is not dwelling in a tent or house in our neighborhood. But he makes his habitation in us and among us as believers and says, "I am holy; you be holy" (1 Peter 1:16, citing Leviticus 11:44-45; 19:2; 20:7).

Once we realize this, the seemingly endless details and instructions of Leviticus become signposts of good news to us: God cares that much about the details of our lives, willing everything in and about us into the transformation that St. Paul later commended:

> So here's what I want you to do, God helping you: Take your everyday, ordinary life—your sleeping, eating, going-to-work, and walking-around life—and place it before God as an offering. Embracing what God does for you is the best thing you can do for him. Don't become so well-adjusted to your culture that you fit into it without even thinking. Instead, fix your attention on God. You'll be changed from the inside out. Readily recognize what he wants from you, and quickly respond to it. Unlike the culture around you, always dragging you down to its level of immaturity, God brings the best out of you, develops well-formed maturity in you. (Romans 12:1-2)

LEVITICUS

1 God called Moses and spoke to him from the Tent of Meeting: "Speak to the People of Israel. Tell them, When anyone presents an offering to God, present an animal from either the herd or the flock.

"If the offering is a Whole-Burnt-Offering from the herd, present a male without a defect at the entrance to the Tent of Meeting that it may be accepted by God. Lay your hand on the head of the Whole-Burnt-Offering so that it may be accepted on your behalf to make atonement for you. Slaughter the bull in God's presence. Aaron's sons, the priests, will make an offering of the blood by splashing it against all sides of the Altar that stands at the entrance to the Tent of Meeting. Next, skin the Whole-Burnt-Offering and cut it up. Aaron's sons, the priests, will prepare a fire on the Altar, carefully laying out the wood, and then arrange the body parts, including the head and the suet, on the wood prepared for the fire on the Altar. Scrub the entrails and legs clean. The priest will burn it all on the Altar: a Whole-Burnt-Offering, a Fire-Gift, a pleasing fragrance to God.

"If the Whole-Burnt-Offering comes from the flock, whether sheep or goat, present a male without defect. Slaughter it on the north side of the Altar in God's presence. The sons of Aaron, the priests, will throw the blood against all sides of the Altar. Cut it up and the priest will arrange the pieces, including the head and the suet, on the wood prepared for burning on the Altar. Scrub the entrails and legs clean. The priest will offer it all, burning it on the Altar: a Whole-Burnt-Offering, a Fire-Gift, a pleasing fragrance to God.

"If a bird is presented to God for the Whole-Burnt-Offering it can be either a dove or a pigeon. The priest will bring it to the Altar, wring off its head, and burn it on the Altar. But he will first drain the blood on the side of the Altar, remove the gizzard and its contents, and throw them on the east side of the Altar where the ashes are piled. Then rip it open by its wings but leave it in one piece and burn it on the Altar on the wood prepared for the fire: a Whole-Burnt-Offering, a Fire-Gift, a pleasing fragrance to God.

GRAIN-OFFERING

2 "When you present a Grain-Offering to GOD, use fine flour. Pour oil on it, put incense on it, and bring it to Aaron's sons, the priests. One of them will take a handful of the fine flour and oil, with all the incense, and burn it on the Altar for a memorial: a Fire-Gift, a pleasing fragrance to GOD. The rest of the Grain-Offering is for Aaron and his sons—a most holy part of the Fire-Gifts to GOD.

"When you present a Grain-Offering of oven-baked loaves, use fine flour, mixed with oil but no yeast. Or present wafers made without yeast and spread with oil.

"If you bring a Grain-Offering cooked on a griddle, use fine flour mixed with oil but without yeast. Crumble it and pour oil on it—it's a Grain-Offering.

"If you bring a Grain-Offering deep-fried in a pan, make it of fine flour with oil.

"Bring the Grain-Offering you make from these ingredients and present it to the priest. He will bring it to the Altar, break off a memorial piece from the Grain-Offering, and burn it on the Altar: a Fire Gift, a pleasing fragrance to GOD. The rest of the Grain-Offering is for Aaron and his sons—a most holy part of the gifts to GOD.

"All the Grain-Offerings that you present to GOD must be made without yeast; you must never burn any yeast or honey as a Fire-Gift to GOD. You may offer them to GOD as an offering of firstfruits but not on the Altar as a pleasing fragrance. Season every presentation of your Grain-Offering with salt. Don't leave the salt of the covenant with your God out of your Grain-Offerings. Present all your offerings with salt.

"If you present a Grain-Offering of firstfruits to GOD, bring crushed heads of the new grain roasted. Put oil and incense on it—it's a Grain-Offering. The priest will burn some of the mixed grain and oil with all the incense as a memorial—a Fire-Gift to GOD.

THE PEACE-OFFERING

3 "If your offering is a Peace-Offering and you present an animal from the herd, either male or female, it must be an animal without any defect. Lay your hand on the head of your offering and slaughter it at the entrance of the Tent of Meeting. Aaron's sons, the priests, will throw the blood on all sides of the Altar. As a Fire-Gift to GOD from the Peace-Offering, present all the fat that covers or is connected to the entrails, the

two kidneys and the fat around them at the loins, and the lobe of the liver that is removed along with the kidneys. Aaron and his sons will burn it on the Altar along with the Whole-Burnt-Offering that is on the wood prepared for the fire: a Fire-Gift, a pleasing fragrance to GOD.

"If your Peace-Offering to GOD comes from the flock, bring a male or female without defect. If you offer a lamb, offer it to GOD. Lay your hand on the head of your offering and slaughter it at the Tent of Meeting. The sons of Aaron will throw its blood on all sides of the Altar. As a Fire-Gift to GOD from the Peace-Offering, present its fat, the entire fat tail cut off close to the backbone, all the fat on and connected to the entrails, the two kidneys and the fat around them on the loins, and the lobe of the liver which is removed along with the kidneys. The priest will burn it on the Altar: a meal, a Fire-Gift to GOD.

"If the offering is a goat, bring it into the presence of GOD, lay your hand on its head and slaughter it in front of the Tent of Meeting. Aaron's sons will throw the blood on all sides of the Altar. As a Fire-Gift to GOD present the fat that covers and is connected to the entrails, the two kidneys and the fat which is around them on the loins, and the lobe of the liver which is removed along with the kidneys. The priest will burn them on the Altar: a meal, a Fire-Gift, a pleasing fragrance.

"All the fat belongs to GOD. This is the fixed rule down through the generations, wherever you happen to live: Don't eat the fat; don't eat the blood. None of it."

THE ABSOLUTION-OFFERING

4 GOD spoke to Moses, "Tell the Israelites: When a person sins unintentionally by straying from any of GOD's commands, breaking what must not be broken, if it's the anointed priest who sins and so brings guilt on the people, he is to bring a bull without defect to GOD as an Absolution-Offering for the sin he has committed. Have him bring the bull to the entrance of the Tent of Meeting in the presence of GOD, lay his hand on the bull's head, and slaughter the bull before GOD. He is then to take some of the bull's blood, bring it into the Tent of Meeting, dip his finger in the blood, and sprinkle some of it seven times before GOD, before the curtain of the Sanctuary. He is to smear some of the blood on the horns of the Altar of Fragrant Incense before GOD which is in the Tent of Meeting. He is to pour the rest of the bull's blood out at the base of the Altar of Whole-Burnt-Offering at the entrance of the Tent of Meeting. He is to remove all the fat from the bull of the

Absolution-Offering, the fat which covers and is connected to the entrails, the two kidneys and the fat that is around them at the loins, and the lobe of the liver which he takes out along with the kidneys — the same procedure as when the fat is removed from the bull of the Peace-Offering. Finally, he is to burn all this on the Altar of Burnt Offering. Everything else — the bull's hide, meat, head, legs, organs, and guts — he is to take outside the camp to a clean place where the ashes are dumped and is to burn it on a wood fire.

"If the whole congregation sins unintentionally by straying from one of the commandments of GOD that must not be broken, they become guilty even though no one is aware of it. When they do become aware of the sin they've committed, the congregation must bring a bull as an Absolution-Offering and present it at the Tent of Meeting. The elders of the congregation will lay their hands on the bull's head in the presence of GOD and one of them will slaughter it before GOD. The anointed priest will then bring some of the blood into the Tent of Meeting, dip his finger in the blood, and sprinkle some of it seven times before GOD in front of the curtain. He will smear some of the blood on the horns of the Altar which is before GOD in the Tent of Meeting and pour the rest of it at the base of the Altar of Whole-Burnt-Offering at the entrance of the Tent of Meeting. He will remove all the fat and burn it on the Altar. He will follow the same procedure with this bull as with the bull for the Absolution-Offering. The priest makes atonement for them and they are forgiven. They then will take the bull outside the camp and burn it just as they burned the first bull. It's the Absolution-Offering for the congregation.

"When a ruler sins unintentionally by straying from one of the commands of his GOD which must not be broken, he is guilty. When he becomes aware of the sin he has committed, he must bring a goat for his offering, a male without any defect, lay his hand on the head of the goat, and slaughter it in the place where they slaughter the Whole-Burnt-Offering in the presence of GOD — it's an Absolution-Offering. The priest will then take some of the blood of the Absolution-Offering with his finger, smear it on the horns of the Altar of Whole-Burnt-Offering, and pour the rest at the base of the Altar. He will burn all its fat on the Altar, the same as with the fat of the Peace-Offering.

"The priest makes atonement for him on account of his sin and he's forgiven.

"When an ordinary member of the congregation sins unintentionally, straying from one of the commandments of GOD which must not be broken, he is guilty. When he is made aware of his sin, he shall bring a goat, a female without any defect, and offer it for his sin, lay his hand on the head of the Absolution-Offering, and slaughter it at the place of the Whole-Burnt-Offering. The priest will take some of its blood with his finger, smear it on the horns of the Altar of Whole-Burnt-Offering, and pour the rest at the base of the Altar. Finally, he'll take out all the fat, the same as with the Peace-Offerings, and burn it on the Altar for a pleasing fragrance to GOD.

"In this way, the priest makes atonement for him and he's forgiven.

"If he brings a lamb for an Absolution-Offering, he shall present a female without any defect, lay his hand on the head of the Absolution-Offering, and slaughter it at the same place they slaughter the Whole-Burnt-Offering. The priest will take some of the blood of the Absolution-Offering with his finger, smear it on the horns of the Altar of Burnt-Offering, and pour the rest at the base of the Altar. He shall remove all the fat, the same as for the lamb of the Peace-Offering. Finally the priest will burn it on the Altar on top of the gifts to GOD.

"In this way, the priest makes atonement for him on account of his sin and he's forgiven.

✛

5 "If you sin by not stepping up and offering yourself as a witness to something you've heard or seen in cases of wrongdoing, you'll be held responsible.

"Or if you touch anything ritually unclean, like the carcass of an unclean animal, wild or domestic, or a dead reptile, and you weren't aware of it at the time, but you're contaminated and you're guilty;

"Or if you touch human uncleanness, any sort of ritually contaminating uncleanness, and you're not aware of it at the time, but later you realize it and you're guilty;

"Or if you impulsively swear to do something, whether good or bad—some rash oath that just pops out—and you aren't aware of what you've done at the time, but later you come to realize it and you're guilty in any of these cases;

"When you are guilty, immediately confess the sin that you've committed and bring as your penalty to GOD for the sin you have committed, a female lamb or goat from the flock for an Absolution-Offering.

"In this way, the priest will make atonement for your sin.

"If you can't afford a lamb, bring as your penalty to GOD for the sin you have committed, two doves or two pigeons, one for the Absolution-Offering and the other for the Whole-Burnt-Offering. Bring them to the priest who will first offer the one for the Absolution-Offering: He'll wring its neck but not sever it, splash some of the blood of the Absolution-Offering against the Altar, and squeeze the rest of it out at the base. It's an Absolution-Offering. He'll then take the second bird and offer it as a Whole-Burnt-Offering, following the procedures step by step.

"In this way, the priest will make atonement for your sin and you're forgiven.

"If you cannot afford the two doves or pigeons, bring two quarts of fine flour for your Absolution-Offering. Don't put oil or incense on it—it's an Absolution-Offering. Bring it to the priest; he'll take a handful from it as a memorial and burn it on the Altar with the gifts for GOD. It's an Absolution-Offering.

"The priest will make atonement for you and any of these sins you've committed and you're forgiven. The rest of the offering belongs to the priest, the same as with the Grain-Offering."

COMPENSATION-OFFERING

GOD spoke to Moses, "When a person betrays his trust and unknowingly sins by straying against any of the holy things of GOD, he is to bring as his penalty to GOD a ram without any defect from the flock, the value of the ram assessed in shekels, according to the Sanctuary shekel for a Compensation-Offering. He is to make additional compensation for the sin he has committed against any holy thing by adding twenty percent to the ram and giving it to the priest.

"Thus the priest will make atonement for him with the ram of the Compensation-Offering and he's forgiven.

"If anyone sins by breaking any of the commandments of GOD which must not be broken, but without being aware of it at the time, the moment he does realize his guilt he is held responsible. He is to bring to the priest a ram without any defect, assessed at the value of the Compensation-Offering.

"Thus the priest will make atonement for him for his error that he was unaware of and he's forgiven. It is a Compensation-Offering; he was surely guilty before God."

6 GOD spoke to Moses, "When anyone sins by betraying trust with GOD by deceiving his neighbor regarding something entrusted to

him, or by robbing or cheating or threatening him; or if he has found something lost and lies about it and swears falsely regarding any of these sins that people commonly commit—when he sins and is found guilty, he must return what he stole or extorted, restore what was entrusted to him, return the lost thing he found, or anything else about which he swore falsely. He must make full compensation, add twenty percent to it, and hand it over to the owner on the same day he brings his Compensation-Offering. He must present to GOD as his Compensation-Offering a ram without any defect from the flock, assessed at the value of a Compensation-Offering.

"Thus the priest will make atonement for him before GOD and he's forgiven of any of the things that one does that bring guilt."

FURTHER INSTRUCTIONS

GOD spoke to Moses, "Command Aaron and his sons. Tell them, These are the instructions for the Whole-Burnt-Offering. Leave the Whole-Burnt-Offering on the Altar hearth through the night until morning, with the fire kept burning on the Altar. Then dress in your linen clothes with linen underwear next to your body. Remove the ashes remaining from the Whole-Burnt-Offering and place them beside the Altar. Then change clothes and carry the ashes outside the camp to a clean place. Meanwhile keep the fire on the Altar burning; it must not go out. Replenish the wood for the fire every morning, arrange the Whole-Burnt-Offering on it, and burn the fat of the Peace-Offering on top of it all. Keep the fire burning on the Altar continuously. It must not go out.

✛

"These are the instructions for the Grain-Offering. Aaron's sons are to present it to GOD in front of the Altar. The priest takes a handful of the fine flour of the Grain-Offering with its oil and all its incense and burns this as a memorial on the Altar, a pleasing fragrance to GOD. Aaron and his sons eat the rest of it. It is unraised bread and so eaten in a holy place—in the Courtyard of the Tent of Meeting. They must not bake it with yeast. I have designated it as their share of the gifts presented to me. It is very holy, like the Absolution-Offering and the Compensation-Offering. Any male descendant among Aaron's sons may eat it. This is a fixed rule regarding GOD's gifts, stretching down the generations. Anyone who touches these offerings must be holy."

174

✠

God spoke to Moses, "This is the offering which Aaron and his sons each are to present to God on the day he is anointed: two quarts of fine flour as a regular Grain-Offering, half in the morning and half in the evening. Prepare it with oil on a griddle. Bring it well-mixed and then present it crumbled in pieces as a pleasing fragrance to God. Aaron's son who is anointed to succeed him offers it to God—this is a fixed rule. The whole thing is burned. Every Grain-Offering of a priest is burned completely; it must not be eaten."

✠

God spoke to Moses, "Tell Aaron and his sons: These are the instructions for the Absolution-Offering. Slaughter the Absolution-Offering in the place where the Whole-Burnt-Offering is slaughtered before God— the offering is most holy. The priest in charge eats it in a holy place, the Courtyard of the Tent of Meeting. Anyone who touches any of the meat must be holy. A garment that gets blood spattered on it must be washed in a holy place. Break the clay pot in which the meat was cooked. If it was cooked in a bronze pot, scour it and rinse it with water. Any male among the priestly families may eat it; it is most holy. But any Absolution-Offering whose blood is brought into the Tent of Meeting to make atonement in the Sanctuary must not be eaten, it has to be burned.

✠

7 "These are the instructions for the Compensation-Offering. It is most holy. Slaughter the Compensation-Offering in the same place that the Whole-Burnt-Offering is slaughtered. Splash its blood against all sides of the Altar. Offer up all the fat: the fat tail, the fat covering the entrails, the two kidneys and the fat encasing them at the loins, and the lobe of the liver that is removed with the kidneys. The priest burns them on the Altar as a gift to God. It is a Compensation-Offering. Any male from among the priests' families may eat it. But it must be eaten in a holy place; it is most holy.

"The Compensation-Offering is the same as the Absolution-Offering—the same rules apply to both. The offering belongs to the priest who makes atonement with it. The priest who presents a Whole-Burnt-Offering for someone gets the hide for himself. Every Grain-Offering baked in an oven or prepared in a pan or on a griddle belongs to the priest who presents it. It's his. Every Grain-Offering, whether dry or mixed with oil, belongs equally to all the sons of Aaron.

✝

"These are the instructions for the Peace-Offering which is presented to GOD. If you bring it to offer thanksgiving, then along with the Thanksgiving-Offering present unraised loaves of bread mixed with oil, unraised wafers spread with oil, and cakes of fine flour, well-kneaded and mixed with oil. Along with the Peace-Offering of thanksgiving, present loaves of yeast bread as an offering. Bring one of each kind as an offering, a Contribution-Offering to GOD; it goes to the priest who throws the blood of the Peace-Offering. Eat the meat from the Peace-Offering of thanksgiving the same day it is offered. Don't leave any of it overnight.

"If the offering is a Votive-Offering or a Freewill-Offering, it may be eaten the same day it is sacrificed and whatever is left over on the next day may also be eaten. But any meat from the sacrifice that is left to the third day must be burned up. If any of the meat from the Peace-Offering is eaten on the third day, the person who has brought it will not be accepted. It won't benefit him a bit—it has become defiled meat. And whoever eats it must take responsibility for his iniquity. Don't eat meat that has touched anything ritually unclean; burn it up. Any other meat can be eaten by those who are ritually clean. But if you're not ritually clean and eat meat from the Peace-Offering for GOD, you will be excluded from the congregation. And if you touch anything ritually unclean, whether human or animal uncleanness or an obscene object, and go ahead and eat from a Peace-Offering for GOD, you'll be excluded from the congregation."

✝

GOD spoke to Moses, "Speak to the People of Israel. Tell them, Don't eat any fat of cattle or sheep or goats. The fat of an animal found dead or torn by wild animals can be put to some other purpose, but you may not eat it. If you eat fat from an animal from which a gift has been presented to GOD, you'll be excluded from the congregation. And don't eat blood, whether of birds or animals, no matter where you end up living. If you eat blood you'll be excluded from the congregation."

✝

GOD spoke to Moses, "Speak to the People of Israel. Tell them: When you present a Peace-Offering to GOD, bring some of your Peace-Offering as a special sacrifice to GOD, a gift to GOD in your own hands. Bring the fat with the breast and then wave the breast before GOD as a Wave-Offering. The priest will burn the fat on the Altar; Aaron and his sons get the breast. Give the right thigh from your Peace-Offerings as a Contribution-Offering to the priest. Give a portion of the right thigh to the son of Aaron who offers the blood and fat of the Peace-Offering as his portion. From the Peace-Offerings of Israel, I'm giving the breast of the Wave-Offering and the thigh of the Contribution-Offering to Aaron the priest and his sons. This is their fixed compensation from the People of Israel."

From the day they are presented to serve as priests to GOD, Aaron and his sons can expect to receive these allotments from the gifts of GOD. This is what GOD commanded the People of Israel to give the priests from the day of their anointing. This is the fixed rule down through the generations.

These are the instructions for the Whole-Burnt-Offering, the Grain-Offering, the Absolution-Offering, the Compensation-Offering, the Ordination-Offering, and the Peace-Offering which GOD gave Moses at Mount Sinai on the day he commanded the People of Israel to present their offerings to GOD in the wilderness of Sinai.

THE ORDINATION OF PRIESTS

8 GOD spoke to Moses. He said, "Take Aaron and with him his sons, the garments, the anointing oil, the bull for the Absolution-Offering, the two rams, and the basket of unraised bread. Gather the entire congregation at the entrance of the Tent of Meeting." Moses did just as GOD commanded him and the congregation gathered at the entrance of the Tent of Meeting.

Moses addressed the congregation: "This is what GOD has commanded to be done."

Moses brought Aaron and his sons forward and washed them with water. He put the tunic on Aaron and tied it around him with a sash. Then he put the robe on him and placed the Ephod on him. He fastened the Ephod with a woven belt, making it snug. He put the Breastpiece on him and put the Urim and Thummim in the pouch of the Breastpiece. He placed the turban on his head with the gold plate fixed

177

to the front of it, the holy crown, just as GOD had commanded Moses.

Then Moses took the anointing oil and anointed The Dwelling and everything that was in it, consecrating them. He sprinkled some of the oil on the Altar seven times, anointing the Altar and all its utensils, the Washbasin and its stand, consecrating them. He poured some of the anointing oil on Aaron's head, anointing him and thus consecrating him.

Moses brought Aaron's sons forward and put tunics on them, belted them with sashes, and put caps on them, just as GOD had commanded Moses.

Moses brought out the bull for the Absolution-Offering. Aaron and his sons placed their hands on its head. Moses slaughtered the bull and purified the Altar by smearing the blood on each of the horns of the Altar with his finger. He poured out the rest of the blood at the base of the Altar. He consecrated it so atonement could be made on it. Moses took all the fat on the entrails and the lobe of liver and the two kidneys with their fat and burned it all on the Altar. The bull with its hide and meat and guts he burned outside the camp, just as GOD had commanded Moses.

Moses presented the ram for the Whole-Burnt-Offering. Aaron and his sons laid their hands on the head of the ram. Moses slaughtered it and splashed the blood against all sides of the Altar. He cut the ram up into pieces and then burned the head, the pieces, and the fat. He washed the entrails and the legs with water and then burned the whole ram on the Altar. It was a Whole-Burnt-Offering, a pleasing fragrance—a gift to GOD, just as GOD had commanded Moses.

Moses then presented the second ram, the ram for the Ordination-Offering. Aaron and his sons laid their hands on the ram's head. Moses slaughtered it and smeared some of its blood on the lobe of Aaron's right ear, on the thumb of his right hand, and on the big toe of his right foot. Then Aaron's sons were brought forward and Moses smeared some of the blood on the lobes of their right ears, on the thumbs of their right hands, and on the big toes of their right feet. Moses threw the remaining blood against each side of the Altar. He took the fat, the fat tail, all the fat that was on the entrails, the lobe of the liver, the two kidneys with their fat, and the right thigh. From the basket of unraised bread that was in the presence of GOD he took one loaf of the unraised bread made with oil and one wafer. He placed these on the fat portions and the right thigh. He put all this in the hands of Aaron and his sons who waved them before GOD as a Wave-Offering. Then Moses took it all back from their hands and burned them on the Altar on top of the Whole-Burnt-Offering. These were the Ordination-Offerings, a pleasing fragrance to GOD, a gift to GOD. Then Moses took the breast and raised it up as a Wave-Offering before GOD; it was Moses' portion from the Ordination-Offering ram, just as GOD had commanded Moses.

Moses took some of the anointing oil and some of the blood from the Altar and sprinkled Aaron and his garments, and his sons and their garments, consecrating Aaron and his garments and his sons and their garments.

Moses spoke to Aaron and his sons: "Boil the meat at the entrance of the Tent of Meeting and eat it there with the bread from the basket of ordination, just as I commanded, saying, 'Aaron and his sons are to eat it.' Burn up the leftovers from the meat and bread. Don't leave through the entrance of the Tent of Meeting for the seven days that will complete your ordination. Your ordination will last seven days. GOD commanded what has been done this day in order to make atonement for you. Stay at the entrance of the Tent of Meeting day and night for seven days. Be sure to do what GOD requires, lest you die. This is what I have been commanded."

Aaron and his sons did everything that GOD had commanded by Moses.

THE PRIESTS GO TO WORK

9 On the eighth day, Moses called in Aaron and his sons and the leaders of Israel. He spoke to Aaron: "Take a bull-calf for your Absolution-Offering and a ram for your Whole-Burnt-Offering, both without defect, and offer them to GOD.

"Then tell the People of Israel, Take a male goat for an Absolution-Offering and a calf and a lamb, both yearlings without defect, for a Whole-Burnt-Offering and a bull and a ram for a Peace-Offering, to be sacrificed before GOD with a Grain-Offering mixed with oil, because GOD will appear to you today."

They brought the things that Moses had ordered to the Tent of Meeting. The whole congregation came near and stood before GOD. Moses said, "This is what GOD commanded you to do so that the Shining Glory of GOD will appear to you."

Moses instructed Aaron, "Approach the Altar and sacrifice your Absolution-Offering and your Whole-Burnt-Offering. Make atonement for yourself and for the people. Sacrifice the offering that is for the people and make atonement for them, just as GOD commanded."

Aaron approached the Altar and slaughtered the calf as an Absolution-Offering for himself. Aaron's sons brought the blood to him. He dipped his finger in the blood and smeared some of it on the horns of the Altar. He poured out the rest of the blood at the base of the Altar. He burned the fat, the kidneys, and the lobe of the liver from the Absolution-Offering on the Altar, just as GOD had commanded Moses. He burned the meat and the skin outside the camp.

Then he slaughtered the Whole-Burnt-Offering. Aaron's sons handed him the blood and he threw it against each side of the Altar. They handed him the pieces and the head and he burned these on the Altar. He washed the entrails and the legs and burned them on top of the Whole-Burnt-Offering on the Altar.

Next Aaron presented the offerings of the people. He took the male goat, the Absolution-Offering for the people, slaughtered it, and offered it as an Absolution-Offering just as he did with the first offering. He presented the Whole-Burnt-Offering following the same procedures. He presented the Grain-Offering by taking a handful of it and burning it on the Altar along with the morning Whole-Burnt-Offering. He slaughtered the bull and the ram, the people's Peace-Offerings. Aaron's sons handed him the blood and he threw it against each side of the Altar. The fat pieces from the bull and the ram—the fat tail and the fat that covers the kidney and the lobe of the liver—they laid on the breasts and Aaron burned it on the Altar. Aaron waved the breasts and the right thigh before GOD as a Wave-Offering, just as GOD commanded.

Aaron lifted his hands over the people and blessed them. Having completed the rituals of the Absolution-Offering, the Whole-Burnt-Offering, and the Peace-Offering, he came down from the Altar. Moses and Aaron entered the Tent of Meeting. When they came out they blessed the people and the Glory of GOD appeared to all the people. Fire blazed out from GOD and consumed the Whole-Burnt-Offering and the fat pieces on the Altar. When all the people saw it happen they cheered loudly and then fell down, bowing in reverence.

NADAB AND ABIHU

10 That same day Nadab and Abihu, Aaron's sons, took their censers, put hot coals and incense in them, and offered "strange" fire to GOD—something GOD had not commanded. Fire blazed out from GOD and consumed them—they died in GOD's presence.

Moses said to Aaron, "This is what GOD meant when he said,

To the one who comes near me,
    I will show myself holy;
Before all the people,
    I will show my glory."

Aaron was silent.

Moses called for Mishael and Elzaphan, sons of Uzziel, Aaron's uncle. He said, "Come. Carry your dead cousins outside the camp, away from the Sanctuary." They came and carried them off, outside the camp, just as Moses had directed.

Moses then said to Aaron and his remaining sons, Eleazar and Ithamar, "No mourning rituals for you—unkempt hair, torn clothes—or you'll also die and GOD will be angry with the whole congregation. Your relatives—all the People of Israel, in fact—will do the mourning over those GOD has destroyed by fire. And don't leave the entrance to the Tent of Meeting lest you die, because GOD's anointing oil is on you."

They did just as Moses said.

✝

GOD instructed Aaron, "When you enter the Tent of Meeting, don't drink wine or strong drink, neither you nor your sons, lest you die. This is a fixed rule down through the generations. Distinguish between the holy and the common, between the ritually clean and unclean. Teach the People of Israel all the decrees that GOD has spoken to them through Moses."

Moses spoke to Aaron and his surviving sons, Eleazar and Ithamar, "Take the leftovers of the Grain-Offering from the Fire-Gifts for GOD and eat beside the Altar that which has been prepared without yeast, for it is most holy. Eat it in the Holy Place because it is your portion and the portion of your sons from the Fire-Gifts for GOD. This is what GOD commanded me. Also, you and your sons and daughters are to eat the breast of the Wave-Offering and the thigh of the Contribution-Offering in a clean place. They are provided as your portion and the portion of your children from the Peace-Offerings presented by the People of Israel. Bring the thigh of the Contribution-Offering and the breast of the Wave-Offering and the fat pieces of the Fire-Gifts and lift them up as a Wave-Offering. This will be the regular share for you and your children as ordered by GOD."

When Moses looked into the matter of the goat of the Absolution-Offering, he found that it had been burned up. He became angry with Eleazar and Ithamar, Aaron's remaining sons, and asked, "Why didn't you eat the Absolution-Offering in the Holy Place since it is most holy? The offering was given to you for taking away the guilt of the community by making atonement for them before GOD. Since its blood was not taken into the Holy Place, you should have eaten the goat in the Sanctuary as I commanded."

Aaron replied to Moses, "Look. They sacrificed their Absolution-Offering and Whole-Burnt-Offering before GOD today, and you see what has happened to me—I've lost two sons. Do you think GOD would have been pleased if I had gone ahead and eaten the Absolution-Offering today?"

When Moses heard this response, he accepted it.

FOODS

11 GOD spoke to Moses and Aaron: "Speak to the People of Israel. Tell them: Of all the animals on Earth, these are the animals that you may eat:

"You may eat any animal that has a split hoof, divided in two, and that chews the cud, but not an animal that only chews the cud or only has a split hoof. For instance, the camel chews the cud but doesn't have a split hoof, so it's unclean. The rock badger chews the cud but doesn't have a split hoof and so it's unclean. The rabbit chews the cud but doesn't have a split hoof so is unclean. The pig has a split hoof, divided in two, but doesn't chew the cud and so is unclean. You may not eat their meat nor touch their carcasses; they are unclean to you.

"Among the creatures that live in the water of the seas and streams, you may eat any that have fins and scales. But anything that doesn't have fins and scales, whether in seas or streams, whether small creatures in the shallows or huge creatures in the deeps, you are to detest. Yes, detest them. Don't eat their meat; detest their carcasses. Anything living in the water that doesn't have fins and scales is detestable to you.

"These are the birds you are to detest. Don't eat them. They are detestable: eagle, vulture, osprey, kite, all falcons, all ravens, ostrich, nighthawk, sea gull, all hawks, owl, cormorant, ibis, water hen, pelican, Egyptian vulture, stork, all herons, hoopoe, bat.

"All flying insects that walk on all fours are detestable to you. But you can eat some of these, namely, those that have jointed legs for hopping on the ground: all locusts, katydids, crickets, and grasshoppers. But all the other flying insects that have four legs you are to detest.

"You will make yourselves ritually unclean until evening if you touch their carcasses. If you pick up one of their carcasses you must wash your clothes and you'll be unclean until evening.

"Every animal that has a split hoof that's not completely divided, or that doesn't chew the cud is unclean for you; if you touch the carcass of any of them you become unclean.

"Every four-footed animal that goes on its paws is unclean for you; if you touch its carcass you are unclean until evening. If you pick up its carcass you must wash your clothes and are unclean until evening. They are unclean for you.

"Among the creatures that crawl on the ground, the following are unclean for you: weasel, rat, all lizards, gecko, monitor lizard, wall lizard, skink, chameleon. Among the crawling creatures, these are unclean for you. If you touch them when they are dead, you are ritually unclean until evening. When one of them dies and falls on something, that becomes unclean no matter what it's used for, whether it's made of wood, cloth, hide, or sackcloth. Put it in the water—it's unclean until evening, and then it's clean. If one of these dead creatures falls into a clay pot, everything in the pot is unclean and you must break the pot. Any food that could be eaten but has water on it from such a pot is unclean, and any liquid that could be drunk from it is unclean. Anything that one of these carcasses falls on is unclean—an oven or cooking pot must be broken up; they're unclean and must be treated as unclean. A spring, though, or a cistern for collecting water remains clean, but if you touch one of these carcasses you're ritually unclean. If a carcass falls on any seeds that are to be planted, they remain clean. But if water has been put on the seed and a carcass falls on it, you must treat it as unclean.

"If an animal that you are permitted to eat dies, anyone who touches the carcass is ritually unclean until evening. If you eat some of the carcass you must wash your clothes and you are unclean until evening. If you pick up the carcass you must wash your clothes and are unclean until evening.

"Creatures that crawl on the ground are detestable and not to be eaten. Don't eat creatures that crawl on the ground, whether on their belly or on all fours or on many feet—they are detestable. Don't make yourselves unclean or be defiled by them, because I am your GOD.

183

"Make yourselves holy for I am holy. Don't make yourselves ritually unclean by any creature that crawls on the ground. I am GOD who brought you up out of the land of Egypt. Be holy because I am holy.

"These are the instructions on animals, birds, fish, and creatures that crawl on the ground. You have to distinguish between the ritually unclean and the clean, between living creatures that can be eaten and those that cannot be eaten."

CHILDBIRTH

12 GOD spoke to Moses: "Tell the People of Israel: A woman who conceives and gives birth to a boy is ritually unclean for seven days, the same as during her menstruation. On the eighth day circumcise the boy. The mother must stay home another thirty-three days for purification from her bleeding. She may not touch anything consecrated or enter the Sanctuary until the days of her purification are complete. If she gives birth to a girl, she is unclean for fourteen days, the same as during her menstruation. She must stay home for sixty-six days for purification from her bleeding.

"When the days for her purification for either a boy or a girl are complete, she will bring a yearling lamb for a Whole-Burnt-Offering and a pigeon or dove for an Absolution-Offering to the priest at the entrance of the Tent of Meeting. He will offer it to GOD and make atonement for her. She is then clean from her flow of blood.

"These are the instructions for a woman who gives birth to either a boy or a girl.

"If she can't afford a lamb, she can bring two doves or two pigeons, one for the Whole-Burnt-Offering and one for the Absolution-Offering. The priest will make atonement for her and she will be clean."

INFECTIONS

13 GOD spoke to Moses and Aaron, "When someone has a swelling or a blister or a shiny spot on the skin that might signal a serious skin disease on the body, bring him to Aaron the priest or to one of his priest sons. The priest will examine the sore on the skin. If the hair in the sore has turned white and the sore appears more than skin deep, it is a serious skin disease and infectious. After the priest has examined it, he will pronounce the person unclean.

"If the shiny spot on the skin is white but appears to be only on the surface and the hair has not turned white, the priest will quarantine the person for seven days. On the seventh day the priest will examine it again; if, in his judgment, the sore is the same and has not spread, the priest will keep him in quarantine for another seven days. On the seventh day the priest will examine him a second time; if the sore has faded and hasn't spread, the priest will declare him clean—it is a harmless rash. The person can go home and wash his clothes; he is clean. But if the sore spreads after he has shown himself to the priest and been declared clean, he must come back again to the priest who will conduct another examination. If the sore has spread, the priest will pronounce him unclean—it is a serious skin disease and infectious.

"Whenever someone has a serious and infectious skin disease, you must bring him to the priest. The priest will examine him; if there is a white swelling in the skin, the hair is turning white, and there is an open sore in the swelling, it is a chronic skin disease. The priest will pronounce him unclean. But he doesn't need to quarantine him because he's already given his diagnosis of unclean. If a serious disease breaks out that covers all the skin from head to foot, wherever the priest looks, the priest will make a thorough examination; if the disease covers his entire body, he will pronounce the person with the sore clean—since it has turned all white, he is clean. But if they are open, running sores, he is unclean. The priest will examine the open sores and pronounce him unclean. The open sores are unclean; they are evidence of a serious skin disease. But if the open sores dry up and turn white, he is to come back to the priest who will reexamine him; if the sores have turned white, the priest will pronounce the person with the sores clean. He is clean.

"When a person has a boil and it heals and in place of the boil there is white swelling or a reddish-white shiny spot, the person must present himself to the priest for an examination. If it looks like it has penetrated the skin and the hair in it has turned white, the priest will pronounce him unclean. It is a serious skin disease that has broken out in the boil. But if the examination shows that there is no white hair in it and it is only skin deep and has faded, the priest will put him in quarantine for seven days. If it then spreads over the skin, the priest will diagnose him as unclean. It is infectious. But if the shiny spot has not changed and hasn't spread, it's only a scar from the boil. The priest will pronounce him clean.

"When a person has a burn on his skin and the raw flesh turns into a reddish-white or white shiny spot, the priest is to examine it. If the hair has turned white in the shiny spot and it looks like it's more than skin deep, a serious skin disease has erupted in the area of the burn. The priest will pronounce him unclean; it is a serious skin disease and infectious. But if on examination there is no white hair in the shiny spot and it doesn't look to be more than skin deep but has faded, the priest will put him in quarantine for seven days. On the seventh day the priest will reexamine him. If by then it has spread over the skin, the priest will diagnose him as unclean; it is a serious skin disease and infectious. If by that time the shiny spot has stayed the same and has not spread but has faded, it is only a swelling from the burn. The priest will pronounce him clean; it's only a scar from the burn.

"If a man or woman develops a sore on the head or chin, the priest will offer a diagnosis. If it looks as if it is under the skin and the hair in it is yellow and thin, he will pronounce the person ritually unclean. It is an itch, an infectious skin disease. But if when he examines the itch, he finds it is only skin deep and there is no black hair in it, he will put the person in quarantine for seven days. On the seventh day he will reexamine the sore; if the itch has not spread, there is no yellow hair in it, and it looks as if the itch is only skin deep, the person must shave, except for the itch; the priest will send him back to quarantine for another seven days. If the itch has not spread, and looks to be only skin deep, the priest will pronounce him clean. The person can go home and wash his clothes; he is clean. But if the itch spreads after being pronounced clean, the priest must reexamine it; if the itch has spread in the skin, he doesn't have to look any farther, for yellow hair, for instance; he is unclean. But if he sees that the itch is unchanged and black hair has begun to grow in it, the itch is healed. The person is clean and the priest will pronounce him clean.

"When a man or woman gets shiny or white shiny spots on the skin, the priest is to make an examination; if the shiny spots are dull white, it is only a rash that has broken out: The person is clean.

"When a man loses his hair and goes bald, he is clean. If he loses his hair from his forehead, he is bald and he is clean. But if he has a reddish-white sore on scalp or forehead, it means a serious skin disease is breaking out. The priest is to examine it; if the swollen sore on his scalp or forehead is reddish-white like the appearance of the sore of a serious skin disease, he has a serious skin disease and is unclean. The priest has to pronounce him unclean because of the sore on his head.

"Any person with a serious skin disease must wear torn clothes, leave his hair loose and unbrushed, cover his upper lip, and cry out, 'Unclean! Unclean!' As long as anyone has the sores, that one continues to be ritually unclean. That person must live alone; he or she must live outside the camp.

✛

"If clothing—woolen or linen clothing, woven or knitted cloth of linen or wool, leather or leatherwork—is infected with a patch of serious fungus and if the spot in the clothing or the leather or the woven or the knitted material or anything made of leather is greenish or rusty, that is a sign of serious fungus. Show it to the priest. The priest will examine the spot and then confiscate the material for seven days. On the seventh day he will reexamine the spot. If it has spread in the garment—the woven or knitted or leather material—it is the spot of a persistent serious fungus and the material is unclean. He must burn the garment. Because of the persistent and contaminating fungus, the material must be burned. But if when the priest examines it the spot has not spread in the garment, the priest will command the owner to wash the material that has the spot, and he will confiscate it for another seven days. He'll then make another examination after it has been washed; if the spot hasn't changed in appearance, even though it hasn't spread, it is still unclean. Burn it up, whether the fungus has affected the back or the front. If, when the priest makes his examination, the spot has faded after it has been washed, he is to tear the spot from the garment. But if it reappears, it is a fresh outbreak—throw whatever has the spot in the fire. If the garment is washed and the spot has gone away, then wash it a second time; it is clean.

"These are the instructions regarding a spot of serious fungus in clothing of wool or linen, woven or knitted material, or any article of leather, for pronouncing them clean or unclean."

✛

14 GOD spoke to Moses, "These are the instructions for the infected person at the time of his cleansing. First, bring him to the priest. The priest will take him outside the camp and make an examination; if the infected person has been healed of the serious skin disease, the priest will order two live, clean birds, some cedar wood, scarlet thread, and hyssop to be brought for the one to be cleansed. The priest will

187

order him to kill one of the birds over fresh water in a clay pot. The priest will then take the live bird with the cedar wood, the scarlet thread, and the hyssop and dip them in the blood of the dead bird over fresh water and then sprinkle the person being cleansed from the serious skin disease seven times and pronounce him clean. Finally, he will release the live bird in the open field. The cleansed person, after washing his clothes, shaving off all his hair, and bathing with water, is clean. Afterwards he may again enter the camp, but he has to live outside his tent for seven days. On the seventh day, he must shave off all his hair—from his head, beard, eyebrows, all of it. He then must wash his clothes and bathe all over with water. He will be clean.

"The next day, the eighth day, he will bring two lambs without defect and a yearling ewe without defect, along with roughly six quarts of fine flour mixed with oil. The priest who pronounces him clean will place him and the materials for his offerings in the presence of GOD at the entrance to the Tent of Meeting. The priest will take one of the lambs and present it and the pint of oil as a Compensation-Offering and lift them up as a Wave-Offering before GOD. He will slaughter the lamb in the place where the Absolution-Offering and the Whole-Burnt-Offering are slaughtered, in the Holy Place, because like the Absolution-Offering, the Compensation-Offering belongs to the priest; it is most holy. The priest will now take some of the blood of the Compensation-Offering and put it on the right earlobe of the man being cleansed, on the thumb of his right hand, and on the big toe of his right foot. Following that he will take some oil and pour it into the palm of his left hand and then with the finger of his right hand sprinkle oil seven times before GOD. The priest will put some of the remaining oil on the right earlobe of the one being cleansed, on the thumb of his right hand, and on the big toe of his right foot, placing it on top of the blood of the Compensation-Offering. He will put the rest of the oil on the head of the man being cleansed and make atonement for him before GOD.

"Finally the priest will sacrifice the Absolution-Offering and make atonement for the one to be cleansed from his uncleanness, slaughter the Whole-Burnt-Offering and offer it with the Grain-Offering on the Altar. He has made atonement for him. He is clean.

"If he is poor and cannot afford these offerings, he will bring one male lamb as a Compensation-Offering to be offered as a Wave-Offering to make atonement for him, and with it a couple of quarts of fine flour mixed with oil for a Grain-Offering, a pint of oil, and two doves or pigeons which he can afford, one for an Absolution-Offering and the other for a Whole-Burnt-Offering.

"On the eighth day he will bring them to the priest at the entrance to the Tent of Meeting before the presence of GOD. The priest will take the lamb for the Compensation-Offering together with the pint of oil and wave them before GOD as a Wave-Offering. He will slaughter the lamb for the Compensation-Offering, take some of its blood and put it on the lobe of the right ear of the one to be cleansed, on the thumb of his right hand, and on the big toe of his right foot. The priest will pour some of the oil into the palm of his left hand, and with his right finger sprinkle some of the oil from his palm seven times before GOD. He will put some of the oil that is in his palm on the same places he put the blood of the Compensation-Offering, on the lobe of the right ear of the one to be cleansed, on the thumb of his right hand, and on the big toe of his right foot. The priest will take what is left of the oil in his palm and put it on the head of the one to be cleansed, making atonement for him before GOD.

"At the last, he will sacrifice the doves or pigeons which are within his means, one as an Absolution-Offering and the other as a Whole-Burnt-Offering along with the Grain-Offering. Following this procedure the priest will make atonement for the one to be cleansed before GOD."

These are the instructions to be followed for anyone who has a serious skin disease and cannot afford the regular offerings for his cleansing.

✠

GOD spoke to Moses and Aaron, "When you enter the land of Canaan, which I'm giving to you as a possession, and I put a serious fungus in a house in the land of your possession, the householder is to go and tell the priest, 'I have some kind of fungus in my house.' The priest is to order the house vacated until he can come to examine the fungus, so that nothing in the house is declared unclean. When the priest comes and examines the house, if the fungus on the walls of the house has greenish or rusty swelling that appears to go deeper than the surface of the wall, the priest is to walk out the door and shut the house up for seven days. On the seventh day he is to come back and conduct another examination; if the fungus has spread in the walls of the house, he is to order that the stones affected by the fungus be torn out and thrown in a garbage dump outside the city. He is to make sure the entire inside of the house is scraped and the plaster that is removed be taken away to the garbage dump outside the city. Then he is to replace the stones and replaster the house.

"If the fungus breaks out again in the house after the stones have been torn out and the house has been scraped and plastered, the priest is to come and conduct an examination; if the fungus has spread, it is a malignant fungus. The house is unclean. The house has to be demolished—its stones, wood, and plaster are to be removed to the garbage dump outside the city. Anyone who enters the house while it is closed up is unclean until evening. Anyone who sleeps or eats in the house must wash his clothes.

"But if when the priest comes and conducts his examination, he finds that the fungus has not spread after the house has been replastered, the priest is to declare that the house is clean; the fungus is cured. He then is to purify the house by taking two birds, some cedar wood, scarlet thread, and hyssop. He will slaughter one bird over fresh water in a clay pot. Then he will take the cedar wood, the hyssop, the scarlet thread, and the living bird, dip them in the blood of the killed bird and the fresh water and sprinkle the house seven times, cleansing the house with the blood of the bird, the fresh water, the living bird, the cedar wood, the hyssop, and the scarlet thread. Last of all, he will let the living bird loose outside the city in the open field. He has made atonement for the house; the house is clean.

"These are the procedures to be followed for every kind of serious skin disease or itch, for mildew or fungus on clothing or in a house, and for a swelling or blister or shiny spot in order to determine when it is unclean and when it is clean. These are the procedures regarding infectious skin diseases and mildew and fungus."

BODILY DISCHARGES

15 GOD spoke to Moses and Aaron, "Speak to the People of Israel. Tell them: When a man has a discharge from his genitals, the discharge is unclean. Whether it comes from a seepage or an obstruction he is unclean. He is unclean all the days his body has a seepage or an obstruction.

"Every bed on which he lies is ritually unclean, everything on which he sits is unclean. If someone touches his bed or sits on anything he's sat on, or touches the man with the discharge, he has to wash his clothes and bathe in water; he remains unclean until evening.

"If the man with the discharge spits on someone who is clean, that person has to wash his clothes and bathe in water; he remains unclean until evening. Every saddle on which the man with the discharge rides is unclean. Whoever touches anything that has been under him becomes unclean until evening. Anyone who carries such an object must wash his clothes and bathe with water; he remains unclean until evening. If the one with the discharge touches someone without first rinsing his hands with water, the one touched must wash his clothes and bathe with water; he remains unclean until evening.

"If a pottery container is touched by someone with a discharge, you must break it; a wooden article is to be rinsed in water.

"When a person with a discharge is cleansed from it, he is to count off seven days for his cleansing, wash his clothes, and bathe in running water. Then he is clean. On the eighth day he is to take two doves or two pigeons and come before GOD at the entrance of the Tent of Meeting and give them to the priest. The priest then offers one as an Absolution-Offering and one as a Whole-Burnt-Offering and makes atonement for him in the presence of GOD because of his discharge.

"When a man has an emission of semen, he must bathe his entire body in water; he remains unclean until evening. Every piece of clothing and everything made of leather which gets semen on it must be washed with water; it remains unclean until evening. When a man sleeps with a woman and has an emission of semen, both are to wash in water; they remain unclean until evening.

"When a woman has a discharge of blood, the impurity of her menstrual period lasts seven days. Anyone who touches her is unclean until evening. Everything on which she lies or sits during her period is unclean. Anyone who touches her bed or anything on which she sits must wash his clothes and bathe in water; he remains unclean until evening.

"If a man sleeps with her and her menstrual blood gets on him, he is unclean for seven days and every bed on which he lies becomes unclean.

"If a woman has a discharge of blood for many days, but not at the time of her monthly period, or has a discharge that continues beyond the time of her period, she is unclean the same as during the time of her period. Every bed on which she lies during the time of the discharge and everything on which she sits becomes unclean the same as in her monthly period. Anyone who touches these things becomes unclean and must wash his clothes and bathe in water; he remains unclean until evening.

"When she is cleansed from her discharge, she is to count off seven days; then she is clean. On the eighth day she is to take two doves and two pigeons and bring them to the priest at the entrance to the Tent of Meeting. The priest will offer one for an Absolution-Offering and the other for a Whole-Burnt-Offering. The priest will make atonement for her in the presence of GOD because of the discharge that made her unclean.

"You are responsible for keeping the People of Israel separate from that which makes them ritually unclean, lest they die in their unclean condition by defiling my Dwelling which is among them.

"These are the procedures to follow for a man with a discharge or an emission of semen that makes him unclean, and for a woman in her menstrual period—any man or woman with a discharge and also for a man who sleeps with a woman who is unclean."

THE DAY OF ATONEMENT

16 After the death of Aaron's two sons—they died when they came before GOD with strange fire—GOD spoke to Moses: "Tell your brother Aaron not to enter into the Holy of Holies, barging inside the curtain that's before the Atonement-Cover on the Chest whenever he feels like it, lest he die, because I am present in the Cloud over the Atonement-Cover.

"This is the procedure for Aaron when he enters the Holy Place: He will bring a young bull for an Absolution-Offering and a ram for a Whole-Burnt-Offering; he will put on the holy linen tunic and the linen underwear, tie the linen sash around him, and put on the linen turban. These are the sacred vestments so he must bathe himself with water before he puts them on. Then from the Israelite community he will bring two male goats for an Absolution-Offering and a Whole-Burnt-Offering.

"Aaron will offer the bull for his own Absolution-Offering in order to make atonement for himself and his household. Then he will set the two goats before GOD at the entrance to the Tent of Meeting and cast lots over the two goats, one lot for GOD and the other lot for Azazel. He will offer the goat on which the lot to GOD falls as an Absolution-Offering. The goat on which the lot for Azazel falls will be sent out into the wilderness to Azazel to make atonement.

"Aaron will present his bull for an Absolution-Offering to make atonement for himself and his household. He will slaughter his bull for the Absolution-Offering. He will take a censer full of burning coals from the Altar before GOD and two handfuls of finely ground aromatic incense and bring them inside the curtain and put the incense on the fire before GOD; the smoke of the incense will cover the Atonement-Cover which is over The Testimony so that he doesn't die. He will take some of the bull's blood and sprinkle it with his finger on the front of the Atonement-Cover, then sprinkle the blood before the Atonement-Cover seven times.

"Next he will slaughter the goat designated as the Absolution-Offering for the people and bring the blood inside the curtain. He will repeat what he does with the bull's blood, sprinkling it on and before the Atonement-Cover. In this way he will make atonement for the Holy of Holies because of the uncleannesses of the Israelites, their acts of rebellion, and all their other sins. He will do the same thing for the Tent of Meeting which dwells among the people in the midst of their uncleanness. There is to be no one in the Tent of Meeting from the time Aaron goes in to make atonement in the Holy of Holies until he comes out, having made atonement for himself, his household, and the whole community of Israel.

"Then he will come out to the Altar that is before GOD and make atonement for it. He will take some of the bull's blood and some of the goat's blood and smear it all around the four horns of the Altar. With his finger he will sprinkle some of the blood on it seven times to purify and consecrate it from the uncleannesses of the Israelites.

"When Aaron finishes making atonement for the Holy of Holies, the Tent of Meeting, and the Altar, he will bring up the live goat, lay both hands on the live goat's head, and confess all the iniquities of the People of Israel, all their acts of rebellion, all their sins. He will put all the sins on the goat's head and send it off into the wilderness, led out by a man standing by and ready. The goat will carry all their iniquities to an empty wasteland; the man will let him loose out there in the wilderness.

"Finally, Aaron will come into the Tent of Meeting and take off the linen clothes in which he dressed to enter the Holy of Holies and leave them there. He will bathe in water in a Holy Place, put on his priestly vestments, offer the Whole-Burnt-Offering for himself and the Whole-Burnt-Offering for the people, making atonement for himself and the people, and burn the fat of the Absolution-Offering on the Altar.

"The man who takes the goat out to Azazel in the wilderness then will wash his clothes and bathe himself with water. After that he will be permitted to come back into the camp. The bull for the Absolution-Offering and the goat for the Absolution-Offering, whose blood has been taken into the Holy of Holies to make atonement, are to be taken outside the camp and burned—their hides, their meat, and their entrails. The man assigned to burn them up will then wash his clothes and bathe himself in water. Then he is free to come back into the camp.

"This is standard practice for you, a perpetual ordinance. On the tenth day of the seventh month, both the citizen and the foreigner living with you are to enter into a solemn fast and refrain from all work, because on this day atonement will be made for you, to cleanse you. In the presence of GOD you will be made clean of all your sins. It is a Sabbath of all Sabbaths. You must fast. It is a perpetual ordinance.

"The priest who is anointed and ordained to succeed his father is to make the atonement:

He puts on the sacred linen garments;

He purges the Holy of Holies by making atonement;

He purges the Tent of Meeting and the Altar by making atonement;

He makes atonement for the priests and all the congregation.

"This is a perpetual ordinance for you: Once a year atonement is to be made for all the sins of the People of Israel."

And Aaron did it, just as GOD commanded Moses.

HOLY LIVING: SACRIFICES AND BLOOD

17 GOD spoke to Moses, "Speak to Aaron and his sons and all the Israelites. Tell them, This is what GOD commands: Any and every man who slaughters an ox or lamb or goat inside or outside the camp instead of bringing it to the entrance of the Tent of Meeting to offer it to GOD in front of The Dwelling of GOD—that man is considered guilty of bloodshed; he has shed blood and must be cut off from his people. This is so the Israelites will bring to GOD the sacrifices that they're in the habit of sacrificing out in the open fields. They must bring them to GOD and the priest at the entrance to the Tent of Meeting and sacrifice them as Peace-Offerings to GOD. The priest will splash the blood on the Altar of GOD at the entrance to the Tent of Meeting and burn the fat as a pleasing fragrance to GOD. They must no longer offer their sacrifices to goat-demons—a kind of religious orgy. This is a perpetual decree down through the generations.

"Tell them: Any Israelite or foreigner living among them who offers a Whole-Burnt-Offering or Peace-Offering but doesn't bring it to the entrance of the Tent of Meeting to sacrifice it to GOD, that person must be cut off from his people.

"If any Israelite or foreigner living among them eats blood, I will disown that person and cut him off from his people, for the life of an animal is in the blood. I have provided the blood for you to make atonement for your lives on the Altar; it is the blood, the life, that makes atonement. That's why I tell the People of Israel, 'Don't eat blood.' The same goes for the foreigner who lives among you, 'Don't eat blood.'

"Any and every Israelite—this also goes for the foreigners—who hunts down an animal or bird that is edible, must bleed it and cover the blood with dirt, because the life of every animal is its blood—the blood is its life. That's why I tell the Israelites, 'Don't eat the blood of any animal because the life of every animal is its blood. Anyone who eats the blood must be cut off.'

"Anyone, whether native or foreigner, who eats from an animal that is found dead or mauled must wash his clothes and bathe in water; he remains unclean until evening and is then clean. If he doesn't wash or bathe his body, he'll be held responsible for his actions."

SEX

18 GOD spoke to Moses, "Speak to the People of Israel. Tell them: I am GOD, your God. Don't live like the people of Egypt where you used to live, and don't live like the people of Canaan where I'm bringing you. Don't do what they do. Obey my laws and live by my decrees. I am your GOD. Keep my decrees and laws: The person who obeys them lives by them. I am GOD.

"Don't have sex with a close relative. I am GOD.

"Don't violate your father by having sex with your mother. She is your mother. Don't have sex with her.

"Don't have sex with your father's wife. That violates your father.

"Don't have sex with your sister, whether she's your father's daughter or your mother's, whether she was born in the same house or elsewhere.

"Don't have sex with your son's daughter or your daughter's daughter. That would violate your own body.

"Don't have sex with the daughter of your father's wife born to your father. She is your sister.

"Don't have sex with your father's sister; she is your aunt, closely related to your father.

"Don't have sex with your mother's sister; she is your aunt, closely related to your mother.

"Don't violate your father's brother, your uncle, by having sex with his wife. She is your aunt.

"Don't have sex with your daughter-in-law. She is your son's wife; don't have sex with her.

"Don't have sex with your brother's wife; that would violate your brother.

"Don't have sex with both a woman and her daughter. And don't have sex with her granddaughters either. They are her close relatives. That is wicked.

"Don't marry your wife's sister as a rival wife and have sex with her while your wife is living.

"Don't have sex with a woman during the time of her menstrual period when she is unclean.

"Don't have sex with your neighbor's wife and violate yourself by her.

"Don't give any of your children to be burned in sacrifice to the god Molech—an act of sheer blasphemy of your God. I am GOD.

"Don't have sex with a man as one does with a woman. That is abhorrent.

"Don't have sex with an animal and violate yourself by it.

"A woman must not have sex with an animal. That is perverse.

"Don't pollute yourself in any of these ways. This is how the nations became polluted, the ones that I am going to drive out of the land before you. Even the land itself became polluted and I punished it for its iniquities—the land vomited up its inhabitants. You must keep my decrees and laws—natives and foreigners both. You must not do any of these abhorrent things. The people who lived in this land before you arrived did all these things and polluted the land. And if you pollute it, the land will vomit you up just as it vomited up the nations that preceded you.

"Those who do any of these abhorrent things will be cut off from their people. Keep to what I tell you; don't engage in any of the abhorrent acts that were practiced before you came. Don't pollute yourselves with them. I am GOD, *your* God."

"I AM GOD, YOUR GOD"

19 GOD spoke to Moses: "Speak to the congregation of Israel. Tell them: Be holy because I, GOD, your God, am holy.

"Every one of you must respect his mother and father.

"Keep my Sabbaths. I am GOD, your God.

"Don't take up with no-god idols. Don't make gods of cast metal. I am GOD, your God.

"When you sacrifice a Peace-Offering to GOD, do it as you've been taught so it is acceptable. Eat it on the day you sacrifice it and the day following. Whatever is left until the third day is to be burned up. If it is eaten on the third day it is polluted meat and not acceptable. Whoever eats it will be held responsible because he has violated what is holy to GOD. That person will be cut off from his people.

"When you harvest your land, don't harvest right up to the edges of your field or gather the gleanings from the harvest. Don't strip your vineyard bare or go back and pick up the fallen grapes. Leave them for the poor and the foreigner. I am GOD, your God.

"Don't steal.

"Don't lie.

"Don't deceive anyone.

"Don't swear falsely using my name, violating the name of your God. I am GOD.

"Don't exploit your friend or rob him.

"Don't hold back the wages of a hired hand overnight.

"Don't curse the deaf; don't put a stumbling block in front of the blind; fear your God. I am GOD.

"Don't pervert justice. Don't show favoritism to either the poor or the great. Judge on the basis of what is right.

"Don't spread gossip and rumors.

"Don't just stand by when your neighbor's life is in danger. I am GOD.

"Don't secretly hate your neighbor. If you have something against him, get it out into the open; otherwise you are an accomplice in his guilt.

"Don't seek revenge or carry a grudge against any of your people.

"Love your neighbor as yourself. I am GOD.

"Keep my decrees.

"Don't mate two different kinds of animals.

"Don't plant your fields with two kinds of seed.

"Don't wear clothes woven of two kinds of material.

"If a man has sex with a slave girl who is engaged to another man but has not yet been ransomed or given her freedom, there must be an investigation. But they aren't to be put to death because she wasn't free. The man must bring a Compensation-Offering to GOD at the entrance to the Tent of Meeting, a ram of compensation. The priest will perform the ritual of atonement for him before GOD with the ram of compensation for the sin he has committed. Then he will stand forgiven of the sin he committed.

"When you enter the land and plant any kind of fruit tree, don't eat the fruit for three years; consider it inedible. By the fourth year its fruit is holy, an offering of praise to GOD. Beginning in the fifth year you can eat its fruit; you'll have richer harvests this way. I am GOD, your God.

"Don't eat meat with blood in it.

"Don't practice divination or sorcery.

"Don't cut the hair on the sides of your head or trim your beard.

"Don't gash your bodies on behalf of the dead.

"Don't tattoo yourselves. I am GOD.

"Don't violate your daughter by making her a whore—the whole country would soon become a brothel, filled with sordid sex.

"Keep my Sabbaths and revere my Sanctuary: I am GOD.

"Don't dabble in the occult or traffic with mediums; you'll pollute your souls. I am GOD, your God.

"Show respect to the aged; honor the presence of an elder; fear your God. I am GOD.

"When a foreigner lives with you in your land, don't take advantage of him. Treat the foreigner the same as a native. Love him like one of your own. Remember that you were once foreigners in Egypt. I am GOD, your God.

"Don't cheat when measuring length, weight, or quantity. Use honest scales and weights and measures. I am GOD, your God. I brought you out of Egypt.

"Keep all my decrees and all my laws. Yes, *do* them. I am GOD."

✛

20 GOD spoke to Moses: "Tell the Israelites, Each and every Israelite and foreigner in Israel who gives his child to the god Molech must be put to death. The community must kill him by stoning. I will resolutely reject that man and cut him off from his people. By giving his child to the god Molech he has polluted my Sanctuary and desecrated my holy name. If the people of the land look the other way as if nothing had happened when that man gives his child to the god Molech and fail to kill him, I will resolutely reject that man and his family, and him and all who join him in prostituting themselves in the rituals of the god Molech I will cut off from their people.

"I will resolutely reject persons who dabble in the occult or traffic with mediums, prostituting themselves in their practices. I will cut them off from their people.

"Set yourselves apart for a holy life. *Live* a holy life, because I am GOD, your God. Do what I tell you; *live* the way I tell you. I am the GOD who makes you holy.

"Any and every person who curses his father or mother must be put to death. By cursing his father or mother he is responsible for his own death.

"If a man commits adultery with another man's wife—the wife, say, of his neighbor—both the man and the woman, the adulterer and adulteress, must be put to death.

"If a man has sex with his father's wife, he has violated his father. Both the man and woman must be put to death; they are responsible for their own deaths.

"If a man has sex with his daughter-in-law, both of them must be put to death. What they have done is perverse. And they are responsible for their own deaths.

"If a man has sex with a man as one does with a woman, both of them have done what is abhorrent. They must be put to death; they are responsible for their own deaths.

"If a man marries both a woman and her mother, that's wicked. All three of them must be burned at the stake, purging the wickedness from the community.

"If a man has sex with an animal, he must be put to death and you must kill the animal.

"If a woman has sex with an animal, you must kill both the woman and the animal. They must be put to death. And they are responsible for their deaths.

"If a man marries his sister, the daughter of either his father or mother, and they have sex, that's a disgrace. They must be publicly cut off from their people. He has violated his sister and will be held responsible.

"If a man sleeps with a woman during her period and has sex with her, he has uncovered her 'fountain' and she has revealed her 'fountain'—both of them must be cut off from their people.

"Don't have sex with your aunt on either your mother's or father's side. That violates a close relative. Both of you are held responsible.

199

"If a man has sex with his aunt, he has dishonored his uncle. They will be held responsible and die childless.

"If a man marries his brother's wife, it's a defilement. He has shamed his brother. They will be childless.

"Do what I tell you, all my decrees and laws; live by them so that the land where I'm bringing you won't vomit you out. You simply must not live like the nations I'm driving out before you. They did all these things and I hated every minute of it.

"I've told you, remember, that you will possess their land, that I'm giving to you as an inheritance, a land flowing with milk and honey. I am GOD, your God, who has distinguished you from the nations. So live like it: Distinguish between ritually clean and unclean animals and birds. Don't pollute yourselves with any animal or bird or crawling thing which I have marked out as unclean for you. Live holy lives before me because I, GOD, am holy. I have distinguished you from the nations to be my very own.

"A man or woman who is a medium or sorcerer among you must be put to death. You must kill them by stoning. They're responsible for their own deaths."

HOLY PRIESTS

21 GOD spoke to Moses: "Speak to the priests, the sons of Aaron. Tell them, A priest must not ritually contaminate himself by touching the dead, except for close relatives: mother, father, son, daughter, brother, or an unmarried sister who is dependent on him since she has no husband; for these he may make himself ritually unclean, but he must not contaminate himself with the dead who are only related to him by marriage and thus profane himself.

"Priests must not shave their heads or trim their beards or gash their bodies. They must be holy to their God and must not profane the name of their God. Because their job is to present the gifts of GOD, the food of their God, they are to be holy.

"Because a priest is holy to his God he must not marry a woman who has been a harlot or a cult prostitute or a divorced woman. Make sure he is holy because he serves the food of your God. Treat him as holy because I, GOD, who make you holy, am holy.

"If a priest's daughter defiles herself in prostitution, she disgraces her father. She must be burned at the stake.

"The high priest, the one among his brothers who has received the anointing oil poured on his head and been ordained to wear the priestly vestments, must not let his hair go wild and tangled nor wear ragged and torn clothes. He must not enter a room where there is a dead body. He must not ritually contaminate himself, even for his father or mother; and he must neither abandon nor desecrate the Sanctuary of his God because of the dedication of the anointing oil which is upon him. I am GOD.

"He is to marry a young virgin, not a widow, not a divorcee, not a cult prostitute—he is only to marry a virgin from his own people. He must not defile his descendants among his people because I am GOD who makes him holy."

GOD spoke to Moses: "Tell Aaron, None of your descendants, in any generation to come, who has a defect of any kind may present as an offering the food of his God. That means anyone who is blind or lame, disfigured or deformed, crippled in foot or hand, hunchbacked or dwarfed, who has anything wrong with his eyes, who has running sores or damaged testicles. No descendant of Aaron the priest who has any defect is to offer gifts to GOD; he has a defect and so must not offer the food of his God. He may eat the food of his God, both the most holy and the holy, but because of his defect he must not go near the curtain or approach the Altar. It would desecrate my Sanctuary. I am GOD who makes them holy."

Moses delivered this message to Aaron, his sons, and to all the People of Israel.

✛

22 GOD spoke to Moses, "Tell Aaron and his sons to treat the holy offerings that the Israelites consecrate to me with reverence so they won't desecrate my holy name. I am GOD.

"Tell them, From now on, if any of your descendants approaches in a state of ritual uncleanness the holy offerings that the Israelites consecrate to GOD, he will be cut off from my presence. I am GOD.

"Each and every one of Aaron's descendants who has an infectious skin disease or a discharge may not eat any of the holy offerings until he is clean. Also, if he touches anything defiled by a corpse, or has an emission of semen, or is contaminated by touching a crawling creature, or touches a person who is contaminated for whatever reason—a person who touches any such thing will be ritually unclean until evening and may not eat any of the holy offerings unless he has washed well with water. After the sun goes down he is clean and may go ahead and eat the holy offerings; they are his food. But he must not contaminate himself by eating anything found dead or torn by wild animals. I am GOD.

"The priests must observe my instructions lest they become guilty and die by treating the offerings with irreverence. I am GOD who makes them holy.

"No layperson may eat anything set apart as holy. Nor may a priest's guest or his hired hand eat anything holy. But if a priest buys a slave, the slave may eat of it; also the slaves born in his house may eat his food. If a priest's daughter marries a layperson, she may no longer eat from the holy contributions. But if the priest's daughter is widowed or divorced and without children and returns to her father's household as before, she may eat of her father's food. But no layperson may eat of it.

"If anyone eats from a holy offering accidentally, he must give back the holy offering to the priest and add twenty percent to it.

"The priests must not treat with irreverence the holy offerings of the Israelites that they contribute to GOD lest they desecrate themselves and make themselves guilty when they eat the holy offerings. I am GOD who makes them holy."

✝

GOD spoke to Moses, "Tell Aaron and his sons and all the People of Israel, Each and every one of you, whether native born or foreigner, who presents a Whole-Burnt-Offering to GOD to fulfill a vow or as a Freewill-Offering, must make sure that it is a male without defect from cattle, sheep, or goats for it to be acceptable. Don't try slipping in some creature that has a defect—it won't be accepted. Whenever anyone brings an offering from cattle or sheep as a Peace-Offering to GOD to fulfill a vow or as a Freewill-Offering, it has to be perfect, without defect, to be acceptable. Don't try giving GOD an animal that is blind, crippled, mutilated, an animal with running sores, a rash, or mange. Don't place any of these on the Altar as a gift to GOD. You may, though, offer an ox or sheep that is deformed or stunted as a Freewill-Offering, but it is not acceptable in fulfilling a vow. Don't offer to GOD an animal with bruised, crushed, torn, or cut-off testicles. Don't do this in your own land but don't accept them from foreigners and present them as food for your GOD either. Because of deformities and defects they will not be acceptable."

GOD spoke to Moses: "When a calf or lamb or goat is born, it is to stay with its mother for seven days. After the eighth day, it is acceptable as an offering, a gift to GOD. Don't slaughter both a cow or ewe and its young on the same day. When you sacrifice a Thanksgiving-Offering to GOD, do it right so it will be acceptable. Eat it on the same day; don't leave any leftovers until morning. I am GOD.

"Do what I tell you; *live* what I tell you. I am GOD.

"Don't desecrate my holy name. I insist on being treated with holy reverence among the People of Israel. I am GOD who makes you holy and brought you out of Egypt to be your God. I am GOD."

THE FEASTS

23 GOD spoke to Moses: "Tell the People of Israel, These are my appointed feasts, the appointed feasts of GOD which you are to decree as sacred assemblies.

"Work six days. The seventh day is a Sabbath, a day of total and complete rest, a sacred assembly. Don't do any work. Wherever you live, it is a Sabbath to GOD.

"These are the appointed feasts of GOD, the sacred assemblies which you are to announce at the times set for them:

"GOD's Passover, beginning at sundown on the fourteenth day of the first month.

"GOD's Feast of Unraised Bread, on the fifteenth day of this same month. You are to eat unraised bread for seven days. Hold a sacred assembly on the first day; don't do any regular work. Offer Fire-Gifts to GOD for seven days. On the seventh day hold a sacred assembly; don't do any regular work."

GOD spoke to Moses: "Tell the People of Israel, When you arrive at the land that I am giving you and reap its harvest, bring to the priest a sheaf of the first grain that you harvest. He will wave the sheaf before GOD for acceptance on your behalf; on the morning after Sabbath, the priest will wave it. On the same day that you wave the sheaf, offer a year-old male lamb without defect for a Whole-Burnt-Offering to GOD and with it the Grain-Offering of four quarts of fine flour mixed with oil—a Fire-Gift to GOD, a pleasing fragrance—and also a Drink-Offering of a quart of wine. Don't eat any bread or roasted or fresh grain until you have presented this offering to your God. This is a perpetual decree for all your generations to come, wherever you live.

"Count seven full weeks from the morning after the Sabbath when you brought the sheaf as a Wave-Offering, fifty days until the morning of the seventh Sabbath. Then present a new Grain-Offering to GOD. Bring from wherever you are living two loaves of bread made from four quarts of fine flour and baked with yeast as a Wave-Offering of the first ripe grain to GOD. In addition to the bread, offer seven yearling male lambs without defect, plus one bull and two rams. They will be a Whole-Burnt-Offering to GOD together with their Grain-Offerings and Drink-Offerings—offered as Fire-Gifts, a pleasing fragrance to GOD. Offer one male goat for an Absolution-Offering and two yearling lambs for a Peace-Offering. The priest will wave the two lambs before GOD as a Wave-Offering, together with the bread of the first ripe grain. They are sacred offerings to GOD for the priest. Proclaim the day as a sacred assembly. Don't do any ordinary work. It is a perpetual decree wherever you live down through your generations.

"When you reap the harvest of your land, don't reap the corners of your field or gather the gleanings. Leave them for the poor and the foreigners. I am GOD, *your* God."

GOD said to Moses: "Tell the People of Israel, On the first day of the seventh month, set aside a day of rest, a sacred assembly—mark it with loud blasts on the ram's horn. Don't do any ordinary work. Offer a Fire-Gift to GOD."

GOD said to Moses, "The tenth day of the seventh month is the Day of Atonement. Hold a sacred assembly, fast, and offer a Fire-Gift to GOD. Don't work on that day because it is a day of atonement to make atonement for you before your GOD. Anyone who doesn't fast on that day must be cut off from his people. I will destroy from among his people anyone who works on that day. Don't do any work that day— none. This is a perpetual decree for all the generations to come, wherever you happen to be living. It is a Sabbath of complete and total rest, a fast day. Observe your Sabbath from the evening of the ninth day of the month until the following evening."

GOD said to Moses, "Tell the People of Israel, GOD's Feast of Booths begins on the fifteenth day of the seventh month. It lasts seven days. The first day is a sacred assembly; don't do any ordinary work. Offer Fire-Gifts to GOD for seven days. On the eighth day hold a sacred assembly and offer a gift to GOD. It is a solemn convocation. Don't do any ordinary work.

"These are the appointed feasts of GOD which you will decree as sacred assemblies for presenting Fire-Gifts to GOD: the Whole-Burnt-Offerings, Grain-Offerings, sacrifices, and Drink-Offerings assigned to each day. These are in addition to offerings for GOD's Sabbaths and also in addition to other gifts connected with whatever you have vowed and all the Freewill-Offerings you give to GOD.

"So, summing up: On the fifteenth day of the seventh month, after you have brought your crops in from your fields, celebrate the Feast of GOD for seven days. The first day is a complete rest and the eighth day is a complete rest. On the first day, pick the best fruit from the best trees; take fronds of palm trees and branches of leafy trees and from willows by the brook and celebrate in the presence of your GOD for seven days—yes, for seven full days celebrate it as a festival to GOD. Every year from now on, celebrate it in the seventh month. Live in booths for seven days—every son and daughter of Israel is to move into booths so that your descendants will know that I made the People of Israel live in booths when I brought them out of the land of Egypt. I am GOD, *your* God."

Moses posted the calendar for the annual appointed feasts of GOD which Israel was to celebrate.

LIGHT AND BREAD

24 GOD spoke to Moses: "Order the People of Israel to bring you virgin olive oil for light so that the lamps may be kept burning continually. Aaron is in charge of keeping these lamps burning in front of the curtain that screens The Testimony in the Tent of Meeting from evening to morning continually before GOD. This is a perpetual decree down through the generations. Aaron is responsible for keeping the lamps burning continually on the Lampstand of pure gold before GOD.

"Take fine flour and bake twelve loaves of bread, using about four quarts of flour to a loaf. Arrange them in two rows of six each on the Table of pure gold before GOD. Along each row spread pure incense, marking the bread as a memorial; it is a gift to GOD. Regularly, every Sabbath, this bread is to be set before GOD, a perpetual covenantal response from Israel. The bread then goes to Aaron and his sons, who are to eat it in a Holy Place. It is their most holy share from the gifts to GOD. This is a perpetual decree."

✝

One day the son of an Israelite mother and an Egyptian father went out among the Israelites. A fight broke out in the camp between him and an Israelite. The son of the Israelite woman blasphemed the Name of GOD and cursed. They brought him to Moses. His mother's name was Shelomith, daughter of Dibri of the tribe of Dan. They put him in custody waiting for GOD's will to be revealed to them.

Then GOD spoke to Moses: "Take the blasphemer outside the camp. Have all those who heard him place their hands on his head; then have the entire congregation stone him. Then tell the Israelites, Anyone who curses God will be held accountable; anyone who blasphemes the Name of GOD must be put to death. The entire congregation must stone him. It makes no difference whether he is a foreigner or a native, if he blasphemes the Name, he will be put to death.

"Anyone who hits and kills a fellow human must be put to death. Anyone who kills someone's animal must make it good—a life for a life. Anyone who injures his neighbor will get back the same as he gave: fracture for fracture, eye for eye, tooth for tooth. What he did to hurt that person will be done to him. Anyone who hits and kills an animal must make it good, but whoever hits and kills a fellow human will be put to death. And no double standards: the same rule goes for foreigners and natives. I am GOD, *your* God."

Moses then spoke to the People of Israel. They brought the blasphemer outside the camp and stoned him. The People of Israel followed the orders GOD had given Moses.

"THE LAND WILL OBSERVE A SABBATH TO GOD"

25 GOD spoke to Moses at Mount Sinai, "Speak to the People of Israel. Tell them: When you enter the land which I am going to give you, the land will observe a Sabbath to GOD. Sow your fields, prune your vineyards, and take in your harvests for six years. But the seventh year the land will take a Sabbath of complete and total rest, a Sabbath to GOD; you will not sow your fields or prune your vineyards. Don't reap what grows of itself; don't harvest the grapes of your untended vines. The land gets a year of complete and total rest. But you can eat from what the land volunteers during the Sabbath year—you and your men and women servants, your hired hands, and the foreigners who live in the country, and, of course, also your livestock and the wild animals in the land can eat from it. Whatever the land volunteers of itself can be eaten.

"The Fiftieth Year Shall Be a Jubilee for You"

"Count off seven Sabbaths of years—seven times seven years: Seven Sabbaths of years adds up to forty-nine years. Then sound loud blasts on the ram's horn on the tenth day of the seventh month, the Day of Atonement. Sound the ram's horn all over the land. Sanctify the fiftieth year; make it a holy year. Proclaim freedom all over the land to everyone who lives in it—a Jubilee for you: Each person will go back to his family's property and reunite with his extended family. The fiftieth year is your Jubilee year: Don't sow; don't reap what volunteers itself in the fields; don't harvest the untended vines because it's the Jubilee and a holy year for you. You're permitted to eat from whatever volunteers itself in the fields.

"In this year of Jubilee everyone returns home to his family property.

"If you sell or buy property from one of your countrymen, don't cheat him. Calculate the purchase price on the basis of the number of years since the Jubilee. He is obliged to set the sale price on the basis of the number of harvests remaining until the next Jubilee. The more years left, the more money; you can raise the price. But the fewer years left, the less money; decrease the price. What you are buying and selling in fact is the number of crops you're going to harvest. Don't cheat each other. Fear your God. I am God, your God.

"Keep my decrees and observe my laws and you will live secure in the land. The land will yield its fruit; you will have all you can eat and will live safe and secure. Do I hear you ask, 'What are we going to eat in the seventh year if we don't plant or harvest?' I assure you, I will send such a blessing in the sixth year that the land will yield enough for three years. While you plant in the eighth year, you will eat from the old crop and continue until the harvest of the ninth year comes in.

"The land cannot be sold permanently because the land is mine and you are foreigners—you're my tenants. You must provide for the right of redemption for any of the land that you own.

"If one of your brothers becomes poor and has to sell any of his land, his nearest relative is to come and buy back what his brother sold. If a man has no one to redeem it but he later prospers and earns enough for its redemption, he is to calculate the value since he sold it and refund the balance to the man to whom he sold it; he can then go back to his own land. If he doesn't get together enough money to repay him, what he sold remains in the possession of the buyer until the year of Jubilee. In the Jubilee it will be returned and he can go back and live on his land.

"If a man sells a house in a walled city, he retains the right to buy it back for a full year after the sale. At any time during that year he can redeem it. But if it is not redeemed before the full year has passed, it becomes the permanent possession of the buyer and his descendants. It is not returned in the Jubilee. However, houses in unwalled villages are treated the same as fields. They can be redeemed and have to be returned at the Jubilee.

"As to the Levitical cities, houses in the cities owned by the Levites are always subject to redemption. Levitical property is always redeemable if it is sold in a town that they hold and reverts to them in the Jubilee, because the houses in the towns of the Levites are their property among the People of Israel. The pastures belonging to their cities may not be sold; they are their permanent possession.

"If one of your brothers becomes indigent and cannot support himself, help him, the same as you would a foreigner or a guest so that he can continue to live in your neighborhood. Don't gouge him with interest charges; out of reverence for your God help your brother to continue to live with you in the neighborhood. Don't take advantage of his plight by running up big interest charges on his loans, and don't give him food for profit. I am your GOD who brought you out of Egypt to give you the land of Canaan and to be your God.

"If one of your brothers becomes indigent and has to sell himself to you, don't make him work as a slave. Treat him as a hired hand or a guest among you. He will work for you until the Jubilee, after which he and his children are set free to go back to his clan and his ancestral land. Because the People of Israel are my servants whom I brought out of Egypt, they must never be sold as slaves. Don't tyrannize them; fear your God.

"The male and female slaves which you have are to come from the surrounding nations; you are permitted to buy slaves from them. You may also buy the children of foreign workers who are living among you temporarily and from their clans which are living among you and have been born in your land. They become your property. You may will them to your children as property and make them slaves for life. But you must not tyrannize your brother Israelites.

"If a foreigner or temporary resident among you becomes rich and one of your brothers becomes poor and sells himself to the foreigner who lives among you or to a member of the foreigner's clan, he still has the right of redemption after he has sold himself. One of his relatives may buy him back. An uncle or cousin or any close relative of his extended family may redeem him. Or, if he gets the money together, he can redeem himself. What happens then is that he and his owner count out the time from the year he sold himself to the year of Jubilee; the buy-back price is set according to the wages of a hired hand for that number of years. If many years remain before the Jubilee, he must pay back a larger share of his purchase price, but if only a few years remain until the Jubilee, he is to calculate his redemption price accordingly. He is to be treated as a man hired from year to year. You must make sure that his owner does not tyrannize him.

"If he is not redeemed in any of these ways, he goes free in the year of Jubilee, he and his children, because the People of Israel are my servants, my servants whom I brought out of Egypt. I am GOD, *your* God.

✝

26 "Don't make idols for yourselves; don't set up an image or a sacred pillar for yourselves, and don't place a carved stone in your land that you can bow down to in worship. I am GOD, *your* God.

"Keep my Sabbaths; treat my Sanctuary with reverence. I am GOD.

"IF YOU LIVE BY MY DECREES . . . "

"If you live by my decrees and obediently keep my commandments, I will send the rains in their seasons, the ground will yield its crops and the trees of the field their fruit. You will thresh until the grape harvest and the grape harvest will continue until planting time; you'll have more than enough to eat and will live safe and secure in your land.

"I'll make the country a place of peace—you'll be able to go to sleep at night without fear; I'll get rid of the wild beasts; I'll eliminate war. You'll chase out your enemies and defeat them: Five of you will chase a hundred, and a hundred of you will chase ten thousand and do away with them. I'll give you my full attention: I'll make sure you prosper, make sure you grow in numbers, and keep my covenant with you in good working order. You'll still be eating from last year's harvest when you have to clean out the barns to make room for the new crops.

"I'll set up my residence in your neighborhood; I won't avoid or shun you; I'll stroll through your streets. I'll be your God; you'll be my people. I am GOD, your personal God who rescued you from Egypt so that you would no longer be slaves to the Egyptians. I ripped off the harness of your slavery so that you can move about freely.

"BUT IF YOU REFUSE TO OBEY ME . . . "

"But if you refuse to obey me and won't observe my commandments, despising my decrees and holding my laws in contempt by your disobedience, making a shambles of my covenant, I'll step in and pour on the trouble: debilitating disease, high fevers, blindness, your life leaking out bit by bit. You'll plant seed but your enemies will eat the crops. I'll turn my back on you and stand by while your enemies defeat you. People who hate you will govern you. You'll run scared even when there's no one chasing you.

"And if none of this works in getting your attention, I'll discipline you seven times over for your sins. I'll break your strong pride: I'll make the skies above you like a sheet of tin and the ground under you like cast iron. No matter how hard you work, nothing will come of it: No crops out of the ground, no fruit off the trees.

"If you defy me and refuse to listen, your punishment will be seven times more than your sins: I'll set wild animals on you; they'll rob you of your children, kill your cattle, and decimate your numbers until you'll think you are living in a ghost town.

"And if even this doesn't work and you refuse my discipline and continue your defiance, then it will be my turn to defy you. I, yes I, will punish you for your sins seven times over: I'll let war loose on you, avenging your breaking of the covenant; when you huddle in your cities for protection, I'll send a deadly epidemic on you and you'll be helpless before your enemies; when I cut off your bread supply, ten women will bake bread in one oven and ration it out. You'll eat, but barely—no one will get enough.

"And if this—*even this!*—doesn't work and you still won't listen, still defy me, I'll have had enough and in hot anger will defy you, punishing you for your sins seven times over: famine will be so severe that you'll end up cooking and eating your sons in stews and your daughters in barbecues; I'll smash your sex-and-religion shrines and all the paraphernalia that goes with them, and then stack your corpses and the idol-corpses in the same piles—I'll abhor you; I'll turn your cities into rubble; I'll clean out your sanctuaries; I'll hold my nose at the "pleasing aroma" of your sacrifices. I'll turn your land into a lifeless moonscape—your enemies who come in to take over will be shocked at what they see. I'll scatter you all over the world and keep after you with the point of my sword in your backs. There'll be nothing left in your land, nothing going on in your cities. With you gone and dispersed in the countries of your enemies, the land, empty of you, will finally get a break and enjoy its Sabbath years. All the time it's left there empty, the land will get rest, the Sabbaths it never got when you lived there.

"As for those among you still alive, I'll give them over to fearful timidity—even the rustle of a leaf will throw them into a panic. They'll run here and there, back and forth, as if running for their lives even though no one is after them, tripping and falling over one another in total confusion. You won't stand a chance against an enemy. You'll perish among the nations; the land of your enemies will eat you up. Any who are left will slowly rot away in the enemy lands. Rot. And all because of their sins, their sins compounded by their ancestors' sins.

"On the Other Hand, If They Confess . . . "

"On the other hand, if they confess their sins and the sins of their ancestors, their treacherous betrayal, the defiance that set off my defiance that sent them off into enemy lands; if by some chance, they soften their hard hearts and make amends for their sin, I'll remember my covenant with Jacob, I'll remember my covenant with Isaac, and, yes, I'll remember my covenant with Abraham. And I'll remember the land.

"The land will be empty of them and enjoy its Sabbaths while they're gone. They'll pay for their sins because they refused my laws and treated my decrees with contempt. But in spite of their behavior, while they are among their enemies I won't reject or abhor or destroy them completely. I won't break my covenant with them: I am God, their God. For their sake I will remember the covenant with their ancestors whom I, with all the nations watching, brought out of Egypt in order to be their God. I am God."

These are the decrees, laws, and instructions that God established between himself and the People of Israel through Moses at Mount Sinai.

Vows, Dedications, and Redemptions

27 God spoke to Moses. He said, "Speak to the People of Israel. Tell them: If anyone wants to vow the value of a person to the service of GOD, set the value of a man between the ages of twenty and sixty at fifty shekels of silver, according to the Sanctuary shekel. For a woman the valuation is thirty shekels. If the person is between the ages of five and twenty, set the value at twenty shekels for a male and ten shekels for a female. If the person is between one month and five years, set the value at five shekels of silver for a boy and three shekels of silver for a girl. If the person is over sixty, set the value at fifteen shekels for a man and ten shekels for a woman. If anyone is too poor to pay the stated amount, he is to present the person to the priest, who will then set the value for him according to what the person making the vow can afford.

"If he vowed an animal that is acceptable as an offering to GOD, the animal is given to GOD and becomes the property of the Sanctuary. He must not exchange or substitute a good one for a bad one, or a bad one for a good one; if he should dishonestly substitute one animal for another, both the original and the substitute become property of the Sanctuary. If what he vowed is a ritually unclean animal, one that is not acceptable as an offering to GOD, the animal must be shown to the priest, who will set its value, either high or low. Whatever the priest sets will be its value. If the owner changes his mind and wants to redeem it, he must add twenty percent to its value.

"If a man dedicates his house to GOD, into the possession of the Sanctuary, the priest assesses its value, setting it either high or low. Whatever value the priest sets, that's what it is. If the man wants to buy it back, he must add twenty percent to its price and then it's his again.

"If a man dedicates to the Lord part of his family land, its value is to be set according to the amount of seed that is needed for it at the rate of fifty shekels of silver to six bushels of barley seed. If he dedicates his field during the year of Jubilee, the set value stays. But if he dedicates it after the Jubilee, the priest will compute the value according to the years left until the next Jubilee, reducing the value proportionately. If the one dedicating it wants to buy it back, he must add twenty percent to its valuation, and then it's his again. But if he doesn't redeem it or sells the field to someone else, it can never be bought back. When the field is released in the Jubilee, it becomes holy to GOD, the possession of the Sanctuary, GOD's field. It goes into the hands of the priests.

"If a man dedicates to GOD a field he has bought, a field which is not part of the family land, the priest will compute its proportionate value in relation to the next year of Jubilee. The man must pay its value on the spot as something that is now holy to GOD, belonging to the

Sanctuary. In the year of Jubilee it goes back to its original owner, the man from whom he bought it. The valuations will be reckoned by the Sanctuary shekel, at twenty gerahs to the shekel.

"No one is allowed to dedicate the firstborn of an animal; the first-born, as firstborn, already belongs to GOD. No matter if it's cattle or sheep, it already belongs to GOD. If it's one of the ritually unclean animals, he can buy it back at its assessed value by adding twenty percent to it. If he doesn't redeem it, it is to be sold at its assessed value.

"But nothing that a man irrevocably devotes to GOD from what belongs to him, whether human or animal or family land, may be either sold or bought back. Everything devoted is holy to the highest degree; it's GOD's inalienable property.

"No human who has been devoted to destruction can be redeemed. He must be put to death.

✛

"A tenth of the land's produce, whether grain from the ground or fruit from the trees, is GOD's. It is holy to GOD. If a man buys back any of the tenth he has given, he must add twenty percent to it. A tenth of the entire herd and flock, every tenth animal that passes under the shepherd's rod, is holy to GOD. He is not permitted to pick out the good from the bad or make a substitution. If he dishonestly makes a substitution, both animals, the original and the substitute, become the possession of the Sanctuary and cannot be redeemed."

These are the commandments that GOD gave to Moses on Mount Sinai for the People of Israel.

NUMBERS

Becoming a truly human community is a long, complex, messy business. Simply growing up as a man or woman demands all the wisdom and patience and courage that we can muster. But growing up with others, parents and siblings and neighbors, to say nothing of odd strangers and mean enemies, immensely complicates the growing up.

The book of Numbers plunges us into the mess of growing up. The pages in this section of the biblical story give us a realistic feel for what is involved in being included in the people of God, which is to say, a human community that honors God, lives out love and justice in daily affairs, learns how to deal with sin in oneself and others, and follows God's commands into a future of blessing. And all this without illusions.

Many of us fondle a romanticized spirituality in our imaginations. The "God's in his heaven/all's right with the world" sort of thing. When things don't go "right" we blame others or ourselves, muddle through as best we can, often with considerable crankiness, and wish that we had been born at a different time — "Bible times" maybe! — when living a holy life was so much easier. That's odd because the Bible, our primary text for showing us what it means to be a human being created by God and called to a life of obedient faith and sacrificial love, nowhere suggests that life is simple or even "natural." We need a lot of help.

We need organizational help. When people live together in community, jobs have to be assigned, leaders appointed, inventories kept. Counting and list-making and rosters are as much a part of being a community of God as prayer and instruction and justice. Accurate arithmetic is an aspect of becoming a people of God.

And we need relational help. The people who find themselves called and led and commanded by God find themselves in the company of men and women who sin a lot — quarrel, bicker, grumble, rebel, fornicate, steal — you name it, we do it. We need help in getting along with each other. Wise discipline is required in becoming a people of God.

It follows that counting and quarreling take up considerable space in the book of Numbers. Because they also continue to be unavoidable aspects of our becoming the people of God, this book is essential in training our imaginations to take in some of these less-than-romantic details by which we are formed into the people of God.

NUMBERS

1 God spoke to Moses in the Wilderness of Sinai at the Tent of Meeting on the first day of the second month in the second year after they had left Egypt. He said, "Number the congregation of the People of Israel by clans and families, writing down the names of every male. You and Aaron are to register, company by company, every man who is twenty years and older who is able to fight in the army. Pick one man from each tribe who is head of his family to help you. These are the names of the men who will help you:

> from Reuben: Elizur son of Shedeur
> from Simeon: Shelumiel son of Zurishaddai
> from Judah: Nahshon son of Amminadab
> from Issachar: Nethanel son of Zuar
> from Zebulun: Eliab son of Helon
> from the sons of Joseph,
>   from Ephraim: Elishama son of Ammihud
>   from Manasseh: Gamaliel son of Pedahzur
> from Benjamin: Abidan son of Gideoni
> from Dan: Ahiezer son of Ammishaddai
> from Asher: Pagiel son of Ocran
> from Gad: Eliasaph son of Deuel
> from Naphtali: Ahira son of Enan."

These were the men chosen from the congregation, leaders of their ancestral tribes, heads of Israel's military divisions.

Moses and Aaron took these men who had been named to help and gathered the whole congregation together on the first day of the second month. The people registered themselves in their tribes according to their ancestral families, putting down the names of those who were twenty years old and older, just as God commanded Moses. He numbered them in the Wilderness of Sinai.

The line of Reuben, Israel's firstborn: The men were counted off head by head, every male twenty years and older who was able to fight in the army, registered by tribes according to their ancestral families. The tribe of Reuben numbered 46,500.

The line of Simeon: The men were counted off head by head, every male twenty years and older who was able to fight in the army, registered by clans and families. The tribe of Simeon numbered 59,300.

The line of Gad: The men were counted off head by head, every male twenty years and older who was able to fight in the army, registered by clans and families. The tribe of Gad numbered 45,650.

The line of Judah: The men were counted off head by head, every male twenty years and older who was able to fight in the army, registered by clans and families. The tribe of Judah numbered 74,600.

The line of Issachar: The men were counted off head by head, every male twenty years and older who was able to fight in the army, registered by clans and families. The tribe of Issachar numbered 54,400.

The line of Zebulun: The men were counted off head by head, every male twenty years and older who was able to fight in the army, registered by clans and families. The tribe of Zebulun numbered 57,400.

The line of Joseph: From son Ephraim the men were counted off head by head, every male twenty years and older who was able to fight in the army, registered by clans and families. The tribe of Ephraim numbered 40,500.

And from son Manasseh the men were counted off head by head, every male twenty years and older who was able to fight in the army, registered by clans and families. The tribe of Manasseh numbered 32,200.

The line of Benjamin: The men were counted off head by head, every male twenty years and older who was able to fight in the army, registered by clans and families. The tribe of Benjamin numbered 35,400.

The line of Dan: The men were counted off head by head, every male twenty years and older who was able to fight in the army, registered by clans and families. The tribe of Dan numbered 62,700.

The line of Asher: The men were counted off head by head, every male twenty years and older who was able to fight in the army, registered by clans and families. The tribe of Asher numbered 41,500.

The line of Naphtali: The men were counted off head by head, every male twenty years and older who was able to fight in the army, registered by clans and families. The tribe of Naphtali numbered 53,400.

These are the numbers of those registered by Moses and Aaron, registered with the help of the leaders of Israel, twelve men, each representing his ancestral family. The sum total of the People of Israel twenty years old and over who were able to fight in the army, counted by ancestral family, was 603,550.

The Levites, however, were not counted by their ancestral family along with the others. GOD had told Moses, "The tribe of Levi is an exception: Don't register them. Don't count the tribe of Levi; don't include them in the general census of the People of Israel. Instead, appoint the Levites to be in charge of The Dwelling of The Testimony— over all its furnishings and everything connected with it. Their job is to carry The Dwelling and all its furnishings, maintain it, and camp around it. When it's time to move The Dwelling, the Levites will take it down, and when it's time to set it up, the Levites will do it. Anyone else who even goes near it will be put to death.

"The rest of the People of Israel will set up their tents in companies, every man in his own camp under its own flag. But the Levites will set up camp around The Dwelling of The Testimony so that wrath will not fall on the community of Israel. The Levites are responsible for the security of The Dwelling of The Testimony."

The People of Israel did everything that God commanded Moses. They did it all.

MARCHING ORDERS

2 GOD spoke to Moses and Aaron. He said, "The People of Israel are to set up camp circling the Tent of Meeting and facing it. Each company is to camp under its distinctive tribal flag."

To the east toward the sunrise are the companies of the camp of Judah under its flag, led by Nahshon son of Amminadab. His troops number 74,600.

The tribe of Issachar will camp next to them, led by Nethanel son of Zuar. His troops number 54,400.

And the tribe of Zebulun is next to them, led by Eliab son of Helon. His troops number 57,400.

The total number of men assigned to Judah, troop by troop, is 186,400. They will lead the march.

To the south are the companies of the camp of Reuben under its flag, led by Elizur son of Shedeur. His troops number 46,500.

The tribe of Simeon will camp next to them, led by Shelumiel son of Zurishaddai. His troops number 59,300.

And the tribe of Gad is next to them, led by Eliasaph son of Deuel. His troops number 45,650.

The total number of men assigned to Reuben, troop by troop, is 151,450. They are second in the order of the march.

The Tent of Meeting with the camp of the Levites takes its place in the middle of the march. Each tribe will march in the same order in which they camped, each under its own flag.

To the west are the companies of the camp of Ephraim under its flag, led by Elishama son of Ammihud. His troops number 40,500.

The tribe of Manasseh will set up camp next to them, led by Gamaliel son of Pedahzur. His troops number 32,200.

And next to him is the camp of Benjamin, led by Abidan son of Gideoni. His troops number 35,400.

The total number of men assigned to the camp of Ephraim, troop by troop, is 108,100. They are third in the order of the march.

To the north are the companies of the camp of Dan under its flag, led by Ahiezer son of Ammishaddai. His troops number 62,700.

The tribe of Asher will camp next to them, led by Pagiel son of Ocran. His troops number 41,500.

And next to them is the tribe of Naphtali, led by Ahira son of Enan. His troops number 53,400.

The total number of men assigned to the camp of Dan number 157,600. They will set out, under their flags, last in the line of the march.

These are the People of Israel, counted according to their ancestral families. The total number in the camps, counted troop by troop, comes to 603,550. Following GOD's command to Moses, the Levites were not counted in with the rest of Israel.

The People of Israel did everything the way GOD commanded Moses: They camped under their respective flags; they marched by tribe with their ancestral families.

THE LEVITES

3 This is the family tree of Aaron and Moses at the time GOD spoke with Moses on Mount Sinai.

The names of the sons of Aaron: Nadab the firstborn, Abihu, Eleazar, and Ithamar—anointed priests ordained to serve as priests. But Nadab and Abihu fell dead in the presence of GOD when they offered unauthorized sacrifice to him in the Wilderness of Sinai. They left no sons, and so only Eleazar and Ithamar served as priests during the lifetime of their father, Aaron.

GOD spoke to Moses. He said, "Bring forward the tribe of Levi and present them to Aaron so they can help him. They shall work for him and the whole congregation at the Tent of Meeting by doing the work of The Dwelling. Their job is to be responsible for all the furnishings of The Dwelling, ministering to the affairs of The Dwelling as the People of Israel come to perform their duties. Turn the Levites over to Aaron and his sons; they are the ones assigned to work full time for him. Appoint Aaron and his sons to minister as priests; anyone else who tries to elbow his way in will be put to death."

GOD spoke to Moses: "I have taken the Levites from among the People of Israel as a stand-in for every Israelite mother's firstborn son. The Levites belong to me. All the firstborn are mine—when I killed all the firstborn in Egypt, I consecrated for my own use every firstborn in Israel, whether human or animal. They belong to me. I am GOD."

GOD spoke to Moses in the Wilderness of Sinai: "Count the Levites by their ancestral families and clans. Count every male a month old and older." Moses counted them just as he was instructed by the mouth of GOD.

These are the names of the sons of Levi: Gershon, Kohath, and Merari.

These are the names of the Gershonite clans: Libni and Shimei.

The sons of Kohath by clan: Amram, Izhar, Hebron, and Uzziel.

The sons of Merari by clan: Mahli and Mushi.

These are the clans of Levi, family by family.

Gershon was ancestor to the clans of the Libnites and Shimeites, known as the Gershonite clans. All the males who were one month and older numbered 7,500. The Gershonite clans camped on the west, behind The Dwelling, led by Eliasaph son of Lael. At the Tent of Meeting the Gershonites were in charge of maintaining The Dwelling and its tent, its coverings, the screen at the entrance to the Tent of Meeting, the hangings of the Courtyard, the screen at the entrance to the Courtyard that surrounded The Dwelling and Altar, and the cords— in short, everything having to do with these things.

Kohath was ancestor to the clans of the Amramites, Izharites, Hebronites, and Uzzielites. These were known as the Kohathite clans. All the males who were one month and older numbered 8,600. The Kohathites were in charge of the Sanctuary. The Kohathite clans camped on the south side of The Dwelling, led by Elizaphan son of Uzziel. They were in charge of caring for the Chest, the Table, the Lampstand, the Altars, the articles of the Sanctuary used in worship, and the screen — everything having to do with these things. Eleazar, the son of Aaron the priest, supervised the leaders of the Levites and those in charge of the Sanctuary.

Merari was ancestor to the clans of the Mahlites and the Mushites, known as the Merarite clans. The males who were one month and older numbered 6,200. They were led by Zuriel son of Abihail and camped on the north side of The Dwelling. The Merarites were in charge of the frames of The Dwelling, its crossbars, posts, bases, and all its equipment — everything having to do with these things, as well as the posts of the surrounding Courtyard with their bases, tent pegs, and cords.

Moses and Aaron and his sons camped to the east of The Dwelling, toward the rising sun, in front of the Tent of Meeting. They were in charge of maintaining the Sanctuary for the People of Israel and the rituals of worship. Anyone else who tried to perform these duties was to be put to death.

The sum total of Levites counted at GOD's command by Moses and Aaron, clan by clan, all the males one month and older, numbered 22,000.

GOD spoke to Moses: "Count all the firstborn males of the People of Israel who are one month and older. List their names. Then set apart for me the Levites — remember, I am GOD — in place of all the firstborn among the People of Israel, also the livestock of the Levites in place of their livestock. I am GOD."

So, just as GOD commanded him, Moses counted all the firstborn of the People of Israel. The total of firstborn males one month and older, listed by name, numbered 22,273.

Again GOD spoke to Moses. He said, "Take the Levites in place of all the firstborn of Israel and the livestock of the Levites in place of their livestock. The Levites are mine, I am GOD. Redeem the 273 firstborn Israelites who exceed the number of Levites by collecting five shekels for each one, using the Sanctuary shekel (the shekel weighing twenty gerahs). Give that money to Aaron and his sons for the redemption of the excess number of Israelites."

So Moses collected the redemption money from those who exceeded the number redeemed by the Levites. From the 273 firstborn Israelites he collected silver weighing 1,365 shekels according to the Sanctuary shekel. Moses turned over the redemption money to Aaron and his sons, as he was commanded by the word of GOD.

DUTIES OF THE KOHATHITES

4 GOD spoke to Moses and Aaron. He said, "Number the Kohathite line of Levites by clan and family. Count all the men from thirty to fifty years of age, all who enter the ministry to work in the Tent of Meeting.

"This is the assigned work of the Kohathites in the Tent of Meeting: care of the most holy things.

"When the camp is ready to set out, Aaron and his sons are to go in and take down the covering curtain and cover the Chest of The Testimony with it. Then they are to cover this with a dolphin skin, spread a solid blue cloth on top, and insert the poles.

"Then they are to spread a blue cloth on the Table of the Presence and set the Table with plates, incense dishes, bowls, and jugs for drink offerings. The bread that is always there stays on the Table. They are to cover these with a scarlet cloth, and on top of that spread the dolphin skin, and insert the poles.

"They are to use a blue cloth to cover the light-giving Lampstand and the lamps, snuffers, trays, and the oil jars that go with it. Then they are to wrap it all in a covering of dolphin skin and place it on a carrying frame.

"They are to spread a blue cloth over the Gold Altar and cover it with dolphin skins and place it on a carrying frame.

"They are to take all the articles used in ministering in the Sanctuary, wrap them in a blue cloth, cover them with dolphin skins, and place them on a carrying frame.

"They are to remove the ashes from the Altar and spread a purple cloth over it. They are to place on it all the articles used in ministering at the Altar—firepans, forks, shovels, bowls; everything used at the Altar—place them on the Altar, cover it with the dolphin skins, and insert the poles.

"When Aaron and his sons have finished covering the holy furnishings and all the holy articles, and the camp is ready to set out, the Kohathites are to come and do the carrying. But they must not touch the holy things or they will die. The Kohathites are in charge of carrying all the things that are in the Tent of Meeting.

"Eleazar son of Aaron the priest, is to be in charge of the oil for the light, the fragrant incense, the regular Grain-Offering, and the anointing oil. He is to be in charge of the entire Dwelling and everything in it, including its holy furnishings and articles."

GOD spoke to Moses and Aaron, "Don't let the tribal families of the Kohathites be destroyed from among the Levites. Protect them so they will live and not die when they come near the most holy things. To protect them, Aaron and his sons are to precede them into the Sanctuary and assign each man his task and what he is to carry. But the Kohathites themselves must not go in to look at the holy things, not even a glance at them, or they will die."

DUTIES OF THE GERSHONITES

GOD spoke to Moses: "Number the Gershonites by tribes according to their ancestral families. Count all the men from thirty to fifty years of age who enter the ministry of work in the Tent of Meeting.

"The Gershonites by family and clan will serve by carrying heavy loads: the curtains of the Sanctuary and the Tent of Meeting; the covering of the Tent and the outer covering of dolphin skins; the screens for the entrance to the Tent; the cords; and all the equipment used in its ministries. The Gershonites have the job of doing the work connected with these things. All their work of lifting and carrying and moving is to be done under the supervision of Aaron and his sons. Assign them specifically what they are to carry. This is the work of the Gershonite clans at the Tent of Meeting. Ithamar son of Aaron the priest is to supervise their work.

DUTIES OF THE MERARITES

"Number the Merarites by their ancestral families. Count all the men from thirty to fifty years of age who enter the ministry of work at the Tent of Meeting.

"This is their assigned duty as they go to work at the Tent of Meeting: to carry the frames of The Dwelling, its crossbars, posts, and bases, as well as the posts of the surrounding Courtyard with their bases, tent pegs, cords, and all the equipment related to their use. Assign to each man exactly what he is to carry. This is the ministry of the

Merarite clans as they work at the Tent of Meeting under the supervision of Ithamar son of Aaron the priest."

⊹

Moses, Aaron, and the leaders of the congregation counted the Kohathites by clan and family. All the men from thirty to fifty years of age who came to serve in the work in the Tent of Meeting, counted by clans, were 2,750. This was the total from the Kohathite clans who served in the Tent of Meeting. Moses and Aaron counted them just as GOD had commanded through Moses.

The Gershonites were counted by clan and family. All the men from thirty to fifty years of age who came to serve in the work in the Tent of Meeting, counted by clan and family, were 2,630. This was the total from the Gershonite clans who served in the Tent of Meeting. Moses and Aaron counted them just as GOD had commanded.

The Merarites were counted by clan and family. All the men from thirty to fifty years of age who came to serve in the work in the Tent of Meeting, counted by clan, were 3,200. This was the total from the Merarite clans. Moses and Aaron counted them just as GOD had commanded through Moses.

So Moses and Aaron and the leaders of Israel counted all the Levites by clan and family. All the men from thirty to fifty years of age who came to do the work of serving and carrying the Tent of Meeting numbered 8,580. At GOD's command through Moses, each man was assigned his work and told what to carry.

And that's the story of their numbering, as GOD commanded Moses.

SOME CAMP RULES

5 GOD spoke to Moses: "Command the People of Israel to ban from the camp anyone who has an infectious skin disease, anyone who has a discharge, and anyone who is ritually unclean from contact with a dead body. Ban male and female alike; send them outside the camp so that they won't defile their camp, the place I live among them."

The People of Israel did this, banning them from the camp. They did exactly what GOD had commanded through Moses.

⊹

GOD spoke to Moses: "Tell the People of Israel, When a man or woman commits any sin, the person has broken trust with GOD, is guilty, and must confess the sin. Full compensation plus twenty percent must be made to whoever was wronged. If the wronged person has no close relative who can receive the compensation, the compensation belongs to GOD and must be given to the priest, along with the ram by which atonement is made. All the sacred offerings that the People of Israel bring to a priest belong to the priest. Each person's sacred offerings are his own, but what one gives to the priest stays with the priest."

⊹

GOD spoke to Moses: "Tell the People of Israel, Say a man's wife goes off and has an affair, is unfaithful to him by sleeping with another man, but her husband knows nothing about it even though she has defiled herself. And then, even though there was no witness and she wasn't caught in the act, feelings of jealousy come over the husband and he suspects that his wife is impure. Even if she is innocent and his jealousy and suspicions are groundless, he is to take his wife to the priest. He must also take an offering of two quarts of barley flour for her. He is to pour no oil on it or mix incense with it because it is a Grain-Offering for jealousy, a Grain-Offering for bringing the guilt out into the open.

"The priest then is to take her and have her stand in the presence of GOD. He is to take some holy water in a pottery jar and put some dust from the floor of The Dwelling in the water. After the priest has her stand in the presence of GOD he is to uncover her hair and place the exposure-offering in her hands, the Grain-Offering for jealousy, while he holds the bitter water that delivers a curse. Then the priest will put the woman under oath and say, 'If no man has slept with you and you have not had an adulterous affair and become impure while married to your husband, may this bitter water that delivers a curse not harm you. But if you have had an affair while married to your husband and have defiled yourself by sleeping with a man other than your husband'— here the priest puts the woman under this curse—'may GOD cause your people to curse and revile you when he makes your womb shrivel and your belly swell. Let this water that delivers a curse enter your body so that your belly swells and your womb shrivels.'

"Then the woman shall say, 'Amen. Amen.'

"The priest is to write these curses on a scroll and then wash the words off into the bitter water. He then is to give the woman the bitter water that delivers a curse. This water will enter her body and cause acute pain. The priest then is to take from her hands a handful of the Grain-Offering for jealousy, wave it before GOD, and bring it to the Altar. The priest then is to take a handful of the Grain-Offering, using it as an exposure-offering, and burn it on the Altar; after this he is to make her drink the water. If she has defiled herself in being unfaithful to her husband, when she drinks the water that delivers a curse, it will enter her body and cause acute pain; her belly will swell and her womb shrivel. She will be cursed among her people. But if she has not defiled herself and is innocent of impurity, her name will be cleared and she will be able to have children.

"This is the law of jealousy in a case where a woman goes off and has an affair and defiles herself while married to her husband, or a husband is tormented with feelings of jealousy because he suspects his wife. The priest is to have her stand in the presence of GOD and go through this entire procedure with her. The husband will be cleared of wrong, but the woman will pay for her wrong."

NAZIRITE VOWS

6 GOD spoke to Moses: "Speak to the People of Israel; tell them, If any of you, man or woman, wants to make a special Nazirite vow, consecrating yourself totally to GOD, you must not drink any wine or beer, no intoxicating drink of any kind, not even the juice of grapes—in fact, you must not even eat grapes or raisins. For the duration of the consecration, nothing from the grapevine—not even the seeds, not even the skin—may be eaten.

"Also, for the duration of the consecration you must not have your hair cut. Your long hair will be a continuing sign of holy separation to GOD.

"Also, for the duration of the consecration to GOD, you must not go near a corpse. Even if it's the body of your father or mother, brother or sister, you must not ritually defile yourself because the sign of consecration to God is on your head.

"For the entire duration of your consecration you are holy to GOD.

"If someone should die suddenly in your presence, so that your consecrated head is ritually defiled, you must shave your head on the day of your purifying, that is, the seventh day. Then on the eighth day bring two doves or two pigeons to the priest at the entrance to the Tent of Meeting. The priest will offer one for the Absolution-Offering and one for the Whole-Burnt-Offering, purifying you from the ritual contamination of the corpse. You resanctify your hair on that day and reconsecrate your Nazirite consecration to GOD by bringing a yearling lamb for a Compensation-Offering. You start over; the previous days don't count because your consecration was ritually defiled.

"These are the instructions for the time set when your special consecration to GOD is up. First, you are to be brought to the entrance to the Tent of Meeting. Then you will present your offerings to GOD: a healthy yearling lamb for the Whole-Burnt-Offering, a healthy yearling ewe for an Absolution-Offering, a healthy ram for a Peace-Offering, a basket of unraised bread made of fine flour, loaves mixed with oil, and crackers spread with oil, along with your Grain-Offerings and Drink-Offerings. The priest will approach GOD and offer up your Absolution-Offering and Whole-Burnt-Offering. He will sacrifice the ram as a Peace-Offering to GOD with the basket of unraised bread, and, last of all, the Grain-Offering and Drink-Offering.

"At the entrance to the Tent of Meeting, shave off the hair you consecrated and put it in the fire that is burning under the Peace-Offering.

"After you have shaved the hair of your consecration, the priest will take a shoulder from the ram, boiled, and a piece of unraised bread and a cracker from the basket and place them in your hands. The priest will then wave them before GOD, a Wave-Offering. They are holy and belong to the priest, along with the breast that was waved and the thigh that was offered.

"Now you are free to drink wine.

"These are the instructions for Nazirites as they bring offerings to GOD in their vow of consecration, beyond their other offerings. They must carry out the vow they have vowed following the instructions for the Nazirite."

THE AARONIC BLESSING

GOD spoke to Moses: "Tell Aaron and his sons, This is how you are to bless the People of Israel. Say to them,

> GOD bless you and keep you,
> GOD smile on you and gift you,
> GOD look you full in the face
>   and make you prosper.
> In so doing, they will place my name on the People of Israel—
>   I will confirm it by blessing them."

OFFERINGS FOR THE DEDICATION

7 When Moses finished setting up The Dwelling, he anointed it and consecrated it along with all that went with it. At the same time he anointed and consecrated the Altar and its accessories.

The leaders of Israel, the heads of the ancestral tribes who had carried out the census, brought offerings. They presented before GOD six covered wagons and twelve oxen, a wagon from each pair of leaders and an ox from each leader.

GOD spoke to Moses: "Receive these so that they can be used to transport the Tent of Meeting. Give them to the Levites according to what they need for their work."

Moses took the wagons and oxen and gave them to the Levites. He gave two wagons and four oxen to the Gershonites for their work and four wagons and eight oxen to the Merarites for their work. They were all under the direction of Ithamar son of Aaron the priest. Moses didn't give any to the Kohathites because they had to carry the holy things for which they were responsible on their shoulders.

When the Altar was anointed, the leaders brought their offerings for its dedication and presented them before the Altar because GOD had instructed Moses, "Each day one leader is to present his offering for the dedication of the Altar."

On the first day, Nahshon son of Amminadab, of the tribe of Judah, brought his offering. His offering was:

a silver plate weighing three and a quarter pounds and a silver bowl weighing one and three-quarter pounds (according to the standard Sanctuary weights), each filled with fine flour mixed with oil as a Grain-Offering;

a gold vessel weighing four ounces, filled with incense;

a young bull, a ram, and a yearling lamb for a Whole-Burnt-Offering;

a he-goat for an Absolution-Offering;

two oxen, five rams, five he-goats, and five yearling lambs to be sacrificed as a Peace-Offering.

This was the offering of Nahshon son of Amminadab.

On the second day, Nethanel son of Zuar, the leader of Issachar, brought his offering. His offering was:

a silver plate weighing three and a quarter pounds and a silver bowl weighing one and three-quarter pounds (according to the standard Sanctuary weights), each filled with fine flour mixed with oil as a Grain-Offering;

a gold vessel weighing four ounces, filled with incense;
a young bull, a ram, and a yearling lamb for a Whole-Burnt-Offering;
a he-goat for an Absolution-Offering;
two oxen, five rams, five he-goats, and five yearling lambs to be sacrificed as a Peace-Offering.
This was the offering of Nethanel son of Zuar.

On the third day, Eliab son of Helon, the leader of the people of Zebulun, brought his offering. His offering was:
a silver plate weighing three and a quarter pounds and a silver bowl weighing one and three-quarter pounds (according to the standard Sanctuary weights), each filled with fine flour mixed with oil as a Grain-Offering;
a gold vessel weighing four ounces, filled with incense;
a young bull, a ram, and a yearling lamb for a Whole-Burnt-Offering;
a he-goat for an Absolution-Offering;
two oxen, five rams, five he-goats, and five yearling lambs to be sacrificed as a Peace-Offering.
This was the offering of Eliab son of Helon.

On the fourth day, Elizur son of Shedeur, the leader of the people of Reuben, brought his offering. His offering was:
a silver plate weighing three and a quarter pounds and a silver bowl weighing one and three-quarter pounds (according to the standard Sanctuary weights), each filled with fine flour mixed with oil as a Grain-Offering;
a gold vessel weighing four ounces, filled with incense;
a young bull, a ram, and a yearling lamb for a Whole-Burnt-Offering;
a he-goat for an Absolution-Offering;
two oxen, five rams, five he-goats, and five yearling lambs to be sacrificed as a Peace-Offering.
This was the offering of Elizur son of Shedeur.

On the fifth day, Shelumiel son of Zurishaddai, the leader of the people of Simeon, brought his offering. His offering was:
a silver plate weighing three and a quarter pounds and a silver bowl weighing one and three-quarter pounds (according to the standard Sanctuary weights), each filled with fine flour mixed with oil as a Grain-Offering;
a gold vessel weighing four ounces, filled with incense;
a young bull, a ram, and a yearling lamb for a Whole-Burnt-Offering;
a he-goat for an Absolution-Offering;

two oxen, five rams, five he-goats, and five yearling lambs to be sacrificed as a Peace-Offering.

This was the offering of Shelumiel son of Zurishaddai.

On the sixth day, Eliasaph son of Deuel, the leader of the people of Gad, brought his offering. His offering was:

a silver plate weighing three and a quarter pounds and a silver bowl weighing one and three-quarter pounds (according to the standard Sanctuary weights), each filled with fine flour mixed with oil as a Grain-Offering;

a gold vessel weighing four ounces, filled with incense;

a young bull, a ram, and a yearling lamb for a Whole-Burnt-Offering;

a he-goat for an Absolution-Offering;

two oxen, five rams, five he-goats, and five yearling lambs to be sacrificed as a Peace-Offering.

This was the offering of Eliasaph son of Deuel.

On the seventh day, Elishama son of Ammihud, the leader of the people of Ephraim, brought his offering. His offering was:

a silver plate weighing three and a quarter pounds and a silver bowl weighing one and three-quarter pounds (according to the standard Sanctuary weights), each filled with fine flour mixed with oil as a Grain-Offering;

a gold vessel weighing four ounces, filled with incense;

a young bull, a ram, and a yearling lamb for a Whole-Burnt-Offering;

a he-goat for an Absolution-Offering;

two oxen, five rams, five he-goats, and five yearling lambs to be sacrificed as a Peace-Offering.

This was the offering of Elishama son of Ammihud.

On the eighth day, Gamaliel son of Pedahzur, the leader of the people of Manasseh, brought his offering. His offering was:

a silver plate weighing three and a quarter pounds and a silver bowl weighing one and three-quarter pounds (according to the standard Sanctuary weights), each filled with fine flour mixed with oil as a Grain-Offering;

a gold vessel weighing four ounces, filled with incense;

a young bull, a ram, and a yearling lamb for a Whole-Burnt-Offering;

a he-goat for an Absolution-Offering;

two oxen, five rams, five he-goats, and five yearling lambs to be sacrificed as a Peace-Offering.

This was the offering of Gamaliel son of Pedahzur.

On the ninth day, Abidan son of Gideoni, the leader of the people of Benjamin, brought his offering. His offering was:

a silver plate weighing three and a quarter pounds and a silver bowl weighing one and three-quarter pounds (according to the standard Sanctuary weights), each filled with fine flour mixed with oil as a Grain-Offering;

a gold vessel weighing four ounces, filled with incense;

a young bull, a ram, and a yearling lamb for a Whole-Burnt-Offering;

a he-goat for an Absolution-Offering;

two oxen, five rams, five he-goats, and five yearling lambs to be sacrificed as a Peace-Offering.

This was the offering of Abidan son of Gideoni.

On the tenth day, Ahiezer son of Ammishaddai, the leader of the people of Dan, brought his offering. His offering was:

a silver plate weighing three and a quarter pounds and a silver bowl weighing one and three-quarter pounds (according to the standard Sanctuary weights), each filled with fine flour mixed with oil as a Grain-Offering;

a gold vessel weighing four ounces, filled with incense;

a young bull, a ram, and a yearling lamb for a Whole-Burnt-Offering;

a he-goat for an Absolution-Offering;

two oxen, five rams, five he-goats, and five yearling lambs to be sacrificed as a Peace-Offering.

This was the offering of Ahiezer son of Ammishaddai.

On the eleventh day, Pagiel son of Ocran, the leader of the people of Asher, brought his offering. His offering was:

a silver plate weighing three and a quarter pounds and a silver bowl weighing one and three-quarter pounds (according to the standard Sanctuary weights), each filled with fine flour mixed with oil as a Grain-Offering;

a gold vessel weighing four ounces, filled with incense;

a young bull, a ram, and a yearling lamb for a Whole-Burnt-Offering;

a he-goat for an Absolution-Offering;

two oxen, five rams, five he-goats, and five yearling lambs to be sacrificed as a Peace-Offering.

This was the offering of Pagiel son of Ocran.

On the twelfth day, Ahira son of Enan, the leader of the people of Naphtali, brought his offering. His offering was:

a silver plate weighing three and a quarter pounds and a silver bowl

230

weighing one and three-quarter pounds (according to the standard Sanctuary weights), each filled with fine flour mixed with oil as a Grain-Offering;
a gold vessel weighing four ounces, filled with incense;
a young bull, a ram, and a yearling lamb for a Whole-Burnt-Offering;
a he-goat for an Absolution-Offering;
two oxen, five rams, five he-goats, and five yearling lambs to be sacrificed as a Peace-Offering.
This was the offering of Ahira son of Enan.

These were the dedication offerings of the leaders of Israel for the anointing of the Altar:

> twelve silver plates,
> twelve silver bowls,
> twelve gold vessels.

Each plate weighed three and a quarter pounds and each bowl one and three-quarter pounds. All the plates and bowls together weighed about sixty pounds (using the official Sanctuary weight). The twelve gold vessels filled with incense weighed four ounces each (using the official Sanctuary weight). Altogether the gold vessels weighed about three pounds.
The sum total of animals used for the Whole-Burnt-Offering together with the Grain-Offering:

> twelve bulls,
> twelve rams,
> twelve yearling lambs.

For the Absolution-Offering:

> twelve he-goats.

The sum total of animals used for the sacrifice of the Peace-Offering:

> twenty-four bulls,
> sixty rams,
> sixty he-goats,
> sixty yearling lambs.

These were the offerings for the dedication of the Altar after it was anointed.

When Moses entered the Tent of Meeting to speak with GOD, he heard the Voice speaking to him from between the two angel-cherubim above the Atonement-Cover on the Chest of The Testimony. He spoke with him.

THE LIGHTS

8 GOD spoke to Moses: "Tell Aaron, Install the seven lamps so they will throw light in front of the Lampstand."

Aaron did just that. He installed the lamps so they threw light in front of the Lampstand, as GOD had instructed Moses. The Lampstand was made of hammered gold from its stem to its petals. It was made precisely to the design GOD had shown Moses.

PURIFYING THE LEVITES

GOD spoke to Moses: "Take the Levites from the midst of the People of Israel and purify them for doing GOD's work. This is the way you will do it: Sprinkle water of absolution on them; have them shave their entire bodies; have them scrub their clothes. Then they will have purified themselves.

"Have them take a young bull with its accompanying Grain-Offering of fine flour mixed with oil, plus a second young bull for an Absolution-Offering. Bring the Levites to the front of the Tent of Meeting and gather the entire community of Israel. Present the Levites before GOD as the People of Israel lay their hands on them. Aaron will present the Levites before GOD as a Wave-Offering from the People of Israel so that they will be ready to do GOD's work.

"Have the Levites place their hands on the heads of the bulls, selecting one for the Absolution-Offering and another for the Whole-Burnt-Offering to GOD to make atonement for the Levites. Then have the Levites stand in front of Aaron and his sons and present them as a Wave-Offering to GOD. This is the procedure for setting apart the Levites from the rest of the People of Israel; the Levites are exclusively for my use.

"After you have purified the Levites and presented them as a Wave-Offering to GOD, they can go to work in the Tent of Meeting. The Levites have been selected out of the People of Israel for my exclusive use; they function in place of every firstborn male born to an Israelite woman. Every firstborn male in Israel, animal or human, is set apart for my use. When I struck down all the firstborn of Egypt, I consecrated them for my holy uses. But now I take the Levites as stand-ins in place of every firstborn son in Israel, selected out of the People of Israel, and I have given the Levites to Aaron and his sons to do all the work involved in the Tent of Meeting on behalf of all the People of Israel and to make atonement for them so that nothing bad will happen to them when they approach the Sanctuary."

Moses, Aaron, and the entire community of the People of Israel carried out these procedures with the Levites, just as GOD had commanded Moses. The Levites purified themselves and scrubbed their clothes. Then Aaron presented them as a Wave-Offering before GOD and made atonement for them to purify them. Only then did the Levites go to work at the Tent of Meeting. Aaron and his sons supervised them following the directions GOD had given.

GOD spoke to Moses: "These are your instructions regarding the Levites: At the age of twenty-five they will join the work force in the Tent of Meeting; at the age of fifty they must retire from the work. They can assist their brothers in the tasks in the Tent of Meeting, but they are not permitted to do the actual work themselves. These are the ground rules for the work of the Levites."

PASSOVER

9 GOD spoke to Moses in the Wilderness of Sinai in the first month of the second year after leaving Egypt: "Have the People of Israel celebrate Passover at the set time. Celebrate it on schedule, on the evening of the fourteenth day of this month, following all the rules and procedures."

Moses told the People of Israel to celebrate the Passover and they did— in the Wilderness of Sinai at evening of the fourteenth day of the first month. The People of Israel did it all just as GOD had commanded Moses.

But some of them couldn't celebrate the Passover on the assigned day because they were ritually unclean on account of a corpse. So they presented themselves before Moses and Aaron on Passover and told Moses, "We have become ritually unclean because of a corpse, but why should we be barred from bringing GOD's offering along with other Israelites on the day set for Passover?"

Moses said, "Give me some time; I'll find out what GOD says in your circumstances."

GOD spoke to Moses: "Tell the People of Israel, If one or another of you is ritually unclean because of a corpse, or you happen to be off on a long trip, you may still celebrate GOD's Passover. But celebrate it on the fourteenth day of the second month at evening. Eat the lamb together with unraised bread and bitter herbs. Don't leave any of it until morning. Don't break any of its bones. Follow all the procedures.

"But a man who is ritually clean and is not off on a trip and still fails to celebrate the Passover must be cut off from his people because he did not present GOD's offering at the set time. That man will pay for his sin.

"Any foreigner living among you who wants to celebrate GOD's Passover is welcome to do it, but he must follow all the rules and procedures. The same procedures go for both foreigner and native-born."

THE CLOUD

The day The Dwelling was set up, the Cloud covered The Dwelling of the Tent of Testimony. From sunset until daybreak it was over The Dwelling. It looked like fire. It was like that all the time, the Cloud over The Dwelling and at night looking like fire.

When the Cloud lifted above the Tent, the People of Israel marched out; and when the Cloud descended the people camped. The People of Israel marched at GOD's command and they camped at his command. As long as the Cloud was over The Dwelling, they camped. Even when the Cloud hovered over The Dwelling for many days, they honored GOD's command and wouldn't march. They stayed in camp, obedient to GOD's command, as long as the Cloud was over The Dwelling, but the moment GOD issued orders they marched. If the Cloud stayed only from sunset to daybreak and then lifted at daybreak, they marched. Night or day, it made no difference—when the Cloud lifted, they marched. It made no difference whether the Cloud hovered over The Dwelling for two days or a month or a year, as long as the Cloud was there, they were there. And when the Cloud went up, they got up and marched. They camped at GOD's command and they marched at GOD's command. They lived obediently by GOD's orders as delivered by Moses.

THE TWO BUGLES

10 GOD spoke to Moses: "Make two bugles of hammered silver. Use them to call the congregation together and give marching orders to the camps. When you blow them, the whole community will meet you at the entrance of the Tent of Meeting.

"When a bugle gives a single, short blast, that's the signal for the leaders, the heads of the clans, to assemble. When it gives a long blast, that's the signal to march. At the first blast the tribes who were camped on the east set out. At the second blast the camps on the south set out. The long blasts are the signals to march. The bugle call that gathers the assembly is different from the signal to march.

"The sons of Aaron, the priests, are in charge of blowing the bugles; it's their assigned duty down through the generations. When you go to war against an aggressor, blow a long blast on the bugle so that GOD will notice you and deliver you from your enemies. Also at times of celebration, at the appointed feasts and New Moon festivals, blow the bugles over your Whole-Burnt-Offerings and Peace-Offerings: they will keep your attention on God. I am GOD, *your* God."

THE MARCH FROM SINAI TO PARAN

In the second year, on the twentieth day of the second month, the Cloud went up from over The Dwelling of The Testimony. At that the People of Israel set out on their travels from the Wilderness of Sinai until the Cloud finally settled in the Wilderness of Paran. They began their march at the command of GOD through Moses.

The flag of the camp of Judah led the way, rank after rank under the command of Nahshon son of Amminadab. Nethanel son of Zuar commanded the forces of the tribe of Issachar, and Eliab son of Helon commanded the forces of the tribe of Zebulun. As soon as The Dwelling was taken down, the Gershonites and the Merarites set out, carrying The Dwelling.

The flag of the camp of Reuben was next with Elizur son of Shedeur in command. Shelumiel son of Zurishaddai commanded the forces of the tribe of Simeon; Eliasaph son of Deuel commanded the forces of the tribe of Gad. Then the Kohathites left, carrying the holy things. By the time they arrived The Dwelling would be set up.

The flag of the tribe of Ephraim moved out next, commanded by Elishama son of Ammihud. Gamaliel son of Pedahzur commanded the forces of the tribe of Manasseh; Abidan son of Gideoni commanded the forces of the tribe of Benjamin.

Finally, under the flag of the tribe of Dan, the rear guard of all the camps marched out with Ahiezer son of Ammishaddai in command. Pagiel son of Ocran commanded the forces of the tribe of Asher; Ahira son of Enan commanded the forces of the tribe of Naphtali.

These were the marching units of the People of Israel. They were on their way.

Moses said to his brother-in-law Hobab son of Reuel the Midianite, Moses' father-in-law, "We're marching to the place about which GOD promised, 'I'll give it to you.' Come with us; we'll treat you well. GOD has promised good things for Israel."

But Hobab said, "I'm not coming; I'm going back home to my own country, to my own family."

Moses countered, "Don't leave us. You know all the best places to camp in the wilderness. We need your eyes. If you come with us, we'll make sure that you share in all the good things GOD will do for us."

And so off they marched. From the Mountain of GOD they marched three days with the Chest of the Covenant of GOD in the lead to scout out a campsite. The Cloud of GOD was above them by day when they marched from the camp. With the Chest leading the way, Moses would say,

> Get up, GOD!
> Put down your enemies!
> Chase those who hate you to the hills!

And when the Chest was set down, he would say,

> Rest with us, GOD,
> Stay with the many,
> Many thousands of Israel.

CAMP TABERAH

11 The people fell to grumbling over their hard life. GOD heard. When he heard his anger flared; then fire blazed up and burned the outer boundaries of the camp. The people cried out for help to Moses; Moses prayed to GOD and the fire died down. They named the place Taberah (Blaze) because fire from GOD had blazed up against them.

CAMP KIBROTH HATTAAVAH

The riff-raff among the people had a craving and soon they had the People of Israel whining, "Why can't we have meat? We ate fish in Egypt—and got it free!—to say nothing of the cucumbers and melons, the leeks and onions and garlic. But nothing tastes good out here; all we get is manna, manna, manna."

Manna was a seedlike substance with a shiny appearance like resin. The people went around collecting it and ground it between stones or pounded it fine in a mortar. Then they boiled it in a pot and shaped it into cakes. It tasted like a delicacy cooked in olive oil. When the dew fell on the camp at night, the manna was right there with it.

Moses heard the whining, all those families whining in front of their tents. GOD's anger blazed up. Moses saw that things were in a bad way.

Moses said to GOD, "Why are you treating me this way? What did I ever do to you to deserve this? Did I conceive them? Was I their mother? So why dump the responsibility of this people on me? Why tell me to carry them around like a nursing mother, carry them all the way to the land you promised to their ancestors? Where am I supposed to get meat for all these people who are whining to me, 'Give us meat; we want meat.' I can't do this by myself—it's too much, all these people. If this is how you intend to treat me, do me a favor and kill me. I've seen enough; I've had enough. Let me out of here."

GOD said to Moses, "Gather together seventy men from among the leaders of Israel, men whom you know to be respected and responsible. Take them to the Tent of Meeting. I'll meet you there. I'll come down and speak with you. I'll take some of the Spirit that is on you and place it on them; they'll then be able to take some of the load of this people—you won't have to carry the whole thing alone.

"Tell the people, Consecrate yourselves. Get ready for tomorrow when you're going to eat meat. You've been whining to GOD, 'We want meat; give us meat. We had a better life in Egypt.' GOD has heard your whining and he's going to give you meat. You're going to eat meat. And it's not just for a day that you'll eat meat, and not two days, or five or ten or twenty, but for a whole month. You're going to eat meat until its coming out your nostrils. You're going to be so sick of meat that you'll throw up at the mere mention of it. And here's why: Because you have rejected GOD who is right here among you, whining to his face, 'Oh, why did we ever have to leave Egypt?'"

Moses said, "I'm standing here surrounded by 600,000 men on foot and you say, 'I'll give them meat, meat every day for a month.' So where's it coming from? Even if all the flocks and herds were butchered, would that be enough? Even if all the fish in the sea were caught, would that be enough?"

GOD answered Moses, "So, do you think I can't take care of you? You'll see soon enough whether what I say happens for you or not."

So Moses went out and told the people what GOD had said. He called together seventy of the leaders and had them stand around the Tent. GOD came down in a cloud and spoke to Moses and took some of the Spirit that was on him and put it on the seventy leaders. When the Spirit rested on them they prophesied. But they didn't continue; it was a onetime event.

⊹

Meanwhile two men, Eldad and Medad, had stayed in the camp. They were listed as leaders but they didn't leave camp to go to the Tent. Still, the Spirit also rested on them and they prophesied in the camp.

A young man ran and told Moses, "Eldad and Medad are prophesying in the camp!"

Joshua son of Nun, who had been Moses' right-hand man since his youth, said, "Moses, master! Stop them!"

But Moses said, "Are you jealous for me? Would that all GOD's people were prophets. Would that GOD would put his Spirit on all of them."

⊹

Then Moses and the leaders of Israel went back to the camp. A wind set in motion by GOD swept quails in from the sea. They piled up to a depth of about three feet in the camp and as far out as a day's walk in every direction. All that day and night and into the next day the people were out gathering the quail—huge amounts of quail; even the slowest person among them gathered at least sixty bushels. They spread them out all over the camp for drying. But while they were still chewing the quail and had hardly swallowed the first bites, GOD's anger blazed out against the people. He hit them with a terrible plague. They ended up calling the place Kibroth Hattaavah (Graves-of-the-Craving). There they buried the people who craved meat.

From Kibroth Hattaavah they marched on to Hazeroth. They remained at Hazeroth.

CAMP HAZEROTH

12 Miriam and Aaron talked against Moses behind his back because of his Cushite wife (he had married a Cushite woman). They said, "Is it only through Moses that GOD speaks? Doesn't he also speak through us?"

GOD overheard their talk.

Now the man Moses was a quietly humble man, more so than anyone living on Earth. GOD broke in suddenly on Moses and Aaron and Miriam saying, "Come out, you three, to the Tent of Meeting." The three went out. GOD descended in a Pillar of Cloud and stood at the entrance to the Tent. He called Aaron and Miriam to him. When they stepped out, he said,

> Listen carefully to what I'm telling you.
>> If there is a prophet of GOD among you,
> I make myself known to him in visions,
>> I speak to him in dreams.
> But I don't do it that way with my servant Moses;
>> he has the run of my entire house;
> I speak to him intimately, in person,
>> in plain talk without riddles:
> He ponders the very form of GOD.
> So why did you show no reverence or respect
>> in speaking against my servant, against Moses?

The anger of GOD blazed out against them. And then he left.

When the Cloud moved off from the Tent, oh! Miriam had turned leprous, her skin like snow. Aaron took one look at Miriam—a leper!

He said to Moses, "Please, my master, please don't come down so hard on us for this foolish and thoughtless sin. Please don't make her like a stillborn baby coming out of its mother's womb with half its body decomposed."

And Moses prayed to GOD:

> Please, God, heal her,
>> please heal her.

GOD answered Moses, "If her father had spat in her face, wouldn't she be ostracized for seven days? Quarantine her outside the camp for seven days. Then she can be readmitted to the camp." So Miriam was in quarantine outside the camp for seven days. The people didn't march on until she was readmitted. Only then did the people march from

Hazeroth and set up camp in the Wilderness of Paran.

Scouting out Canaan

13 God spoke to Moses: "Send men to scout out the country of Canaan that I am giving to the People of Israel. Send one man from each ancestral tribe, each one a tried-and-true leader in the tribe."

So Moses sent them off from the Wilderness of Paran at the command of God. All of them were leaders in Israel, one from each tribe. These were their names:

> from Reuben: Shammua son of Zaccur
> from Simeon: Shaphat son of Hori
> from Judah: Caleb son of Jephunneh
> from Issachar: Igal son of Joseph
> from Ephraim: Hoshea son of Nun
> from Benjamin: Palti son of Raphu
> from Zebulun: Gaddiel son of Sodi
> from Manasseh (a Joseph tribe): Gaddi son of Susi
> from Dan: Ammiel son of Gemalli
> from Asher: Sethur son of Michael
> from Naphtali: Nahbi son of Vophsi
> from Gad: Geuel son of Maki

These are the names of the men Moses sent to scout out the land. Moses gave Hoshea (Salvation) son of Nun a new name—Joshua (God-Saves).

When Moses sent them off to scout out Canaan, he said, "Go up through the Negev and then into the hill country. Look the land over, see what it is like. Assess the people: Are they strong or weak? Are there few or many? Observe the land: Is it pleasant or harsh? Describe the towns where they live: Are they open camps or fortified with walls? And the soil: Is it fertile or barren? Are there forests? And try to bring back a sample of the produce that grows there—this is the season for the first ripe grapes."

With that they were on their way. They scouted out the land from the Wilderness of Zin as far as Rehob toward Lebo Hamath. Their route went through the Negev Desert to the town of Hebron. Ahiman, Sheshai, and Talmai, descendants of the giant Anak, lived there. Hebron had been built seven years before Zoan in Egypt. When they arrived at the Eshcol Valley they cut off a branch with a single cluster of grapes—it took two men to carry it—slung on a pole. They also picked some pomegranates and figs. They named the place Eshcol Valley (Grape-Cluster-Valley) because of the huge cluster of grapes they had cut down there. After forty days of scouting out the land, they returned home.

They presented themselves before Moses and Aaron and the whole congregation of the People of Israel in the Wilderness of Paran at Kadesh. They reported to the whole congregation and showed them the fruit of the land. Then they told the story of their trip:

"We went to the land to which you sent us and, oh! It *does* flow with milk and honey! Just look at this fruit! The only thing is that the people who live there are fierce, their cities are huge and well fortified. Worse yet, we saw descendants of the giant Anak. Amalekites are spread out in the Negev; Hittites, Jebusites, and Amorites hold the hill country; and the Canaanites are established on the Mediterranean Sea and along the Jordan."

Caleb interrupted, called for silence before Moses and said, "Let's go up and take the land—now. We can do it."

But the others said, "We can't attack those people; they're way stronger than we are." They spread scary rumors among the People of Israel. They said, "We scouted out the land from one end to the other—it's a land that swallows people whole. Everybody we saw was huge. Why, we even saw the Nephilim giants (the Anak giants come from the Nephilim). Alongside them we felt like grasshoppers. And they looked down on us as if we were grasshoppers."

✛

14 The whole community was in an uproar, wailing all night long. All the People of Israel grumbled against Moses and Aaron. The entire community was in on it: "Why didn't we die in Egypt? Or in this wilderness? Why has GOD brought us to this country to kill us? Our wives and children are about to become plunder. Why don't we just head back to Egypt? And right now!"

Soon they were all saying it to one another: "Let's pick a new leader; let's head back to Egypt."

Moses and Aaron fell on their faces in front of the entire community, gathered in emergency session.

Joshua son of Nun and Caleb son of Jephunneh, members of the scouting party, ripped their clothes and addressed the assembled People of Israel: "The land we walked through and scouted out is a very good land—very good indeed. If GOD is pleased with us, he will lead us into that land, a land that flows, as they say, with milk and honey. And he'll give it to us. Just don't rebel against GOD! And don't be afraid of those people. Why, we'll have them for lunch! They have no protection and GOD is on our side. Don't be afraid of them!"

But, up in arms now, the entire community was talking of hurling stones at them.

Just then the bright Glory of GOD appeared at the Tent of Meeting. Every Israelite saw it. GOD said to Moses, "How long will these people treat me like dirt? How long refuse to trust me? And with all these signs I've done among them! I've had enough—I'm going to hit them with a plague and kill them. But I'll make you into a nation bigger and stronger than they ever were."

But Moses said to GOD, "The Egyptians are going to hear about this! You delivered this people from Egypt with a great show of strength, and now this? The Egyptians will tell everyone. They've already heard that you are GOD, that you are on the side of this people, that you are present among them, that they see you with their own eyes in your Cloud that hovers over them, in the Pillar of Cloud that leads them by day and the Pillar of Fire at night. If you kill this entire people in one stroke, all the nations that have heard what has been going on will say, 'Since GOD couldn't get these people into the land which he had promised to give them, he slaughtered them out in the wilderness.'

"Now, please, let the power of the Master expand, enlarge itself greatly, along the lines you have laid out earlier when you said,

> GOD, slow to get angry and huge in loyal love,
>   forgiving iniquity and rebellion and sin;
> Still, never just whitewashing sin.
>   But extending the fallout of parents' sins
> to children into the third,
>   even the fourth generation.

"Please forgive the wrongdoing of this people out of the extravagance of your loyal love just as all along, from the time they left Egypt, you have been forgiving this people."

GOD said, "I forgive them, honoring your words. But as I live and as the Glory of GOD fills the whole Earth—not a single person of those who saw my Glory, saw the miracle signs I did in Egypt and the wilderness, and who have tested me over and over and over again, turning a deaf ear to me—not one of them will set eyes on the land I so solemnly promised to their ancestors. No one who has treated me with such repeated contempt will see it.

"But my servant Caleb—this is a different story. He has a different spirit; he follows me passionately. I'll bring him into the land that he scouted and his children will inherit it.

"Since the Amalekites and Canaanites are so well established in the valleys, for right now change course and head back into the wilderness following the route to the Red Sea."

GOD spoke to Moses and Aaron: "How long is this going to go on, all this grumbling against me by this evil-infested community? I've had my fill of complaints from these grumbling Israelites. Tell them, As I live—GOD's decree—here's what I'm going to do: Your corpses are going to litter the wilderness—every one of you twenty years and older who was counted in the census, this whole generation of grumblers and grousers. Not one of you will enter the land and make your home there, the firmly and solemnly promised land, except for Caleb son of Jephunneh and Joshua son of Nun.

"Your children, the very ones that you said would be taken for plunder, I'll bring in to enjoy the land you rejected while your corpses will be rotting in the wilderness. These children of yours will live as shepherds in the wilderness for forty years, living with the fallout of your whoring unfaithfulness until the last of your generation lies a corpse in the wilderness. You scouted out the land for forty days; your punishment will be a year for each day, a forty-year sentence to serve for your sins—a long schooling in my displeasure.

"I, GOD, have spoken. I will most certainly carry out these things against this entire evil-infested community which has banded together against me. In this wilderness they will come to their end. There they will die."

So it happened that the men Moses sent to scout out the land returned to circulate false rumors about the land causing the entire community to grumble against Moses—all these men died. Having spread false rumors of the land, they died in a plague, confronted by GOD. Only Joshua son of Nun and Caleb son of Jephunneh were left alive of the men who went to scout out the land.

When Moses told all of this to the People of Israel, they mourned long and hard. But early the next morning they started out for the high hill country, saying, "We're here; we're ready—let's go up and attack the land that GOD promised us. We sinned, but now we're ready."

But Moses said, "Why are you crossing GOD's command yet again? This won't work. Don't attack. GOD isn't with you in this—you'll be beaten badly by your enemies. The Amalekites and Canaanites are ready for you and they'll kill you. Because you have left off obediently following GOD, GOD is not going to be with you in this."

But they went anyway; recklessly and arrogantly they climbed to the high hill country. But the Chest of the Covenant and Moses didn't budge from the camp. The Amalekites and the Canaanites who lived in the hill country came out of the hills and attacked and beat them, a rout all the way down to Hormah.

MATTERS OF WORSHIP

15 GOD spoke to Moses: "Speak to the People of Israel. Tell them, When you enter your homeland that I am giving to you and sacrifice a Fire-Gift to GOD, a Whole-Burnt-Offering or any sacrifice from the herd or flock for a Vow-Offering or Freewill-Offering at one of the appointed feasts, as a pleasing fragrance for GOD, the one bringing the offering shall present to GOD a Grain-Offering of two quarts of fine flour mixed with a quart of oil. With each lamb for the Whole-Burnt-Offering or other sacrifice, prepare a quart of oil and a quart of wine as a Drink-Offering.

"For a ram prepare a Grain-Offering of four quarts of fine flour mixed with one and a quarter quarts of oil and one and a quarter quarts of wine as a Drink-Offering. Present it as a pleasing fragrance to GOD.

"When you prepare a young bull as a Whole-Burnt-Offering or sacrifice for a special vow or a Peace-Offering to GOD, bring with the bull a Grain-Offering of six quarts of fine flour and two quarts of oil. Also bring two quarts of wine as a Drink-Offering. It will be a Fire-Gift, a pleasing fragrance to GOD.

"Each bull or ram, each lamb or young goat, is to be prepared in this same way. Carry out this procedure for each one, no matter how many you have to prepare.

"Every native-born Israelite is to follow this procedure when he brings a Fire-Gift as a pleasing fragrance to GOD. In future generations, when a foreigner or visitor living at length among you presents a Fire-Gift as a pleasing fragrance to GOD, the same procedures must be followed. The community has the same rules for you and the foreigner living among you. This is the regular rule for future generations. You and the foreigner are the same before GOD. The same laws and regulations apply to both you and the foreigner who lives with you."

GOD spoke to Moses: "Speak to the People of Israel. Tell them, When you enter the land into which I'm bringing you, and you eat the food of that country, set some aside as an offering for GOD. From the first batch of bread dough make a round loaf for an offering—an offering from the threshing floor. Down through the future generations make this offering to GOD from each first batch of dough.

⁜

"But if you should get off the beaten track and not keep the commands which GOD spoke to Moses, any of the things that GOD commanded you under the authority of Moses from the time that GOD first commanded you right up to this present time, and if it happened more or less by mistake, with the congregation unaware of it, then the whole congregation is to sacrifice one young bull as a Whole-Burnt-Offering, a pleasing fragrance to GOD, accompanied by its Grain-Offering and Drink-Offering as stipulated in the rules, and a he-goat as an Absolution-Offering. The priest is to atone for the entire community of the People of Israel and they will stand forgiven. The sin was not deliberate, and they offered to GOD the Fire-Gift and Absolution-Offering for their inadvertence. The whole community of Israel including the foreigners living there will be absolved, because everyone was involved in the error.

"But if it's just one person who sins by mistake, not realizing what he's doing, he is to bring a yearling she-goat as an Absolution-Offering. The priest then is to atone for the person who accidentally sinned, to make atonement before GOD so that it won't be held against him.

"The same standard holds for everyone who sins by mistake; the native-born Israelites and the foreigners go by the same rules.

"But the person, native or foreigner, who sins defiantly, deliberately blaspheming GOD, must be cut off from his people: He has despised GOD's word, he has violated GOD's command; that person must be kicked out of the community, ostracized, left alone in his wrongdoing."

✠

Once, during those wilderness years of the People of Israel, a man was caught gathering wood on the Sabbath. The ones who caught him hauled him before Moses and Aaron and the entire congregation. They put him in custody until it became clear what to do with him. Then GOD spoke to Moses: "Give the man the death penalty. Yes, kill him, the whole community hurling stones at him outside the camp."

So the whole community took him outside the camp and threw stones at him, an execution commanded by GOD and given through Moses.

✠

GOD spoke to Moses: "Speak to the People of Israel. Tell them that from now on they are to make tassels on the corners of their garments and to mark each corner tassel with a blue thread. When you look at these tassels you'll remember and keep all the commandments of GOD, and not get distracted by everything you feel or see that seduces you into infidelities. The tassels will signal remembrance and observance of all my commandments, to live a holy life to GOD. I am your GOD who rescued you from the land of Egypt to be your personal God. Yes, I am GOD, *your* God."

THE REBELS

16 Getting on his high horse one day, Korah son of Izhar, the son of Kohath, the son of Levi, along with a few Reubenites—Dathan and Abiram sons of Eliab, and On son of Peleth—rebelled against Moses. He had with him 250 leaders of the congregation of Israel, prominent men with positions in the Council. They came as a group and confronted Moses and Aaron, saying, "You've overstepped yourself. This entire community is holy and GOD is in their midst. So why do you act like you're running the whole show?"

On hearing this, Moses threw himself face-down on the ground.

Then he addressed Korah and his gang: "In the morning GOD will make clear who is on his side, who is holy. GOD will take his stand with the one he chooses.

"Now, Korah, here's what I want you, you and your gang, to do: Tomorrow, take censers. In the presence of GOD, put fire in them and then incense. Then we'll see who is holy, see whom GOD chooses. Sons of Levi, you've overstepped *yourselves*!"

Moses continued with Korah, "Listen well now, sons of Levi. Isn't it enough for you that the God of Israel has selected you out of the congregation of Israel to bring you near him to serve in the ministries of The Dwelling of GOD, and to stand before the congregation to minister to them? He has brought you and all your brother Levites into his inner circle, and now you're grasping for the priesthood too. It's GOD you've ganged up against, not us. What do you have against Aaron that you're bad-mouthing him?"

Moses then ordered Dathan and Abiram, sons of Eliab, to appear, but they said, "We're not coming. Isn't it enough that you yanked us out of a land flowing with milk and honey to kill us in the wilderness? And now you keep trying to boss us around! Face it, you haven't produced: You haven't brought us into a land flowing with milk and honey, you haven't given us the promised inheritance of fields and vineyards. You'd have to poke our eyes out to keep us from seeing what's going on. Forget it, we're not coming."

Moses' temper blazed white-hot. He said to GOD, "Don't accept their Grain-Offering. I haven't taken so much as a single donkey from them; I haven't hurt a single hair of their heads."

Moses said to Korah, "Bring your people before GOD tomorrow. Appear there with them and Aaron. Have each man bring his censer filled with incense and present it to GOD—all 250 censers. And you and Aaron do the same, bring your censers."

So they all did it. They brought their censers filled with fire and incense and stood at the entrance of the Tent of Meeting. Moses and Aaron did the same.

It was Korah and his gang against Moses and Aaron at the entrance of the Tent of Meeting. The entire community could see the Glory of GOD.

GOD said to Moses and Aaron, "Separate yourselves from this congregation so that I can finish them off and be done with them."

They threw themselves on their faces and said, "O God, God of everything living, when one man sins are you going to take it out on the whole community?"

GOD spoke to Moses: "Speak to the community. Tell them, Back off from the tents of Korah, Dathan, and Abiram."

Moses got up and went to Dathan and Abiram. The leaders of Israel followed him. He then spoke to the community: "Back off from the tents of these bad men; don't touch a thing that belongs to them lest you be carried off on the flood of their sins."

So they all backed away from the tents of Korah, Dathan, and Abiram. Dathan and Abiram by now had come out and were standing at the entrance to their tents with their wives, children, and babies.

Moses continued to address the community: "This is how you'll know that it was GOD who sent me to do all these things and that it wasn't anything I cooked up on my own. If these men die a natural death like all the rest of us, you'll know that it wasn't GOD who sent me. But if GOD does something unprecedented—if the ground opens up and swallows the lot of them and they are pitched alive into Sheol—then you'll know that these men have been insolent with GOD."

The words were hardly out of his mouth when the Earth split open. Earth opened its mouth and in one gulp swallowed them down, the men and their families, all the human beings connected with Korah, along with everything they owned. And that was the end of them, pitched alive into Sheol. The Earth closed up over them and that was the last the community heard of them.

At the sound of their cries everyone around ran for dear life, shouting, "We're about to be swallowed up alive!"

Then GOD sent lightning. The fire cremated the 250 men who were offering the incense.

GOD spoke to Moses: "Tell Eleazar son of Aaron the priest, Gather up the censers from the smoldering cinders and scatter the coals a distance away for these censers have become holy. Take the censers of the men who have sinned and are now dead and hammer them into thin sheets for covering the Altar. They have been offered to GOD and are holy to GOD. Let them serve as a sign to Israel, evidence of what happened this day."

So Eleazar gathered all the bronze censers that belonged to those who had been burned up and had them hammered flat and used to overlay the Altar, just as GOD had instructed him by Moses. This was to serve as a sign to Israel that only descendants of Aaron were allowed to burn incense before GOD; anyone else trying it would end up like Korah and his gang.

Grumbling broke out the next day in the community of Israel, grumbling against Moses and Aaron: "You have killed GOD's people!"

But it so happened that when the community got together against Moses and Aaron, they looked over at the Tent of Meeting and there was the Cloud—the Glory of GOD for all to see.

Moses and Aaron stood at the front of the Tent of Meeting. GOD spoke to Moses: "Back away from this congregation so that I can do away with them this very minute."

They threw themselves face-down on the ground.

Moses said to Aaron, "Take your censer and fill it with incense, along with fire from the Altar. Get to the congregation as fast as you can: make atonement for them. Anger is pouring out from GOD—the plague has started!"

Aaron grabbed the censer, as directed by Moses, and ran into the midst of the congregation. The plague had already begun. He put burning incense into the censer and atoned for the people. He stood there between the living and the dead and stopped the plague.

Fourteen thousand seven hundred people died from the plague, not counting those who died in the affair of Korah. Aaron then went back to join Moses at the entrance to the Tent of Meeting. The plague was stopped.

AARON'S STAFF

17 GOD spoke to Moses: "Speak to the People of Israel. Get staffs from them—twelve staffs in all, one from the leader of each of their ancestral tribes. Write each man's name on his staff. Start with Aaron; write Aaron's name on the staff of Levi and then proceed with the rest, a staff for the leader of each ancestral tribe. Now lay them out in the Tent of Meeting in front of The Testimony where I keep appointments with you. What will happen next is this: The staff of the man I choose will sprout. I'm going to put a stop to this endless grumbling by the People of Israel against you."

Moses spoke to the People of Israel. Their leaders handed over twelve staffs, one for the leader of each tribe. And Aaron's staff was one of them. Moses laid out the staffs before GOD in the Tent of Testimony.

Moses walked into the Tent of Testimony the next day and saw that Aaron's staff, the staff of the tribe of Levi, had in fact sprouted—buds, blossoms, and even ripe almonds! Moses brought out all the staffs from GOD's presence and presented them to the People of Israel. They took a good look. Each leader took the staff with his name on it.

GOD said to Moses, "Return Aaron's staff to the front of The Testimony. Keep it there as a sign to rebels. This will put a stop to the grumbling against me and save their lives."

Moses did just as GOD commanded him.

The People of Israel said to Moses, "We're as good as dead. This is our death sentence. Anyone who even gets close to The Dwelling of GOD is as good as dead. Are we all doomed?"

DUTIES IN THE TENT OF TESTIMONY

18 GOD said to Aaron, "You and your sons, along with your father's family, are responsible for taking care of sins having to do with the Sanctuary; you and your sons are also responsible for sins involving the priesthood. So enlist your brothers of the tribe of Levi to join you and assist you and your sons in your duties in the Tent of Testimony. They will report to you as they go about their duties related to the Tent, but they must not have anything to do with the holy things of the Altar under penalty of death—both they and you will die! They are to work with you in taking care of the Tent of Meeting, whatever work is involved in the Tent. Outsiders are not allowed to help you.

"Your job is to take care of the Sanctuary and the Altar so that there will be no more outbreaks of anger on the People of Israel. I personally have picked your brothers, the Levites, from Israel as a whole. I'm giving them to you as a gift, a gift of GOD, to help with the work of the Tent of Meeting. But only you and your sons may serve as priests, working around the Altar and inside the curtain. The work of the priesthood is my exclusive gift to you; it cannot be delegated—anyone else who invades the Sanctuary will be executed."

GOD spoke to Aaron, "I am personally putting you in charge of my contributions, all the holy gifts I get from the People of Israel. I am turning them over to you and your children for your personal use. This is the standing rule. You and your sons get what's left from the offerings, whatever hasn't been totally burned up on the Altar—the leftovers from Grain-Offerings, Absolution-Offerings, and Compensation-Offerings. Eat it reverently; it is most holy; every male may eat it. Treat it as holy.

"You also get the Wave-Offerings from the People of Israel. I present them to you and your sons and daughters as a gift. This is the standing rule. Anyone in your household who is ritually clean may eat it. I also give you all the best olive oil, the best new wine, and the grain that is offered to GOD as the firstfruits of their harvest—all the firstfruits they offer to GOD are yours. Anyone in your household who is ritually clean may eat it.

"You get every Totally-Devoted gift. Every firstborn that is offered to GOD, whether animal or person, is yours. Except you don't get the firstborn itself, but its redemption price; firstborn humans and ritually clean animals are bought back and you get the redemption price. When the firstborn is a month old it must be redeemed at the redemption price of five shekels of silver, using the standard of the Sanctuary shekel, which weighs twenty gerahs.

"On the other hand, you don't redeem a firstborn ox, sheep, or goat—they are holy. Instead splash their blood on the Altar and burn their fat as a Fire-Gift, a pleasing fragrance to GOD. But you get the meat, just as you get the breast from the Wave-Offering and the right thigh. All the holy offerings that the People of Israel set aside for GOD, I'm turning over to you and your children. That's the standard rule and includes both you and your children—a Covenant-of-Salt, eternal and unchangeable before GOD."

GOD said to Aaron, "You won't get any inheritance in land, not so much as a small plot of ground: I am your plot of ground, I am your inheritance among the People of Israel.

"I'm giving the Levites all the tithes of Israel as their pay for the work they do in the Tent of Meeting. Starting now, the rest of the People of Israel cannot wander in and out of the Tent of Meeting; they'll be penalized for their sin and the penalty is death. It's the Levites and only the Levites who are to work in the Tent of Meeting and they are responsible for anything that goes wrong. This is the regular rule for all time. They get no inheritance among the People of Israel; instead I turn over to them the tithes that the People of Israel present as an offering to GOD. That's why I give the ruling: They are to receive no land-inheritance among the People of Israel."

✠

GOD spoke to Moses: "Speak to the Levites. Tell them, When you get the tithe from the People of Israel, the inheritance that I have assigned to you, you must tithe that tithe and present it as an offering to GOD. Your offerings will be treated the same as other people's gifts of grain from the threshing floor or wine from the wine vat. This is your procedure for making offerings to GOD from all the tithes you get from the People of Israel: give GOD's portion from these tithes to Aaron the priest. Make sure that GOD's portion is the best and holiest of everything you get.

"Tell the Levites, When you offer the best part, the rest will be treated the same as grain from the threshing floor or wine from the wine vat that others give. You and your households are free to eat the rest of it anytime and anyplace—it's your wages for your work at the Tent of Meeting. By offering the best part, you'll avoid guilt, you won't desecrate the holy offerings of the People of Israel, and you won't die."

THE RED COW

19 GOD spoke to Moses and Aaron: "This is the rule from the Revelation that GOD commands: Tell the People of Israel to get a red cow, a healthy specimen, ritually clean, that has never been in harness. Present it to Eleazar the priest, then take it outside the camp and butcher it while he looks on. Eleazar will take some of the blood on his finger and splash it seven times in the direction of the Tent of Meeting.

"Then under Eleazar's supervision burn the cow, the whole thing— hide, meat, blood, even its dung. The priest then will take a stick of cedar, some sprigs of hyssop, and a piece of scarlet material and throw them on the burning cow. Afterwards the priest must wash his clothes and bathe well with water. He can then come into the camp but he remains ritually unclean until evening. The man who burns the cow must also wash his clothes and bathe with water. He also is unclean until evening.

"Then a man who is ritually clean will gather the ashes of the cow and place them in a ritually clean place outside the camp. The congregation of Israel will keep them to use in the Water-of-Cleansing, an Absolution-Offering.

"The man who gathered up the ashes must scrub his clothes; he is ritually unclean until evening. This is to be a standing rule for both native-born Israelites and foreigners living among them.

"Anyone who touches a dead body is ritually unclean for seven days. He must purify himself with the Water-of-Cleansing on the third day; on the seventh day he will be clean. But if he doesn't follow the procedures for the third and seventh days, he won't be clean. Anyone who touches the dead body of anyone and doesn't get cleansed desecrates GOD's Dwelling and is to be excommunicated. For as long as the Water-of-Cleansing has not been sprinkled on him, he remains ritually unclean.

"This is the rule for someone who dies in his tent: Anyone who enters the tent or is already in the tent is ritually unclean for seven days, and every open container without a lid is unclean.

"Anyone out in the open field who touches a corpse, whether dead from violent or natural causes, or a human bone or a grave is unclean for seven days. For this unclean person, take some ashes from the burned Absolution-Offering and add some fresh water to it in a bowl. Find a ritually clean man to dip a sprig of hyssop into the water and sprinkle the tent and all its furnishings, the persons who were in the tent, the one who touched the bones of the person who was killed or died a natural death, and whoever may have touched a grave. Then he is to sprinkle the unclean person on the third and seventh days. On the seventh day he is considered cleansed. The cleansed person must then scrub his clothes and take a bath; by evening he is clean. But if an unclean person does not go through these cleansing procedures, he must be excommunicated from the community; he has desecrated the Sanctuary of GOD. The Water-of-Cleansing has not been sprinkled on him and he is ritually unclean. This is the standing rule for these cases.

"The man who sprinkles the Water-of-Cleansing has to scrub his clothes; anyone else who touched the Water-of-Cleansing is also ritually unclean until evening.

"Anything the ritually unclean man touches becomes unclean, and the person who touches what he touched is unclean until evening."

CAMP KADESH

20 In the first month, the entire company of the People of Israel arrived in the Wilderness of Zin. The people stayed in Kadesh.

Miriam died there, and she was buried.

There was no water there for the community, so they ganged up on Moses and Aaron. They attacked Moses: "We wish we'd died when the rest of our brothers died before GOD. Why did you haul this congregation of GOD out here into this wilderness to die, people and cattle alike? And why did you take us out of Egypt in the first place, dragging us into this miserable country? No grain, no figs, no grapevines, no pomegranates—and now not even any water!"

Moses and Aaron walked from the assembled congregation to the Tent of Meeting and threw themselves face-down on the ground. And they saw the Glory of GOD.

GOD spoke to Moses: "Take the staff. Assemble the community, you and your brother Aaron. Speak to that rock that's right in front of them and it will give water. You will bring water out of the rock for them; congregation and cattle will both drink."

Moses took the staff away from GOD's presence, as commanded.

He and Aaron rounded up the whole congregation in front of the rock. Moses spoke: "Listen, rebels! Do we have to bring water out of this rock for you?"

With that Moses raised his arm and slammed his staff against the rock—once, twice. Water poured out. Congregation and cattle drank.

GOD said to Moses and Aaron, "Because you didn't trust me, didn't treat me with holy reverence in front of the People of Israel, you two aren't going to lead this company into the land that I am giving them."

These were the Waters of Meribah (Bickering) where the People of Israel bickered with GOD, and he revealed himself as holy.

✛

Moses sent emissaries from Kadesh to the king of Edom with this message: "A message from your brother Israel: You are familiar with all the trouble we've run into. Our ancestors went down to Egypt and lived there a long time. The Egyptians viciously abused both us and our ancestors. But when we cried out for help to GOD, he heard our cry. He sent an angel and got us out of Egypt. And now here we are at Kadesh, a town at the border of your land.

"Will you give us permission to cut across your land? We won't trespass through your fields or orchards and we won't drink out of your wells; we'll keep to the main road, the King's Road, straying neither right nor left until we've crossed your border."

The king of Edom answered, "Not on your life. If you so much as set a foot on my land, I'll kill you."

The People of Israel said, "Look, we'll stay on the main road. If we or our animals drink any water, we'll pay you for it. We're harmless— just a company of footsore travelers."

He answered again: "No. You may *not* come through." And Edom came out and blocked the way with a crowd of people brandishing weapons. Edom refused to let them cross through his land. So Israel had to detour around him.

CAMP HOR

The People of Israel, the entire company, set out from Kadesh and traveled to Mount Hor.

GOD said to Moses and Aaron at Mount Hor at the border of Edom,

"It's time for Aaron to be gathered into the company of his ancestors. He will not enter the land I am giving to the People of Israel because you both rebelled against my orders at the Waters of Meribah. So take Aaron and his son Eleazar and lead them up Mount Hor. Remove Aaron's clothes from him and put them on his son Eleazar. Aaron will be gathered there; Aaron will die."

Moses obeyed GOD's command. They climbed Mount Hor as the whole congregation watched. Moses took off Aaron's clothes and put them on his son Eleazar. Aaron died on top of the mountain. Then Moses and Eleazar came down from the mountain. The whole congregation, getting the news that Aaron had died, went into thirty days of mourning for him.

HORMAH

21 The Canaanite king of Arad, ruling in the Negev, heard that Israel was advancing up the road to Atharim. He attacked Israel and took prisoners of war.

Israel vowed a vow to GOD: "If you will give this people into our power, we'll destroy their towns and present the ruins to you as a holy destruction."

GOD listened to Israel's prayer and gave them the Canaanites. They destroyed both them and their towns, a holy destruction. They named the place Hormah (Holy Destruction).

THE SNAKE OF FIERY COPPER

They set out from Mount Hor along the Red Sea Road, a detour around the land of Edom. The people became irritable and cross as they traveled. They spoke out against God and Moses: "Why did you drag us out of Egypt to die in this godforsaken country? No decent food; no water—we can't stomach this stuff any longer."

So GOD sent poisonous snakes among the people; they bit them and many in Israel died. The people came to Moses and said, "We sinned when we spoke out against GOD and you. Pray to GOD; ask him to take these snakes from us."

Moses prayed for the people.

GOD said to Moses, "Make a snake and put it on a flagpole: Whoever is bitten and looks at it will live."

So Moses made a snake of fiery copper and put it on top of a flagpole. Anyone bitten by a snake who then looked at the copper snake lived.

CAMPING ON THE WAY TO MOAB

The People of Israel set out and camped at Oboth. They left Oboth and camped at Iye Abarim in the wilderness that faces Moab on the east. They went from there and pitched camp in the Zered Valley. Their next camp was alongside the Arnon River, which marks the border between Amorite country and Moab. The Book of the Wars of GOD refers to this place:

> Waheb in Suphah,
>   the canyons of Arnon;
> Along the canyon ravines
>   that lead to the village Ar
> And lean hard against
>   the border of Moab.

They went on to Beer (The Well), where GOD said to Moses, "Gather the people; I'll give them water." That's where Israel sang this song:

> Erupt, Well!
> Sing the Song of the Well,
>   the well sunk by princes,
> Dug out by the peoples' leaders
>   digging with their scepters and staffs.

From the wilderness their route went from Mattanah to Nahaliel to Bamoth (The Heights) to the valley that opens into the fields of Moab from where Pisgah (The Summit) rises and overlooks Jeshimon (Wasteland).

Israel sent emissaries to Sihon, king of the Amorites, saying, "Let us cross your land. We won't trespass into your fields or drink water in your vineyards. We'll keep to the main road, the King's Road, until we're through your land."

But Sihon wouldn't let Israel go through. Instead he got his army together and marched into the wilderness to fight Israel. At Jahaz he attacked Israel. But Israel fought hard, beat him soundly, and took possession of his land from the Arnon all the way to the Jabbok right up to the Ammonite border. They stopped there because the Ammonite border was fortified. Israel took and occupied all the Amorite cities, including Heshbon and all its surrounding villages. Heshbon was the capital city of Sihon king of the Amorites. He had attacked the former king of Moab and captured all his land as far north as the river Arnon. That is why the folk singers sing,

> Come to Heshbon to rebuild the city,
>   restore Sihon's town.

> Fire once poured out of Heshbon,
>   flames from the city of Sihon;
> Burning up Ar of Moab,
>   the natives of Arnon's heights.
> Doom, Moab!
>   The people of Chemosh, done for!
> Sons turned out as fugitives, daughters abandoned as captives
>   to the king of the Amorites, to Sihon.

> Oh, but we finished them off:
>   Nothing left of Heshbon as far as Dibon;
> Devastation as far off as Nophah,
>   scorched earth all the way to Medeba.

Israel moved in and lived in Amorite country. Moses sent men to scout out Jazer. They captured its villages and drove away the Amorites who lived there.

Then they turned north on the road to Bashan. Og king of Bashan marched out with his entire army to meet Moses in battle at Edrei.

GOD said to Moses, "Don't be afraid of him. I'm making a present of him to you, him and all his people and his land. Treat him the same as Sihon king of the Amorites who ruled in Heshbon."

So they attacked him, his sons, and all the people—there was not a single survivor. Israel took the land.

BALAAM

22 The People of Israel marched on and camped on the Plains of Moab at Jordan-Jericho.

Balak son of Zippor learned of all that Israel had done to the

Amorites. The people of Moab were in a total panic because of Israel. There were so many of them! They were terrorized.

Moab spoke to the leaders of Midian: "Look, this mob is going to clean us out—a bunch of crows picking a carcass clean."

Balak son of Zippor, who was king of Moab at that time, sent emissaries to get Balaam son of Beor, who lived at Pethor on the banks of the Euphrates River, his homeland.

Balak's emissaries said, "Look. A people has come up out of Egypt, and they're all over the place! And they're pressing hard on me. Come and curse them for me—they're too much for me. Maybe then I can beat them; we'll attack and drive them out of the country. You have a reputation: Those you bless stay blessed; those you curse stay cursed."

The leaders of Moab and Midian were soon on their way, with the fee for the cursing tucked safely in their wallets. When they got to Balaam, they gave him Balak's message.

"Stay here for the night," Balaam said. "In the morning I'll deliver the answer that GOD gives me."

The Moabite nobles stayed with him.

Then God came to Balaam. He asked, "So who are these men here with you?"

Balaam answered, "Balak son of Zippor, king of Moab, sent them with a message: 'Look, the people that came up out of Egypt are all over the place! Come and curse them for me. Maybe then I'll be able to attack and drive them out of the country.'"

God said to Balaam, "Don't go with them. And don't curse the others—they are a blessed people."

The next morning Balaam got up and told Balak's nobles, "Go back home; GOD refuses to give me permission to go with you."

So the Moabite nobles left, came back to Balak, and said, "Balaam wouldn't come with us."

Balak sent another group of nobles, higher ranking and more distinguished. They came to Balaam and said, "Balak son of Zippor says, 'Please, don't refuse to come to me. I will honor and reward you lavishly—anything you tell me to do, I'll do; I'll pay anything—only come and curse this people.'"

Balaam answered Balak's servants: "Even if Balak gave me his house stuffed with silver and gold, I wouldn't be able to defy the orders of my GOD to do anything, whether big or little. But come along and stay with me tonight as the others did; I'll see what GOD will say to me this time."

God came to Balaam that night and said, "Since these men have come all this way to see you, go ahead and go with them. But make sure you do absolutely nothing other than what I tell you."

Balaam got up in the morning, saddled his donkey, and went off with the noblemen from Moab. As he was going, though, God's anger flared. The angel of GOD stood in the road to block his way. Balaam was riding his donkey, accompanied by his two servants. When the donkey saw the angel blocking the road and brandishing a sword, she veered off the road into the ditch. Balaam beat the donkey and got her back on the road.

But as they were going through a vineyard, with a fence on either side, the donkey again saw GOD's angel blocking the way and veered into the fence, crushing Balaam's foot against the fence. Balaam hit her again.

GOD's angel blocked the way yet again—a very narrow passage this time; there was no getting through on the right or left. Seeing the angel, Balaam's donkey sat down under him. Balaam lost his temper; he beat the donkey with his stick.

Then GOD gave speech to the donkey. She said to Balaam: "What have I ever done to you that you have beat me these three times?"

Balaam said, "Because you've been playing games with me! If I had a sword I would have killed you by now."

The donkey said to Balaam, "Am I not your trusty donkey on whom you've ridden for years right up until now? Have I ever done anything like this to you before? Have I?"

He said, "No."

Then GOD helped Balaam see what was going on: He saw GOD's angel blocking the way, brandishing a sword. Balaam fell to the ground, his face in the dirt.

GOD's angel said to him: "Why have you beaten your poor donkey these three times? I have come here to block your way because you're getting way ahead of yourself. The donkey saw me and turned away from me these three times. If she hadn't, I would have killed you by this time, but not the donkey. I would have let her off."

Balaam said to GOD's angel, "I have sinned. I had no idea you were standing in the road blocking my way. If you don't like what I'm doing, I'll head back."

But GOD's angel said to Balaam, "Go ahead and go with them. But only say what I tell you to say—absolutely no other word."

And so Balaam continued to go with Balak's nobles.

When Balak heard that Balaam was coming, he went out to meet him in the Moabite town that was on the banks of the Arnon, right on the boundary of his land.

Balak said to Balaam, "Didn't I send an urgent message for help? Why didn't you come when I called? Do you think I can't pay you enough?"

Balaam said to Balak, "Well, I'm here now. But I can't tell you just anything. I can speak only words that God gives me—no others."

Balaam then accompanied Balak to Kiriath Huzoth (Street-Town). Balak slaughtered cattle and sheep for sacrifices and presented them to Balaam and the nobles who were with him.

At daybreak Balak took Balaam up to Bamoth Baal (The Heights of Baal) so that he could get a good view of some of the people.

23 Balaam said, "Build me seven altars here, and then prepare seven bulls and seven rams."

Balak did it. Then Balaam and Balak sacrificed a bull and a ram on each of the altars.

Balaam instructed Balak: "Stand watch here beside your Whole-Burnt-Offering while I go off by myself. Maybe GOD will come and meet with me. Whatever he shows or tells me, I'll report to you." Then he went off by himself.

God did meet with Balaam. Balaam said, "I've set up seven altars and offered a bull and a ram on each altar."

Then GOD gave Balaam a message: "Return to Balak and give him this message."

He went back and found him stationed beside his Whole-Burnt-Offering and with him all the nobles of Moab. Then Balaam spoke his message-oracle:

Balak led me here from Aram,
    the king of Moab all the way from the eastern mountains.
"Go, curse Jacob for me;
    go, damn Israel."

How can I curse whom God has not cursed?
How can I damn whom GOD has not damned?
From rock pinnacles I see them,
from hilltops I survey them:
Look! a people camping off by themselves,
thinking themselves outsiders among nations.
But who could ever count the dust of Jacob
or take a census of cloud-of-dust Israel?
I want to die like these right-living people!
I want an end just like theirs!

Balak said to Balaam, "What's this? I brought you here to curse my enemies, and all you've done is bless them."

Balaam answered, "Don't I have to be careful to say what GOD gives me to say?"

✠

Balak said to him, "Go with me to another place from which you can only see the outskirts of their camp—you won't be able to see the whole camp. From there, curse them for my sake."

So he took him to Watchmen's Meadow at the top of Pisgah. He built seven altars there and offered a bull and a ram on each altar.

Balaam said to Balak, "Take up your station here beside your Whole-Burnt-Offering while I meet with him over there."

GOD met with Balaam and gave him a message. He said, "Return to Balak and give him the message."

Balaam returned and found him stationed beside his Whole-Burnt-Offering and the nobles of Moab with him. Balak said to him, "What did GOD say?" Then Balaam spoke his message-oracle:

On your feet, Balak. Listen,
listen carefully son of Zippor:
God is not man, one given to lies,
and not a son of man changing his mind.
Does he speak and not do what he says?
Does he promise and not come through?
I was brought here to bless;
and now he's blessed—how can I change that?
He has no bone to pick with Jacob,

261

he sees nothing wrong with Israel.
GOD is with them,
and they're with him, shouting praises to their King.
God brought them out of Egypt,
rampaging like a wild ox.
No magic spells can bind Jacob,
no incantations can hold back Israel.
People will look at Jacob and Israel and say,
"What a great thing has God done!"
Look, a people rising to its feet, stretching like a lion,
a king-of-the-beasts, aroused,
Unsleeping, unresting until its hunt is over
and it's eaten and drunk its fill.

Balak said to Balaam, "Well, if you can't curse them, at least don't bless them."

Balaam replied to Balak, "Didn't I tell you earlier: 'All God speaks, and only what he speaks, I speak'?"

✛

Balak said to Balaam, "Please, let me take you to another place; maybe we can find the right place in God's eyes where you'll be able to curse them for me." So Balak took Balaam to the top of Peor, with a vista over the Jeshimon (Wasteland).

Balaam said to Balak, "Build seven altars for me here and prepare seven bulls and seven rams for sacrifice."

Balak did it and presented an offering of a bull and a ram on each of the altars.

24 By now Balaam realized that GOD wanted to bless Israel. So he didn't work in any sorcery as he had done earlier. He turned and looked out over the wilderness. As Balaam looked, he saw Israel camped tribe by tribe. The Spirit of God came on him, and he spoke his oracle-message:

Decree of Balaam son of Beor,
yes, decree of a man with 20/20 vision;
Decree of a man who hears God speak,
who sees what The Strong God shows him,

Who falls on his face in worship,
    who sees what's really going on.

What beautiful tents, Jacob,
    oh, your homes, Israel!
Like valleys stretching out in the distance,
    like gardens planted by rivers,
Like sweet herbs planted by the gardener GOD,
    like red cedars by pools and springs,
Their buckets will brim with water,
    their seed will spread life everywhere.
Their king will tower over Agag and his ilk,
    their kingdom surpassingly majestic.
God brought them out of Egypt,
    rampaging like a wild ox,
Gulping enemies like morsels of meat,
    crushing their bones, snapping their arrows.
Israel crouches like a lion and naps,
    king-of-the-beasts—who dares disturb him?
Whoever blesses you is blessed,
    whoever curses you is cursed.

Balak lost his temper with Balaam. He shook his fist. He said to Balaam: "I got you in here to curse my enemies and what have you done? Blessed them! Blessed them three times! Get out of here! Go home! I told you I would pay you well, but you're getting nothing. You can blame GOD."

Balaam said to Balak, "Didn't I tell you up front when you sent your emissaries, 'Even if Balak gave me his palace stuffed with silver and gold, I couldn't do anything on my own, whether good or bad, that went against GOD's command'? I'm leaving for home and my people, but I warn you of what this people will do to your people in the days to come." Then he spoke his oracle-message:

Decree of Balaam son of Beor,
    decree of the man with 20/20 vision,
Decree of the man who hears godly speech,
    who knows what's going on with the High God,
Who sees what The Strong God reveals,

who bows in worship and sees what's real.
I see him, but not right now,
    I perceive him, but not right here;
A star rises from Jacob
    a scepter from Israel,
Crushing the heads of Moab,
    the skulls of all the noisy windbags;
I see Edom sold off at auction,
    enemy Seir marked down at the flea market,
    while Israel walks off with the trophies.
A ruler is coming from Jacob
    who'll destroy what's left in the city.

✝

Then Balaam spotted Amalek and delivered an oracle-message. He said,

Amalek, you're in first place among nations right now,
    but you're going to come in last, ruined.

✝

He saw the Kenites and delivered his oracle-message to them:

Your home is in a nice secure place,
    like a nest high on the face of a cliff.
Still, you Kenites will look stupid
    when Asshur takes you prisoner.

✝

Balaam spoke his final oracle-message:

Doom! Who stands a chance
    when God starts in?
Sea-Peoples, raiders from across the sea,
    will harass Asshur and Eber,
But they'll also come to nothing,
    just like all the rest.

Balaam got up and went home. Balak also went on his way.

THE ORGY AT SHITTIM

25 While Israel was camped at Shittim (Acacia Grove), the men began to have sex with the Moabite women. It started when the women invited the men to their sex-and-religion worship. They ate together and then worshiped their gods. Israel ended up joining in the worship of the Baal of Peor. GOD was furious, his anger blazing out against Israel.

GOD said to Moses, "Take all the leaders of Israel and kill them by hanging, leaving them publicly exposed in order to turn GOD's anger away from Israel."

Moses issued orders to the judges of Israel: "Each of you must execute the men under your jurisdiction who joined in the worship of Baal Peor."

Just then, while everyone was weeping in penitence at the entrance of the Tent of Meeting, an Israelite man, flaunting his behavior in front of Moses and the whole assembly, paraded a Midianite woman into his family tent. Phinehas son of Eleazar, the son of Aaron the priest, saw what he was doing, grabbed his spear, and followed them into the tent. With one thrust he drove the spear through the two of them, the man of Israel and the woman, right through their private parts. That stopped the plague from continuing among the People of Israel. But 24,000 had already died.

GOD spoke to Moses: "Phinehas son of Eleazar, son of Aaron the priest, has stopped my anger against the People of Israel. Because he was as zealous for my honor as I myself am, I didn't kill all the People of Israel in my zeal. So tell him that I am making a Covenant-of-Peace with him. He and his descendants are joined in a covenant of eternal priesthood, because he was zealous for his God and made atonement for the People of Israel."

The name of the man of Israel who was killed with the Midianite woman was Zimri son of Salu, the head of the Simeonite family. And the name of the Midianite woman who was killed was Cozbi daughter of Zur, a tribal chief of a Midianite family.

GOD spoke to Moses: "From here on make the Midianites your enemies. Fight them tooth and nail. They turned out to be your enemies when they seduced you in the business of Peor and that woman Cozbi, daughter of a Midianite leader, the woman who was killed at the time of the plague in the matter of Peor."

CENSUS ON THE PLAINS OF MOAB

26 After the plague GOD said to Moses and Eleazar son of Aaron the priest, "Number the entire community of Israel by families— count every person who is twenty years and older who is able to serve in the army of Israel."

Obeying GOD's command, Moses and Eleazar the priest addressed them on the Plains of Moab at Jordan-Jericho: "Count off from age twenty and older."

The People of Israel who came out of the land of Egypt:
Reuben, Israel's firstborn. The sons of Reuben were:
   Hanoch and the Hanochite clan,
   Pallu and the Palluite clan,
   Hezron and the Hezronite clan,
   Carmi and the Carmite clan.
These made up the Reubenite clans. They numbered 43,730.
   The son of Pallu: Eliab.
   The sons of Eliab: Nemuel, Dathan, and Abiram. (These were the same Dathan and Abiram, community leaders from Korah's gang, who rebelled against Moses and Aaron in the Korah Rebellion against GOD. The Earth opened its jaws and swallowed them along with Korah's gang who died when the fire ate them up, all 250 of them. After all these years, they're still a warning sign. But the line of Korah did not die out.)

The sons of Simeon by clans:
   Nemuel and the Nemuelite clan,
   Jamin and the Jaminite clan,
   Jakin and the Jakinite clan,
   Zerah and the Zerahite clan,
   Shaul and the Shaulite clan.
These were the clans of Simeon. They numbered 22,200 men.

The sons of Gad by clans:
   Zephon and the Zephonite clan,
   Haggi and the Haggite clan,
   Shuni and the Shunite clan,
   Ozni and the Oznite clan,

Eri and the Erite clan,
Arodi and the Arodite clan,
Areli and the Arelite clan.
These were the clans of Gad. They numbered 40,500 men.

Er and Onan were sons of Judah who died early on in Canaan. The sons of Judah by clans:
Shelah and the Shelanite clan,
Perez and the Perezite clan,
Zerah and the Zerahite clan.
The sons of Perez:
Hezron and the Hezronite clan,
Hamul and the Hamulite clan.
These were the clans of Judah. They numbered 76,500.

The sons of Issachar by clans:
Tola and the Tolaite clan,
Puah and the Puite clan,
Jashub and the Jashubite clan,
Shimron and the Shimronite clan.
These were the clans of Issachar. They numbered 64,300.

The sons of Zebulun by clans:
Sered and the Seredite clan,
Elon and the Elonite clan,
Jahleel and the Jahleelite clan.
These were the clans of Zebulun. They numbered 60,500.

The sons of Joseph by clans through Manasseh and Ephraim. Through Manasseh:
Makir and the Makirite clan
(now Makir was the father of Gilead),
Gilead and the Gileadite clan.
The sons of Gilead:
Iezer and the Iezerite clan,
Helek and the Helekite clan,
Asriel and the Asrielite clan,
Shechem and the Shechemite clan,
Shemida and the Shemidaite clan,

Hepher and the Hepherite clan.

Zelophehad son of Hepher had no sons, only daughters.

Their names were Mahlah, Noah, Hoglah, Milcah, and Tirzah.

These were the clans of Manasseh. They numbered 52,700.

The sons of Ephraim by clans:

Shuthelah and the Shuthelahite clan,

Beker and the Bekerite clan,

Tahan and the Tahanite clan.

The sons of Shuthelah:

Eran and the Eranite clan.

These were the clans of Ephraim. They numbered 32,500.

These are all the sons of Joseph by their clans.

The sons of Benjamin by clans:

Bela and the Belaite clan,

Ashbel and the Ashbelite clan,

Ahiram and the Ahiramite clan,

Shupham and the Shuphamite clan,

Hupham and the Huphamite clan.

The sons of Bela through Ard and Naaman:

Ard and the Ardite clan,

Naaman and the Naamite clan.

These were the clans of Benjamin. They numbered 45,600.

The sons of Dan by clan:

Shuham and the Shuhamite clan.

These are the clans of Dan, all Shuhamite clans. They numbered 64,400.

The sons of Asher by clan:

Imnah and the Imnite clan,

Ishvi and the Ishvite clan,

Beriah and the Beriite clan.

The sons of Beriah:

Heber and the Heberite clan,

Malkiel and the Malkielite clan.

Asher also had a daughter, Serah.

These were the clans of Asher. They numbered 53,400.

The sons of Naphtali by clans:
    Jahzeel and the Jahzeelite clan,
    Guni and the Gunite clan,
    Jezer and the Jezerite clan,
    Shillem and the Shillemite clan.
These were the clans of Naphtali. They numbered 45,400.

The total number of the People of Israel: 601,730.

✠

GOD spoke to Moses: "Divide up the inheritance of the land based on population. A larger group gets a larger inheritance; a smaller group gets a smaller inheritance — each gets its inheritance based on the population count.

"Make sure that the land is assigned by lot.

"Each group's inheritance is based on population, the number of names listed in its ancestral tribe, divided among the many and the few by lot."

✠

These are the numberings of the Levites by clan:
    Gershon and the Gershonite clan,
    Kohath and the Kohathite clan,
    Merari and the Merarite clan.
The Levite clans also included:
    the Libnite clan,
    the Hebronite clan,
    the Mahlite clan,
    the Mushite clan,
    the Korahite clan.
Kohath was the father of Amram. Amram's wife was Jochebed, a descendant of Levi, born into the Levite family during the Egyptian years. Jochebed bore Aaron, Moses, and their sister Miriam to Amram. Aaron was the father of Nadab and Abihu, Eleazar and Ithamar; however, Nadab and Abihu died when they offered unauthorized sacrifice in the presence of GOD.

The numbering of Levite males one month and older came to 23,000. They hadn't been counted in with the rest of the People of Israel because they didn't inherit any land.

269

These are the ones numbered by Moses and Eleazar the priest, the People of Israel counted in the Plains of Moab at Jordan-Jericho. Not one of them had been among those counted by Moses and Aaron the priest in the census of the People of Israel taken in the Wilderness of Sinai. For GOD had said of them, "They'll die, die in the wilderness—not one of them will be left except for Caleb son of Jephunneh, and Joshua son of Nun."

THE DAUGHTERS OF ZELOPHEHAD

27 The daughters of Zelophehad showed up. Their father was the son of Hepher son of Gilead son of Makir son of Manasseh, belonging to the clans of Manasseh son of Joseph. The daughters were Mahlah, Noah, Hoglah, Milcah, and Tirzah.

They came to the entrance of the Tent of Meeting. They stood before Moses and Eleazar the priest and before the leaders and the congregation and said, "Our father died in the wilderness. He wasn't part of Korah's rebel anti-GOD gang. He died for his own sins. And he left no sons. But why should our father's name die out from his clan just because he had no sons? So give us an inheritance among our father's relatives."

Moses brought their case to GOD.

GOD ruled: "Zelophehad's daughters are right. Give them land as an inheritance among their father's relatives. Give them their father's inheritance.

"Then tell the People of Israel, If a man dies and leaves no son, give his inheritance to his daughter. If he has no daughter, give it to his brothers. If he has no brothers, give it to his father's brothers. If his father had no brothers, give it to the nearest relative so that the inheritance stays in the family. This is the standard procedure for the People of Israel, as commanded by GOD through Moses."

JOSHUA

GOD said to Moses, "Climb up into the Abarim Mountains and look over at the land that I am giving to the People of Israel. When you've had a good look you'll be joined to your ancestors in the grave—yes, you also along with Aaron your brother. This goes back to the day when the congregation quarreled in the Wilderness of Zin and you didn't honor me in holy reverence before them in the matter of the waters, the Waters of Meribah (Quarreling) at Kadesh in the Wilderness of Zin."

Moses responded to GOD: "Let GOD, the God of the spirits of everyone living, set a man over this community to lead them, to show the way ahead and bring them back home so GOD's community will not be like sheep without a shepherd."

GOD said to Moses, "Take Joshua the son of Nun—the Spirit is in him!—and place your hand on him. Stand him before Eleazar the priest in front of the entire congregation and commission him with everyone watching. Pass your magisterial authority over to him so that the whole congregation of the People of Israel will listen obediently to him. He is to consult with Eleazar the priest who, using the oracle-Urim, will prayerfully advise him in the presence of GOD. He will command the People of Israel, the entire community, in all their comings and goings."

Moses followed GOD's orders. He took Joshua and stood him before Eleazar the priest in front of the entire community. He laid his hands on him and commissioned him, following the procedures GOD had given Moses.

OFFERINGS

28 GOD spoke to Moses: "Command the People of Israel. Tell them, You're in charge of presenting my food, my Fire-Gifts of pleasing fragrance, at the set times. Tell them, This is the Fire-Gift that you are to present to GOD: two healthy yearling lambs each day as a regular Whole-Burnt-Offering. Sacrifice one lamb in the morning, the other in the evening, together with two quarts of fine flour mixed with a quart of olive oil for a Grain-Offering. This is the standard Whole-Burnt-Offering instituted at Mount Sinai as a pleasing fragrance, a Fire-Gift to GOD. The Drink-Offering that goes with it is a quart of strong beer with each lamb. Pour out the Drink-Offering before GOD in the Sanctuary. Sacrifice the second lamb in the evening with the Grain-Offering and Drink-Offering the same as in the morning—a Fire-Gift of pleasing fragrance for GOD.

☩

"On the Sabbath, sacrifice two healthy yearling lambs, together with the Drink-Offering and the Grain-Offering of four quarts of fine flour mixed with oil. This is the regular Sabbath Whole-Burnt-Offering, in addition to the regular Whole-Burnt-Offering and its Drink-Offering.

☩

"On the first of the month offer a Whole-Burnt-Offering to GOD: two young bulls, one ram, and seven male yearling lambs—all healthy.

"A Grain-Offering of six quarts of fine flour mixed with oil goes with each bull, four quarts of fine flour mixed with oil with the ram, and two quarts of fine flour mixed with oil with each lamb. This is for a Whole-Burnt-Offering, a pleasing fragrance, a Fire-Gift to GOD. Also, Drink-Offerings of two quarts of wine for each bull, one and a quarter quarts of wine for the ram, and a quart of wine for each lamb are to be poured out.

"This is the first of the month Whole-Burnt-Offering to be made throughout the year. In addition to the regular Whole-Burnt-Offering with its accompanying Drink-Offering, a he-goat is to be offered to GOD as an Absolution-Offering.

✝

"GOD'S Passover is to be held on the fourteenth day of the first month. On the fifteenth day of this month hold a festival.

"For seven days, eat only unraised bread: Begin the first day in holy worship; don't do any regular work that day. Bring a Fire-Gift to GOD, a Whole-Burnt-Offering: two young bulls, one ram, and seven male yearling lambs—all healthy. Prepare a Grain-Offering of six quarts of fine flour mixed with oil for each bull, four quarts for the ram, and two quarts for each lamb, plus a goat as an Absolution-Offering to atone for you.

"Sacrifice these in addition to the regular morning Whole-Burnt-Offering. Prepare the food this way for the Fire-Gift, a pleasing fragrance to GOD, every day for seven days. Prepare it in addition to the regular Whole-Burnt-Offering and Drink-Offering.

"Conclude the seventh day in holy worship; don't do any regular work on that day.

✝

"On the Day of Firstfruits when you bring an offering of new grain to GOD on your Feast-of-Weeks, gather in holy worship and don't do any regular work. Bring a Whole-Burnt-Offering of two young bulls, one ram, and seven male yearling lambs as a pleasing fragrance to GOD. Prepare a Grain-Offering of six quarts of fine flour mixed with oil for each bull, four quarts for the ram, and two quarts for each lamb, plus a he-goat as an Absolution-Offering to atone for you.

272

"These are all over and above the daily Whole-Burnt-Offering and its Grain-Offering and the Drink-Offering. Remember, the animals must be healthy.

✠

29 "On the first day of the seventh month, gather in holy worship and do no regular work. This is your Day-of-Trumpet-Blasts. Sacrifice a Whole-Burnt-Offering: one young bull, one ram, and seven male yearling lambs—all healthy—as a pleasing fragrance to GOD. Prepare a Grain-Offering of six quarts of fine flour mixed with oil for the bull, four quarts for the ram, and two quarts for each lamb, plus a he-goat as an Absolution-Offering to atone for you.

"These are all over and above the monthly and daily Whole-Burnt-Offerings with their Grain-Offerings and Drink-Offerings as prescribed, a pleasing fragrance, a Fire-Gift to GOD.

✠

"On the tenth day of this seventh month, gather in holy worship, humble yourselves and do no work.

"Bring a Whole-Burnt-Offering to GOD as a pleasing fragrance: one young bull, one ram, and seven yearling male lambs—all healthy. Prepare a Grain-Offering of six quarts of fine flour mixed with oil for the bull, four quarts for the ram, and two quarts for each of the seven lambs. Also bring a he-goat as an Absolution-Offering to atone for you in addition to the regular Whole-Burnt-Offering with its Grain-Offering and Drink-Offering.

✠

"Gather in holy worship on the fifteenth day of the seventh month; do no regular work. Celebrate a Festival to GOD for seven days. Bring a Whole-Burnt-Offering, a Fire-Gift of pleasing fragrance to GOD: thirteen young bulls, two rams, and fourteen yearling male lambs—all healthy. Prepare a Grain-Offering of six quarts of fine flour mixed with oil for each of the bulls, four quarts for each ram, and two quarts for each of the fourteen lambs. Also bring a he-goat as an Absolution-Offering in addition to the regular Whole-Burnt-Offering with its Grain-Offering and Drink-Offering.

"On the second day: twelve young bulls, two rams, and fourteen year-ling male lambs—all healthy. Prepare Grain-Offerings and Drink-Offerings to go with the bulls, rams, and lambs following the prescribed recipes. And bring a he-goat as an Absolution-Offering in addition to the regular Whole-Burnt-Offering with its Grain-Offering and Drink-Offering.

"On the third day: eleven bulls, two rams, and fourteen male yearling lambs—all healthy. Prepare Grain-Offerings and Drink-Offerings to go with the bulls, rams, and lambs following the prescribed recipes. And bring a he-goat as an Absolution-Offering in addition to the regular Whole-Burnt-Offering with its Grain-Offering and Drink-Offering.

"On the fourth day: ten bulls, two rams, and fourteen male yearling lambs—all healthy. Prepare Grain-Offerings and Drink-Offerings to go with the bulls, rams, and lambs following the prescribed recipes. And bring a he-goat as an Absolution-Offering in addition to the regular Whole-Burnt-Offering with its Grain-Offering and Drink-Offering.

"On the fifth day: nine bulls, two rams, and fourteen male yearling lambs—all healthy. Prepare Grain-Offerings and Drink-Offerings to go with the bulls, rams, and lambs following the prescribed recipes. And bring a he-goat as an Absolution-Offering in addition to the regular Whole-Burnt-Offering with its Grain-Offering and Drink-Offering.

"On the sixth day: eight bulls, two rams, and fourteen male yearling lambs—all healthy. Prepare Grain-Offerings and Drink-Offerings to go with the bulls, rams, and lambs following the prescribed recipes. And bring a he-goat as an Absolution-Offering in addition to the regular Whole-Burnt-Offering with its Grain-Offering and Drink-Offering.

"On the seventh day: seven bulls, two rams, and fourteen male yearling lambs—all healthy. Prepare Grain-Offerings and Drink-Offerings to go with the bulls, rams, and lambs following the prescribed recipes. And bring a he-goat as an Absolution-Offering in addition to the regular Whole-Burnt-Offering with its Grain-Offering and Drink-Offering.

"On the eighth day: Gather in holy worship; do no regular work. Bring a Fire-Gift of pleasing fragrance to GOD, a Whole-Burnt-Offering: one bull, one ram, and seven male yearling lambs—all healthy. Prepare Grain-Offerings and Drink-Offerings to go with the bulls, rams, and lambs following the prescribed recipes. And bring a he-goat as an Absolution-Offering in addition to the regular Whole-Burnt-Offering with its Grain-Offering and Drink-Offering.

"Sacrifice these to GOD as a congregation at your set feasts: your Whole-Burnt-Offerings, Grain-Offerings, Drink-Offerings, and Peace-Offerings. These are all over and above your personal Vow-Offerings and Freewill-Offerings."

Moses instructed the People of Israel in all that GOD commanded him.

VOWS

30 Moses spoke to the heads of the tribes of the People of Israel: "This is what GOD commands: When a man makes a vow to GOD or binds himself by an oath to do something, he must not break his word; he must do exactly what he has said.

"When a woman makes a vow to GOD and binds herself by a pledge as a young girl still living in her father's house, and her father hears of her vow or pledge but says nothing to her, then she has to make good on all her vows and pledges. But if her father holds her back when he hears of what she has done, none of her vows and pledges are valid. GOD will release her since her father held her back.

"If she marries after she makes a vow or has made some rash promise or pledge, and her husband hears of it but says nothing to her, then she has to make good on whatever she vowed or pledged. But if her husband intervenes when he hears of it, he cancels the vow or rash promise that binds her. And GOD will release her.

"Any vow or pledge taken by a widow or divorced woman is binding on her.

"When a woman who is living with her husband makes a vow or takes a pledge under oath and her husband hears about it but says nothing and doesn't say she can't do it, then all her vows and pledges are valid. But if her husband cancels them when he hears about them, then none of the vows and pledges that she made are binding. Her husband has cancelled them and GOD will release her. Any vow and pledge that she makes that may be to her detriment can be either affirmed or annulled by her husband. But if her husband is silent and doesn't speak up day after day, he confirms her vows and pledges — she has to make good on them. By saying nothing to her when he hears of them, he binds her to them. If, however, he cancels them sometime after he hears of them, he takes her guilt on himself."

These are the rules that GOD gave Moses regarding conduct between a man and his wife and between a father and his young daughter who is still living at home.

THE MIDIANITE WAR

31 GOD spoke to Moses: "Avenge the People of Israel on the Midianites. Afterward you will go to be with your dead ancestors."

Moses addressed the people: "Recruit men for a campaign against Midian, to exact GOD's vengeance on Midian, a thousand from each tribe of Israel to go to war."

A fighting force of a thousand from each tribe of Israel—twelve thousand in all—was recruited. Moses sent them off to war, a thousand from each tribe, and also Phinehas son of Eleazar, who went as priest to the army, in charge of holy vessels and the signaling bugles.

They attacked Midian, just as GOD had commanded Moses, and killed every last man. Among the fallen were Evi, Rekem, Zur, Hur, and Reba—the five kings of Midian. They also killed Balaam son of Beor with the sword. The People of Israel took the Midianite women and children captive and took all their animals and herds and goods as plunder. They burned to the ground all the towns in which Midianites lived and also their tent camps. They looted and plundered everything and everyone—stuff and people and animals. They took it all—captives and booty and plunder—back to Moses and Eleazar the priest and the company of Israel where they were camped on the Plains of Moab, at Jordan-Jericho.

Moses, Eleazar, and all the leaders of the congregation went to meet the returning army outside the camp. Moses was furious with the army officers—the commanders of thousands and commanders of hundreds—as they came back from the battlefield: "What's this! You've let these women live! They're the ones who, under Balaam's direction, seduced the People of Israel away from GOD in that mess at Peor, causing the plague that hit GOD's people. Finish your job: kill all the boys. Kill every woman who has slept with a man. The younger women who are virgins you can keep alive for yourselves.

"Now here's what you are to do: Pitch tents outside the camp. All who have killed anyone or touched a corpse must stay outside the camp for seven days. Purify yourselves and your captives on the third and seventh days. Purify every piece of clothing and every utensil—everything made of leather, goat hair, or wood."

Eleazar the priest then spoke to the soldiers who had fought in the battle: "This is the ruling from the Revelation that GOD gave Moses: Gold, silver, bronze, iron, tin, and lead—and anything else that can survive fire—must be passed through the fire; then it will be ritually purified. It must also be ritually washed in the Water-of-Cleansing. Further, whatever cannot survive fire must be put through that water. On the seventh day scrub your clothes; you will be ritually clean. Then you can return to camp."

✝

GOD said to Moses, "I want you and Eleazar the priest and the family leaders in the community to count the captives, people and animals. Split the plunder between the soldiers who fought the battle and the rest of the congregation.

"Then tax the booty that goes to the soldiers at the rate of one life out of five hundred, whether humans, cattle, donkeys, or sheep. It's a GOD-tax taken from their half-share to be turned over to Eleazar the priest on behalf of GOD. Tax the congregation's half-share at the rate of one life out of fifty, whether persons, cattle, donkeys, sheep, goats, or other animals. Give this to the Levites who are in charge of the care of GOD's Dwelling."

Moses and Eleazar followed through with what GOD had commanded Moses.

The rest of the plunder taken by the army:
675,000 sheep
72,000 cattle
61,000 donkeys
32,000 women who were virgins
The half-share for those who had fought in the war:
337,500 sheep, with a tax of 675 for GOD
36,000 cattle, with a tax of 72 for GOD
30,500 donkeys, with a tax of 61 for GOD
16,000 people, with a tax of 32 for GOD
Moses turned the tax over to Eleazar the priest as GOD's part, following GOD's instructions to Moses.

The other half-share for the Israelite community that Moses set apart from what was given to the men who fought the war was:
337,500 sheep
36,000 cattle
30,500 donkeys
16,000 people
From the half-share going to the People of Israel, Moses, just as GOD had instructed him, picked one out of every fifty persons and animals and gave them to the Levites, who were in charge of maintaining GOD's Dwelling.

The military officers—commanders of thousands and commanders of hundreds—came to Moses and said, "We have counted the soldiers under our command and not a man is missing. We've brought offerings to GOD from the gold jewelry we got—armlets, bracelets, rings, earrings, ornaments—to make atonement for our lives before GOD."

Moses and Eleazar the priest received the gold from them, all that fine-crafted jewelry. In total, the gold from the commanders of thousands and hundreds that Moses and Eleazar offered as a gift to GOD weighed about six hundred pounds, all donated by the soldiers who had taken the booty. Moses and Eleazar took the gold from the commanders of thousands and hundreds and brought it to the Tent of Meeting, to serve as a reminder for the People of Israel before GOD.

TRIBES EAST OF THE JORDAN

32 The families of Reuben and Gad had huge herds of livestock. They saw that the country of Jazer and Gilead was just the place for grazing livestock. And so they came, the families of Gad and of Reuben, and spoke to Moses and Eleazar the priest and the leaders of the congregation, saying, "Ataroth, Dibon, Jazer, Nimrah, Heshbon, Elealeh, Sebam, Nebo, and Beon—the country that GOD laid low before the community of Israel—is a country just right for livestock, and we have livestock."

They continued, "If you think we've done a good job so far, give us this country for our inheritance. Don't make us go across the Jordan."

Moses answered the families of Gad and Reuben: "Do you mean that you are going to leave the fighting that's ahead to your brothers while you settle down here? Why would you even think of letting the People of Israel down, demoralizing them just as they're about to move into the land GOD gave them? That's exactly what your ancestors did when I sent them from Kadesh Barnea to survey the country. They went as far as the Valley of Eshcol, took one look and quit. They completely demoralized the People of Israel from entering the land GOD had given them. And GOD got angry—oh, did he get angry! He swore: 'They'll never get to see it; none of those who came up out of Egypt who are twenty years and older will ever get to see the land that I promised to Abraham, Isaac, and Jacob. They weren't interested in following me—their hearts weren't in it. None, except for Caleb son of Jephunneh the Kenizzite, and Joshua son of Nun; they followed me—their hearts were in it.'

"GOD's anger smoked against Israel. He made them wander in the

wilderness for forty years, until that entire generation that acted out evil in his sight had died out.

"And now here you are, just one more mob of sinners stepping up to replace your ancestors, throwing fuel on the already blazing anger of GOD against Israel. If you won't follow him, he'll do it again. He'll dump them in the desert and the disaster will be all your fault."

They came close to him and said, "All we want to do is build corrals for our livestock and towns for our families. Then we'll take up arms and take the front lines, leading the People of Israel to their place. We'll be able to leave our families behind, secure in fortified towns, safe from those who live in the land. But we won't go back home until every Israelite is in full possession of his inheritance. We won't expect any inheritance west of the Jordan; we are claiming all our inheritance east of the Jordan."

Moses said, "If you do what you say, take up arms before GOD for battle and together go across the Jordan ready, before GOD, to fight until GOD has cleaned his enemies out of the land, then when the land is secure you will have fulfilled your duty to GOD and Israel. Then this land will be yours to keep before GOD.

"But if you don't do what you say, you will be sinning against GOD; you can be sure that your sin will track you down. So, go ahead. Build towns for your families and corrals for you livestock. Do what you said you'd do."

The families of Gad and Reuben told Moses: "We will do as our master commands. Our children and wives, our flocks and herds will stay behind here in the towns of Gilead. But we, every one of us fully armed, will cross the river to fight for GOD, just as our master has said."

So Moses issued orders for them to Eleazar the priest, Joshua the son of Nun, and the heads of the ancestral tribes of the People of Israel. Moses said, "If the families of Gad and Reuben cross the Jordan River with you and before GOD, all armed and ready to fight, then after the land is secure, you may give them the land of Gilead as their inheritance. But if they don't cross over with you, they'll have to settle up with you in Canaan."

The families of Gad and Reuben responded: "We will do what GOD has said. We will cross the Jordan before GOD, ready and willing to fight. But the land we inherit will be here, to the east of the Jordan."

Moses gave the families of Gad, Reuben, and the half-tribe of Manasseh son of Joseph the kingdom of Sihon, king of the Amorites, and the kingdom of Og, king of Bashan—the land, its towns, and all the territories connected with them—the works.

The Gadites rebuilt Dibon, Ataroth, Aroer, Atroth Shophan, Jazer, Jogbehah, Beth Nimrah, and Beth Haran as fortified cities; they also built corrals for their animals.

The Reubenites rebuilt Heshbon, Elealeh, and Kiriathaim, also Nebo and Baal Meon and Sibmah. They renamed the cities that they rebuilt.

The family of Makir son of Manasseh went to Gilead, captured it, and drove out the Amorites who lived there. Moses then gave Gilead to the Makirites, the descendants of Manasseh. They moved in and settled there.

Jair, another son of Manasseh, captured some villages and named them Havvoth Jair (Jair's Tent-Camps).

Nobah captured Kenath and its surrounding camps. He renamed it after himself, Nobah.

CAMPSITES FROM RAMESES TO JORDAN-JERICHO

33 These are the camping sites in the journey of the People of Israel after they left Egypt, deployed militarily under the command of Moses and Aaron. Under GOD's instruction Moses kept a log of every time they moved, camp by camp:

They marched out of Rameses the day after the Passover. It was the fifteenth day of the first month. They marched out heads high and confident. The Egyptians, busy burying their firstborn whom GOD had killed, watched them go. GOD had exposed the nonsense of their gods.

The People of Israel:

left Rameses and camped at Succoth;

left Succoth and camped at Etham at the edge of the wilderness;

left Etham, circled back to Pi Hahiroth east of Baal Zephon, and camped near Migdol;

left Pi Hahiroth and crossed through the Sea into the wilderness; three days into the Wilderness of Etham they camped at Marah;

left Marah and came to Elim where there were twelve springs and seventy palm trees; they camped there;

left Elim and camped by the Red Sea;

left the Red Sea and camped in the Wilderness of Sin;

left the Wilderness of Sin and camped at Dophkah;

left Dophkah and camped at Alush;

left Alush and camped at Rephidim where there was no water for the people to drink;

left Rephidim and camped in the Wilderness of Sinai;

left the Wilderness of Sinai and camped at Kibroth Hattaavah;

left Kibroth Hattaavah and camped at Hazeroth;

left Hazeroth and camped at Rithmah;

left Rithmah and camped at Rimmon Perez;

left Rimmon Perez and camped at Libnah;

left Libnah and camped at Rissah;

left Rissah and camped at Kehelathah;

left Kehelathah and camped at Mount Shepher;

left Mount Shepher and camped at Haradah;

left Haradah and camped at Makheloth;

left Makheloth and camped at Tahath;

left Tahath and camped at Terah;

left Terah and camped at Mithcah;

left Mithcah and camped at Hashmonah;

left Hashmonah and camped at Moseroth;

left Moseroth and camped at Bene Jaakan;

left Bene Jaakan and camped at Hor Haggidgad;

left Hor Haggidgad and camped at Jotbathah;

left Jotbathah and camped at Abronah;

left Abronah and camped at Ezion Geber;

left Ezion Geber and camped at Kadesh in the Wilderness of Zin.

After they left Kadesh and camped at Mount Hor at the border of Edom, Aaron the priest climbed Mount Hor at GOD's command and died there. It was the first day of the fifth month in the fortieth year after the People of Israel had left Egypt. Aaron was 123 years old when he died on Mount Hor.

✠

The Canaanite king of Arad—he ruled in the Negev of Canaan—heard that the People of Israel had arrived.

They left Mount Hor and camped at Zalmonah;

left Zalmonah and camped at Punon;

left Punon and camped at Oboth;

left Oboth and camped at Iye Abarim on the border of Moab;

left Iyim and camped at Dibon Gad;

left Dibon Gad and camped at Almon Diblathaim;

left Almon Diblathaim and camped in the mountains of Abarim (Across-the-River), within sight of Nebo.

After they left the mountains of Abarim they camped on the Plains of Moab at Jordan-Jericho. On the Plains of Moab their camp stretched along the banks of the Jordan from Beth Jeshimoth to Abel Shittim (Acacia Meadow).

GOD spoke to Moses on the Plains of Moab at Jordan-Jericho: "Tell the People of Israel, When you cross the Jordan into the country of Canaan, drive out the native population before you, destroy their carved idols, destroy their cast images, level their worship-mounds so that you take over the land and make yourself at home in it; I've given it to you. It's yours.

"Divide up the land by lot according to the size of your clans: Large clans will get large tracts of land, small clans will get smaller tracts of land. However the lot falls, that's it. Divide it up according to your ancestral tribes.

"But if you don't drive out the native population, everyone you let stay there will become a cinder in your eye and a splinter in your foot. They'll give you endless trouble right in your own backyards. And I'll start treating you the way I planned to treat them."

LAND INHERITANCE

34 GOD spoke to Moses: "Command the People of Israel. Tell them: When you enter Canaan, these are the borders of the land you are getting as an inheritance:

"Your southern border will take in some of the Wilderness of Zin where it touches Edom. It starts in the east at the Dead Sea, curves south of Scorpion Pass and on to Zin, continues south of Kadesh Barnea, then to Hazar Addar and on to Azmon, where it takes a turn to the northwest to the Brook of Egypt and on to the Mediterranean Sea.

"Your western border will be the Mediterranean Sea.

"Your northern border runs on a line from the Mediterranean Sea to Mount Hor, and from Mount Hor to Lebo Hamath, connects to Zedad, continues to Ziphron, and ends at Hazar Enan. This is your northern border.

"Your eastern border runs on a line from Hazar Enan to Shepham. The border goes south from Shepham to Riblah to the east of Ain, and continues along the slopes east of the Sea of Galilee. The border then follows the Jordan River and ends at the Dead Sea.

"This is your land with its four borders."

Moses then commanded the People of Israel: "This is the land: Divide up the inheritance by lot. GOD has ordered it to be given to the nine and a half tribes. The tribe of Reuben, the tribe of Gad, and the half-tribe of Manasseh have already received their inheritance; the two tribes and the half-tribe got their inheritance east of Jordan-Jericho, facing the sunrise."

☩

GOD spoke to Moses: "These are the men who will be in charge of distributing the inheritance of the land: Eleazar the priest and Joshua son of Nun. Assign one leader from each tribe to help them in distributing the land. Assign these:

Caleb son of Jephunneh from the tribe of Judah;

Shemuel son of Ammihud from the tribe of Simeon;

Elidad son of Kislon from the tribe of Benjamin;

Bukki son of Jogli, leader from the tribe of Dan;

Hanniel son of Ephod, leader from the tribe of Manasseh son of Joseph;

Kemuel son of Shiphtan, leader from the tribe of Ephraim son of Joseph;

Elizaphan son of Parnach, leader from the tribe of Zebulun;

Paltiel son of Azzan, leader from the tribe of Issachar;

Ahihud son of Shelomi, leader from the tribe of Asher;

Pedahel son of Ammihud, leader from the tribe of Naphtali."

These are the men GOD commanded to hand out the assignments of land-inheritance to the People of Israel in the country of Canaan.

CITIES FOR LEVITES AND ASYLUM-CITIES

35 Then GOD spoke to Moses on the Plains of Moab at Jordan-Jericho: "Command the People of Israel to give the Levites as their part of the total inheritance towns to live in. Make sure there is plenty of pasture around the towns. Then they will be well taken care of with towns to live in and pastures for their cattle, flocks, and other livestock.

"The pasture surrounding the Levites' towns is to extend 1,500 feet in each direction from the city wall. The outside borders of the pasture are to measure three thousand feet on each of the four sides—east, south, west, and north—with the town at the center. Each city will be supplied with pasture.

"Six of these towns that you give the Levites will be asylum-cities to which anyone who accidentally kills another person may flee for asylum. In addition, you will give them forty-two other towns—forty-eight towns in all, together with their pastures. The towns that you give the Levites from the common inheritance of the People of Israel are to be taken in proportion to the size of each tribe—many towns from a tribe that has many, few from a tribe that has few."

GOD spoke to Moses: "Speak to the People of Israel. Tell them, When you cross the River Jordan into the country of Canaan, designate your asylum-cities, towns to which a person who accidentally kills someone can flee for asylum. They will be places of refuge from the avenger so that the alleged murderer won't be killed until he can appear before the community in court. Provide six asylum-cities. Designate three of the towns to the east side of the Jordan, the other three in Canaan proper—asylum-cities for the People of Israel, for the foreigner, and for any occasional visitors or guests—six asylum-cities to run to for anyone who accidentally kills another.

"But if the killer has used an iron object, that's just plain murder; he's obviously a murderer and must be put to death.

"Or if he has a rock in his hand big enough to kill and the man dies, that's murder; he's a murderer and must be put to death.

"Or if he's carrying a wooden club heavy enough to kill and the man dies, that's murder; he's a murderer and must be put to death.

"In such cases the avenger has a right to kill the murderer when he meets him—he can kill him on the spot.

"And if out of sheer hatred a man pushes another or from ambush throws something at him and he dies, or angrily hits him with his fist and kills him, that's murder—he must be put to death. The avenger has a right to kill him when he gets him.

"If, however, he impulsively pushes someone and there is no history of hard feelings, or he impetuously picks up something and throws it, or he accidentally drops a stone tool—a maul or hammer, say—and it hits and kills someone he didn't even know was there, and there's no suspicion that there was bad blood between them, the community is to judge between the killer and the avenger following these guidelines. It's the task of the community to save the killer from the hand of the avenger—the community is to return him to his asylum-city to which he fled. He must stay there until the death of the High Priest who was anointed with the holy oil. But if the murderer leaves the asylum-city to which he has fled, and the avenger finds him outside the borders of his asylum-city, the avenger has a right to kill the murderer. And he's not considered guilty of murder.

"So it's important that he stay in his asylum-city until the death of the High Priest. After the death of the High Priest he is free to return to his own place.

⁜

"These are the procedures for making judgments from now on, wherever you live.

"Anyone who kills another may be executed only on the testimony of eyewitnesses. But no one can be executed on the testimony of only one witness.

"Don't accept bribe money in exchange for the life of a murderer. He's guilty and deserves the death penalty. Put him to death.

"And don't accept bribe money for anyone who has fled to an asylum-city so as to permit him to go back and live in his own place before the death of the High Priest.

"Don't pollute the land in which you live. Murder pollutes the land. The land can't be cleaned up of the blood of murder except through the blood of the murderer.

"Don't desecrate the land in which you live. I live here too—I, GOD, live in the same neighborhood with the People of Israel."

THE DAUGHTERS OF ZELOPHEHAD

36 The heads of the ancestral clan of Gilead son of Makir, the son of Manasseh—they were from the clans of the descendants of Joseph—approached Moses and the leaders who were heads of the families in the People of Israel.

They said, "When GOD commanded my master to hand over the inheritance-lands by lot to the People of Israel, my master was also commanded by GOD to hand over the inheritance-land of Zelophehad our brother to his daughters. But what happens if they marry into another tribe in the People of Israel? Their inheritance-land will be taken out of our ancestral tribe and get added into the tribe into which they married. And then when the Year of Jubilee comes for the People of Israel their inheritance will be lumped in with the inheritance of the tribe into which they married—their land will be removed from our ancestors' inheritance!"

Moses, at GOD's command, issued this order to the People of Israel: "What the tribe of the sons of Joseph says is right. This is GOD's command to Zelophehad's daughters: They are free to marry anyone they choose as long as they marry within their ancestral clan. The inheritance-land of the People of Israel must not get passed around from tribe to tribe. No, keep the tribal inheritance-land in the family. Every daughter who inherits land, regardless of the tribe she is in, must marry a man from within her father's tribal clan. Every Israelite is responsible for making sure the inheritance stays within the ancestral tribe. No inheritance-land may be passed from tribe to tribe; each tribe of the People of Israel must hold tight to its own land."

Zelophehad's daughters did just as GOD commanded Moses. Mahlah, Tirzah, Hoglah, Milcah, and Noah, Zelophehad's daughters, all married their cousins on their father's side. They married within the families of Manasseh son of Joseph and their inheritance-lands stayed in their father's family.

These are the commands and regulations that GOD commanded through the authority of Moses to the People of Israel on the Plains of Moab at Jordan-Jericho.

DEUTERONOMY

Deuteronomy is a sermon—actually a series of sermons. It is the longest sermon in the Bible and maybe the longest sermon ever. Deuteronomy presents Moses, standing on the Plains of Moab with all Israel assembled before him, preaching. It is his last sermon. When he completes it, he will leave his pulpit on the plains, climb a mountain, and die.

The setting is stirring and emotion-packed. Moses had entered the biblical story of salvation as a little baby born in Egypt under a death threat. Now, 120 years later, eyesight sharp as ever and walking with "a spring in his step," he preaches this immense sermon and dies, still brimming with words and life.

This sermon does what all sermons are intended to do: Take God's words, written and spoken in the past, take the human experience, ancestral and personal, of the listening congregation, then reproduce the words and experience as a single event right now, in this present moment. No word that God has spoken is a mere literary artifact to be studied; no human experience is dead history merely to be regretted or admired. The continuous and insistent Mosaic repetitions of "today" and "this day" throughout these sermons keep attentions taut and responsive. The complete range of human experience is brought to life and salvation by the full revelation of God: Live this! Now!

The Plains of Moab are the last stop on the forty-year journey from Egyptian slavery to Promised Land freedom. The People of Israel have experienced a lot as a congregation: deliverance, wanderings, rebellions, wars, providence, worship, guidance. The People of Israel have heard a lot from God: commandments, covenant conditions, sacrificial procedures. And now, poised at the River Jordan, ready to cross over and possess the new land, Moses, preaching his great Plains of Moab sermon, makes sure that they don't leave any of it behind, not so much as one detail of their experience or God's revelation: He puts their entire experience of salvation and providence into the present tense (chapters 1-11); he puts the entire revelation of commandment and covenant into the present tense (chapters 12-28); and then he wraps it all up in a charge and a song and a blessing to launch them into today's obedience and believing (chapters 29-34).

"Let's go."

DEUTERONOMY

1 These are the sermons Moses preached to all Israel when they were east of the Jordan River in the Arabah Wilderness, opposite Suph, in the vicinity of Paran, Tophel, Laban, Hazeroth, and Dizahab. It takes eleven days to travel from Horeb to Kadesh Barnea following the Mount Seir route.

✝

It was on the first day of the eleventh month of the fortieth year when Moses addressed the People of Israel, telling them everything GOD had commanded him concerning them. This came after he had defeated Sihon king of the Amorites, who ruled from Heshbon, and Og king of Bashan, who ruled from Ashtaroth in Edrei. It was east of the Jordan in the land of Moab that Moses set out to explain this Revelation.

MOSES PREACHES TO ISRAEL ON THE PLAINS OF MOAB
He said:

Back at Horeb, GOD, our God, spoke to us: "You've stayed long enough at this mountain. On your way now. Get moving. Head for the Amorite hills, wherever people are living in the Arabah, the mountains, the foothills, the Negev, the seashore—the Canaanite country and the Lebanon all the way to the big river, the Euphrates. Look, I've given you this land. Now go in and take it. It's the land GOD promised to give your ancestors Abraham, Isaac, and Jacob and their children after them."

At the time I told you, "I can't do this, can't carry you all by myself. GOD, your God, has multiplied your numbers. Why, look at you—you rival the stars in the sky! And may GOD, the God-of-Your-Fathers, keep it up and multiply you another thousand times, bless you just as he promised. But how can I carry, all by myself, your troubles and burdens and quarrels? So select some wise, understanding, and seasoned men from your tribes, and I will commission them as your leaders."

You answered me, "Good! A good solution."

So I went ahead and took the top men of your tribes, wise and seasoned, and made them your leaders—leaders of thousands, of hundreds, of fifties, and of tens, officials adequate for each of your tribes.

At the same time I gave orders to your judges: "Listen carefully to complaints and accusations between your fellow Israelites. Judge fairly between each person and his fellow or foreigner. Don't play favorites; treat the little and the big alike; listen carefully to each. Don't be impressed by big names. This is *God's* judgment you're dealing with. Hard cases you can bring to me; I'll deal with them."

I issued orders to you at that time regarding everything you would have to deal with.

Then we set out from Horeb and headed for the Amorite hill country, going through that huge and frightening wilderness that you've had more than an eyeful of by now—all under the command of GOD, our God,—and finally arrived at Kadesh Barnea. There I told you, "You've made it to the Amorite hill country that GOD, our God, is giving us. Look, GOD, your God, has placed this land as a gift before you. Go ahead and take it now. GOD, the God-of-Your-Fathers, promised it to you. Don't be afraid. Don't lose heart."

But then you all came to me and said, "Let's send some men on ahead to scout out the land for us and bring back a report on the best route to take and the kinds of towns we can expect to find."

That seemed like a good idea to me, so I picked twelve men, one from each tribe. They set out, climbing through the hills. They came to the Eshcol Valley and looked it over. They took samples of the produce of the land and brought them back to us, saying, "It's a good land that GOD, our God, is giving us!"

But then you weren't willing to go up. You rebelled against GOD, your God's plain word. You complained in your tents: "GOD hates us. He hauled us out of Egypt in order to dump us among the Amorites— a death sentence for sure! How can we go up? We're trapped in a dead end. Our brothers took all the wind out of our sails, telling us, 'The people are bigger and stronger than we are; their cities are huge, their defenses massive—we even saw Anakite giants there!'"

I tried to relieve your fears: "Don't be terrified of them. GOD, your God, is leading the way; he's fighting for you. You saw with your own eyes what he did for you in Egypt; you saw what he did in the wilderness, how GOD, your God, carried you as a father carries his child, carried you the whole way until you arrived here. But now that you're here, you won't trust GOD, your God,—this same GOD who goes ahead of you in your travels to scout out a place to pitch camp, a fire by night and a cloud by day to show you the way to go."

When GOD heard what you said, he exploded in anger. He swore,

"Not a single person of this evil generation is going to get so much as a look at the good land that I promised to give to your parents. Not one—except for Caleb son of Jephunneh. He'll see it. I'll give him and his descendants the land he walked on because he was all for following GOD, heart and soul."

But I also got it. Because of you GOD's anger spilled over onto me. He said, "You aren't getting in either. Your assistant, Joshua son of Nun, will go in. Build up his courage. He's the one who will claim the inheritance for Israel. And your babies of whom you said, 'They'll be grabbed for plunder,' and all these little kids who right now don't even know right from wrong—they'll get in. I'll give it to them. Yes, they'll be the new owners. But not you. Turn around and head back into the wilderness following the route to the Red Sea."

You spoke up, "We've sinned against GOD. We'll go up and fight, following all the orders that GOD, our God, has commanded." You took your weapons and dressed for battle—you thought it would be so easy going into those hills!

But GOD told me, "Tell them, 'Don't do it; don't go up to fight—I'm not with you in this. Your enemies will waste you.'"

I told you but you wouldn't listen. You rebelled at the plain word of GOD. You threw out your chests and strutted into the hills. And those Amorites, who had lived in those hills all their lives, swarmed all over you like a hive of bees, chasing you from Seir all the way to Hormah, a stinging defeat. You came back and wept in the presence of GOD, but he didn't pay a bit of attention to you; GOD didn't give you the time of day. You stayed there in Kadesh a long time, about as long as you had stayed there earlier.

2 Then we turned around and went back into the wilderness following the route to the Red Sea, as GOD had instructed me. We worked our way in and around the hills of Seir for a long, long time.

☩

Then GOD said, "You've been going around in circles in these hills long enough; go north. Command the people, You're about to cut through the land belonging to your relatives, the People of Esau who settled in Seir. They are terrified of you, but restrain yourselves. Don't try and start a fight. I am not giving you so much as a square inch of their land. I've already given all the hill country of Seir to Esau—he owns it all.

Pay them up front for any food or water you get from them."

GOD, your God, has blessed you in everything you have done. He has guarded you in your travels through this immense wilderness. For forty years now, GOD, your God, has been right here with you. You haven't lacked one thing.

So we detoured around our brothers, the People of Esau who live in Seir, avoiding the Arabah Road that comes up from Elath and Ezion Geber; instead we used the road through the Wilderness of Moab.

GOD told me, "And don't try to pick a fight with the Moabites. I am not giving you any of their land. I've given ownership of Ar to the People of Lot."

The Emites (Monsters) used to live there — mobs of hulking giants, like Anakites. Along with the Anakites they were lumped in with the Rephaites (Ghosts) but in Moab they were called Emites. Horites also used to live in Seir, but the descendants of Esau took over and destroyed them, the same as Israel did in the land GOD gave them to possess.

GOD said, "It's time now to cross the Brook Zered." So we crossed the Brook Zered.

It took us thirty-eight years to get from Kadesh Barnea to the Brook Zered. That's how long it took for the entire generation of soldiers from the camp to die off, as GOD had sworn they would. GOD was relentless against them until the last one was gone from the camp.

When the last of these soldiers had died, GOD said to me, "This is the day you cut across the territory of Moab, at Ar. When you approach the People of Ammon, don't try and pick a fight with them because I'm not giving you any of the land of the People of Ammon for yourselves — I've already given it to the People of Lot." It is also considered to have once been the land of the Rephaites. Rephaites lived there long ago — the Ammonites called them Zamzummites (Barbarians) — huge mobs of them, giants like the Anakites. GOD destroyed them and the Ammonites moved in and took over. It was the same with the People of Esau who live in Seir — GOD got rid of the Horites who lived there earlier and they moved in and took over, as you can see. Regarding the Avvites who lived in villages as far as Gaza, the Caphtorites who came from Caphtor (Crete) wiped them out and moved in.

✢

"On your feet now. Get started. Cross the Brook Arnon. Look: Here's Sihon the Amorite king of Heshbon and his land. I'm handing it over to you— it's all yours. Go ahead take it. Go to war with him. Before the day is out, I'll make sure that all the people around here are thoroughly terrified. Rumors of you are going to spread like wildfire; they'll totally panic."

From the Wilderness of Kedemoth, I sent messengers to Sihon, king of Heshbon. They carried a friendly message: "Let me cross through your land on the highway. I'll stay right on the highway; I won't trespass right or left. I'll pay you for any food or water we might need. Let me walk through.

"The People of Esau who live in Seir and the Moabites who live in Ar did this, helping me on my way until I can cross the Jordan and enter the land that GOD, our God, is giving us."

But Sihon king of Heshbon wouldn't let us cross his land. GOD, your God, turned his spirit mean and his heart hard so he could hand him over to you, as you can see that he has done.

Then GOD said to me, "Look, I've got the ball rolling—Sihon and his land are soon yours. Go ahead. Take it. It's practically yours!"

So Sihon and his entire army confronted us in battle at Jahaz. GOD handed him, his sons, and his entire army over to us and we utterly crushed them. While we were at it we captured all his towns and totally destroyed them, a holy destruction—men, women, and children. No survivors. We took the livestock and the plunder from the towns we had captured and carried them off for ourselves. From Aroer on the edge of the Brook Arnon and the town in the gorge, as far as Gilead, not a single town proved too much for us; GOD, our God, gave every last one of them to us.

The only land you didn't take, obeying GOD's command, was the land of the People of Ammon, the land along the Jabbok and around the cities in the hills.

✢

3 Then we turned north and took the road to Bashan. Og king of Bashan, he and all his people, came out to meet us in battle at Edrei.

GOD said to me, "Don't be afraid of him; I'm turning him over to you, along with his whole army and his land. Treat him the way you treated Sihon king of the Amorites who ruled from Heshbon."

So GOD, our God, also handed Og king of Bashan over to us—Og and all his people—and we utterly crushed them. Again, no survivors. At the same time we took all his cities. There wasn't one of the sixty cities that we didn't take—the whole region of Argob, Og's kingdom in Bashan. All these cities were fortress cities with high walls and barred gates. There were also numerous unwalled villages. We totally destroyed them—a holy destruction. It was the same treatment we gave to Sihon king of Heshbon, a holy destruction of every city, man, woman, and child. But all the livestock and plunder from the cities we took for ourselves.

Throughout that time we took the land from under the control of the two kings of the Amorites who ruled the country east of the Jordan, all the way from the Brook Arnon to Mount Hermon. (Sirion is the name given Hermon by the Sidonians; the Amorites call it Senir.) We took all the towns of the plateau, everything in Gilead, everything in Bashan, as far as Salecah and Edrei, the border towns of Bashan, Og's kingdom.

Og king of Bashan was the last remaining Rephaite. His bed, made of iron, was over thirteen feet long and six wide. You can still see it on display in Rabbah of the People of Ammon.

✝

Of the land that we possessed at that time, I gave the Reubenites and the Gadites the territory north of Aroer along the Brook Arnon and half the hill country of Gilead with its towns.

I gave the half-tribe of Manasseh the rest of Gilead and all of Bashan, Og's kingdom—all the region of Argob, which takes in all of Bashan. This used to be known as the Land of the Rephaites.

Jair, a son of Manasseh, got the region of Argob to the borders of the Geshurites and Maacathites. He named the Bashan villages after himself, Havvoth Jair (Jair's Tent-Villages). They're still called that.

I gave Gilead to Makir.

I gave the Reubenites and Gadites the land from Gilead down to the Brook Arnon, whose middle was the boundary, and as far as the Jabbok River, the boundary line of the People of Ammon. The western boundary was the Jordan River in the Arabah all the way from the Kinnereth (the Sea of Galilee) to the Sea of the Arabah (the Salt Sea or Dead Sea) at the base of the slopes of Mount Pisgah on the east.

✝

I commanded you at that time, "GOD, your God, has given you this land to possess. Your men, fit and armed for the fight, are to cross the river in advance of their brothers, the People of Israel. Only your wives, children, and livestock (I know you have much livestock) may go ahead and settle down in the towns I have already given you until GOD secures living space for your brothers as he has for you and they have taken possession of the country west of the Jordan that GOD, your God, is giving them. After that, each man may return to the land I've given you here."

✛

I commanded Joshua at that time, "You've seen with your own two eyes everything GOD, your God, has done to these two kings. GOD is going to do the same thing to all the kingdoms over there across the river where you're headed. Don't be afraid of them. GOD, your God, — he's fighting for you."

At that same time, I begged GOD: "GOD, my Master, you let me in on the beginnings, you let me see your greatness, you let me see your might— what god in Heaven or Earth can do anything like what you've done! Please, let me in also on the endings, let me cross the river and see the good land over the Jordan, the lush hills, the Lebanon mountains."

But GOD was still angry with me because of you. He wouldn't listen. He said, "Enough of that. Not another word from you on this. Climb to the top of Mount Pisgah and look around: look west, north, south, east. Take in the land with your own eyes. Take a good look because you're not going to cross this Jordan.

"Then command Joshua: Give him courage. Give him strength. Single-handed he will lead this people across the river. Single-handed he'll cause them to inherit the land at which you can only look."

That's why we have stayed in this valley near Beth Peor.

✛

4 Now listen, Israel, listen carefully to the rules and regulations that I am teaching you to follow so that you may live and enter and take possession of the land that GOD, the God-of-Your-Fathers, is giving to you. Don't add a word to what I command you, and don't remove a word from it. Keep the commands of GOD, your God, that I am commanding you.

You saw with your own eyes what GOD did at Baal Peor, how GOD destroyed from among you every man who joined in the Baal Peor orgies. But you, the ones who held tight to GOD, your God, are alive and well, every one of you, today.

Pay attention: I'm teaching you the rules and regulations that GOD commanded me, so that you may live by them in the land you are entering to take up ownership. Keep them. Practice them. You'll become wise and understanding. When people hear and see what's going on, they'll say, "What a great nation! So wise, so understanding! We've never seen anything like it."

Yes. What other great nation has gods that are intimate with them the way GOD, our God, is with us, always ready to listen to us? And what other great nation has rules and regulations as good and fair as this Revelation that I'm setting before you today?

Just make sure you stay alert. Keep close watch over yourselves. Don't forget anything of what you've seen. Don't let your heart wander off. Stay vigilant as long as you live. Teach what you've seen and heard to your children and grandchildren.

That day when you stood before GOD, your God, at Horeb, GOD said to me, "Assemble the people in my presence to listen to my words so that they will learn to fear me in holy fear for as long as they live on the land, and then they will teach these same words to their children."

You gathered. You stood in the shadow of the mountain. The mountain was ablaze with fire, blazing high into the very heart of Heaven. You stood in deep darkness and thick clouds. GOD spoke to you out of the fire. You heard the sound of words but you saw nothing — no form, only a voice. He announced his covenant, the Ten Words, by which he commanded you to live. Then he wrote them down on two slabs of stone.

And GOD commanded me at that time to teach you the rules and regulations that you are to live by in the land which you are crossing over the Jordan to possess.

You saw no form on the day GOD spoke to you at Horeb from out of the fire. Remember that. Carefully guard yourselves so that you don't turn corrupt and make a form, carving a figure that looks male or female, or looks like a prowling animal or a flying bird or a slithering snake or a fish in a stream. And also carefully guard yourselves so that you don't look up into the skies and see the sun and moon and stars, all the constellations of the skies, and be seduced into worshiping and serving them. GOD set them out for everybody's benefit, everywhere. But you — GOD took you right out of the iron furnace, out of Egypt, to become the people of his inheritance — and that's what you are this very day.

But GOD was angry with me because of you and the things you

said. He swore that I'd never cross the Jordan, never get to enter the good land that GOD, your God, is giving you as an inheritance. This means that I am going to die here. I'm not crossing the Jordan. But you will cross; you'll possess the good land.

So stay alert. Don't for a minute forget the covenant which GOD, your God, made with you. And don't take up with any carved images, no forms of any kind—GOD, your God, issued clear commands on that. GOD, your God, is not to be trifled with—he's a consuming fire, a jealous God.

When the time comes that you have children and grandchildren, put on years, and start taking things for granted, if you then become corrupt and make any carved images, no matter what their form, by doing what is sheer evil in GOD's eyes and provoking his anger— I can tell you right now, with Heaven and Earth as witnesses, that it will be all over for you. You'll be kicked off the land that you're about to cross over the Jordan to possess. Believe me, you'll have a very short stay there. You'll be ruined, completely ruined. GOD will scatter you far and wide; a few of you will survive here and there in the nations where GOD will drive you. There you can worship your homemade gods to your hearts' content, your wonderful gods of wood and stone that can't see or hear or eat or smell.

But even there, if you seek GOD, your God, you'll be able to find him if you're serious, looking for him with your whole heart and soul. When troubles come and all these awful things happen to you, in future days you will come back to GOD, your God, and listen obediently to what he says. GOD, your God, is above all a compassionate God. In the end he will not abandon you, he won't bring you to ruin, he won't forget the covenant with your ancestors which he swore to them.

Ask questions. Find out what has been going on all these years before you were born. From the day God created man and woman on this Earth, and from the horizon in the east to the horizon in the west— as far back as you can imagine and as far away as you can imagine— has as great a thing as this ever happened? Has anyone ever heard of such a thing? Has a people ever heard, as you did, a god speaking out of the middle of the fire and lived to tell the story?

Or has a god ever tried to select for himself a nation from within a nation using trials, miracles, and war, putting his strong hand in, reaching his long arm out, a spectacle awesome and staggering, the way GOD, your God, did it for you in Egypt while you stood right there and watched?

You were shown all this so that you would know that GOD is, well,

God. He's the only God there is. He's it. He made it possible for you to hear his voice out of Heaven to discipline you. Down on Earth, he showed you the big fire and again you heard his words, this time out of the fire. He loved your ancestors and chose to work with their children. He personally and powerfully brought you out of Egypt in order to displace bigger and stronger and older nations with you, bringing you out and turning their land over to you as an inheritance. And now it's happening. This very day.

Know this well, then. Take it to heart right now: GOD is in Heaven above; GOD is on Earth below. He's the only God there is. Obediently live by his rules and commands which I'm giving you today so that you'll live well and your children after you — oh, you'll live a long time in the land that GOD, your God, is giving you.

‡

Then Moses set aside three towns in the country on the east side of the Jordan to which someone who had unintentionally killed a person could flee and find refuge. If the murder was unintentional and there was no history of bad blood, the murderer could flee to one of these cities and save his life:

Bezer in the wilderness on the tableland for the Reubenites, Ramoth in Gilead for the Gadites, and Golan in Bashan for the Manassites.

‡

This is the Revelation that Moses presented to the People of Israel. These are the testimonies, the rules and regulations Moses spoke to the People of Israel after their exodus from Egypt and arrival on the east side of the Jordan in the valley near Beth Peor. It was the country of Sihon king of the Amorites who ruled from Heshbon. Moses and the People of Israel fought and beat him after they left Egypt and took his land. They also took the land of Og king of Bashan. The two Amorite kings held the country on the east of the Jordan from Aroer on the bank of the Brook Arnon as far north as Mount Siyon, that is, Mount Hermon, all the Arabah plain east of the Jordan, and as far south as the Sea of the Arabah (the Dead Sea) beneath the slopes of Mount Pisgah.

MOSES TEACHES ISRAEL ON THE PLAINS OF MOAB

5 Moses called all Israel together. He said to them,

Attention, Israel. Listen obediently to the rules and regulations I am delivering to your listening ears today. Learn them. Live them.

GOD, our God, made a covenant with us at Horeb. GOD didn't just make this covenant with our parents; he made it also with us, with all of us who are alive right now. GOD spoke to you personally out of the fire on the mountain. At the time I stood between GOD and you, to tell you what GOD said. You were afraid, remember, of the fire and wouldn't climb the mountain. He said:

> I am GOD, your God,
> who brought you out of the land of Egypt,
> out of a house of slaves.

No other gods, only me.

No carved gods of any size, shape, or form of anything whatever, whether of things that fly or walk or swim. Don't bow down to them and don't serve them because I am GOD, your God, and I'm a most jealous God. I hold parents responsible for any sins they pass on to their children to the third, and yes, even to the fourth generation. But I'm lovingly loyal to the thousands who love me and keep my commandments.

No using the name of GOD, your God, in curses or silly banter; GOD won't put up with the irreverent use of his name.

No working on the Sabbath; keep it holy just as GOD, your God, commanded you. Work six days, doing everything you have to do, but the seventh day is a Sabbath, a Rest Day—no work: not you, your son, your daughter, your servant, your maid, your ox, your donkey (or any of your animals), and not even the foreigner visiting your town. That way your servants and maids will get the same rest as you. Don't ever forget that you were slaves in Egypt and GOD, your God, got you out of there in a powerful show of strength. That's why GOD, your God, commands you to observe the day of Sabbath rest.

Respect your father and mother—GOD, your God, commands it! You'll have a long life; the land that God is giving you will treat you well.

No murder.

No adultery.

No stealing.

No lies about your neighbor.

No coveting your neighbor's wife. And no lusting for his house, field, servant, maid, ox, or donkey either—nothing that belongs to your neighbor!

These are the words that GOD spoke to the whole congregation at the mountain. He spoke in a tremendous voice from the fire and cloud and dark mist. And that was it. No more words. Then he wrote them on two slabs of stone and gave them to me.

As it turned out, when you heard the Voice out of that dark cloud and saw the mountain on fire, you approached me, all the heads of your tribes and your leaders, and said,

"Our GOD has revealed to us his glory and greatness. We've heard him speak from the fire today! We've seen that God can speak to humans and they can still live. But why risk it further? This huge fire will devour us if we stay around any longer. If we hear GOD's voice anymore, we'll die for sure. Has anyone ever known of anyone who has heard the Voice of GOD the way we have and lived to tell the story?

"From now on, *you* go and listen to what GOD, our God, says and then tell us what GOD tells you. We'll listen and we'll do it."

GOD heard what you said to me and told me, "I've heard what the people said to you. They're right—good and true words. What I wouldn't give if they'd always feel this way, continuing to revere me and always keep all my commands; they'd have a good life forever, they and their children!

"Go ahead and tell them to go home to their tents. But you, you stay here with me so I can tell you every commandment and all the rules and regulations that you must teach them so they'll know how to live in the land that I'm giving them as their own."

So be very careful to act exactly as GOD commands you. Don't veer off to the right or the left. Walk straight down the road GOD commands so that you'll have a good life and live a long time in the land that you're about to possess.

6 This is the commandment, the rules and regulations, that GOD, your God, commanded me to teach you to live out in the land you're about to cross into to possess. This is so that you'll live in deep reverence before GOD life-long, observing all his rules and regulations that I'm commanding you, you and your children and your grandchildren, living good long lives.

Listen obediently, Israel. Do what you're told so that you'll have a good life, a life of abundance and bounty, just as GOD promised, in a land abounding in milk and honey.

Attention, Israel!

GOD, our God! GOD the one and only!

Love GOD, your God, with your whole heart: love him with all that's in you, love him with all you've got!

Write these commandments that I've given you today on your hearts. Get them inside of you and then get them inside your children. Talk about them wherever you are, sitting at home or walking in the street; talk about them from the time you get up in the morning to when you fall into bed at night. Tie them on your hands and foreheads as a reminder; inscribe them on the doorposts of your homes and on your city gates.

When GOD, your God, ushers you into the land he promised through your ancestors Abraham, Isaac, and Jacob to give you, you're going to walk into large, bustling cities you didn't build, well-furnished houses you didn't buy, come upon wells you didn't dig, vineyards and olive orchards you didn't plant. When you take it all in and settle down, pleased and content, make sure you don't forget how you got there—GOD brought you out of slavery in Egypt.

Deeply respect GOD, your God. Serve and worship him exclusively. Back up your promises with his name only. Don't fool around with other gods, the gods of your neighbors, because GOD, your God, who is alive among you is a jealous God. Don't provoke him, igniting his hot anger that would burn you right off the face of the Earth. Don't push GOD, your God, to the wall as you did that day at Massah, the Testing-Place. Carefully keep the commands of GOD, your God, all the requirements and regulations he gave you. Do what is right; do what is good in GOD's sight so you'll live a good life and be able to march in and take this pleasant land that GOD so solemnly promised through your ancestors, throwing out your enemies left and right—exactly as GOD said.

The next time your child asks you, "What do these requirements and regulations and rules that GOD, our God, has commanded mean?" tell your child, "We were slaves to Pharaoh in Egypt and GOD powerfully intervened and got us out of that country. We stood there and watched as GOD delivered miracle-signs, great wonders, and evil-visitations on Egypt, on Pharaoh and his household. He pulled us out of there so he could bring us here and give us the land he so solemnly promised to our ancestors. That's why GOD commanded us to follow all these rules, so that we would live reverently before GOD, our God, as he gives us this good life, keeping us alive for a long time to come.

"It will be a set-right and put-together life for us if we make sure that we do this entire commandment in the Presence of GOD, our God, just as he commanded us to do."

⸶

7 When GOD, your God, brings you into the country that you are about to enter and take over, he will clear out the super powers that were there before you: the Hittite, the Girgashite, the Amorite, the Canaanite, the Perizzite, the Hivite, and the Jebusite. Those seven nations are all bigger and stronger than you are. GOD, your God, will turn them over to you and you will conquer them. You must completely destroy them, offering them up as a holy destruction to GOD.

Don't make a treaty with them.

Don't let them off in any way.

Don't marry them: Don't give your daughters to their sons and don't take their daughters for your sons—before you know it they'd involve you in worshiping their gods, and GOD would explode in anger, putting a quick end to you.

Here's what you are to do:

> Tear apart their altars stone by stone,
> smash their phallic pillars,
> chop down their sex-and-religion Asherah groves,
> set fire to their carved god-images.

Do this because you are a people set apart as holy to GOD, your God. GOD, your God, chose you out of all the people on Earth for himself as a cherished, personal treasure.

GOD wasn't attracted to you and didn't choose you because you were big and important—the fact is, there was almost nothing to you. He did it out of sheer love, keeping the promise he made to your ancestors. GOD stepped in and mightily bought you back out of that world of slavery, freed you from the iron grip of Pharaoh king of Egypt. Know this: GOD, your God, is God indeed, a God you can depend upon. He keeps his covenant of loyal love with those who love him and observe his commandments for a thousand generations. But he also pays back those who hate him, pays them the wages of death; he isn't slow to pay them off—those who hate him, he pays right on time.

301

So keep the command and the rules and regulations that I command you today. Do them.

And this is what will happen: When you, on your part, will obey these directives, keeping and following them, GOD, on his part, will keep the covenant of loyal love that he made with your ancestors:

> He will love you,
> he will bless you,
> he will increase you.

He will bless the babies from your womb and the harvest of grain, new wine, and oil from your fields; he'll bless the calves from your herds and lambs from your flocks in the country he promised your ancestors that he'd give you. You'll be blessed beyond all other peoples: no sterility or barrenness in you or your animals. GOD will get rid of all sickness. And all the evil afflictions you experienced in Egypt he'll put not on you but on those who hate you.

You'll make mincemeat of all the peoples that GOD, your God, hands over to you. Don't feel sorry for them. And don't worship their gods—they'll trap you for sure.

You're going to think to yourselves, "Oh! We're outnumbered ten to one by these nations! We'll never even make a dent in them!" But I'm telling you, Don't be afraid. Remember, yes, remember in detail what GOD, your God, did to Pharaoh and all Egypt. Remember the great contests to which you were eyewitnesses: the miracle-signs, the wonders, GOD's mighty hand as he stretched out his arm and took you out of there. GOD, your God, is going to do the same thing to these people you're now so afraid of.

And to top it off, the Hornet. GOD will unleash the Hornet on them until every survivor-in-hiding is dead.

So don't be intimidated by them. GOD, your God, is among you— GOD majestic, GOD awesome. GOD, your God, will get rid of these nations, bit by bit. You won't be permitted to wipe them out all at once lest the wild animals take over and overwhelm you. But GOD, your God, will move them out of your way—he'll throw them into a huge panic until there's nothing left of them. He'll turn their kings over to you and you'll remove all trace of them under Heaven. Not one person will be able to stand up to you; you'll put an end to them all.

Make sure you set fire to their carved gods. Don't get greedy for the veneer of silver and gold on them and take it for yourselves—you'll get trapped by it for sure. GOD hates it; it's an abomination to GOD, your God. And don't dare bring one of these abominations home or you'll end up just like it, burned up as a holy destruction. No: It is forbidden! Hate it. Abominate it. Destroy it and preserve GOD's holiness.

✝

8 Keep and live out the entire commandment that I'm commanding you today so that you'll live and prosper and enter and own the land that GOD promised to your ancestors. Remember every road that GOD led you on for those forty years in the wilderness, pushing you to your limits, testing you so that he would know what you were made of, whether you would keep his commandments or not. He put you through hard times. He made you go hungry. Then he fed you with manna, something neither you nor your parents knew anything about, so you would learn that men and women don't live by bread only; we live by every word that comes from GOD's mouth. Your clothes didn't wear out and your feet didn't blister those forty years. You learned deep in your heart that GOD disciplines you in the same ways a father disciplines his child.

So it's paramount that you keep the commandments of GOD, your God, walk down the roads he shows you and reverently respect him. GOD is about to bring you into a good land, a land with brooks and rivers, springs and lakes, streams out of the hills and through the valleys. It's a land of wheat and barley, of vines and figs and pomegranates, of olives, oil, and honey. It's land where you'll never go hungry—always food on the table and a roof over your head. It's a land where you'll get iron out of rocks and mine copper from the hills.

After a meal, satisfied, bless GOD, your God, for the good land he has given you.

Make sure you don't forget GOD, your God, by not keeping his commandments, his rules and regulations that I command you today. Make sure that when you eat and are satisfied, build pleasant houses and settle in, see your herds and flocks flourish and more and more money come in, watch your standard of living going up and up—make sure you don't become so full of yourself and your things that you forget GOD, your God,

the God who delivered you from Egyptian slavery;
the God who led you through that huge and fearsome wilderness,

those desolate, arid badlands crawling with fiery snakes and
scorpions;

the God who gave you water gushing from hard rock;

the God who gave you manna to eat in the wilderness, something your ancestors had never heard of, in order to give you
a taste of the hard life, to test you so that you would be prepared to live well in the days ahead of you.

If you start thinking to yourselves, "I did all this. And all by myself.
I'm rich. It's all mine!" — well, think again. Remember that GOD, your
God, gave you the strength to produce all this wealth so as to confirm
the covenant that he promised to your ancestors — as it is today.

If you forget, forget GOD, your God, and start taking up with other
gods, serving and worshiping them, I'm on record right now as giving you
firm warning: that will be the end of you; I mean it — destruction. You'll
go to your doom — the same as the nations GOD is destroying before you;
doom because you wouldn't obey the Voice of GOD, your God.

⊹

9 Attention, Israel!
This very day you are crossing the Jordan to enter the land and
dispossess nations that are much bigger and stronger than you are.
You're going to find huge cities with sky-high fortress-walls and gigan-
tic people, descendants of the Anakites — you've heard all about them;
you've heard the saying, "No one can stand up to an Anakite."

Today know this: GOD, your God, is crossing the river ahead of
you — he's a consuming fire. He will destroy the nations, he will put
them under your power. You will dispossess them and very quickly
wipe them out, just as GOD promised you would.

But when GOD pushes them out ahead of you, don't start thinking
to yourselves, "It's because of all the good I've done that GOD has
brought me in here to dispossess these nations." Actually it's because
of all the evil these nations have done. No, it's nothing good that you've
done, no record for decency that you've built up, that got you here; it's
because of the vile wickedness of these nations that GOD, your God, is
dispossessing them before you so that he can keep his promised word
to your ancestors, to Abraham, Isaac, and Jacob.

Know this and don't ever forget it: It's not because of any good that
you've done that GOD is giving you this good land to own. Anything but!

You're stubborn as mules. Keep in mind and don't ever forget how angry you made GOD, your God, in the wilderness. You've kicked and screamed against GOD from the day you left Egypt until you got to this place, rebels all the way. You made GOD angry at Horeb, made him so angry that he wanted to destroy you. When I climbed the mountain to receive the slabs of stone, the tablets of the covenant that GOD made with you, I stayed there on the mountain forty days and nights: I ate no food; I drank no water. Then GOD gave me the two slabs of stone, engraved with the finger of God. They contained word for word everything that GOD spoke to you on the mountain out of the fire, on the day of the assembly.

It was at the end of the forty days and nights that GOD gave me the two slabs of stone, the tablets of the covenant. GOD said to me, "Get going, and quickly. Get down there, because your people whom you led out of Egypt have ruined everything. In almost no time at all they have left the road that I laid out for them and gone off and made for themselves a cast god."

GOD said, "I look at this people and all I see are hardheaded, hardhearted rebels. Get out of my way now so I can destroy them. I'm going to wipe them off the face of the map. Then I'll start over with you to make a nation far better and bigger than they could ever be."

I turned around and started down the mountain—by now the mountain was blazing with fire—carrying the two tablets of the covenant in my two arms. That's when I saw it: There you were, sinning against GOD, your God,—you had made yourselves a cast god in the shape of a calf! So soon you had left the road that GOD had commanded you to walk on. I held the two stone slabs high and threw them down, smashing them to bits as you watched.

Then I prostrated myself before GOD, just as I had at the beginning of the forty days and nights. I ate no food; I drank no water. I did this because of you, all your sins, sinning against GOD, doing what is evil in GOD's eyes and making him angry. I was terrified of GOD's furious anger, his blazing anger. I was sure he would destroy you. But once again GOD listened to me. And Aaron! How furious he was with Aaron—ready to destroy him. But I prayed also for Aaron at that same time.

But that sin-thing that you made, that calf-god, I took and burned in the fire, pounded and ground it until it was crushed into a fine powder, then threw it into the stream that comes down the mountain.

And then there was Camp Taberah (Blaze), Massah (Testing-Place), and Camp Kibroth Hattaavah (Graves-of-the-Craving)—more occasions when you made God furious with you.

The most recent was when GOD sent you out from Kadesh Barnea, ordering you: "Go. Possess the land that I'm giving you." And what did you do? You rebelled. Rebelled against the clear orders of GOD, your God. Refused to trust him. Wouldn't obey him. You've been rebels against GOD from the first day I knew you.

When I was on my face, prostrate before GOD those forty days and nights after GOD said he would destroy you, I prayed to GOD for you, "My Master, GOD, don't destroy your people, your inheritance whom, in your immense generosity, you redeemed, using your enormous strength to get them out of Egypt.

"Remember your servants Abraham, Isaac, and Jacob; don't make too much of the stubbornness of this people, their evil and their sin, lest the Egyptians from whom you rescued them say, 'GOD couldn't do it; he got tired and wasn't able to take them to the land he promised them. He ended up hating them and dumped them in the wilderness to die.'

"They are your people still, your inheritance whom you powerfully and sovereignly rescued."

10 GOD responded. He said, "Shape two slabs of stone similar to the first ones. Climb the mountain and meet me. Also make yourself a wooden chest. I will engrave the stone slabs with the words that were on the first ones, the ones you smashed. Then you will put them in the Chest."

So I made a chest out of acacia wood, shaped two slabs of stone, just like the first ones, and climbed the mountain with the two slabs in my arms. He engraved the stone slabs the same as he had the first ones, the Ten Words that he addressed to you on the mountain out of the fire on the day of the assembly. Then GOD gave them to me. I turned around and came down the mountain. I put the stone slabs in the Chest that I made and they've been there ever since, just as GOD commanded me.

✙

The People of Israel went from the wells of the Jaakanites to Moserah. Aaron died there and was buried. His son Eleazar succeeded him as priest. From there they went to Gudgodah, and then to Jotbathah, a land of streams of water.

That's when GOD set apart the tribe of Levi to carry GOD's Covenant Chest, to be on duty in the Presence of GOD, to serve him, and to bless in his name, as they continue to do today. And that's why Levites don't have a piece of inherited land as their kinsmen do. GOD is their inheritance, as GOD, your God, promised them.

I stayed there on the mountain forty days and nights, just as I did the first time. And GOD listened to me, just as he did the first time: GOD decided not to destroy you.

GOD told me, "Now get going. Lead your people as they resume the journey to take possession of the land that I promised their ancestors that I'd give to them."

So now Israel, what do you think GOD expects from you? Just this: Live in his presence in holy reverence, follow the road he sets out for you, love him, serve GOD, your God, with everything you have in you, obey the commandments and regulations of GOD that I'm commanding you today—live a good life.

Look around you: Everything you see is GOD's—the heavens above and beyond, the Earth, and everything on it. But it was your ancestors that GOD fell in love with; he picked their children—that's *you!*—out of all the other peoples. That's where we are right now. So cut away the thick calluses from your heart and stop being so willfully hardheaded. GOD, your God, is the God of all gods, he's the Master of all masters, a God immense and powerful and awesome. He doesn't play favorites, takes no bribes, makes sure orphans and widows are treated fairly, takes loving care of foreigners by seeing that they get food and clothing.

> You must treat foreigners with the same loving care—
>   remember, you were once foreigners in Egypt.
> Reverently respect GOD, your God, serve him, hold tight to him,
>   back up your promises with the authority of his name.
> He's your praise! He's your God!
> He did all these tremendous, these staggering things
>   that you saw with your own eyes.

When your ancestors entered Egypt, they numbered a mere seventy souls. And now look at you—you look more like the stars in the night skies in number. And your GOD did it.

☩

11

So love GOD, your God;
    guard well his rules and regulations;
    obey his commandments for the rest of time.

Today it's very clear that it isn't your children who are front and center here: They weren't in on what GOD did, didn't see the acts, didn't experience the discipline, didn't marvel at his greatness, the way he displayed his power in the miracle-signs and deeds that he let loose in Egypt on Pharaoh king of Egypt and all his land, the way he took care of the Egyptian army, its horses and chariots, burying them in the waters of the Red Sea as they pursued you. GOD drowned them. And you're standing here today alive. Nor was it your children who saw how GOD took care of you in the wilderness up until the time you arrived here, what he did to Dathan and Abiram, the sons of Eliab son of Reuben, how the Earth opened its jaws and swallowed them with their families—their tents, and everything around them—right out of the middle of Israel. Yes, it was you—your eyes—that saw every great thing that GOD did.

So it's you who are in charge of keeping the entire commandment that I command you today so that you'll have the strength to invade and possess the land that you are crossing the river to make your own. Your obedience will give you a long life on the soil that GOD promised to give your ancestors and their children, a land flowing with milk and honey.

The land you are entering to take up ownership isn't like Egypt, the land you left, where you had to plant your own seed and water it yourselves as in a vegetable garden. But the land you are about to cross the river and take for your own is a land of mountains and valleys; it drinks water that rains from the sky. It's a land that GOD, your God, personally tends—he's the gardener—he alone keeps his eye on it all year long.

From now on if you listen obediently to the commandments that I am commanding you today, love GOD, your God, and serve him with everything you have within you, he'll take charge of sending the rain at the right time, both autumn and spring rains, so that you'll be able to harvest your grain, your grapes, your olives. He'll make sure there's plenty of grass for your animals. You'll have plenty to eat.

But be vigilant, lest you be seduced away and end up serving and worshiping other gods and GOD erupts in anger and shuts down Heaven so there's no rain and nothing grows in the fields, and in no time at all you're starved out—not a trace of you left on the good land that GOD is giving you.

Place these words on your hearts. Get them deep inside you. Tie them on your hands and foreheads as a reminder. Teach them to your children. Talk about them wherever you are, sitting at home or walking in the street; talk about them from the time you get up in the morning until you fall into bed at night. Inscribe them on the doorposts and gates of your cities so that you'll live a long time, and your children with you, on the soil that GOD promised to give your ancestors for as long as there is a sky over the Earth.

That's right. If you diligently keep all this commandment that I command you to obey—love GOD, your God, do what he tells you, stick close to him—GOD on his part will drive out all these nations that stand in your way. Yes, he'll drive out nations much bigger and stronger than you. Every square inch on which you place your foot will be yours. Your borders will stretch from the wilderness to the mountains of Lebanon, from the Euphrates River to the Mediterranean Sea. No one will be able to stand in your way. Everywhere you go, GOD-sent fear and trembling will precede you, just as he promised.

I've brought you today to the crossroads of Blessing and Curse.

The Blessing: if you listen obediently to the commandments of GOD, your God, which I command you today.

The Curse: if you don't pay attention to the commandments of GOD, your God, but leave the road that I command you today, following other gods of which you know nothing.

Here's what comes next: When GOD, your God, brings you into the land you are going into to make your own, you are to give out the Blessing from Mount Gerizim and the Curse from Mount Ebal. After you cross the Jordan River, follow the road to the west through Canaanite settlements in the valley near Gilgal and the Oaks of Moreh.

You are crossing the Jordan River to invade and take the land that GOD, your God, is giving you. Be vigilant. Observe all the regulations and rules I am setting before you today.

✝

12 These are the rules and regulations that you must diligently observe for as long as you live in this country that GOD, the God-of-Your-Fathers, has given you to possess.

Ruthlessly demolish all the sacred shrines where the nations that you're driving out worship their gods—wherever you find them, on hills and mountains or in groves of green trees. Tear apart their altars. Smash their phallic pillars. Burn their sex-and-religion Asherah shrines. Break up their carved gods. Obliterate the names of those god sites.

Stay clear of those places—don't let what went on there contaminate the worship of GOD, your God.

Instead find the site that GOD, your God, will choose and mark it with his name as a common center for all the tribes of Israel. Assemble there. Bring to that place your Absolution-Offerings and sacrifices, your tithes and Tribute-Offerings, your Vow-Offerings, your Freewill-Offerings, and the firstborn of your herds and flocks. Feast there in the Presence of GOD, your God. Celebrate everything that you and your families have accomplished under the blessing of GOD, your God.

Don't continue doing things the way we're doing them at present, each of us doing as we wish. Until now you haven't arrived at the goal, the resting place, the inheritance that GOD, your God, is giving you. But the minute you cross the Jordan River and settle into the land GOD, your God, is enabling you to inherit, he'll give you rest from all your surrounding enemies. You'll be able to settle down and live in safety.

From then on, at the place that GOD, your God, chooses to mark with his name as the place where you can meet him, bring everything that I command you: your Absolution-Offerings and sacrifices, tithes and Tribute-Offerings, and the best of your Vow-Offerings that you vow to GOD. Celebrate there in the Presence of GOD, your God, you and your sons and daughters, your servants and maids, including the Levite living in your neighborhood because he has no place of his own in your inheritance.

Be extra careful: Don't offer your Absolution-Offerings just any place that strikes your fancy. Offer your Absolution-Offerings only in the place that GOD chooses in one of your tribal regions. There and only there are you to bring all that I command you.

It's permissible to slaughter your non-sacrificial animals like gazelle and deer in your towns and eat all you want from them with the blessing of GOD, your God. Both the ritually clean and unclean may eat.

But you may not eat the blood. Pour the blood out on the ground like water. Nor may you eat there the tithe of your grain, new wine, or olive oil; nor the firstborn of your herds and flocks; nor any of the Vow-Offerings that you vow; nor your Freewill-Offerings and Tribute-Offerings. All these you must eat in the Presence of GOD, your God, in the place GOD, your God, chooses—you, your son and daughter, your servant and maid, and the Levite who lives in your neighborhood. You are to celebrate in the Presence of GOD, your God, all the things you've been able to accomplish.

And make sure that for as long as you live on your land you never, never neglect the Levite.

When GOD, your God, expands your territory as he promised he would do, and you say, "I'm hungry for meat," because you happen to be craving meat at the time, go ahead and eat as much meat as you want. If you're too far away from the place that GOD, your God, has marked with his name, it's all right to slaughter animals from your herds and flocks that GOD has given you, as I've commanded you. In your own towns you may eat as much of them as you want. Just as the non-sacrificial animals like the gazelle and deer are eaten, you may eat them; the ritually unclean and clean may eat them at the same table.

Only this: Absolutely no blood. Don't eat the blood. Blood is life; don't eat the life with the meat. Don't eat it; pour it out on the ground like water. Don't eat it; then you'll have a good life, you and your children after you. By all means, do the right thing in GOD's eyes.

And this: Lift high your Holy-Offerings and your Vow-Offerings and bring them to the place GOD designates. Sacrifice your Absolution-Offerings, the meat and blood, on the Altar of GOD, your God; pour out the blood of the Absolution-Offering on the Altar of GOD, your God; then you can go ahead and eat the meat.

Be vigilant, listen obediently to these words that I command you so that you'll have a good life, you and your children, for a long, long time, doing what is good and right in the eyes of GOD, your God.

When GOD, your God, cuts off the nations whose land you are invading, shoves them out of your way so that you displace them and settle in their land, be careful that you don't get curious about them after they've been destroyed before you. Don't get fascinated with their gods, thinking, "I wonder what it was like for them, worshiping their gods. I'd like to try that myself." Don't do this to GOD, your God. They commit every imaginable abomination with their gods. GOD hates it all with a passion. Why, they even set their children on fire as offerings to their gods!

Diligently do everything I command you, the way I command you: don't add to it; don't subtract from it.

✠

13 When a prophet or visionary gets up in your community and gives out a miracle-sign or wonder, and the miracle-sign or wonder that he gave out happens and he says, "Let's follow other gods" (these are gods you know nothing about), "let's worship them," don't pay any attention to what that prophet or visionary says. GOD, your God, is testing you to find out if you totally love him with everything you have in you. You are to follow only GOD, your God, hold him in deep reverence, keep his commandments, listen obediently to what he says, serve him—hold on to him for dear life!

And that prophet or visionary must be put to death. He has urged mutiny against GOD, your God, who rescued you from Egypt, who redeemed you from a world of slavery and put you on the road on which GOD, your God, has commanded you to walk. Purge the evil from your company.

And when your brother or son or daughter, or even your dear wife or lifelong friend, comes to you in secret and whispers, "Let's go and worship some other gods" (gods that you know nothing about, neither you nor your ancestors, the gods of the peoples around you near and far, from one end of the Earth to the other), don't go along with him; shut your ears. Don't feel sorry for him and don't make excuses for him. Kill him. That's right, kill him. You throw the first stone. Take action at once and swiftly with everybody in the community getting in on it at the end. Stone him with stones so that he dies. He tried to turn you traitor against GOD, your God, the one who got you out of Egypt and the world of slavery.

Every man, woman, and child in Israel will hear what's been done and be in awe. No one will dare to do an evil thing like this again.

When word comes in from one of your cities that GOD, your God, is giving you to live in, reporting that evil men have gotten together with some of the citizens of the city and have broken away, saying, "Let's go and worship other gods" (gods you know nothing about), then you must conduct a careful examination. Ask questions, investigate. If it turns out that the report is true and this abomination did in fact take place in your community, you must execute the citizens of that town. Kill them, setting that city apart for holy destruction: the city and everything in it including its animals. Gather the plunder in the middle of the town square and burn it all—town and plunder together up in smoke, a holy sacrifice to GOD, your God. Leave it there, ashes and ruins. Don't build on that site again. And don't let any of the plunder devoted to holy destruction stick to your fingers. Get rid of it so that GOD may turn from anger to compassion, generously making you prosper, just as he promised your ancestors.

Yes. Obediently listen to GOD, your God. Keep all his commands that I am giving you today. Do the right thing in the eyes of GOD, your God.

✝

14 You are children of GOD, your God, so don't mutilate your bodies or shave your heads in funeral rites for the dead. You only are a people holy to GOD, your God; GOD chose you out of all the people on Earth as his cherished personal treasure.

Don't eat anything abominable. These are the animals you may eat: ox, sheep, goat, deer, gazelle, roebuck, wild goat, ibex, antelope, mountain sheep — any animal that has a cloven hoof and chews the cud. But you may not eat camels, rabbits, and rock badgers because they chew the cud but they don't have a cloven hoof — that makes them ritually unclean. And pigs: Don't eat pigs — they have a cloven hoof but don't chew the cud, which makes them ritually unclean. Don't even touch a pig's carcass.

This is what you may eat from the water: anything that has fins and scales. But if it doesn't have fins or scales, you may not eat it. It's ritually unclean.

You may eat any ritually clean bird. These are the exceptions, so don't eat these: eagle, vulture, black vulture, kite, falcon, the buzzard family, the raven family, ostrich, nighthawk, the hawk family, little owl, great owl, white owl, pelican, osprey, cormorant, stork, the heron family, hoopoe, bat.

Winged insects are ritually unclean; don't eat them. But ritually clean winged creatures are permitted.

Because you are a people holy to GOD, your God, don't eat anything that you find dead. You can, though, give it to a foreigner in your neighborhood for a meal or sell it to a foreigner.

Don't boil a kid in its mother's milk.

Make an offering of ten percent, a tithe, of all the produce which grows in your fields year after year. Bring this into the Presence of GOD, your God, at the place he designates for worship and there eat the tithe from your grain, wine, and oil and the firstborn from your herds and flocks. In this way you will learn to live in deep reverence before GOD, your God, as long as you live. But if the place GOD, your God, designates for worship is too far away and you can't carry your tithe that far, GOD, your God, will still bless you: exchange your tithe for money and take the money to the place GOD, your God, has chosen to be worshiped. Use the money to buy anything you want: cattle, sheep, wine, or beer—anything that looks good to you. You and your family can then feast in the Presence of GOD, your God, and have a good time.

Meanwhile, don't forget to take good care of the Levites who live in your towns; they won't get any property or inheritance of their own as you will.

At the end of every third year, gather the tithe from all your produce of that year and put it aside in storage. Keep it in reserve for the Levite who won't get any property or inheritance as you will, and for the foreigner, the orphan, and the widow who live in your neighborhood. That way they'll have plenty to eat and GOD, your God, will bless you in all your work.

15 At the end of every seventh year, cancel all debts. This is the procedure: Everyone who has lent money to a neighbor writes it off. You must not press your neighbor or his brother for payment: All-Debts-Are-Canceled—GOD says so. You may collect payment from foreigners, but whatever you have lent to your fellow Israelite you must write off.

There must be no poor people among you because GOD is going to bless you lavishly in this land that GOD, your God, is giving you as an inheritance, your very own land. But only if you listen obediently to the Voice of GOD, your God, diligently observing every commandment that I command you today. Oh yes—GOD, your God, will bless you just as he promised. You will lend to many nations but won't borrow from any; you'll rule over many nations but none will rule over you.

When you happen on someone who's in trouble or needs help among your people with whom you live in this land that GOD, your God, is giving you, don't look the other way pretending you don't see him. Don't keep a tight grip on your purse. No. Look at him, open your purse, lend whatever and as much as he needs. Don't count the cost. Don't listen to that selfish voice saying, "It's almost the seventh year, the year of All-Debts-Are-Cancelled," and turn aside and leave your needy neighbor in the lurch, refusing to help him. He'll call GOD's attention to you and your blatant sin.

Give freely and spontaneously. Don't have a stingy heart. The way you handle matters like this triggers GOD, your God's, blessing in everything you do, all your work and ventures. There are always going to be poor and needy people among you. So I command you: Always be generous, open purse and hands, give to your neighbors in trouble, your poor and hurting neighbors.

If a Hebrew man or Hebrew woman was sold to you and has served you for six years, in the seventh year you must set him or her free, released into a free life. And when you set them free don't send them off empty-handed. Provide them with some animals, plenty of bread and wine and oil. Load them with provisions from all the blessings with which GOD, your God, has blessed you. Don't for a minute forget that you were once slaves in Egypt and GOD, your God, redeemed you from that slave world.

For that reason, this day I command you to do this.

But if your slave, because he loves you and your family and has a good life with you, says, "I don't want to leave you," then take an awl and pierce through his earlobe into the doorpost, marking him as your slave forever. Do the same with your women slaves who want to stay with you.

Don't consider this an unreasonable hardship, this setting your slave free. After all, he's worked six years for you at half the cost of a hired hand.

Believe me, GOD, your God, will bless you in everything you do.

⊹

Consecrate to GOD, your God, all the firstborn males in your herds and flocks. Don't use the firstborn from your herds as work animals; don't shear the firstborn from your flocks. These are for you to eat every year, you and your family, in the Presence of GOD, your God, at the place that GOD designates for worship. If the animal is defective, lame, say, or blind—anything wrong with it—don't slaughter it as a sacrifice to GOD, your God. Stay at home and eat it there. Both the ritually clean and unclean may eat it, the same as with a gazelle or a deer. Only you must not eat its blood. Pour the blood out on the ground like water.

⊹

16 Observe the month of Abib by celebrating the Passover to GOD, your God. It was in the month of Abib that GOD, your God, delivered you by night from Egypt. Offer the Passover-Sacrifice to GOD, your

315

God, at the place GOD chooses to be worshiped by establishing his name there. Don't eat yeast bread with it; for seven days eat it with unraised bread, hard-times bread, because you left Egypt in a hurry—that bread will keep the memory fresh of how you left Egypt for as long as you live. There is to be no sign of yeast anywhere for seven days. And don't let any of the meat that you sacrifice in the evening be left over until morning.

Don't sacrifice the Passover in any of the towns that GOD, your God, gives you other than the one GOD, your God, designates for worship; there and there only you will offer the Passover-Sacrifice at evening as the sun goes down, marking the time that you left Egypt. Boil and eat it at the place designated by GOD, your God. Then, at daybreak, turn around and go home.

Eat unraised bread for six days. Set aside the seventh day as a holiday; don't do any work.

Starting from the day you put the sickle to the ripe grain, count out seven weeks. Celebrate the Feast-of-Weeks to GOD, your God, by bringing your Freewill-Offering—give as generously as GOD, your God, has blessed you. Rejoice in the Presence of GOD, your God: you, your son, your daughter, your servant, your maid, the Levite who lives in your neighborhood, the foreigner, the orphan and widow among you; rejoice at the place GOD, your God, will set aside to be worshiped.

Don't forget that you were once a slave in Egypt. So be diligent in observing these regulations.

Observe the Feast-of-Booths for seven days when you gather the harvest from your threshing-floor and your wine-vat. Rejoice at your festival: you, your son, your daughter, your servant, your maid, the Levite, the foreigner, and the orphans and widows who live in your neighborhood. Celebrate the Feast to GOD, your God, for seven days at the place GOD designates. GOD, your God, has been blessing you in your harvest and in all your work, so make a day of it—really celebrate!

All your men must appear before GOD, your God, three times each year at the place he designates: at the Feast-of-Unraised-Bread (Passover), at the Feast-of-Weeks, and at the Feast-of-Booths. No one is to show up in the Presence of GOD empty-handed; each man must bring as much as he can manage, giving generously in response to the blessings of GOD, your God.

✛

Appoint judges and officers, organized by tribes, in all the towns that GOD, your God, is giving you. They are to judge the people fairly and honestly. Don't twist the law. Don't play favorites. Don't take a bribe—a bribe blinds even a wise person; it undermines the intentions of the best of people.

The right! The right! Pursue only what's right! It's the only way you can really live and possess the land that GOD, your God, is giving you.

✛

Don't plant fertility Asherah trees alongside the Altar of GOD, your God, that you build. Don't set up phallic sex pillars—GOD, your God, hates them.

17And don't sacrifice to GOD, your God, an ox or sheep that is defective or has anything at all wrong with it. That's an abomination, an insult to GOD, your God.

✛

If you find anyone within the towns that GOD, your God, is giving you doing what is wrong in GOD's eyes, breaking his covenant by going off to worship other gods, bowing down to them—the sun, say, or the moon, or any rebel sky-gods—look at the evidence and investigate carefully. If you find that it is true, that, in fact, an abomination has been committed in Israel, then you are to take the man or woman who did this evil thing outside your city gates and stone the man or the woman. Hurl stones at the person until dead.

But only on the testimony of two or three witnesses may a person be put to death. No one may be put to death on the testimony of one witness. The witnesses must throw the first stones in the execution, then the rest of the community joins in. You have to purge the evil from your community.

When matters of justice come up that are too much for you—hard cases regarding homicides, legal disputes, fights—take them up to the central place of worship that GOD, your God, has designated. Bring them to the Levitical priests and the judge who is in office at the time. Consult them and they will hand down the decision for you.

Then carry out their verdict at the place designated by GOD, your

God. Do what they tell you, in exactly the way they tell you. Follow their instructions precisely: Don't leave out anything; don't add anything. Anyone who presumes to override or twist the decision handed down by the priest or judge who was acting in the Presence of GOD, your God, is as good as dead—root him out, rid Israel of the evil. Everyone will take notice and be impressed. That will put an end to presumptuous behavior.

✢

When you enter the land that GOD, your God, is giving you and take it over and settle down, and then say, "I'm going to get me a king, a king like all the nations around me," make sure you get yourself a king whom GOD, your God, chooses. Choose your king from among your kinsmen; don't take a foreigner—only a kinsman. And make sure he doesn't build up a war machine, amassing military horses and chariots. He must not send people to Egypt to get more horses, because GOD told you, "You'll never go back there again!" And make sure he doesn't build up a harem, collecting wives who will divert him from the straight and narrow. And make sure he doesn't pile up a lot of silver and gold.

This is what must be done: When he sits down on the throne of his kingdom, the first thing he must do is make himself a copy of this Revelation on a scroll, copied under the supervision of the Levitical priests. That scroll is to remain at his side at all times; he is to study it every day so that he may learn what it means to fear his GOD, living in reverent obedience before these rules and regulations by following them. He must not become proud and arrogant, changing the commands at whim to suit himself or making up his own versions. If he reads and learns, he will have a long reign as king in Israel, he and his sons.

✢

18 The Levitical priests—that's the entire tribe of Levi—don't get any land-inheritance with the rest of Israel. They get the Fire-Gift-Offerings of GOD—they will live on that inheritance. But they don't get land-inheritance like the rest of their kinsmen. GOD is their inheritance.

This is what the priests get from the people from any offering of an ox or a sheep: the shoulder, the two cheeks, and the stomach. You must also give them the firstfruits of your grain, wine, and oil and the first fleece of your sheep, because GOD, your God, has chosen only them and their children out of all your tribes to be present and serve always in the name of GOD, your God.

If a Levite moves from any town in Israel—and he is quite free to move wherever he desires—and comes to the place GOD designates for worship, he may serve there in the name of GOD along with all his brother Levites who are present and serving in the Presence of GOD. And he will get an equal share to eat, even though he has money from the sale of his parents' possessions.

✝

When you enter the land that GOD, your God, is giving you, don't take on the abominable ways of life of the nations there. Don't you dare sacrifice your son or daughter in the fire. Don't practice divination, sorcery, fortune-telling, witchery, casting spells, holding seances, or channeling with the dead. People who do these things are an abomination to GOD. It's because of just such abominable practices that GOD, your God, is driving these nations out before you.

Be completely loyal to GOD, your God. These nations that you're about to run out of the country consort with sorcerers and witches. But not you. GOD, your God, forbids it.

GOD, your God, is going to raise up a prophet for you. GOD will raise him up from among your kinsmen, a prophet like me. Listen obediently to him. This is what you asked GOD, your God, for at Horeb on the day you were all gathered at the mountain and said, "We can't hear any more from GOD, our God; we can't stand seeing any more fire. We'll die!"

And GOD said to me, "They're right; they've spoken the truth. I'll raise up for them a prophet like you from their kinsmen. I'll tell him what to say and he will pass on to them everything I command him. And anyone who won't listen to my words spoken by him, I will personally hold responsible.

"But any prophet who fakes it, who claims to speak in my name something I haven't commanded him to say, or speaks in the name of other gods, that prophet must die."

You may be wondering among yourselves, "How can we tell the difference, whether it was GOD who spoke or not?" Here's how: If what the prophet spoke in GOD's name doesn't happen, then obviously GOD wasn't behind it; the prophet made it up. Forget about him.

✝

19 When GOD, your God, throws the nations out of the country that GOD, your God, is giving you and you settle down in their cities and houses, you are to set aside three easily accessible cities in the land that GOD, your God, is giving you as your very own. Divide your land into thirds, this land that GOD, your God, is giving you to possess, and build roads to the towns so that anyone who accidentally kills another can flee there.

This is the guideline for the murderer who flees there to take refuge: He has to have killed his neighbor without premeditation and with no history of bad blood between them. For instance, a man goes with his neighbor into the woods to cut a tree; he swings the ax, the head slips off the handle and hits his neighbor, killing him. He may then flee to one of these cities and save his life. If the city is too far away, the avenger of blood racing in hot-blooded pursuit might catch him since it's such a long distance, and kill him even though he didn't deserve it. It wasn't his fault. There was no history of hatred between them. Therefore I command you: Set aside the three cities for yourselves.

When GOD, your God, enlarges your land, extending its borders as he solemnly promised your ancestors, by giving you the whole land he promised them because you are diligently living the way I'm commanding you today, namely, to love GOD, your God, and do what he tells you all your life; and when that happens, then add three more to these three cities so that there is no chance of innocent blood being spilt in your land. GOD, your God, is giving you this land as an inheritance—you don't want to pollute it with innocent blood and bring bloodguilt upon yourselves.

On the other hand, if a man with a history of hatred toward his neighbor waits in ambush, then jumps him, mauls and kills him, and then runs to one of these cities, that's a different story. The elders of his own city are to send for him and have him brought back. They are to hand him over to the avenger of blood for execution. Don't feel sorry for him. Clean out the pollution of wrongful murder from Israel so that you'll be able to live well and breathe clean air.

✝

Don't move your neighbor's boundary markers, the longstanding landmarks set up by your pioneer ancestors defining their property.

✝

You cannot convict anyone of a crime or sin on the word of one witness. You need two or three witnesses to make a case.

If a hostile witness stands to accuse someone of a wrong, then both parties involved in the quarrel must stand in the Presence of GOD before the priests and judges who are in office at that time. The judges must conduct a careful investigation; if the witness turns out to be a false witness and has lied against his fellow Israelite, give him the same medicine he intended for the other party. Clean the polluting evil from your company. People will hear of what you've done and be impressed; that will put a stop to this kind of evil among you. Don't feel sorry for the person: It's life for life, eye for eye, tooth for tooth, hand for hand, foot for foot.

⊹

20 When you go to war against your enemy and see horses and chariots and soldiers far outnumbering you, do not recoil in fear of them; GOD, your God, who brought you up out of Egypt is with you. When the battle is about to begin, let the priest come forward and speak to the troops. He'll say, "Attention, Israel. In a few minutes you're going to do battle with your enemies. Don't waver in resolve. Don't fear. Don't hesitate. Don't panic. GOD, your God, is right there with you, fighting with you against your enemies, fighting to win."

Then let the officers step up and speak to the troops: "Is there a man here who has built a new house but hasn't yet dedicated it? Let him go home right now lest he die in battle and another man dedicate it. And is there a man here who has planted a vineyard but hasn't yet enjoyed the grapes? Let him go home right now lest he die in battle and another man enjoy the grapes. Is there a man here engaged to marry who hasn't yet taken his wife? Let him go home right now lest he die in battle and another man take her."

The officers will then continue, "And is there a man here who is wavering in resolve and afraid? Let him go home right now so that he doesn't infect his fellows with his timidity and cowardly spirit."

When the officers have finished speaking to the troops, let them appoint commanders of the troops who shall muster them by units.

When you come up against a city to attack it, call out, "Peace?" If they answer, "Yes, peace!" and open the city to you, then everyone found there will be conscripted as forced laborers and work for you. But if they don't settle for peace and insist on war, then go ahead and attack.

GOD, your God, will give them to you. Kill all the men with your swords. But don't kill the women and children and animals. Everything inside the town you can take as plunder for you to use and eat—GOD, your God, gives it to you. This is the way you deal with the distant towns, the towns that don't belong to the nations at hand.

But with the towns of the people that GOD, your God, is giving you as an inheritance, it's different: don't leave anyone alive. Consign them to holy destruction: the Hittites, Amorites, Canaanites, Perizzites, Hivites, and Jebusites, obeying the command of GOD, your God. This is so there won't be any of them left to teach you to practice the abominations that they engage in with their gods and you end up sinning against GOD, your God.

When you mount an attack on a town and the siege goes on a long time, don't start cutting down the trees, swinging your axes against them. Those trees are your future food; don't cut them down. Are trees soldiers who come against you with weapons? The exception can be those trees which don't produce food; you can chop them down and use the timbers to build siege engines against the town that is resisting you until it falls.

✙

21 If a dead body is found on the ground, this ground that GOD, your God, has given you, lying out in the open, and no one knows who killed him, your leaders and judges are to go out and measure the distance from the body to the nearest cities. The leaders and judges of the city that is nearest the corpse will then take a heifer that has never been used for work, never had a yoke on it. The leaders will take the heifer to a valley with a stream, a valley that has never been plowed or planted, and there break the neck of the heifer. The Levitical priests will then step up. GOD has chosen them to serve him in these matters by settling legal disputes and violent crimes and by pronouncing blessings in GOD's name. Finally, all the leaders of that town that is nearest the body will wash their hands over the heifer that had its neck broken at the stream and say, "We didn't kill this man and we didn't see who did it. Purify your people Israel whom you redeemed, O GOD. Clear your people Israel from any guilt in this murder."

That will clear them from any responsibility in the murder. By following these procedures you will have absolved yourselves of any part in the murder because you will have done what is right in GOD's sight.

✠

When you go to war against your enemies and GOD, your God, gives you victory and you take prisoners, and then you notice among the prisoners of war a good-looking woman whom you find attractive and would like to marry, this is what you do: Take her home; have her trim her hair, cut her nails, and discard the clothes she was wearing when captured. She is then to stay in your home for a full month, mourning her father and mother. Then you may go to bed with her as husband and wife. If it turns out you don't like her, you must let her go and live wherever she wishes. But you can't sell her or use her as a slave since you've humiliated her.

✠

When a man has two wives, one loved and the other hated, and they both give him sons, but the firstborn is from the hated wife, at the time he divides the inheritance with his sons he must not treat the son of the loved wife as the firstborn, cutting out the son of the hated wife, who is the actual firstborn. No, he must acknowledge the inheritance rights of the real firstborn, the son of the hated wife, by giving him a double share of the inheritance: that son is the first proof of his virility; the rights of the firstborn belong to him.

✠

When a man has a stubborn son, a real rebel who won't do a thing his mother and father tell him, and even though they discipline him he still won't obey, his father and mother shall forcibly bring him before the leaders at the city gate and say to the city fathers, "This son of ours is a stubborn rebel; he won't listen to a thing we say. He's a glutton and a drunk."

Then all the men of the town are to throw rocks at him until he's dead. You will have purged the evil pollution from among you. All Israel will hear what's happened and be in awe.

✠

When a man has committed a capital crime, been given the death sentence, executed and hung from a tree, don't leave his dead body hanging overnight from the tree. Give him a decent burial that same day so that you don't desecrate your GOD-given land—a hanged man is an insult to God.

323

22 If you see your kinsman's ox or sheep wandering off loose, don't look the other way as if you didn't see it. Return it promptly. If your fellow Israelite is not close by or you don't know whose it is, take the animal home with you and take care of it until your fellow asks about it. Then return it to him. Do the same if it's his donkey or a piece of clothing or anything else your fellow Israelite loses. Don't look the other way as if you didn't see it.

If you see your fellow's donkey or ox injured along the road, don't look the other way. Help him get it up and on its way.

A woman must not wear a man's clothing, nor a man wear women's clothing. This kind of thing is an abomination to GOD, your God.

When you come across a bird's nest alongside the road, whether in a tree or on the ground, and the mother is sitting on the young or on the eggs, don't take the mother with the young. You may take the babies, but let the mother go so that you will live a good and long life.

When you build a new house, make a parapet around your roof to make it safe so that someone doesn't fall off and die and your family become responsible for the death.

Don't plant two kinds of seed in your vineyard. If you do, you will forfeit what you've sown, the total production of the vineyard.

Don't plow with an ox and a donkey yoked together.

Don't wear clothes of mixed fabrics, wool and linen together.

Make tassels on the four corners of the cloak you use to cover yourself.

If a man marries a woman, sleeps with her, and then turns on her, calling her a slut, giving her a bad name, saying, "I married this woman, but when I slept with her I discovered she wasn't a virgin," then the father and mother of the girl are to take her with the proof of her virginity to the town leaders at the gate. The father is to tell the leaders, "I gave my daughter to this man as wife and he turned on her, rejecting her. And now he has slanderously accused her, claiming that she wasn't a virgin. But look at this, here is the proof of my daughter's virginity." And then he is to spread out her blood-stained wedding garment before the leaders for their examination. The town leaders then are to take the husband, whip him, fine him a hundred pieces of silver, and give it to the father of the girl. The man gave a virgin girl of Israel a bad name. He has to keep her as his wife and can never divorce her.

But if it turns out that the accusation is true and there is no evidence of the girl's virginity, the men of the town are to take her to the door of her father's house and stone her to death. She acted disgracefully in Israel. She lived like a whore while still in her parents' home. Purge the evil from among you.

If a man is found sleeping with another man's wife, both must die. Purge that evil from Israel.

If a man comes upon a virgin in town, a girl who is engaged to another man, and sleeps with her, take both of them to the town gate and stone them until they die—the girl because she didn't yell out for help in the town and the man because he raped her, violating the fiancée of his neighbor. You must purge the evil from among you.

But if it was out in the country that the man found the engaged girl and grabbed and raped her, only the man is to die, the man who raped her. Don't do anything to the girl; she did nothing wrong. This is similar to the case of a man who comes across his neighbor out in the country and murders him; when the engaged girl yelled out for help, there was no one around to hear or help her.

When a man comes upon a virgin who has never been engaged and grabs and rapes her and they are found out, the man who raped her has to give her father fifty pieces of silver. He has to marry her because he took advantage of her. And he can never divorce her.

A man may not marry his father's ex-wife—that would violate his father's rights.

⊹

23 No eunuch is to enter the congregation of GOD.
No bastard is to enter the congregation of GOD, even to the tenth generation, nor any of his children.

No Ammonite or Moabite is to enter the congregation of GOD, even to the tenth generation, nor any of his children, ever. Those nations didn't treat you with hospitality on your travels out of Egypt, and on top of that they also hired Balaam son of Beor from Pethor in Mesopotamia to curse you. GOD, your God, refused to listen to Balaam but turned the curse into a blessing—how GOD, your God, loves you! Don't even try to get along with them or do anything for them, ever.

But don't spurn an Edomite; he's your kin.

And don't spurn an Egyptian; you were a foreigner in his land.

Children born to Edomites and Egyptians may enter the congregation of GOD in the third generation.

✝

When you are camped out, at war with your enemies, be careful to keep yourself from anything ritually defiling. If one of your men has become ritually unclean because of a nocturnal emission, he must go outside the camp and stay there until evening when he can wash himself, returning to the camp at sunset.

Mark out an area outside the camp where you can go to relieve yourselves. Along with your weapons have a stick with you. After you relieve yourself, dig a hole with the stick and cover your excrement. GOD, your God, strolls through your camp; he's present to deliver you and give you victory over your enemies. Keep your camp holy; don't permit anything indecent or offensive in GOD's eyes.

✝

Don't return a runaway slave to his master; he's come to you for refuge. Let him live wherever he wishes within the protective gates of your city. Don't take advantage of him.

No daughter of Israel is to become a sacred prostitute; and no son of Israel is to become a sacred prostitute. And don't bring the fee of a sacred whore or the earnings of a priest-pimp to the house of GOD, your God, to pay for any vow—they are both an abomination to GOD, your God.

Don't charge interest to your kinsmen on any loan: not for money or food or clothing or anything else that could earn interest. You may charge foreigners interest, but you may not charge your brothers interest; that way GOD, your God, will bless all the work that you take up and the land that you are entering to possess.

When you make a vow to GOD, your God, don't put off keeping it; GOD, your God, expects you to keep it and if you don't you're guilty. But if you don't make a vow in the first place, there's no sin. If you say you're going to do something, do it. Keep the vow you willingly vowed to GOD, your God. You promised it, so do it.

When you enter your neighbor's vineyard, you may eat all the grapes you want until you're full, but you may not put any in your bucket or bag. And when you walk through the ripe grain of your neighbor, you may pick the heads of grain, but you may not swing your sickle there.

24 If a man marries a woman and then it happens that he no longer likes her because he has found something wrong with her, he may give her divorce papers, put them in her hand, and send her off. After she leaves, if she becomes another man's wife and he also comes to hate her and this second husband also gives her divorce papers, puts them in her hand, and sends her off, or if he should die, then the first husband who divorced her can't marry her again. She has made herself ritually unclean, and her remarriage would be an abomination in the Presence of GOD and defile the land with sin, this land that GOD, your God, is giving you as an inheritance.

When a man takes a new wife, he is not to go out with the army or be given any business or work duties. He gets one year off simply to be at home making his wife happy.

Don't seize a handmill or an upper millstone as collateral for a loan. You'd be seizing someone's very life.

If a man is caught kidnapping one of his kinsmen, someone of the People of Israel, to enslave or sell him, the kidnapper must die. Purge that evil from among you.

Warning! If a serious skin disease breaks out, follow exactly the rules set down by the Levitical priests. Follow them precisely as I commanded them. Don't forget what GOD, your God, did to Miriam on your way out of Egypt.

When you make a loan of any kind to your neighbor, don't enter his house to claim his pledge. Wait outside. Let the man to whom you made the pledge bring the pledge to you outside. And if he is destitute, don't use his cloak as a bedroll; return it to him at nightfall so that he can sleep in his cloak and bless you. In the sight of GOD, your God, that will be viewed as a righteous act.

Don't abuse a laborer who is destitute and needy, whether he is a fellow Israelite living in your land and in your city. Pay him at the end of each workday; he's living from hand to mouth and needs it now. If you hold back his pay, he'll protest to GOD and you'll have sin on your books.

Parents shall not be put to death for their children, nor children for their parents. Each person shall be put to death for his own sin.

Make sure foreigners and orphans get their just rights. Don't take the cloak of a widow as security for a loan. Don't ever forget that you were once slaves in Egypt and GOD, your God, got you out of there. I command you: Do what I'm telling you.

When you harvest your grain and forget a sheaf back in the field, don't go back and get it; leave it for the foreigner, the orphan, and the widow so that GOD, your God, will bless you in all your work. When you shake the olives off your trees, don't go back over the branches and strip them bare—what's left is for the foreigner, the orphan, and the widow. And when you cut the grapes in your vineyard, don't take every last grape—leave a few for the foreigner, the orphan, and the widow. Don't ever forget that you were a slave in Egypt. I command you: Do what I'm telling you.

25 When men have a legal dispute, let them go to court; the judges will decide between them, declaring one innocent and the other guilty. If the guilty one deserves punishment, the judge will have him prostrate himself before him and lashed as many times as his crime deserves, but not more than forty. If you hit him more than forty times, you will degrade him to something less than human.

Don't muzzle an ox while it is threshing.

When brothers are living together and one of them dies without having had a son, the widow of the dead brother shall not marry a stranger from outside the family; her husband's brother is to come to her and marry her and do the brother-in-law's duty by her. The first son that she bears shall be named after her dead husband so his name won't die out in Israel.

But if the brother doesn't want to marry his sister-in-law, she is to go to the leaders at the city gate and say, "My brother-in-law refuses to keep his brother's name alive in Israel; he won't agree to do the brother-in-law's duty by me." Then the leaders will call for the brother and confront him. If he stands there defiant and says, "I don't want her," his sister-in-law is to pull his sandal off his foot, spit in his face, and say, "This is what happens to the man who refuses to build up the family of his brother—his name in Israel will be Family-No-Sandal."

When two men are in a fight and the wife of the one man, trying to rescue her husband, grabs the genitals of the man hitting him, you are to cut off her hand. Show no pity.

Don't carry around with you two weights, one heavy and the other light, and don't keep two measures at hand, one large and the other small. Use only one weight, a true and honest weight, and one measure, a true and honest measure, so that you will live a long time on the land that GOD, your God, is giving you. Dishonest weights and measures are an abomination to GOD, your God,—all this corruption in business deals!

Don't forget what Amalek did to you on the road after you left Egypt, how he attacked you when you were tired, barely able to put one foot in front of another, mercilessly cut off your stragglers, and had no regard for God. When GOD, your God, gives you rest from all the enemies that surround you in the inheritance-land GOD, your God, is giving you to possess, you are to wipe the name of Amalek from off the Earth. Don't forget!

26 Once you enter the land that GOD, your God, is giving you as an inheritance and take it over and settle down, you are to take some of all the firstfruits of what you grow in the land that GOD, your God, is giving you, put them in a basket and go to the place GOD, your God, sets apart for you to worship him. At that time, go to the priest who is there and say, "I announce to GOD, your God, today that I have entered the land that GOD promised our ancestors that he'd give to us." The priest will take the basket from you and place it on the Altar of GOD, your God. And there in the Presence of GOD, your God, you will recite,

> A wandering Aramean was my father,
> he went down to Egypt and sojourned there,
> he and just a handful of his brothers at first, but soon
> they became a great nation, mighty and many.
> The Egyptians abused and battered us,
> in a cruel and savage slavery.
> We cried out to GOD, the God-of-Our-Fathers:
> He listened to our voice, he saw
> our destitution, our trouble, our cruel plight.
> And GOD took us out of Egypt
> with his strong hand and long arm, terrible and great,
> with signs and miracle-wonders.
> And he brought us to this place,
> gave us this land flowing with milk and honey.
> So here I am. I've brought the firstfruits
> of what I've grown on this ground you gave me, O GOD.

Then place it in the Presence of GOD, your God. Prostrate yourselves in the Presence of GOD, your God. And rejoice! Celebrate all the good things that GOD, your God, has given you and your family; you and the Levite and the foreigner who lives with you.

✛

Every third year, the year of the tithe, give a tenth of your produce to the Levite, the foreigner, the orphan, and the widow so that they may eat their fill in your cities. And then, in the Presence of GOD, your God, say this:

> I have brought the sacred share,
> I've given it to the Levite, foreigner, orphan, and widow.
> What you commanded, I've done.
> I haven't detoured around your commands,
> I haven't forgotten a single one.
> I haven't eaten from the sacred share while mourning,
> I haven't removed any of it while ritually unclean,
> I haven't used it in funeral feasts.

I have listened obediently to the Voice of God, my God,
I have lived the way you commanded me.

Look down from your holy house in Heaven!
Bless your people Israel and the ground you gave us,
just as you promised our ancestors you would,
this land flowing with milk and honey.

✛

This very day God, your God, commands you to follow these rules and regulations, to live them out with everything you have in you. You've renewed your vows today that God is your God, that you'll live the way he shows you; do what he tells you in the rules, regulations, and commandments; and listen obediently to him.

And today God has reaffirmed that you are dearly-held treasure just as he promised, a people entrusted with keeping his commandments, a people set high above all other nations that he's made, high in praise, fame, and honor: you're a people holy to God, your God. That's what he has promised.

✛

27 Moses commanded the leaders of Israel and charged the people: Keep every commandment that I command you today. On the day you cross the Jordan into the land that God, your God, is giving you, erect large stones and coat them with plaster. As soon as you cross over the river, write on the stones all the words of this Revelation so that you'll enter the land that God, your God, is giving you, that land flowing with milk and honey that God, the God-of-Your-Fathers, promised you.

So when you've crossed the Jordan, erect these stones on Mount Ebal. Then coat them with plaster. Build an Altar of stones for God, your God, there on the mountain. Don't use an iron tool on the stones; build the Altar to God, your God, with uncut stones and offer your Whole-Burnt-Offerings on it to God, your God. When you sacrifice your Peace-Offerings you will also eat them there, rejoicing in the Presence of God, your God.

Write all the words of this Revelation on the stones. Incise them sharply.

Moses and the Levitical priests addressed all Israel: Quiet. Listen obediently, Israel. This very day you have become the people of GOD, your God. Listen to the Voice of GOD, your God. Keep his commandments and regulations that I'm commanding you today.

That day Moses commanded: After you've crossed the Jordan, these tribes will stand on Mount Gerizim to bless the people: Simeon, Levi, Judah, Issachar, Joseph, and Benjamin. And these will stand on Mount Ebal for the curse: Reuben, Gad, Asher, Zebulun, Dan, and Naphtali.

The Levites, acting as spokesmen and speaking loudly, will address Israel:

GOD's curse on anyone who carves or casts a god-image—an abomination to GOD made by a craftsman—and sets it up in secret.
All respond: *Yes. Absolutely.*
GOD's curse on anyone who demeans a parent.
All respond: *Yes. Absolutely.*
GOD's curse on anyone who moves his neighbor's boundary marker.
All respond: *Yes. Absolutely.*
GOD's curse on anyone who misdirects a blind man on the road.
All respond: *Yes. Absolutely.*
GOD's curse on anyone who interferes with justice due the foreigner, orphan, or widow.
All respond: *Yes. Absolutely.*
GOD's curse on anyone who has sex with his father's wife; he has violated the woman who belongs to his father.
All respond: *Yes. Absolutely.*
GOD's curse on anyone who has sex with an animal.
All respond: *Yes. Absolutely.*
GOD's curse on anyone who has sex with his sister, the daughter of his father or mother.
All respond: *Yes. Absolutely.*
GOD's curse on anyone who has sex with his mother-in-law.
All respond: *Yes. Absolutely.*
GOD's curse on anyone who kills his neighbor in secret.
All respond: *Yes. Absolutely.*
GOD's curse on anyone who takes a bribe to kill an innocent person.
All respond: *Yes. Absolutely.*
GOD's curse on whoever does not give substance to the words of

this Revelation by living them.
  All respond: *Yes. Absolutely.*

✝

28 If you listen obediently to the Voice of GOD, your God, and heartily obey all his commandments that I command you today, GOD, your God, will place you on high, high above all the nations of the world. All these blessings will come down on you and spread out beyond you because you have responded to the Voice of GOD, your God:

> GOD's blessing inside the city,
> GOD's blessing in the country;
> GOD's blessing on your children,
>> the crops of your land,
>> the young of your livestock,
>> the calves of your herds,
>> the lambs of your flocks.
> GOD's blessing on your basket and bread bowl;
> GOD's blessing in your coming in,
> GOD's blessing in your going out.

GOD will defeat your enemies who attack you. They'll come at you on one road and run away on seven roads.

GOD will order a blessing on your barns and workplaces; he'll bless you in the land that GOD, your God, is giving you.

GOD will form you as a people holy to him, just as he promised you, if you keep the commandments of GOD, your God, and live the way he has shown you.

All the peoples on Earth will see you living under the Name of GOD and hold you in respectful awe.

GOD will lavish you with good things: children from your womb, offspring from your animals, and crops from your land, the land that GOD promised your ancestors that he would give you. GOD will throw open the doors of his sky vaults and pour rain on your land on schedule and bless the work you take in hand. You will lend to many nations but you yourself won't have to take out a loan. GOD will make you the head, not the tail; you'll always be the top dog, never the bottom dog, as you obediently listen to and diligently keep the commands of GOD,

333

your God, that I am commanding you today. Don't swerve an inch to the right or left from the words that I command you today by going off following and worshiping other gods.

Here's what will happen if you don't obediently listen to the Voice of GOD, your God, and diligently keep all the commandments and guidelines that I'm commanding you today. All these curses will come down hard on you:

> GOD's curse in the city,
> GOD's curse in the country;
> GOD's curse on your basket and bread bowl;
> GOD's curse on your children,
>> the crops of your land,
>> the young of your livestock,
>> the calves of your herds,
>> the lambs of your flocks.
> GOD's curse in your coming in,
> GOD's curse in your going out.

GOD will send The Curse, The Confusion, The Contrariness down on everything you try to do until you've been destroyed and there's nothing left of you—all because of your evil pursuits that led you to abandon me.

GOD will infect you with The Disease, wiping you right off the land that you're going in to possess.

GOD will set consumption and fever and rash and seizures and dehydration and blight and jaundice on you. They'll hunt you down until they kill you.

The sky over your head will become an iron roof, the ground under your feet, a slab of concrete. From out of the skies GOD will rain ash and dust down on you until you suffocate.

GOD will defeat you by enemy attack. You'll come at your enemies on one road and run away on seven roads. All the kingdoms of Earth will see you as a horror. Carrion birds and animals will boldly feast on your dead body with no one to chase them away.

GOD will hit you hard with the boils of Egypt, hemorrhoids, scabs, and an incurable itch. He'll make you go crazy and blind and senile. You'll grope around in the middle of the day like a blind person feeling his way through a lifetime of darkness; you'll never get to where you're going. Not a day will go by that you're not abused and robbed. And no one is going to help you.

You'll get engaged to a woman and another man will take her for his mistress; you'll build a house and never live in it; you'll plant a garden and never eat so much as a carrot; you'll watch your ox get butchered and not get a single steak from it; your donkey will be stolen from in front of you and you'll never see it again; your sheep will be sent off to your enemies and no one will lift a hand to help you.

Your sons and daughters will be shipped off to foreigners; you'll wear your eyes out looking vainly for them, helpless to do a thing. Your crops and everything you work for will be eaten and used by foreigners; you'll spend the rest of your lives abused and knocked around. What you see will drive you crazy.

GOD will hit you with painful boils on your knees and legs and no healing or relief from head to foot.

GOD will lead you and the king you set over you to a country neither you nor your ancestors have heard of; there you'll worship other gods, no-gods of wood and stone. Among all the peoples where GOD will take you, you'll be treated as a lesson or a proverb—a horror!

You'll plant sacks and sacks of seed in the field but get almost nothing—the grasshoppers will devour it. You'll plant and hoe and prune vineyards but won't drink or put up any wine—the worms will devour them. You'll have groves of olive trees everywhere, but you'll have no oil to rub on your face or hands—the olives will have fallen off. You'll have sons and daughters but they won't be yours for long—they'll go off to captivity. Locusts will take over all your trees and crops.

The foreigner who lives among you will climb the ladder, higher and higher, while you go deeper and deeper into the hole. He'll lend to you; you won't lend to him. He'll be the head; you'll be the tail.

All these curses are going to come on you. They're going to hunt you down and get you until there's nothing left of you because you didn't obediently listen to the Voice of GOD, your God, and diligently keep his commandments and guidelines that I commanded you. The curses will serve as signposts, warnings to your children ever after.

Because you didn't serve GOD, your God, out of the joy and goodness of your heart in the great abundance, you'll have to serve your enemies whom GOD will send against you. Life will be famine and drought, rags and wretchedness; then he'll put an iron yoke on your neck until he's destroyed you.

Yes, GOD will raise up a faraway nation against you, swooping down on you like an eagle, a nation whose language you can't understand, a mean-faced people, cruel to grandmothers and babies alike. They'll ravage the young of your animals and the crops from your fields until you're destroyed. They'll leave nothing behind: no grain, no wine, no oil, no calves, no lambs—and finally, no *you*. They'll lay siege to you while you're huddled behind your town gates. They'll knock those high, proud walls flat, those walls behind which you felt so safe. They'll lay siege to your fortified cities all over the country, this country that GOD, your God, has given you.

And you'll end up cannibalizing your own sons and daughters that GOD, your God, has given you. When the suffering from the siege gets extreme, you're going to eat your own babies. The most gentle and caring man among you will turn hard, his eye evil, against his own brother, his cherished wife, and even the rest of his children who are still alive, refusing to share with them a scrap of meat from the cannibal child-stew he is eating. He's lost everything, even his humanity, in the suffering of the siege that your enemy mounts against your fortified towns.

And the most gentle and caring woman among you, a woman who wouldn't step on a wildflower, will turn hard, her eye evil, against her cherished husband, against her son, against her daughter, against even the afterbirth of her newborn infants; she plans to eat them in secret— she does eat them!—because she has lost everything, even her humanity, in the suffering of the siege that your enemy mounts against your fortified towns.

If you don't diligently keep all the words of this Revelation written in this book, living in holy awe before This Name glorious and terrible, GOD, your God, then GOD will pound you with catastrophes, you and your children, huge interminable catastrophes, hideous interminable illnesses. He'll bring back and stick you with every old Egyptian malady that once terrorized you. And yes, every disease and catastrophe imaginable— things not even written in the Book of this Revelation—GOD will bring on you until you're destroyed.

Because you didn't listen obediently to the Voice of GOD, your God, you'll be left with a few pitiful stragglers in place of the dazzling stars-in-the-heavens multitude you had become.

And this is how things will end up: Just as GOD once enjoyed you, took pleasure in making life good for you, giving you many children, so GOD will enjoy getting rid of you, clearing you off the Earth. He'll weed you out of the very soil that you are entering in to possess. He'll scatter you to the four winds, from one end of the Earth to the other. You'll worship all kinds of other gods, gods neither you nor your parents ever heard of, wood and stone no-gods. But you won't find a home there, you'll not be able to settle down. GOD will give you a restless heart, longing eyes, a homesick soul. You will live in constant jeopardy, terrified of every shadow, never knowing what you'll meet around the next corner.

In the morning you'll say, "I wish it were evening." In the evening you'll say, "I wish it were morning." Afraid, terrorized at what's coming next, afraid of the unknown, because of the sights you've witnessed.

GOD will ship you back to Egypt by a road I promised you'd never see again. There you'll offer yourselves for sale, both men and women, as slaves to your enemies. And not a buyer to be found.

These are the terms of the Covenant that GOD commanded Moses to make with the People of Israel in the land of Moab, renewing the Covenant he made with them at Horeb.

MOSES BLESSES ISRAEL ON THE PLAINS OF MOAB

29 Moses called all Israel together and said, You've seen with your own eyes everything that GOD did in Egypt to Pharaoh and his servants, and to the land itself—the massive trials to which you were eyewitnesses, the great signs and miracle-wonders. But GOD didn't give you an understanding heart or perceptive eyes or attentive ears until right now, this very day.

I took you through the wilderness for forty years and through all that time the clothes on your backs didn't wear out, the sandals on your feet didn't wear out, and you lived well without bread and wine and beer, proving to you that I am in fact GOD, your God.

When you arrived here in this place, Sihon king of Heshbon and Og king of Bashan met us primed for war but we beat them. We took their land and gave it as an inheritance to the Reubenites, the Gadites, and the half-tribe of Manasseh.

Diligently keep the words of this Covenant. Do what they say so that you will live well and wisely in every detail.

You are all standing here today in the Presence of GOD, your God,—
the heads of your tribes, your leaders, your officials, all Israel: your
babies, your wives, the resident foreigners in your camps who fetch
your firewood and water—ready to cross over into the solemnly sworn
Covenant that GOD, your God, is making with you today, the Covenant
that this day confirms that you are his people and he is GOD, your God,
just as he promised you and your ancestors Abraham, Isaac, and Jacob.

I'm not making this Covenant and its oath with you alone. I *am*
making it with you who are standing here today in the Presence of
GOD, our God, yes, but also with those who are not here today. You
know the conditions in which we lived in Egypt and how we criss-
crossed through nations in our travels. You got an eyeful of their obscen-
ities, their wood and stone, silver and gold junk-gods. Don't let down
your guard lest even now, today, someone—man or woman, clan or
tribe—gets sidetracked from GOD, our God, and gets involved with
the no-gods of the nations; lest some poisonous weed sprout and spread
among you, a person who hears the words of the Covenant-oath but
exempts himself, thinking, "I'll live just the way I please, thank you,"
and ends up ruining life for everybody. GOD won't let him off the hook.
GOD's anger and jealousy will erupt like a volcano against that person.
The curses written in this book will bury him. GOD will delete his name
from the records. GOD will separate him out from all the tribes of Israel
for special punishment, according to all the curses of the Covenant
written in this Book of Revelation.

The next generation, your children who come after you and the
foreigner who comes from a far country, will be appalled when they
see the widespread devastation, how GOD made the whole land sick.
They'll see a fire-blackened wasteland of brimstone and salt flats, nothing planted, nothing growing, not so much as a blade of grass anywhere—like the overthrow of Sodom and Gomorrah, Admah and
Zeboiim, which GOD overthrew in fiery rage.

All the nations will ask, "Why did GOD do this to this country?
What on earth could have made him this angry?"

Your children will answer, "Because they abandoned the Covenant
of the GOD of their ancestors that he made with them after he got them
out of Egypt; they went off and worshiped other gods, submitted to
gods they'd never heard of before, gods they had no business dealing
with. So GOD's anger erupted against that land and all the curses written in this book came down on it. GOD, furiously angry, pulled them,

roots and all, out of their land and dumped them in another country, as you can see."

GOD, our God, will take care of the hidden things but the revealed things are our business. It's up to us and our children to attend to all the terms in this Revelation.

30 Here's what will happen. While you're out among the nations where GOD has dispersed you and the blessings and curses come in just the way I have set them before you, and you and your children take them seriously and come back to GOD, your God, and obey him with your whole heart and soul according to everything that I command you today, GOD, your God, will restore everything you lost; he'll have compassion on you; he'll come back and pick up the pieces from all the places where you were scattered. No matter how far away you end up, GOD, your God, will get you out of there and bring you back to the land your ancestors once possessed. It will be yours again. He will give you a good life and make you more numerous than your ancestors.

GOD, your God, will cut away the thick calluses on your heart and your children's hearts, freeing you to love GOD, your God, with your whole heart and soul and live, really live. GOD, your God, will put all these curses on your enemies who hated you and were out to get you.

And you will make a new start, listening obediently to GOD, keeping all his commandments that I'm commanding you today. GOD, your God, will outdo himself in making things go well for you: you'll have babies, get calves, grow crops, and enjoy an all-around good life. Yes, GOD will start enjoying you again, making things go well for you just as he enjoyed doing it for your ancestors.

But only if you listen obediently to GOD, your God, and keep the commandments and regulations written in this Book of Revelation. Nothing halfhearted here; you must return to GOD, your God, totally, heart and soul, holding nothing back.

This commandment that I'm commanding you today isn't too much for you, it's not out of your reach. It's not on a high mountain—you don't have to get mountaineers to climb the peak and bring it down to your level and explain it before you can live it. And it's not across the ocean—you don't have to send sailors out to get it, bring it back, and then explain it before you can live it. No. The word is right here and now—as near as the tongue in your mouth, as near as the heart in your chest. Just do it!

> Look at what I've done for you today: I've placed in front of you
> > Life and Good
> > Death and Evil.

And I command you today: Love GOD, your God. Walk in his ways. Keep his commandments, regulations, and rules so that you will live, really live, live exuberantly, blessed by GOD, your God, in the land you are about to enter and possess.

But I warn you: If you have a change of heart, refuse to listen obediently, and willfully go off to serve and worship other gods, you will most certainly die. You won't last long in the land that you are crossing the Jordan to enter and possess.

I call Heaven and Earth to witness against you today: I place before you Life and Death, Blessing and Curse. Choose life so that you and your children will live. And love GOD, your God, listening obediently to him, firmly embracing him. Oh yes, he is life itself, a long life settled on the soil that GOD, your God, promised to give your ancestors, Abraham, Isaac, and Jacob.

THE CHARGE

31 Moses went on and addressed these words to all Israel. He said, "I'm 120 years old today. I can't get about as I used to. And GOD told me, 'You're not going to cross this Jordan River.'

"GOD, your God, will cross the river ahead of you and destroy the nations in your path so that you may dispossess them. (And Joshua will cross the river before you, as GOD said he would.) GOD will give the nations the same treatment he gave the kings of the Amorites, Sihon and Og, and their land; he'll destroy them. GOD will hand the nations over to you, and you'll treat them exactly as I have commanded you.

"Be strong. Take courage. Don't be intimidated. Don't give them a second thought because GOD, your God, is striding ahead of you. He's right there with you. He won't let you down; he won't leave you."

Then Moses summoned Joshua. He said to him with all Israel watching, "Be strong. Take courage. You will enter the land with this people, this land that GOD promised their ancestors that he'd give them. You will make them the proud possessors of it. GOD is striding ahead of you. He's right there with you. He won't let you down; he won't leave you. Don't be intimidated. Don't worry."

☩

Moses wrote out this Revelation and gave it to the priests, the sons of Levi, who carried the Chest of the Covenant of GOD, and to all the leaders of Israel. And he gave these orders: "At the end of every seven years, the Year-All-Debts-Are-Canceled, during the pilgrim Festival of Booths when everyone in Israel comes to appear in the Presence of GOD, your God, at the place he designates, read out this Revelation to all Israel, with everyone listening. Gather the people together—men, women, children, and the foreigners living among you—so they can listen well, so they may learn to live in holy awe before GOD, your God, and diligently keep everything in this Revelation. And do this so that their children, who don't yet know all this, will also listen and learn to live in holy awe before GOD, your God, for as long as you live on the land that you are crossing over the Jordan to possess."

GOD spoke to Moses: "You are about to die. So call Joshua. Meet me in the Tent of Meeting so that I can commission him."

So Moses and Joshua went and stationed themselves in the Tent of Meeting. GOD appeared in the Tent in a Pillar of Cloud. The Cloud was near the entrance of the Tent of Meeting.

GOD spoke to Moses: "You're about to die and be buried with your ancestors. You'll no sooner be in the grave than this people will be up and whoring after the foreign gods of this country that they are entering. They will abandon me and violate my Covenant that I've made with them. I'll get angry, oh so angry! I'll walk off and leave them on their own, won't so much as look back at them. Then many calamities and disasters will devastate them because they are defenseless. They'll say, 'Isn't it because our God wasn't here that all this evil has come upon us?' But I'll stay out of their lives, keep looking the other way because of all their evil: they took up with other gods!

"But for right now, copy down this song and teach the People of Israel to sing it by heart. They'll have it then as my witness against them. When I bring them into the land that I promised to their ancestors, a land flowing with milk and honey, and they eat and become full and get fat and then begin fooling around with other gods and worshiping them, and then things start falling apart, many terrible things happening, this song will be there with them as a witness to who they are and what went wrong. Their children won't forget this song; they'll be singing it. Don't think I don't know what they are already scheming to do, and they're not even in the land yet, this land I promised them."

So Moses wrote down this song that very day and taught it to the People of Israel.

Then GOD commanded Joshua son of Nun saying, "Be strong. Take courage. You will lead the People of Israel into the land I promised to give them. And I'll be right there with you."

After Moses had finished writing down the words of this Revelation in a book, right down to the last word, he ordered the Levites who were responsible for carrying the Chest of the Covenant of GOD, saying, "Take this Book of Revelation and place it alongside the Chest of the Covenant of GOD, your God. Keep it there as a witness.

"I know what rebels you are, how stubborn and willful you can be. Even today, while I'm still alive and present with you, you're rebellious against GOD. How much worse when I've died! So gather the leaders of the tribes and the officials here. I have something I need to say directly to them with Heaven and Earth as witnesses. I know that after I die you're going to make a mess of things, abandoning the way I commanded, inviting all kinds of evil consequences in the days ahead. You're determined to do evil in defiance of GOD—I know you are—deliberately provoking his anger by what you do."

So with everyone in Israel gathered and listening, Moses taught them the words of this song, from start to finish.

THE SONG

32 Listen, Heavens, I have something to tell you.
Attention, Earth, I've got a mouth full of words.
My teaching, let it fall like a gentle rain,
my words arrive like morning dew,
Like a sprinkling rain on new grass,
like spring showers on the garden.
For it's GOD's Name I'm preaching—
respond to the greatness of our God!
The Rock: His works are perfect,
and the way he works is fair and just;
A God you can depend upon, no exceptions,
a straight-arrow God.

His messed-up, mixed-up children, his non-children,
    throw mud at him but none of it sticks.

Don't you realize it is GOD you are treating like this?
    This is crazy; don't you have any sense of reverence?
Isn't this your father who created you,
    who made you and gave you a place on Earth?
Read up on what happened before you were born;
    dig into the past, understand your roots.
Ask your parents what it was like before you were born;
    ask the old-ones, they'll tell you a thing or two.

When the High God gave the nations their stake,
    gave them their place on Earth,
He put each of the peoples within boundaries
    under the care of divine guardians.
But GOD himself took charge of his people,
    took Jacob on as his personal concern.

He found him out in the wilderness,
    in an empty, windswept wasteland.
He threw his arms around him, lavished attention on him,
    guarding him as the apple of his eye.
He was like an eagle hovering over its nest,
    overshadowing its young,
Then spreading its wings, lifting them into the air,
    teaching them to fly.
GOD alone led him;
    there was not a foreign god in sight.
GOD lifted him on to the hilltops,
    so he could feast on the crops in the fields.
He fed him honey from the rock,
    oil from granite crags,
Curds of cattle and the milk of sheep,
    the choice cuts of lambs and goats,
Fine Bashan rams, high quality wheat,
    and the blood of grapes: you drank good wine!

Jeshurun put on weight and bucked;
    you got fat, became obese, a tub of lard.

He abandoned the God who made him,
    he mocked the Rock of his salvation.
They made him jealous with their foreign newfangled gods,
    and with obscenities they vexed him no end.
They sacrificed to no-god demons,
    gods they knew nothing about,
The latest in gods, fresh from the market,
    gods your ancestors would never call "gods."
You walked out on the Rock who gave you your life,
    forgot the birth-God who brought you into the world.

GOD saw it and turned on his heel,
    angered and hurt by his sons and daughters.
He said, "From now on I'm looking the other way.
    Wait and see what happens to them.
Oh, they're a turned-around, upside-down generation!
    Who knows what they'll do from one moment to the next?
They've goaded me with their no-gods,
    infuriated me with their hot-air gods;
I'm going to goad them with a no-people,
    with a hollow nation incense them.
My anger started a fire,
    a wildfire burning deep down in Sheol,
Then shooting up and devouring the Earth and its crops,
    setting all the mountains, from bottom to top, on fire.
I'll pile catastrophes on them,
    I'll shoot my arrows at them:
Starvation, blistering heat, killing disease;
    I'll send snarling wild animals to attack from the forest
    and venomous creatures to strike from the dust.
Killing in the streets,
    terror in the houses,
Young men and virgins alike struck down,
    and yes, breast-feeding babies and gray-haired old men."

I could have said, "I'll hack them to pieces,
    wipe out all trace of them from the Earth,"
Except that I feared the enemy would grab the chance
    to take credit for all of it,

Crowing, "Look what we did!
     GOD had nothing to do with this."

They are a nation of ninnies,
     they don't know enough to come in out of the rain.
If they had any sense at all, they'd know this;
     they would see what's coming down the road.
How could one soldier chase a thousand enemies off,
     or two men run off two thousand,
Unless their Rock had sold them,
     unless GOD had given them away?
For their rock is nothing compared to our Rock;
     even our enemies say that.
They're a vine that comes right out of Sodom,
     who they are is rooted in Gomorrah;
Their grapes are poison grapes,
     their grape-clusters bitter.
Their wine is rattlesnake venom,
     mixed with lethal cobra poison.

Don't you realize that I have my shelves
     well stocked, locked behind iron doors?
I'm in charge of vengeance and payback,
     just waiting for them to slip up;
And the day of their doom is just around the corner,
     sudden and swift and sure.

Yes, GOD will judge his people,
     but oh how compassionately he'll do it.
When he sees their weakened plight
     and there is no one left, slave or free,
He'll say, "So where are their gods,
     the rock in which they sought refuge,
The gods who feasted on the fat of their sacrifices
     and drank the wine of their drink-offerings?
Let them show their stuff and help you,
     let them give you a hand!

"Do you see it now? Do you see that I'm the one?
    Do you see that there's no other god beside me?
I bring death and I give life, I wound and I heal—
    there is no getting away from or around me!
I raise my hand in solemn oath;
    I say, 'I'm always around. By that very life I promise:
When I sharpen my lightning sword
    and execute judgment,
I take vengeance on my enemies
    and pay back those who hate me.
I'll make my arrows drunk with blood,
    my sword will gorge itself on flesh,
Feasting on slain and captive alike,
    the proud and vain enemy corpses.'"

Celebrate, nations, join the praise of his people.
    He avenges the deaths of his servants,
Pays back his enemies with vengeance,
    and cleanses his land for his people.

Moses came and recited all the words of this song in the hearing of the people, he and Joshua son of Nun. When Moses had finished saying all these words to all Israel, he said, "Take to heart all these words to which I give witness today and urgently command your children to put them into practice, every single word of this Revelation. Yes. This is no small matter for you; it's your life. In keeping this word you'll have a good and long life in this land that you're crossing the Jordan to possess."

That same day GOD spoke to Moses: "Climb the Abarim Mountains to Mount Nebo in the land of Moab, overlooking Jericho, and view the land of Canaan that I'm giving the People of Israel to have and hold. Die on the mountain that you climb and join your people in the ground, just as your brother Aaron died on Mount Hor and joined his people.
    "This is because you broke faith with me in the company of the People of Israel at the Waters of Meribah Kadesh in the Wilderness of Zin—you didn't honor my Holy Presence in the company of the People of Israel. You'll look at the land spread out before you but you won't enter it, this land that I am giving to the People of Israel."

346

THE BLESSING

33 Moses, man of God, blessed the People of Israel with this blessing before his death. He said,

> GOD came down from Sinai,
>> he dawned from Seir upon them;
> He radiated light from Mount Paran,
>> coming with ten thousand holy angels
> And tongues of fire
>> streaming from his right hand.
> Oh, how you love the people,
>> all his holy ones are palmed in your left hand.
> They sit at your feet,
>> honoring your teaching,
> The Revelation commanded by Moses,
>> as the assembly of Jacob's inheritance.
> Thus GOD became king in Jeshurun
>> as the leaders and tribes of Israel gathered.

Reuben:
> "Let Reuben live and not die,
>> but just barely, in diminishing numbers."

Judah:
> "Listen, GOD, to the Voice of Judah,
>> bring him to his people;
> Strengthen his grip,
>> be his helper against his foes."

Levi:
> "Let your Thummim and Urim
>> belong to your loyal saint;
> The one you tested at Massah,
>> whom you fought with at the Waters of Meribah,
> Who said of his father and mother,
>> 'I no longer recognize them.'
> He turned his back on his brothers
>> and neglected his children,

347

Because he was guarding your sayings
    and watching over your Covenant.
Let him teach your rules to Jacob
    and your Revelation to Israel,
Let him keep the incense rising to your nostrils
    and the Whole-Burnt-Offerings on your Altar.
GOD bless his commitment,
    stamp your seal of approval on what he does;
Disable the loins of those who defy him,
    make sure we've heard the last from those who hate him."

Benjamin:
"GOD's beloved;
    GOD's permanent residence.
Encircled by GOD all day long,
    within whom GOD is at home."

Joseph:
"Blessed by GOD be his land:
    The best fresh dew from high heaven,
    and fountains springing from the depths;
The best radiance streaming from the sun
    and the best the moon has to offer;
Beauty pouring off the tops of the mountains
    and the best from the everlasting hills;
The best of Earth's exuberant gifts,
    the smile of the Burning-Bush Dweller.
All this on the head of Joseph,
    on the brow of the consecrated one among his brothers.
In splendor he's like a firstborn bull,
    his horns the horns of a wild ox;
He'll gore the nations with those horns,
    push them all to the ends of the Earth.
Ephraim by the ten thousands will do this,
    Manasseh by the thousands will do this."

Zebulun and Issachar:
"Celebrate, Zebulun, as you go out,
    and Issachar, as you stay home.

They'll invite people to the Mountain
    and offer sacrifices of right worship,
For they will have hauled riches in from the sea
    and gleaned treasures from the beaches."

Gad:
"Blessed is he who makes Gad large.
    Gad roams like a lion,
    tears off an arm, rips open a skull.
He took one look and grabbed the best place for himself,
    the portion just made for someone in charge.
He took his place at the head,
    carried out GOD's right ways
    and his rules for life in Israel."

Dan:
"Dan is a lion's cub
    leaping out of Bashan."

Naphtali:
"Naphtali brims with blessings,
    spills over with GOD's blessings
As he takes possession
    of the sea and southland."

Asher:
"Asher, best blessed of the sons!
    May he be the favorite of his brothers,
    his feet massaged in oil.
Safe behind iron-clad doors and gates,
    your strength like iron as long as you live."

✝

There is none like God, Jeshurun,
    riding to your rescue through the skies,
    his dignity haloed by clouds.
The ancient God is home
    on a foundation of everlasting arms.
He drove out the enemy before you

and commanded, "Destroy!"
Israel lived securely,
    the fountain of Jacob undisturbed
In grain and wine country
    and, oh yes, his heavens drip dew.

Lucky Israel! Who has it as good as you?
    A people *saved* by GOD!
The Shield who defends you,
    the Sword who brings triumph.
Your enemies will come crawling on their bellies
    and you'll march on their backs.

THE DEATH OF MOSES

34 Moses climbed from the Plains of Moab to Mount Nebo, the peak of Pisgah facing Jericho. GOD showed him all the land from Gilead to Dan, all Naphtali, Ephraim, and Manasseh; all Judah reaching to the Mediterranean Sea; the Negev and the plains which encircle Jericho, City of Palms, as far south as Zoar.

Then and there GOD said to him, "This is the land I promised to your ancestors, to Abraham, Isaac, and Jacob with the words 'I will give it to your descendants.' I've let you see it with your own eyes. There it is. But you're not going to go in."

Moses died there in the land of Moab, Moses the servant of GOD, just as GOD said. God buried him in the valley in the land of Moab opposite Beth Peor. No one knows his burial site to this very day.

Moses was 120 years old when he died. His eyesight was sharp; he still walked with a spring in his step. The People of Israel wept for Moses in the Plains of Moab thirty days. Then the days of weeping and mourning for Moses came to an end.

Joshua son of Nun was filled with the spirit of wisdom because Moses had laid his hands on him. The People of Israel listened obediently to him and did the same as when GOD had commanded Moses.

No prophet has risen since in Israel like Moses, whom GOD knew face-to-face. Never since has there been anything like the signs and miracle-wonders that GOD sent him to do in Egypt, to Pharaoh, to all his servants, and to all his land—nothing to compare with that all-powerful hand of his and all the great and terrible things Moses did as every eye in Israel watched.